Sharing News Online

Fiona Martin • Tim Dwyer

Sharing News Online

Commendary Cultures and Social Media News
Ecologies

Fiona Martin
Department of Media and
Communications
University of Sydney
Sydney, NSW, Australia

Tim Dwyer
Department of Media and
Communications
University of Sydney
Sydney, NSW, Australia

ISBN 978-3-030-17905-2   ISBN 978-3-030-17906-9   (eBook)
https://doi.org/10.1007/978-3-030-17906-9

Cover image: Bloomberg Creative Photos / Getty images
Cover design: Tjasa Krivec and eStudioCalamar

This Palgrave Macmillan imprint is published by the registered company Springer Nature
Switzerland AG
The registered company address is: Gewerbestrasse 11, 6330 Cham, Switzerland

For Ruth, Jim, Jamilla and Rosie who all know the power and delight of social news sharing.
For Susan

ACKNOWLEDGEMENTS

This book has had a long gestation through several news analytics projects, but is primarily the outcome of an Australian Research Council Linkage grant, *Sharing News Online: Analysing the Significance of a Social Media Phenomenon* (LP140100148). We are indebted to our industry partners, the Share Wars team of Hal Crawford, Andrew Hunter and Dominic Filipovic for introducing us to the Likeable Engine and to Nine News Australia for supporting this research. The detailed social media analytics was made possible by our colleagues Professor James Curran and Dr Joel Nothman, of the University of Sydney's School of Information Technology, who were thoughtful, challenging collaborators. We are also grateful for the chapter contributions from linguist Associate Professor Monika Bednarek and audience researcher Associate Professor Virginia Nightingale, who expanded our conceptions of why people might share news.

Our research assistants Tim Koskie, Weiwei Xu, Penelope Thomas and Marion McCutcheon were endlessly helpful and inventive. Special thanks to Joel Nothman who compiled the text for Chap. 6 and Penelope who corrected the data manually. Finally many thanks go to Mr Steven Hayes and Dr Ian Johnson, who gave us access to the University's Heurist Scholar database, were patient when we nearly broke it with the weight of news ingested and started us on the path of digital methods research.

The chapters contain material adapted from previously published news and journal articles including:

Chapters 3, 4 and 7: Dwyer, Tim and Fiona Martin. 2017. Sharing News Online: social media news analytics and their implications for media pluralism policies, *Digital Journalism*, 5:8, 1080–1100. https://doi.org/10.1080/21670811.2017.1338527.

Chapter 6: Bednarek, Monika. 2016. Investigating evaluation and news values in news items that are shared through social media. *Corpora: corpus-based language learning, language processing and linguistics*, 11(2): 227–257.

Bednarek, Monika and Helen Caple. 2017. 'All the news that's fit to share': news values in 'most shared' news, In *The Discourse of News Values: how organisations create newsworthiness*, 195–223. Oxford: Oxford University Press. https://doi.org/10.1093/acprof:oso/9780190653934.001.0001.

Chapter 8: Dwyer, Tim and Weiwei Xu. 'Tianjin Disaster Takes Social News. Sharing to New Levels in China.' *The Conversation*, August 25, 2015.   https://theconversation.com/tianjin-disaster-takes-social-news-sharing-to-new-levels-in-china-46401.

CONTENTS

About the Authors

Fiona Martin is Senior Lecturer in Online Media at the Department of Media & Communications, University of Sydney. She studies digital journalism and the uses, politics and regulation of internet media. She is co-editor and author, with Gregory F. Lowe, of *The Value of Public Service Media* (Nordicom 2014).

Tim Dwyer is an Associate Professor at the Department of Media & Communications, University of Sydney. He studies media and communications industries, media diversity and pluralism, regulation and policy in an era of convergent media and algorithmic mediatisation. He is the author of *Convergent Media and Privacy* (Palgrave 2016).

About the Contributors

Monika Bednarek is an Associate Professor in the Department of Linguistics, University of Sydney, Australia. She is the co-author of *The Discourse of News Values* (2017).

Virginia Nightingale was formerly Associate Professor in Media and Communication at the University of Western Sydney. She retired in 2010.

LIST OF FIGURES

LIST OF TABLES

In the Suicide Forest: How Social Media News Sharing Is Affecting News Journalism

Fiona Martin

On New Year's Eve 2017, popular US YouTuber Logan Paul's New Year message to his more than 15 million subscribers featured a crass encounter with an apparently dead man. The video shows Paul discovering the man's body hanging from a tree in Japan's Aokigahara park, otherwise known as the 'Suicide Forest' (Paul 2017). The vlogger later argued his post, which started by showing an apparently comedic attempt to camp with friends in the eerie location, was designed to create awareness of suicide. However Paul's video was internationally condemned for exploiting his macabre discovery to gain views and subscribers.[1] YouTube did not remove the post, even though it clearly violated its community standards but, after 48 hours of backlash, Paul deleted the offensive footage, posting several apologies (Paul 2018). Other YouTubers however created reaction and attack videos which reposted edited segments of his post in disjointed iterations. The public debate about Paul's dubious media ethics and the consequences of his vlog spilled onto Twitter, Tumblr, Instagram and Reddit, with users translating each other's messages from English to Japanese and back and subtitling the footage in other languages. Days afterwards, the world's major legacy media—New York Times, BBC and

---

[1] Paul says he did not 'monetise' the post due to its sensitive content. However, he did enable ads to run against his subsequent apology and clarifications.

© The Author(s) 2019
F. Martin, T. Dwyer, *Sharing News Online*,
https://doi.org/10.1007/978-3-030-17906-9_1

1

News Corp publications—caught up with the scandal, reporting Paul's belated attempts to say sorry and his temporary withdrawal from vlogging.

The backlash saw YouTube remove Paul from its Red streaming project, temporarily cut his ad revenues and suspend him from its Google preferred ads programme, which previously allowed him to place ads with the top 5% of YouTube influencers. Yet, a year on, he remained in the top ten of the highest earning figures on the platform (Robehmed 2018).

This moment starkly illustrates the new networked political economy and cultural politics of social media news sharing. In the last decade, the consumption, production and distribution of news has been radically altered by the dynamics of social media use and industry development. More people are discovering news on social media. In 2017, the Reuters Digital News survey indicated that social media platforms have become the primary news source for 33% of people under 25 in most developed countries (Newman et al. 2017). In the latest survey, 53% of young people reported accessing news on social media during the previous week (Newman et al. 2018). While much of that news content still emanates from legacy brands, the old news business is virtually hostage to the new, with social media sharing driving anywhere between 7 and 50% of traffic to major news websites depending on their business model. 'Dark social', web referrals via email, apps or messaging systems, made up much of the rest. In 2015, social sharing from Facebook exceeded Google search as a source of that referred traffic (Ingram 2015), although this dynamic has since reversed following Facebook's demotion of news media content in its feeds.[2]

More users also report recirculating digital news than creating it, making online news 'sharing' a more significant form of cultural production than citizen journalism. For example, the 2014 Pew Research Center *State of the News Media* report notes that half of the US social network users surveyed (50%) had shared or reposted news content and 46% had commented on the news, while only 12% posted videos of newsworthy events that they had created and only 11% of online news consumers had submitted original content such as photos or stories to news websites or blogs (Pew Research Center 2014: 5). Overall, 24% of the participants in Reuters' 2016 world survey said they share news regularly on social media (Newman et al. 2016: 11), although this figure varies by country and

---

[2] In 2018 Facebook decreased the level of professional news visible in its feeds in favour of family and friend posts (Facebook 2018).

platform. Sixty-six per cent of US Twitter users said they shared news regularly with their followers (Rosenstiel et al. 2015). In countries like Turkey and Hong Kong where social media is censored, messaging services like WhatsApp and WeChat increasingly allow users to share news privately (even though news sharing on the latter platform is often censored). During Hong Kong's 'Umbrella Revolution', pictured on the cover of this book, protestors' use of the mesh networking app FireChat enabled them to share information and mobilise despite government surveillance (Anthony 2014; Lin 2016).

This book investigates the potent nature of social media news sharing, why so many have embraced it so enthusiastically and so quickly, how it has been commodified and what impact *commendary culture* is having on the news media internationally. It will explore aspects of corporate and technological interdependence that characterise the news sharing ecology, and the role of second wave automation and social analytics in the redistribution of news on social media platforms. Importantly, this book will query common assumptions about the types of stories that trigger news sharing, drawing on research into what news genres and topics people share and what motivates their sharing behaviours. We demonstrate, for example, that politics is still a more important subject worldwide than celebrity or sports. We also reveal that news sharing is not simply driven by egocentric objectives but also by affective, emotional relations to story content, a finding that offers fertile territory for our discursive analysis of most shared stories, the language they employ and the news values they embody. Our chapters on the policy and political implications of social news sharing then show how this activity is shaping our social and cultural worlds.

Sharing News Online concentrates on the fate of news journalism, but our work will be of interest to lobbyists, activists, marketers and communications practitioners—anyone with an interest in what goes viral, or who hopes to influence others to exchange information online. All of these actors have a stake in the future of digital journalism, its shifting boundaries, and its historic claims to legitimacy, authority, privilege and—most significantly—public trust. They depend on news media to credibly amplify their messages. Yet the 2017 Cambridge Analytica scandal, where researchers acquired Facebook user data and provided it to a third-party company which then tried to manipulate political processes in the US and UK, alongside subsequent, widespread instances of social media misinformation campaigns (Allcott et al. 2019; Chadwick and Viccari 2019), have reduced trust in both the platforms and the media more broadly (Edelmann 2018; Knight Foundation 2018).

Critically, this damage comes on top of social media's economic destabilisation of the legacy news media and the historic financial model for news journalism. Using personalised, behaviourally targeted advertising models, social media platforms have appropriated much of the old media's advertising revenue—already diminished by the migration of classifieds to specialised web services like EBay, Envato and Craigslist. Social media advertising is finely directed to individual users based on analyses of what they talk about, view, search for, like, buy and repost from other media, as well as metadata about their location, the time of day they choose to interact and on which device. The platforms also sponsor digital influencers like Logan Paul, whose lifestyle commentaries attract millions more subscribers than would pay for traditional news publications. Through these paid vloggers, or digital influencers, the platforms gather even more data on users' interests and their relationships with those celebrities, who in turn promote brand engagement in ways that traditional news has eschewed. As a result, in 2017, Facebook and Google had reportedly captured half of the world's online advertising revenue and around 20% of its total advertising spend (Kollewe 2017; Reuters 2017). The drift of advertising income to social media platforms has left legacy journalism in economic freefall, with news organisations restructuring operations and cutting staff, bureaux and publications across the globe. While subscriptions, native advertising, events and sales are beginning to fill the gap, platform engagement is essential to ensure audience reach (Küng 2018). Meanwhile Alphabet, the parent company of Google, Instagram and Snapchat, has become the world's largest media company by revenues, with Facebook ranked ninth, China's Tencent Holdings fourteenth and Microsoft eighteenth (Institute for Media and Communication Policy 2017).[3]

The popular turn to social platforms for news consumption and distribution has also had significant impacts on journalism processes, practices and pay. Inside newsrooms, social sharing of news has affected the types of stories that are commissioned and reported, the timing and placement of their publication and the measurement of their worth. Social media analytics services such as Chartbeat and Parse.ly provide tools that assess which stories are shared, where, with what audiences and what extent of reach. Headlines, images and story structures are reworked, with the aim of making stories more shareable, or 'spreadable', as Jenkins et al. (2013) term it.

---

[3] Digital media businesses Apple, Alphabet, Microsoft, Amazon and Facebook also made up the top five of the largest companies in the US by market capitalisation.

Journalists can gauge their work's appeal in social mentions—shares, likes and tweets—and in the mounting page views that accompany news virality. Their pay may include traffic bonuses for attracting significant attention or encouraging certain types of user engagement. Their engagement with audiences may boost their personal profile beyond their publication and make them marketable brands.

Yet, while much research has probed why news stories might go viral on social networks, and under what conditions, little is known about what we share in the everyday, what types of narrative forms we prefer and what added features, videos, interactives or comments might boost the scale and scope of our information exchange. Similarly, journalists and editors might be curious about how shareable news correlates with traditional markers of newsworthiness, the news values that guide editorial decision making. In light of debates about the dangers of social media metrics driving editorial decision making (Petre 2015), and shaping news agendas based on popular tastes rather than diverse information (Bruns 2018: 230–236), it is critical to analyse what information sharing signals convey to journalists and how they then might shape the news. We need to consider how social media news sharing differs between individuals and platform cultures, to explore what people think they are doing when they share stories, and add their personal evaluation of the contents, and to critically analyse how their actions are guided by human and machine processes.

The need to better understand our information sharing habits, their significance and impacts, has always been central to media or communications research—but research on social media news sharing has far wider implications. As Director of the Tow Centre, Emily Bell (2016) has said "Social media hasn't just swallowed journalism, it has swallowed everything … political campaigns, banking systems, personal histories, the leisure industry, retail, even government and security." The barriers to obtaining business information, to entrepreneurship, marketing and public communications, have all been lowered via social media publishing. DIY creativity is celebrated and commercialised. Social networking is reinventing the way we seek finance, buy and rent goods, manage healthcare and respond to disasters. From Donald Trump's tweets to Narendra Modi's Instagram pictures, politics is increasingly being played out in symbolic exchanges, to global audiences, and power plays fought using 'fake news', troll armies and issues-based advertising campaigns.

Sharing News Online aims to explore the fundamental dynamics of that power shift. It draws on a two-year multidisciplinary project with an Australian news start-up called Share Wars and one of the country's most popular news services, ninemsn (now Nine.com). Together we have charted the rise and domination of social media services in the news business using insights drawn from digital media and cultural studies, computing science, linguistics, sociology and political science. Much of our empirical research analyses data captured from Facebook and Twitter, but we will also explore case studies from other platforms and start-ups, as well as co-created phenomena such as hashtags. Finally while other studies have envisioned the future of news as a co-production with global audiences and transnational platforms, shifting political and cultural power away from national legacy news media, we also consider the way in which social sharing has national characteristics and triggers national regulatory responses.

Finding a framework to ground this type of multidisciplinary enterprise is never a simple task, and is only partially realised in this collaboration. Since mid-last century at least, scholars have been working to transcend the limitations of disciplinarity and its tendency to fragment academic vision (Osborne 2015). Yet, at some moments, particular disciplinary expertise, such as the computational science that underpins our news sharing analysis in Chap. 4 or the corpus linguistics in Chap. 5, is essential to our methodological hybridity. Here, we are trying to repurpose the very same tools used by the platforms to inform their commercial strategies and build their ecologies, to probe less obviously profitable aspects of social sharing.

As a whole though, the book projects a systematic overview of social media news sharing, which connects aspects of structure and agency, regulation and autonomy, adaptability and stasis. It connects the macro interests of political economy (ownership, competition, labour and regulation) with the more micro concerns of critical cultural media studies, which aim to understand how our cultural activities construct, contest and transform power relations in society.

The name we give our approach is *critical media ecology*. In the coming chapters, we set out to explore several aspects of the online news sharing ecology:

- the factors that bring together the many and diverse actors in our internetworked information, communication and representational systems, which are now integrated into so much of our work, home life and play, and our political, economic, social and cultural worlds.

- the historic, situated interdependencies between these actors that come about as a result of user goals and motivations, cultural identity and allegiances, business models and missions and specific social contexts.
- the way those relationships are shaped by the economic, legal and ethical parameters of different social media platforms, apps, websites and internet providers and by black boxed algorithmic processes.
- the extent to which these associations respond to, and are influenced by, structural factors in the news media and information technology industries, regionally or globally.

As critical media ecologists, we share an interest in the evolution of media technologies with the US schools of media ecology, based on the work of Harold Innis, Marshall McLuhan and Walter Ong. However, unlike them, we are more concerned with the political and economic implications of social media use and platform operations, the actors who have built networked power through their corporate and social alliances and the ways in which corporate uses of social media data affect the character and quality of independent, public interest journalism. Where the North American media ecologists have a sociological focus on the systemic ways in which technology impacts on human cognition and behaviour, we investigate how social media business and cultural relations are constructed around news journalism and how they affect the news media's pursuit of collective, normative ideals such as democracy, social inclusion and cultural diversity.

News is a commodity wrapped in ideology, mythology and contest, so studying how it is being shaped by social media companies, uses and users requires we first position our understanding of its social and political purpose, before we delve into its changing meaning and value in the digital era. Emeritus Professor Melvin Mencher, renowned Western journalism educator, tells us that news is the reporting of information that breaks with the normal flow of events and helps people make sound decisions about their lives (2011: 56). However, we think of news journalism more critically as a normatively conceived system of producing publicly useful information that is driven by a mix of commercial imperatives, ideological interests, professional ideals and social and cultural expectations. It is differently configured from country to country by historical events, markets and political interventions. Political scientists tell us we should be concerned about the quality and diversity of news journalism, as it monitors the operations of government and business and informs citizens about issues of public interest so they can make more informed choices about how they act in society. This is the normative 'watchdog' or fourth estate imaginary of journalism's social purpose.

Yet, as sociologist Herbert Gans (1979) revealed when he studied how news was made by US television networks, it is most often about the doings of elites—celebrities, politicians, business tycoons and public officials—and shaped by institutional forces such as government and market decisions. The lives of most ordinary people "never come into the news except as statistics. How ordinary people work, what they do outside working hours, in their families, churches, clubs and other organizations and how they relate to government and public agencies hardly ever make the news" (1979: 15). Researchers have since continually verified this status bias and highlighted other biases of the mainstream news media: its Anglo ethnocentrism, masculinist and heteronormative tendencies, and its tendency to marginalise social activism, as well as its common resort to mythic figures and narratives to affirm dominant beliefs and values. Some scholars suggest that audiences themselves are complicit in the commercial news media's focus on entertainment and sensationalism, as they are more interested in celebrity and lifestyle news than the worthy forms of political and civic journalism that reporters value (Boczkowski and Mitchelstein 2013). In the last decade though, social media sharing has enabled ordinary people to show the diversity of what interests them in news' cavalcade of power, scandal and fame. They can now promote what matters to them among their social networks, ostensibly lending some degree of democratic intervention to journalism's elite bias. For that reason, one of our interests in this book is to examine how online news sharing incorporates everyday preferences, tastes, ideas, attitudes and emotions and what impacts this is having on institutional media agendas and operations.

Our focus on news as the exemplar of socially valuable journalism is symbolic rather than exclusive of other forms of journalism. In the account that follows, we will talk about the social sharing of many forms of factual reporting, short and long form, from the informative and investigative to the editorial and analytic. Curiously, as we will reveal, the widespread industry predictions that online audiences, in the face of proliferating information, will demand more analysis and more long-form, deep dive reporting does not necessarily relate to what they share most on social media platforms. As Chap. 4 indicates, what we share online may have more to do with participating in everyday public debates and alerting our networks to key issues as a means to educate others about what we think is important and to express our opinions about world events.

News sharing, as the platforms have recognised, is now a daily ritual of social and cultural participation that gives us visibility, connection and belonging in an increasingly noisy, mediated world—where our communications contexts have converged and, as Zizi Papacharissi argues, "sociocultural, economic, and political tendencies and tensions are collapsed" (2015: 117). Paying attention to news is a metre of our engagement with the social world. Sharing it with others is both an act of self-actualisation and a bid for relevance and relatedness.

Given the platforms' apparently tight grip on the future of the news media, there are contrasting views on the possible long-term outcomes of social sharing for factual journalism. Optimists tend to foreground the ways in which sharing has democratised news distribution and diversified flows and consumption. As our Share Wars colleagues have noted, in the last century at least, journalistic agendas have been determined by a narrow set of professionals, with the final say on what is published going to those 'alpha male' editors that tended to run legacy newsrooms (Crawford et al. 2015: 10–14). Online, however, we share news that defines both our professional and private worlds and those of our friends, family and colleagues—and this spread of subject matter may be more pluralist than the broadcast bulletins or front pages of traditional news media, depending on the composition of our social networks. It is also possible that social media use incidentally exposes users to news sources that they wouldn't normally encounter and provides them with more political diversity in their media consumption (Fletcher and Kleis 2017). In their book, *All Your Friends Like This*, the Share Wars team argue that studying what the audience wants to share generally makes journalism *better*. It helps journalists determine the subject matter that people publicly identify with and what they value, enabling them to deliver more timely, relevant, diverse information to their audiences. Social media metrics, based on real time monitoring of consumption and sharing, have brought valuable insights to commissioning and reporting, with a Reuters Institute report (Cherubini and Kleis Nielsen 2016) noting that they inform story discovery, production, revision, release time and promotion. Digital-born companies such as *Buzzfeed*, *Upworthy* and the now defunct *Gawker* have based their business models on crafting content that increases measures of user attention and interaction.

Pessimists and sceptics have questioned the impact of the news media too closely following, and replicating, what does well on social media. They highlight the limits to consumer sovereignty and giving people what they want, warning that algorithmically defined echo chambers and the proliferation of clickbait are evidence that editors need to maintain a critical mindset about using social sharing metrics to determine editorial agendas. As the US Congressional inquiry into the 2016 US election confirmed, the social media news sharing business has also ushered in an era of paid mis- and disinformation, where partisans, propagandists and hoaxers play to our prejudices and undermine our capacity to make effective, informed political and economic judgments. Just as search usurped the gatekeeping authority, verification and legitimation practices of journalism (Carlson 2007), so too has social sharing enabled any user to circulate bogus narratives globally without the expert scrutiny or interference of editors and reporters. Reporters too, working under increased pressure to churn out copy, are potential recyclers of this misinformation (Wardle 2017). Claire Wardle's typology of fake news reminds us that even genuine news can be misleading if it's circulated in a false or altered context. The intensification of fake news circulating on social media in recent years, exposed during Craig Silverman's (2016; Silverman and Alexander 2016) investigation into the rise of pro-Trump sites in Macedonia, has opened a lively debate about the extent to which social news sharing can be manipulated for political and economic gain. Others highlight the tendency for news sharing to reinforce sender and receiver confirmation biases, reducing the likelihood that they will post on topics they don't agree with and fostering echo chamber effects.

Our book explores these rugged, often unpredictable contours of news transformation via the evolution of the social media news sharing business. In doing so, it surveys the differing motivations for and uses of sharing exchanges and their cultural consequences.

Chapter 2 connects the value we derive from sharing news, including characteristics of information gifts and the moral economies of web 2.0, with the logic of the attention economy and its exploitation of news consumers' affective relations with story content. It introduces two sides to sharing commodification—the commercial development of recommendation technologies for signalling taste, promoting choices, redistributing and contesting ideas, and the evolution of analytics tools to collate and categorise data on our topical preferences and consumption activities, which then influence reporting, agenda setting and newsroom resource allocation, alongside news production and placement, distribution and redistribution.

Rather than interpreting users as informational or affective labourers, we see them as evaluative intermediaries—in an unequal but interdependent relationship with the platforms that shapes their development and focus. This chapter explores how social media platforms provide access to communicative affordances and simultaneously use automation, notification technologies and reward systems to trigger and promote social sharing of news and information, in order to collect intimate, personalised user knowledge that they can commodify. The commendary signals we send when sharing news, via links, likes and favourites, emojis and hashtags, are aggregated and analysed to demonstrate the specificity and scope of audience interest to advertisers. Through individual profiling and aggregate profile patterning, social media companies and their analytics partners can then provide advertisers and publishers remarkably fine data about human behaviour online. Automating this process, so that platform users willingly input that data and build an everyday culture of commending news, allows social media companies to provide audience metrics at a scale never before possible.

However, as we discuss, the reasons we share news are complex, and the ways diverse, that *commendary culture* varies greatly across different news sharing platforms and social phenomena. Chapter 1 considers how it is structured around diverse means of quantifying and commodifying, as well as building, rewarding and managing, social relations—with a focus on Twitter's follower status and Reddit's karma points system. We then explore how tools for measuring and interpreting commendary activity have been adopted and implemented by news journalists, with a case study from our research partners Nine News and Share Wars, whose Likeable Engine was a prototype for integrating social media analytics into the routines of news gathering and production.

Chapter 3 explores how social sharing is analysed, measured and valued, and how it impacts on journalism work. It charts the evolution of social media metrics, the industry development undertaken using public application programming interfaces (APIs) and the wars over the development of new digital audience measurement standards. In this chapter, we also outline a new form of information commodification which underpins the value of social media news sharing, and shapes the corporate entanglements of digital media companies. Alongside the traditional news and audience commodities, we chart the rise of the *metadata commodity*, and the trade in data about news use and usage contexts.

In investigating the metrification of journalism, we question the clarity, stability and transparency of platform metrics such as Facebook's 'like' and consider how commendary signals have come to represent such potent indicators of audience approval and journalistic worth. Problematising the accuracy and reliability of sharing measurements allows us to critique the techniques of control used by the tech giants to transform the news business, and to explore their lack of openness about how they manipulate sharing activities manually and algorithmically. Worldwide, as this is written, there is a growing public push for algorithmic transparency as a human rights issue in order to force corporations to reveal the ways in which their programming assumptions embed social disadvantage, surveillance, unfair competition and other negative social outcomes.

From examining how social news sharing is organised, operationalised and monetised in different cultural settings, we move to mapping its industrial planes, networks and nodes. Chapter 4 analyses the political economics of news sharing, investigating how social media companies and analytics services are transforming journalism, news production and distribution. Just as social networking and media services are co-constructed with their users, so too have these platforms relied on the interdependencies of start-up culture, and vertical integration of small, interlinked companies in order to consolidate their capacities to track our actions and interests.

This raises questions about the activities of the companies that control and exchange this information, and their strategies for exploiting it. The chapter then explores their business activities and alliances through the notion of *critical media ecology*, examining the complexly imbricated business models, ownership patterns and industrial power of key players such as Facebook, YouTube, Reddit and Gigya. It examines the variety of smaller actors that support what Nardi and O'Day (1999) would call the 'predator' species of the social media ecosystem, the major social sharing platforms. These intermediary companies include news analytics firms, identity management companies, native advertising or content placement services and dialogic media and community management services, alongside bookmarking and link shortening operations. Each of these plays a role in facilitating the easy, personalised, monitored and analysed use of social media news sharing platforms in a relatively open, if proprietary, ecosystem of digital intermediaries. To contrast this, we offer a glimpse into the more closed ecosystem of China's social media market, where the government and platform corporations work hand in hand to ensure social surveillance and control.

Finally, in light of Facebook's dealings with Cambridge Analytica, we consider the lack of public information about which businesses platforms share our information with, and on what terms. This leads to a broader discussion of algorithmic culture, and the extent of its influence on news distribution and visibility.

The lack of transparency about how platform algorithms work to curate and place news in people's feeds has invited researchers to reverse engineer their actions (Diakopolous 2013; Gehl 2014) and to explore aspects of their operation and meaning that lie outside social media's commercial imperatives. In our case, we have been interested in using data analytics to discover what types of news people shared most, what topics they preferenced, what forms of commendary action they engaged in and how this compared to previous studies of digital news consumption.

Chapter 5 details the findings of a genre and topic analysis conducted of most shared news on Facebook and Twitter. The data was captured by Share Wars' Likeable Engine from these platforms' then-public application programming interfaces (APIs) and matched to stories from over 100 English language news sites internationally. The final list of shared stories was then hand coded for story form, social purpose, style and keyword topic, as well as the presence of multimedia comments, other forms of participatory features. The resulting analysis explores which story genres and which topics trigger high-volume news sharing and what constitutes everyday low-volume sharing. It also considers whether interactive, multimedia and participative features increase the likelihood that stories will be shared. Importantly, this study questions the so-called news gap theory, which posits that audiences favour light, lifestyles stories over the more serious hard news journalism that the legacy news media promote as their raison d'etre. Instead, we make the case that what we share, we care about—and that include politics and current affairs.

Digging deeper then into the packaging of most highly shared news, Chap. 6 demonstrates what corpus linguistics can tell us about the language of these stories. Given that the social media era has been characterised by the search for a virality formula, it is surprising that more public attention hasn't been paid to the syntax and semantics of highly shared news. There are certainly some industry studies that look at aspects of story construction, such as the headline phrases that gain most Facebook engagement (Rayson 2017). Analysing 100 million news headlines shared on Facebook over a two-month period, Buzzsumo concluded that the words "will make you" comprised the most engaging headline phrase based on cumulative shares, likes and comments. This phrase, director Steve Rayson argues, "promises that the content will have a direct impact on the reader, often an emotional reaction", picking up on earlier research that shows sharing is often triggered by emotional reaction and physiological arousal (Berger and Milkman 2010, 2012). Yet this study, which also explores the worst performing phrases, the top headline starters and ends and the optimum length of headlines, tells us nothing about the rest of the stories that prompted users to signal their approval on Facebook. Rather, it is designed to promote the corporation's services.

By way of contrast, our colleague Monika Bednarek's analysis reveals the variety and contextual complexity of what we share. She also draws on quantitative and qualitative analyses to underscore the significance of traditional news values like eliteness, superlativeness, unexpectedness and negativity in most shared stories. These findings suggest the types of story framing that might attract attention on social media and the local contexts that can affect virality.

These issues are taken up again from an audience research perspective in Chap. 7. Here, we report on a study of ninemsn.com.au news consumers, the audience for one of Australia's most popular news services. It explores the critical role emotional or affective responses play in shaping their news sharing decisions and reflects on differences in these responses across demographic groups. It explores two key questions: what motivates people to recirculate the news they find online, and what feelings are involved in their decision to share a story?

This study indicates variations in triggers to sharing and the importance of pedagogical and caring impulses in motivating action, rather than the desire to amuse, inspire or amaze—although there are marked gender and age differences in sharing motivation. Findings suggest that emerging social media editorial strategies need to closely consider cultural differences in user interests, and less sensationalist motivations for sharing than might be signalled by click-driven metrics.

Chapter 8 looks at how online news sharing is affecting policy thinking about media pluralism and control of the media in Western democracies. We re-examine the proposition that news sharing is able to produce a democratising effect on the news media, in giving ordinary people the capacity to recommend and redistribute the news they find socially significant. The chapter explores how policy makers and media researchers might assess the veracity of that claim against historic notions of media diversity, and the central role of that concept in media policy. It revisits and expands on some of the questions raised throughout the book about the power of social media platforms to control political news sharing and to influence political agenda setting. In doing so it further investigates how *news intermediaries* are reshaping the mediascape and provides new resources for exploring the measurement of voice plurality and information quality questions in digital news.

Chapter 9 then considers how viral news differs from everyday news sharing, and how it impacts on the formation of public opinion in different political, social and cultural contexts: China, Australia and the US It explores how the undifferentiated notion of virality can be differently conceived of, and analysed, using case studies of the Tianjin port explosions of 2015, the Queensland floods of 2011 and the Boston Marathon bombing of 2013. This chapter investigates different government responses to these disasters, the dynamics of control and coordination around social media news sharing, and how these shaped interactions with social media users and platforms.

There are several fine books about media sharing that inform our discussion throughout, and which are central to our argument about the politics of commendary culture and its intersection with the transformation of news. Nicholas John's *The Age of Sharing,* Graham Meikle's *Social Media: Communication, Sharing and Visibility* and *Spreadable Media* by Henry Jenkins, Sam Ford and Joshua Green, all traverse social and cultural territory that informs our analysis of the social media ecology, its industry relationships, labour models, preoccupations, values and ideologies.

We also owe a great deal of thanks to our Share Wars partners, Hal Crawford, Andrew Hunter and Domagoj Filipovic, for great discussion and generous access to the Nine newsroom and their Share Wars research. Hal's investigation of fake news purveyors in the US and Australia (Crawford et al. 2015) predates many of the debates that emerged around the Trump election, and reveals a range of financial and creative rationales for peddling misinformation that emanate from dot-com libertarianism.

The account that follows investigates the impacts of popular digital redistribution on the news media. It has entered its own spooky realm of uncertainty, dire predictions and despair thanks to the rise of social media and influencers like Logan Paul, and the gravitation of audience attention to platform feeds. Outside the film and television industries, media distribution is a sorely under-researched cultural activity, partly because the print, radio and music sectors had relatively stable contours during the analogue media decades during which media studies developed. However, the coming of internet, web, mobile and social media technologies has enabled every connected person to be a global publisher, disrupting historic methods and measures of media dissemination and creating opportunities for the rapidly evolving information technology industry to capitalise on its internetworking expertise.[4]

Since around 2008, the social media platforms have established a parallel media distribution system; one which relies on their users finding, assessing and recommending stories to others. Each of us in this scenario is a potential critic and taste maker, or *cultural intermediator* in the Bourdieusian (1984) sense. Our power to influence others' news consumption is determined not only by our own social and cultural clout, but also by our interest in pursuing others' attention, within and beyond our social circles. Combine our capacity to quickly rate and recommend news with the ability to recirculate it globally, without the regulatory constraints of analogue media, and it is easy to see how the platforms have enabled their users to assume a greater degree of control over how journalism is seen, interpreted and valued than in the previous century. At the same time, the platforms benefit through the aggregation and trade of data about our cultural preferences. It is this commendary dynamic, the dialectic of gifting and accumulation, that we will explore as a prelude to analysing the business of news sharing.

References

Allcott, Hunt, Matthew Gentzkow, and Chuan Yu. 2019. Trends in the Diffusion of Misinformation on Social Media. *Research & Politics* 6 (2). https://doi.org/10.1177/2053168019848554.

Anthony, Sebastian. 2014. Hong Kong Protesters Turn to Mesh Networks to Evade China's Censorship. *Extreme Tech.* September 30. http://www.extreme-tech.com/extreme/191118-hongkong-protesters-turn-to-mesh-networks-to-evade-chinascensorship.

Bell, Emily. 2016. The End of the News as We Know It: How Facebook Swallowed Journalism. *Medium.* March 7. https://medium.com/tow-center/the-end-of-the-news-as-we-know-it-how-facebook-swallowed-journalism-60344fa50962

Berger, Jonah, and Katherine L. Milkman. 2010. Virality: What Gets Shared and Why. In *Advances in Consumer Research*, ed. Margaret C. Campbell, Jeff

---

[4] Except where this appears to violate traditional legal principles of copyright, for example, peer to peer networking.

Inman, and Rik Pieters, vol. 37, 118–121. Duluth, MN: Association for Consumer Research.

———. 2012. What Makes Online Content Viral? *Journal of Marketing Research* 49 (2): 192–205.

Boczkowski, Pablo J., and Eugenia Mitchelstein. 2013. *The News Gap: When the Information Preferences of the Media and the Public Diverge.* Cambridge, MA: The MIT Press.

Bourdieu, Pierre. 1984. *Distinction: A Cultural Critique of the Judgement of Taste.* Translated by Richard Nice. London: Routledge.

Bruns, Axel. 2018. *Gatewatching and News Curation: Journalism, Social Media, and the Public Sphere.* New York: Peter Lang.

Carlson, Matt. 2007. Order versus Access: News Search Engines and the Challenge to Traditional Journalistic Roles. *Media, Culture and Society* 29 (6): 1014–1030.

Chadwick, Andrew, and Christian Viccari. 2019. *News Sharing on UK Social Media: Misinformation, Disinformation, and Correction.* Survey Report. Online Civic Culture Centre. Loughborough University. https://www.lboro. ac.uk/media/media/research/o3c/Chadwick%20Vaccari%20O3C-1%20 News%20Sharing%20on%20UK%20Social%20Media.pdf.

Cherubini, Federica, and Rasmus Kleis Nielsen. 2016. *Editorial Analytics: How News Media Are Developing and Using Audience Data and Metrics.* Oxford: Reuters Institute for the Study of Journalism, February 23.

Crawford, Hal, Andrew Hunter, and Domagoj Filipovic. 2015. *All Your Friends Like This: How Social Networks Took over News.* Sydney: HarperCollins.

Diakopolous, Nick. 2013. Rage Against the Algorithms. *The Atlantic.* October 3. http://www.theatlantic.com/technology/archive/2013/10/rage-against-the-algorithms/280255/.

Edelman. 2018. *2018 Edelman Trust Barometer Global Report.* http://cms.edelman.com/sites/default/files/2018-02/2018_Edelman_Trust_Barometer_ Global_Report_FEB.pdf.

Fletcher, Richard, and Rasmus Kleis Nielsen. 2017. Using Social Media Appears to Diversify Your News Diet, Not Narrow It. *Nieman Lab.* June 21. http://www. niemanlab.org/2017/06/using-social-media-appears-to-diversify-your-news-diet-not-narrow-it/.

Gans, Herbert J. 1979. *Deciding What's News: A Study of CBS Evening News, NBC Nightly News, Newsweek, and Time.* New York: Pantheon Books.

Gehl, Robert W. 2014. *Reverse Engineering Social Media: Software, Culture, and Political Economy in New Media Capitalism.* Philadelphia, PA: Temple University Press.

Ingram, Matthew. 2015. Facebook Has Taken over from Google as a Traffic Source for News. *Fortune.* August 19. http://fortune.com/2015/08/18/ facebook-google/.

Institute for Media and Communication Policy. 2017. *Ranking - The 100 Largest Media Companies 2017.* Cologne: Institute for Media and Communication Policy.

https://www.mediadb.eu/de/datenbanken/internationale-medienkonzerne.
html.

Jenkins, Henry, Sam Ford, and Joshua Green. 2013. *Spreadable Media: Creating Value and Meaning in a Networked Culture.* New York: New York University Press.

Knight Foundation. 2018. *American Views: Trust, Media And Democracy. Gallup/Knight Foundation.* January 1. https://knightfoundation.org/reports/american-views-trust-media-and-democracy.

Kollewe, Julia. 2017. Google and Facebook Bring in One-Fifth of Global Ad Revenue. *The Guardian.* May 17. https://www.theguardian.com/media/2017/may/02/google-and-facebook-bring-in-one-fifth-of-global-ad-revenue.

Küng, Lucy. 2018. *Digital Transformation. The Organisational Challenge – Creating a Roadmap for Change.* Oxford: Reuters Institute/Thomson Reuters. https://agency.reuters.com/en/insights/industryreports/going-digital-a-roadmap-for-organizational-transformation.html.

Lin, Zhongxuan. 2016. Traditional Media, Social Media, and Alternative Media in Hong Kong's Umbrella Movement. *Asian Politics & Policy* 8 (2): 365–372.

Mencher, Melvin. 2011. *Melvin Mencher's News Reporting and Writing.* New York: McGraw-Hill Higher Education.

Nardi, Bonnie A., and Vicki L. O'Day. 1999. *Information Ecologies.* Cambridge, MA: MIT Press.

Newman, Nic, Richard Fletcher, David A. Levy, and Rasmus Kleis Nielsen. 2016. *Digital News Report 2016.* Oxford: Reuters Institute.

Newman, Nic, Richard Fletcher, Antonis Kalogeropoulos, David A. Levy, and Rasmus Kleis Nielsen. 2017. *Digital News Report 2017.* Oxford: Reuters Institute.

———. 2018. *Digital News Report 2018.* Oxford: Reuters Institute.

Osborne, Peter. 2015. Problematizing Disciplinarity, Transdisciplinary Problematics. *Theory, Culture & Society* 32 (5–6): 3–35. https://doi.org/10.1177/0263276415592245.

Papacharissi, Zizi. 2015. *Affective Publics: Sentiment, Technology, and Politics.* Oxford; New York: Oxford University Press.

Paul, Logan. 2017. We Found a Dead Body in the Japanese Suicide Forest. Logan Paul Vlogs. *YouTube.* December 31. Video Taken Down and URL Not Available.

———. 2018. So Sorry. Logan Paul Vlogs. *YouTube.* January 2. https://www.youtube.com/watch?v=QwZT7T-TXT0.

Petre, Caitlin. 2015. *The Traffic Factories: Metrics at Chartbeat, Gawker Media, and The New York Times.* New York: Tow Center for Digital Journalism.

Pew Research Center. 2014. *State of the News Media.* March 26. http://assets.pewresearch.org/wp-content/uploads/sites/13/2017/05/30142556/state-of-the-news-media-report-2014-final.pdf.

Rayson, Steve. 2017. We Analyzed 100 Million Headlines. Here's What We Learned (New Research). *Buzzsumo*. June 26. http://buzzsumo.com/blog/most-shared-headlines-study/.

Reuters. 2017. Why Google and Facebook Prove the Digital Ad Market Is a Duopoly. *Fortune*. July 28. http://fortune.com/2017/07/28/google-facebook-digital-advertising/.

Robehmed, Natalie. 2018. Highest-Paid YouTube Stars 2018: Markiplier, Jake Paul, PewDiePie And More. *Forbes*. December 3. https://www.forbes.com/sites/natalierobehmed/2018/12/03/highest-paid-youtube-stars-2018-markiplier-jake-paul-pewdiepie-and-more/#77753232909a.

Rosenstiel, Tom, Jeff Sonderman, Kevin Loker, Maria Ivancin, and Nina Kjarval. 2015. *Twitter and the News: How People Use the Social Network to Learn about the World*. American Press Institute and Twitter. September 1. https://www.americanpressinstitute.org/publications/reports/survey-research/how-people-use-twitter-news/.

Silverman, Craig. 2016. This Analysis Shows How Viral Fake Election News Stories Outperformed Real News on Facebook. *Buzzfeed*. November 17. https://www.buzzfeed.com/craigsilverman/viral-fake-election-news-outperformed-real-news-on-facebook.

Silverman, Craig, and Lawrence Alexander. 2016. How Teens in the Balkans are Duping Trump Supporters with Fake News. *Buzzfeed*. November 4. https://www.buzzfeed.com/craigsilverman/how-macedonia-became-a-global-hub-for-pro-trump-misinfo.

Wardle, Claire. 2017. Fake News: It's Complicated. *First Draft*. February 16. https://firstdraftnews.com/fake-news-complicated/.

CHAPTER 2

Commendary Cultures

Fiona Martin

Social sharing of news has a critical economic and cultural function in an attention economy. It reveals our personal interests, beliefs and tastes to the array of publications trying to win our interest and identifies to them and our social networks what is valuable to us in the cascades of data that we negotiate every day. Through our shares, likes and favourites we help the social platforms determine what is popular and profitable in advertising terms. We also elevate certain events and issues in public debate, and reinforce opinions and attitudes in our social circles. Thus, if most mainstream media users are more likely to redistribute, like or recommend news than to create it, then news sharing is potentially as important a phenomenon to study as participatory or citizen journalism.

This makes it imperative for reporters, editors and news executives to understand, beyond the metrics they might receive about Facebook or Twitter trends, what motivates news sharing in different contexts, as well as how and why we are likely to share stories we come across online. It is also important to recognise how the platforms have ensured news sharing is imbricated in the rhythms of everyday life online and integrated into the editorial processes of news rooms. This shift is driving the reorganisation of news production, consumption and distribution, and redirecting economic, political and cultural power away from the legacy media and towards the platforms.

It's easy to focus on social media platforms as the primary site of news sharing, as they are designed precisely for that purpose: the easy personal exchange of information with what passes for a self-built social network

© The Author(s) 2019
F. Martin, T. Dwyer, *Sharing News Online*,
https://doi.org/10.1007/978-3-030-17906-9_2

(although recommendation algorithms play a big role in helping us constructing that sociality). Social media companies make sharing simple to encourage us to disclose more about our everyday lives, so they can analyse that routine evidence of activities and preferences to create more effective forms of advertising. It's a twenty-first-century design for a radical, globalised consumer sovereignty that seeks to make as much social behaviour as possible accessible to corporate scrutiny or, as Facebook's most durable first decade mission statement more altruistically puts it, "To give people the power to share and make the world more open and connected" (Reagan 2009).

Yet, news sharing also takes place via email, apps, forums and other online channels, just through the posting of hyperlinks—a practice as old as the World Wide Web, and which has its basis in earlier hypertext systems. Each time we post a link to a news story, we are curating from our own feeds what might be of interest to others, recommending what they should attend to and demonstrating something of our own concerns and biases. Link sharing is not always an endorsement of the content, but demands those who click through consider its meaning and worth. So, this chapter explores how social news sharing has become central to the creation of commendary cultures online, where ordinary people take on the representational and distributive roles of the news media, as well as something of journalism's filtering and evaluative functions. It explores the pre-history and evolution of news sharing technologies and the emergence of different ideas about what sharing means, why we do it and how it's affecting digital journalism.

If link sharing is the basis for online news exchange, how then did social media become synonymous with this practice, to the extent that people around the globe now see these channels as key news sources? To answer this question, we first need to establish what qualifies as 'social media'. As new media scholar Graham Meikle notes this term evokes "a particular set of technological affordances, a particular set of business models and corporate practices, a particular set of organisations, and a particular set of cultural habits, practices and expectations" (2016: x). The organisations are well recognised worldwide and becoming virtual monopolies in their various niches by virtue of their transnational scale and market dominance. By late 2016, Alphabet (owner of Google and YouTube), Facebook (with WhatsApp and Instagram) and Microsoft (LinkedIn and Yammer) were among the largest companies internationally by market capitalisation, bigger than the finance and energy companies they had succeeded on that list

(Flew et al. 2019). Facebook is now the world's most popular social media platform, with around 2.19 billion monthly active users in the first quarter of 2018. In the same period, WeChat has reached 1 billion Chinese users alone, more than Twitter has worldwide, while YouTube dominates video sharing and video on demand advertising globally.

While each company has a distinct business model, on the whole, the biggest players' economic success has been based in five factors:

1. broadening the base of production to every subscriber;
2. making global communication and publishing easier through templating and automation;
3. reducing or removing the geographic boundaries to social and business transactions;
4. aggregating and analysing user created data to create more efficient, individually targeted advertising sales models; and
5. operating as international information technology companies rather than national media publishers, which has until recently put them outside traditional media content regulations and allowed them to publish content that others could or would not.

Economist Yochai Benkler (2004) suggests internetworked social sharing of information has proved a more efficient form of distribution than historic market forces. It is decentralised, avoiding the strictures, conventions and routines of corporate news gatekeepers; autonomous, allowing anyone and everyone with network access to take part, and personalised, in tying the act of recirculating news to communicative rituals and social conventions of information gifting and reciprocation.

Social media companies' technological affordances have enabled us to increase our everyday news sharing, extending it to large, curated social networks. Starting with Six Degrees, launched back in 1997, and then Friendster in 2002, social networking applications allowed users to create public or semi-public personal profiles, to build a list of social connections that they could easily navigate, and to communicate publicly or privately with those people using templated publishing tools (Hinton and Hjorth 2013). Later social media technologies also enabled users to create, aggregate, evaluate and share media, to create groups and audiences for this content, and to monitor user analytics based on that service interaction. From 2006, Facebook and others provided widgets or limited functionality scripts for publishers to embed in their sites so users could subscribe to news publishers' social media channels, or share a story link directly on reading it on a branded website, and later, mobile apps for continuous access to this sharing capacity.

All of these strategies were designed to simultaneously extend our customised communicative reach and to automatically co-opt more users and publishers into the orbit of platform analysis, in what critical media studies scholars Jose van Dijck and Poell (2013: 8) calls a "double logic" of connectivity. Platform analytics are not only "perpetually operational" and so pervasive that we don't notice them (as Kennedy [2016: 25] suggests), but are also designed to reward and reinforce our participation; to make it addictive using a series of behaviour reinforcing communication strategies (Alter 2017). Alerts or notifications from our social media feeds tell us how much attention our posts are getting, and detail our network members' activities, to encourage our reciprocity and to routinise our sharing activity. Sometimes, gamification is built into the systems, so that we are notified where in a hierarchy of users we are placed as a result of our activity. We are encouraged to move to the next status level by posting more. In these ways, platforms cultivate habits of documentation, declaration, discussion and debate, through constant visual and auditory reminders of their presence. They recommend related posts and stories we should like, given our past consumption and interaction history, and make others invisible, through algorithmic processes that maximise our exposure to popular content, personalised advertising and online services.

So, while social media platforms are not the simplest or only ways to share news stories, they do provide a widely accessible suite of portable tools for customising our news consumption, accelerating the scale and scope of its distribution and exposing it to the scrutiny of algorithmic tracking, classification and assessment which allows them to monetise any insights into our behaviour and interests.

In positioning themselves as IT companies and carriers of content rather than publishers, social media companies historically have avoided having to conform to the content regulation laws and accountability measures set up for legacy media, or to worry overly about what their users post on their platforms. For example, the U.S. Digital Millennium Copyright Act includes a safe harbour provision, which protects them from liability for the content their users might post—as long as they act to remove any illegal content about which they are informed (Flew et al. 2019). There is, as yet, no legal mechanism for forcing platforms to reveal how their algorithms structure the content we see, and that we don't see, or what human editorial decision making takes place in content management. Recent national and regional moves to regulate the content we share, like Germany's Network Enforcement Act (German Law Archive 2017) and the European Commission's (2016) Code of Conduct on Countering Illegal Hate Speech have put some pressure on the major platforms to remove violent and extreme political speech (Goggin et al. 2017). However, on the whole, what we share online is determined by the guidelines that they set, and which they are not answerable for—even to us.

From this relatively unassailable legal position, and in possession of audience knowledge that the old media could only dream of, major social media platforms have been in a position to influence both cultural production and the production of culture, especially news media culture.

THE IMPORTANCE OF COMMENDARY CULTURE

As a source of traffic to news websites, social media's influence on news distribution may well have peaked and passed. Certainly its 2015 dominance of referred news traffic was a blip on the metrics radar. Since then, Google search has reasserted its place as the number one online news referral source. Following the 2016 election misinformation scandal, Facebook also demoted news page content in people's feeds (Facebook 2018), leading some industry observers to argue that publishers should reorient their strategy away from that platform (Filloux 2018) and engage more deeply with their audiences rather than using social media channels to push out links to stories (Elizabeth 2017).

Yet, some media commentators still argue that social media sharing may have profound effects on the future of journalism. They note that young people's turn to social media as a primary news source together with social media companies' capacity to imperceptibly select, filter and promote the news that gets seen could have three immediate impacts: eroding journalism's power to connect directly with audiences, to deliver what they need to know in the public interest and to ensure the accuracy and quality of the news they consume (Bell 2016; Bell and Taylor 2017). They worry that there is little platform accountability for what news gets seen, and by whom, and how much revenue is shared as a result (Newman 2018). Some see journalists as being locked into reporting what gets likes and shares, tailoring the news to social media metrics and "dancing to the popular music of consumer driven logic" (Tandoc 2014: 572). Others, like digital media theorist Jodi Dean (2005, 2014), have positioned social media users as unpaid labourers in the platforms' bid for informational dominance, questioning whether their circulation of ideas can do much to affect the democratic process (as well-informed citizens might hope to), or is attenuated instead in technological fetishism. From this perspective, news sharing may be just so much symbolic chaff, spread in lieu of political engagement or action. From the standpoint of critical political economics, Christian Fuchs has noted that some moments, "where social media become tools that support politics" are interesting in terms of providing alternative forms of political news, "but commercial social media's democratic and political potentials should not be overestimated" (2014: 61). More recently he has positioned Facebook CEO Mark Zuckerberg's claim that "the goal of the company is to help people share more in order to make the world more open and help promote understanding between people", as a ruse that belies a ruthless commercial business model (Fuchs 2018: 172).

The more hopeful call social media news sharing a new form of media democracy and creativity, enabling a greater diversity of people to signal to newsmakers and our social networks what's truly significant to them, in both local contexts and globally. Ostensibly, social signalling should guide journalists to report on what we value most, and on more varied conceptions of that value. In an ideal world, that would make journalism more socially responsive and culturally diverse. This techno-optimist shift is characterised in Henry Jenkins (1992) notion of participatory culture, and his newer concept of "spreadability", where "new tools have proliferated the means by which people can circulate material, word of mouth recommendations and the sharing of media content" and facilitated the diffusion of cultural artefacts and practices (Jenkins et al. 2013: 2–3). It is also embraced in Bruns' (2005, 2018) idea of "gatewatching", where ordinary users publicise news, rather than reporting or publishing it. Bruns sees news sharing as a demotic, habitual practice for most people, and core to the emergence of new forms of expertise. But while these claims may have some basis, we need to know far more about the political economics and cultural forms of shared news, as well as the real-time network dynamics and contexts for its production and consumption, before we can understand its ramifications for the news media or its role in our societies.

Up until now citizen journalism has had far more attention in media research than sharing. Most book-length studies of participatory news cultures to date have focused on novel forms of news creation: blogging, produsage and gatewatching (Bruns 2005, 2008, 2018), user-generated content (Singer et al. 2011), citizen journalism (Allan and Thorsen 2009; Miller 2014), citizen witnessing (Allan 2013) and maker and hacker culture (Usher 2016), rather than the new modes of distribution such as aggregation and sharing. Alfred Hermida's #TellEveryone: why we share and why it matters, a lively journalism studies account of how everyday social news sharing works, concentrates on the sociology of sharing, leaving the broader questions of cultural change and platform power, their shape and impacts largely unaddressed. In Axel Bruns' more theoretically engaged Gatewatching and News Curation, he devotes considerable energy to analysing news sharing, but tends to focus on the relationships between users, journalists and platforms, rather than the more complex industrial and regulatory relationships emerging in the social media news ecology. These books are important interventions in social media research, but the study of news sharing remains a relatively understudied transformation of cultural production, and one whose complex power dynamics remain obscure.

Rather than taking one or other polar position on how our social media engagement will affect the future of news, we adopt a critical media perspective on news sharing's meanings for journalism in society. That is, we want to examine how our online news sharing has been commodified, what role our actions, beliefs and proclivities have played in that process and what impact it will have on the institutional notion of journalism and the new cultures of digital news consumption.

The rest of this chapter examines the rich meanings of sharing, and how they have shifted to accommodate our new socially networked interactions and the commodification of that sociality. It then investigates why we share news online and how, exploring how our motivations for promoting certain types of news and the nature of our interactions is reshaping the way news generally is selected, reported and distributed, and in different ways on different platforms. In these senses, it is an account of the cultural politics of news sharing, or the ways that our cultural practices affect the exercise of news media power, and vice versa. As Angus and Jhally (1989) argued, it is important to understand "the manner in which institutional and ideological structures act as limits to the possibilities of cultural practices" and how cultural activity supports the emergence of new forms of power such as those of the transnational social media platforms.

So, instead of focusing on people's impulse to create media online or to participate in public debate, as most participatory journalism studies have done to date, we are exploring the rise of a more everyday use of internet technologies—to commend, recommend or condemn the news. In the first instance, news sharing seeks to draw people's attention to a news item by extending its reach. Sharers will often tell others what they think about their shared item to rationalise the reposting, and seek or expect some sort of response from their social networks. They may hope to engage others in discussing or debating or acting on the judgement they have expressed. But they may share with little or no comment, and without even reading what they've commended, leaving the interpretation to their friends and followers.

The term *commendary culture*, used here to describe the rituals, beliefs, norms and practices associated with sharing pre-existing messages online, is drawn from the two fourteenth-century Latin meanings of *commendare*: to entrust someone or something to the care of others, and to commit to writing. These days, the acts of commending and recommending have the same positive connotation of praising the object in question. Those stronger positive associations have developed in contradistinction to the concept of condemnation, criticism or censure, yet to commend something originally meant simply to note it as worthy of attention. The study of commendary culture then, is concerned with all acts of elevating media to the attention of others, regardless of the conclusion drawn about that material. It understands news sharing as a social and cultural practice which seeks to amplify messages, to capture the attention of interested others, and to engage them in a reciprocal evaluative process. It is also interested in the socio-technical systems that allow this sharing of symbolic goods, preferences and opinions, and the means of making sense of these acts—the techniques of measuring and analysing commendary activities.

As the title of this books suggests, the commendation of news stories to our social networks is commonly described as news 'sharing'. Sharing is such a polysemic and widely used term in online contexts that it demands some deconstruction before we look at why it is such a compelling activity.

WHAT IS SHARING?

As Nicholas John (2017) reveals in his absorbing cultural history of sharing, the phrase 'to share' has three different root meanings: to distribute or divide, to have something in common with and to communicate one's personal experience or feelings. Like marketing scholar Russell Belk, John is intrigued by the association of sharing with economic behaviours, and particularly prosocial internet use.

Belk (2010), from an anthropological perspective, originally argued that sharing is a form of consumption within practices of commodity exchange and gifting, based in mutual association, shared possession or collaborative ownership, and caring relationships with others. For this perspective in sharing news online, we are not losing our share of anything, but expanding what he calls our sense of an 'extended self', the projection of our identity in the world through external means (p. 724).[1] However, he saw sharing as a non-commodity relationship, which it clearly is not in the contemporary sense, when social media companies reap both advertising data and attention from our information sharing activities. Thus, while Belk later modified his definition of sharing to include industrial models of collaborative consumption and short-term rental (Belk 2014), John's work is more relevant to our purposes. He sets out to explore how tech corporations have appropriated the idea of sharing to fuel the expansion of digital capitalism via the 'sharing economy'—a key concept enabling social media companies to appropriate our personal data, our social connections and our interests.

John (2017: 62–64) proposes that sharing has acquired new meanings in the age of social networking, associated with the reach, scale, morality and emotional intimacy of online communication. The first has come via the new organisational techniques of early computing, including practices like time sharing and file sharing, which point to sharing's networked or *distributive potential.* Wadbring and Ödmark (2016) argue that there is a difference between the news media's deliberate distribution strategies, which are designed to attract, hold and measure audiences, and social sharing's 'circulatory', participative logics. We disagree with that assessment. As we will argue, platforms have their own deliberate, quantified distribution logics which seek to reach as many as possible with the most popular content their algorithms identify.

The second meaning for news sharing is reproductive, as online messaging collapses sharing's two primary meanings of communication and distribution. In sharing news, we are simultaneously engaged in an interpersonal act of telling others about ourselves *and* publishing that information for an audience to read. Sharing in these reproductive senses is also enabled by what Meikle (2016: 26) calls the "intrinsic" capacity of computational technologies to produce perfect copies, which means we can give information without losing it and in a non-rivalrous manner, as the original is still around for others to consume. Despite the culture industries' ongoing legal proceedings to assert their digital rights in music and film file sharing (Borschke 2017) and in news aggregation (Martin 2015), the capacity to make and exchange digital copies has established online media sharing as a commonplace, even virtuous act—especially where it challenges the constrictive licencing regimes of media and publishing con-

[1] See also Belk (1988) Possessions and the Extended Self.

glomerates. Meikle quotes programmer and former Reddit co-owner Aaron Swartz arguing that "sharing isn't immoral—it's a moral imperative. Only those blinded by greed would refuse to let a friend make a copy" (Swartz 2015).

This *reproductive potential* underpins the third and most potent reason for sharing's expropriation by Silicon Valley—what John calls "its positive connotations of equality, selflessness and giving" (John 2017: 63). This beneficial sense of online sharing, he notes, accords neatly with origin mythologies of the internet as a democratic force, a network for free, transparent and non-hierarchical exchange of information. So, news sharing has an *egalitarian potential* that makes us feel good about commending coverage of events and ideas to others.

Fourthly, a factor that John briefly alludes to and Meikle develops, is sharing as intimacy, and immediate personal exchange. We most often share online with our friends, family and workmates, people with whom we have some close, emotional or intellectual connections, and these bonds influence what we share and why we share it in networked circumstances. We share to build, affirm, maintain or repair relationships (Goh et al. 2017; Meikle 2016: 26). As we will see in Chap. 6, the users of an online news service who we surveyed primarily share news to show they care about a topic. They do it to express their feelings about a subject and sometimes to provoke a reaction from their friends or followers. This *affective potential* of sharing is key to understanding the topics people will respond to, and what types of stories might go viral on a social platform (see Fig. 2.1).

Over time, social media companies have recognised how to capitalise on these semantic potentials, with Facebook in particular promoting our information sharing as a "mechanism for improving human relations and making the world a better place" (John 2017: 65–66). As John critically observes, they also tend to use the term sharing to underplay the commodity exchanges they have with third-party advertisers or developers, with whom they also 'share' our personal information. This appropriation of the positive meanings for sharing to legitimate purely commercial and wholly privatised trade activity is meant to divert user attention from the potential privacy implications of this activity.

The corporate intention is to promote sharing as collectively oriented, authentic and socially productive. Reddit's 2018 homepage states it is "home to thousands of communities, endless conversation, and authentic human connection". Twitter too wants us to "spark a global conversation".

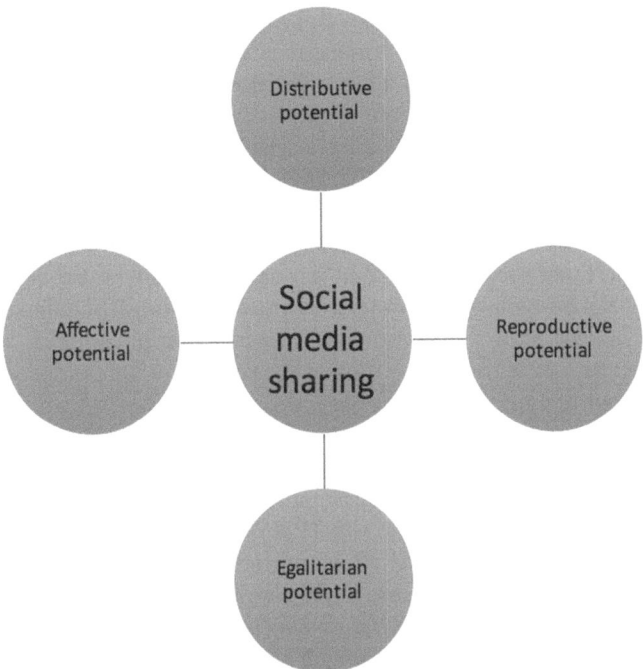

Fig. 2.1   The semantic associations of social media sharing. Image: Fiona R Martin

Facebook is "giving people the power to build community and bringing the world close together" (Zuckerberg 2017). In this focus on dialogue and community, the platforms are tapping into an old understanding of sharing as a means of intensifying social relations through personal and emotional disclosure. According to media studies researcher Jenny Kennedy (2016), social intensification is one of the three main discourses of sharing in literature on technologically networked exchange.[2] She uses Wittel's (2011) sociological analysis to argue that the exchange of immaterial goods, such as news, is 'inherently social', as it only serves to invite responses from those in the sharer's network and to accelerate interaction

[2] The other two being sharing as an economic exchange, which embraces different types of research on how we allocate access to resources, and sharing as scaled distribution, which explores the extension and contestation of ownership in sharing systems.

(2016: 468). In short, we share to connect more and more often. Platforms certainly seek to intensify our connective impulses by engineering rituals of information sharing. They send us regular, repeated daily alerts—who is tweeting what, who you should follow, how many responses you have had. To ignore these is to deny a basic drive to sociality, or so they would have us believe.

The concept of social intensification also alludes to a marriage of old and new meanings for sharing online: the search for connection with like minds, and the increased speed and scale of messaging possible in networked systems. Social media analytics now measure 'social velocity' to understand the intensity of news sharing (and other social signals) as a measure of informational relevance. The proposition is that the faster and more often we share, like or favourite a breaking story, the more engaged we are with the topic, and the more important it is to the news media's agenda. In 2016, Chartbeat subsidiary NewsWhip patented its social velocity algorithm, which it claimed at the time was used to identify breaking news and guide editorial decision making in 300 newsrooms worldwide (PR Web 2016).

This industrial interest in the gauging and valuing of social intensity speaks to the way in which our map of sharing's semantic evolution is still incomplete. Our research suggests that social media sharing is interesting to journalists and editors for the way it signals the popular worth of stories, and magnifies their reproduction and distribution, supporting the so-called virality of highly shared content. Online we can not only share stories but with more people than we ever could face-to-face, and more quickly. Due to the exponential distribution effect enabled (and encouraged) by online networks (Kelly 1997) sharing can extend the reach and amplify the impact of false, shocking or scandalous news, with potentially significant effects. In India, for example, social media rumours and disinformation campaigns have recently resulted in riots and lynching (Tharoor 2018). In social media contexts, then, news sharing then not only distributes and reproduces, but *amplifies*.

Further, to share something immaterial is to seek wider recognition of that report, analysis, idea or opinion. We recommend (and hope) that our friends and followers attend to what we post. From a Bakhtinian perspective, we speak with anticipation of an audience and a response.[3] In a social media system, we may add comments to a link or tag it so it is discoverable as part of larger discussions on a platform. We lift this item out of the flows

---

[3] See Mikhail Bakhtin (1981) *The Dialogic Imagination: four essays*, (Ed. Michael Holquist), University of Texas Press, Austin.

and try to make it more *visible*. Our success of course is contingent on our playing the social game—sharing regularly, interacting lots with other users, sharing what is already popular, tagging posts with popular keywords, 'optimising' them for search-engine discoverability. And while Google argues that social signals do not influence a news story's visibility in search rankings, they do influence, for example, a post's Facebook 'relevancy score' (Oremus 2016). At Menlo Park, Facebook's Silicon Valley headquarters, your past performance in signalling what's important to you is one of the hundreds of factors that play into the platform's algorithmic prediction of what will then show up in your news feed, and be subject to on-sharing.

So, in sharing news on social media systems we are not only signalling what we think about that material, but making it available for evaluation by others. Sharing is a collaborative *evaluative* process: we amplify and draw attention to a story, our contacts register their assessment (thumbs up, smiley face, heart, downvote), the platform registers, collates and analyses our reactions, and shows us more of what we like. We are entangled in a process of promoting and assessing information, a commentary circuit, which feeds social media companies' understanding of how audiences behave and express desire, and enables personalised targeting of its behavioural advertising (see Fig. 2.2).

In socially networked environments, news sharing accrues meaning through its annotation and iteration. Users will normally frame the link to, an excerpt or copy of, a story with either an iconic evaluation, a like or an emoji, a comment about it, or a discursive categorisation such as a hashtag or category tag. Each type of annotation has different effects in terms of the way that the news item is then indexed, and its relative value is measured by the social system involved. Comments give companies richer data about our opinions and attitudes, so Facebook users are urged to "Say something about it", while Twitter gives us the option to retweet with a comment. These evaluative gestures set the agenda for any subsequent interpretation and discussion of that material within a social network, and provide the data for the algorithmic placement of those items in the news feeds of the users' social network. Hashtags, which are now used on Twitter, Facebook and Instagram to organise information flows, also act to amplify the reach of any original share, by making the item visible to interested parties. Thus, it is difficult to interpret the impact of any one act of sharing without also analysing its diffusion, and the accumulation of these incremental social signals.

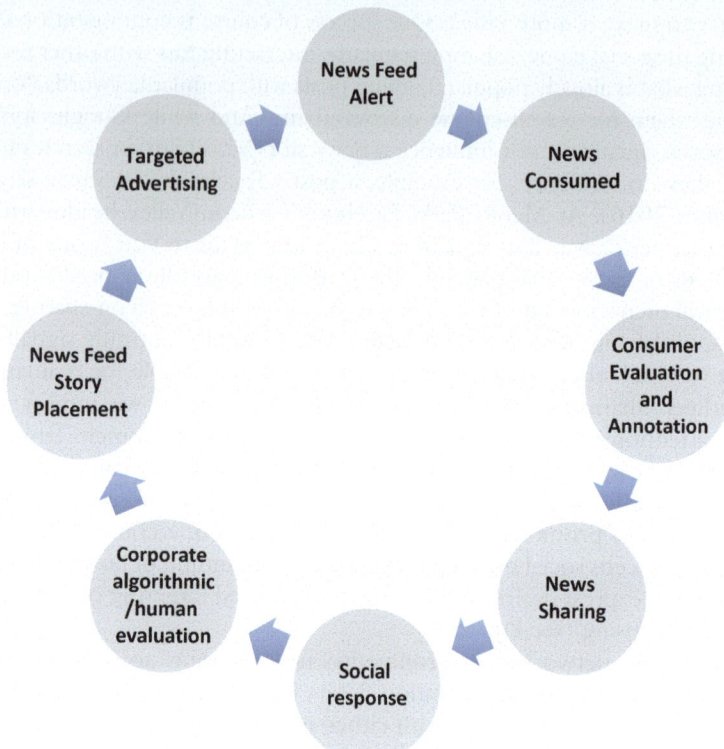

Fig. 2.2   The commendary circuit of news sharing. Image: Fiona R Martin

The other problem for news organisations trying to promote this commendary activity is that social media users seem to favour the entertaining over the newsworthy. In 2017, there were no news organisations on YouTube's top ten most viewed and subscribed channels, none in Instagram's most viewed stories list, and only four news articles and two research features in the top fifteen most shared Facebook posts. One study of the best performing WeChat accounts found 24% were 'media' companies, but another noted that only 24% of users posted trending news content on Moments (tagline: "Share your life with friends"), and only 16.6% wanted to view this type of content, compared to 66.8% who posted personal life records and 62.7% who wanted to see that material. Only Twitter and Reddit stand out as systems that sustain significant reposting of news journalism (Bastos 2015; Barthel et al. 2016). The Pew Research Center found that 78% of Reddit users relied on its threads for news, either via information from other users or links and excerpts on the site (Barthel et al. 2016).

What then do we know about why people might share news rather than celebrity shots, funny pet videos and political memes, and why they might gravitate to particular news platforms?

WHY WE SHARE NEWS ONLINE

As many journalism texts will argue, news fulfils a basic human need to know about the actions of others, our place in the society and our capacity to act in the world. Exchanging news with others is fundamental to establishing and maintaining our social connections, to building and demonstrating social (and cultural) capital—and beyond those motivations is a way of projecting ourselves into the world, as self-determining individuals and agents of change. A recent and extensive survey of literature looking at news sharing motivations suggested they fell into three broad categories: we seek to attract attention, promote our reputation and gain social status; to socialise with others, discussing and developing ideas; and to share important information, not just altruistically but in order to process it better and in the hope that others will reciprocate (Kümpel et al. 2015).

While study participants are sometimes unwilling to characterise themselves as self-serving, research by boyd et al. (2010), Lee et al. (2012) and Ihm and Kim (2018) found that there are strong presentational and impression management aspects to news sharing. People will carefully choose what they share to construct an ideal self-image, one that will attract approval from friends and peers. Some are keen to build their followers, or to get a response from a more visible actor in the network. Those who are highly motivated by self-presentation are more likely to share news, and on several platforms, than those who are less motivated by attracting recognition and acknowledgement (Ihm and Kim 2018: 14). This is likely because the more people we share new, credible and arresting information with, the higher our social visibility and the potential for building influence. The need to develop a reputation as a valuable news source applies most strongly when people are building professional networks on platforms like Twitter or LinkedIn. But self-presentation factors may not be as broadly important in news sharing as social motives (Picone et al. 2016).

danah boyd and her colleagues found that people retweeted news for a range of social outcomes: as "an act of friendship, loyalty or homage", to validate others' ideas, and to recognise less visible participants in a conversation (boyd et al. 2010). A widely cited New York Times study also found the primary motives for their readers to share news were social: to improve the lives of people they cared about and to build and maintain relationships (NYT 2011). They hoped to help others have good experiences (or to avoid bad ones), to save money and to give them information about products that they'd be interested in. Readers also derived enjoyment from giving people useful news, from the responses they received and the sense of connection they felt to the world. Eighty per cent used news sharing as a way of keeping in touch with others, while 73% wanted to connect with those who shared their interests.

The NYT study also found evidence of a strong informational motive for news sharing: three in four of their surveyed readers "process information more deeply, thoroughly and thoughtfully as a result of sharing it with others" and said responses from their network helped them to interpret its meaning (NYT 2011: 6). Importantly, the survey suggested politics was key, as people share news about causes they want to promote. A UK study (Chadwick and Viccari 2019: 11) suggests people share political news to express their opinions, to inform and influence others, and to explore ideas or provoke discussions, all facets of political engagement. Indeed many studies that show the centrality of social sharing in mobilising political activity (see Hermida 2016; Papacharissi and de Fatima Oliveira 2012; Halpern et al. 2017; Kahne and Bowyer 2018).

However, context is clearly central to why we share. In cases of natural disasters, we share to express our emotions and to establish how we can best act to respond to the crisis (Shaw et al. 2013). In therapeutic communities, where people gather to self-manage illness, they exchange news about research which might aid their treatment. Pedagogical groups share news about teaching, and which may be of use in the classroom (Swart et al. 2018). In an extensive survey of news sharing literature, researchers also found that people who most often share news on social media "perceive themselves as opinion leaders and tend to have lots of friends or followers", consume a variety of news, especially on social media and follow news organisations (Kümpel et al. 2015: 5).

We certainly share news to influence others' opinions, and intimate sharing is very effective in this sense. Both political and sociological studies have shown social recommendations have significant power to shape our belief in news, and the likelihood of us commending news to others. An American Press Institute study (Media Insight Project 2017) argues that

Americans evaluate the trustworthiness of news based on who shares it, rather than where it comes from. If they trust the sharer, they are more likely to "recommend the news source to friends, follow the source on social media and sign up to news alerts from that source" (p. 1). This is particularly the case for young people. Boczkowski and his colleagues (Boczkowski et al. 2017) found that much of the news young people encounter is 'incidental news', seen in the process of following their social feed rather than accessed from a trusted brand as part of a deliberate news search strategy. In this environment, news appears as part of an undifferentiated flow of social and informational content, its value mediated by social recommendations.

As the fake news moment testifies, some people share news to deceive. In analysing the false stories that she saw circulating online during the 2016 Trump election campaign, digital journalism researcher Clair Wardle found seven different kinds of 'fake news'—or mis-, dis- and mal-information, as she more accurately labels it (Wardle and Derakhshan 2017). There were items that made false connections or presented false context, as well as manipulated, misleading, imposter and fabricated content, and satire or parody (Wardle 2017). However, it is a moot point whether much of this deceptive material stemmed from ordinary individuals with unhappy intentions. Subsequent academic research suggests that politicised institutional and economic rationales have been driving the circulation of deliberately deceptive news—not in the least the notorious Internet Research Agency of St Petersburg, once Russia's most prominent trolling operation, which a Guardian investigation (Hern et al. 2017) showed was posting supposed witness accounts from disasters and crime scenes that were picked up by UK and US publications including the Telegraph, BuzzFeed, the Daily Mail, the Huffington Post and the BBC.

Journalists being fooled by imposter accounts is one problem, but a larger concern, which Wardle and Derakhshan (2017) highlight in a report for the Council of Europe, is whether and how ordinary social media users can identify a hoax post. The templating of social media items and their random appearance in our feeds, means that a post from a legitimate news source can look similar to a story from a conspiracy site, and equally shareworthy. They cite political scientists Messing and Westwood's (2014) observations that social media content is decontextualised, since the focus is the story content, not the source. The Reuters Institute found that less than half of those they surveyed in 2017 usually recognised the brand of news content when they access news from social platforms (Kalogeropoulos and Newman 2017). Thus, without rich indicators of quality or origin, people are left to their social networks to help them identify and critique what's authentic and what's not.

Unfortunately, misinformation is far more likely to be recirculated than the truth because it makes a claim that is unexpected and contradicts what people know about the world. Its novel, unusual nature makes it more interesting to share (Vosoughi et al. 2018). Researchers at MIT's Laboratory for Social Machines found that the average 'fake' news item took 10 hours to spread to 1500 users on Twitter, whereas a verified story took 60 hours to reach the same number of people. They also found it travelled "farther … deeper, and more broadly than the truth", partly because of the strong emotional reactions people had to it (Aral 2018). This points to an interesting aspect of virality that will be explored further in Chaps. 6 and 8—that news we feel strongly about is more likely to be shared.

Research from the last decade indicates that whether we share news will depend on how we feel about what we're viewing. As Jonah Berger (2011) showed in a ground-breaking marketing psychology study, we are more likely to share information that stimulates or arouses us emotionally, whether we feel positively or negatively about that content. His work with Katherine Milkman (2012), which suggests that arousal increases the speed of news sharing, triggered a wave of studies that have explored how our emotional or affective states influence the sentiment of news we share, and the rate at which it spreads. As Chap. 6 indicates though, this research has provided some confusing and contradictory results.

For a start, it is not clear whether emotional reactions make us more inclined to share positive or negative stories. Decades of research on legacy news distribution has suggested journalists and consumers pay more attention to bad news than good (Galtung and Ruge 1965; Glasgow University Media Group 1980; Trussler and Soroka 2014), a trend reflected in news sharing on Twitter (Hansen et al. 2011). Yet Berger (2013) has argued that if we have a choice we prefer to pass on good news rather than bad, and this is supported by a recent study showing Twitter users share 'overwhelming positive' viral news (Al-Rawi 2017). Meanwhile, another group who set out to determine whether everyday bad news is likely to travel faster than good found that it did—at least as far as Brexit news on Twitter was concerned (Fang and Ben-Miled 2017).

It is clear, though, that sharing news is very much an affective pursuit, an immediate reaction to socially significant events, issues and actions. It invites others in our social network to identify with or dispute ideas and helps us to mobilise others around causes or campaigns. Zizi Papacharissi (2015) notes affective publics form around networked expressions of sentiment about news, supporting large-scale, pluralised responses to it, and connective—if not collective—action on it. Social sharing is a move away from the controlled, centralised representative agendas of analogue news, which offered limited means to publicly express our feelings, in our ways about important changes in our worlds. As Chap. 6 will argue, sharing news enables users to place themselves in the news matrix, integrating or contesting the concepts, symbols and ideologies of news narratives in ways particular to themselves and their cultural identities.

How We Share News Online

Just as our motives for news sharing vary, we have many ways to do the sharing. People will use any networked communicative tool they read news on to flag or repost the URLs of content they find interesting or valuable, and there are many competing systems designed to allow us to do that. Much news sharing is done via email clients, from secure forums or using messaging apps like WeChat, WhatsApp, LINE or Facebook Messenger. The problem is that these channels, together with a range of mobile social apps, such as those belonging to Reddit, Facebook and Instagram, don't generate traffic referral information in their message headers. That means measuring and understanding how people share news via these 'dark social' avenues is a difficult pursuit, and one that has become more pressing with the upswing in mobile traffic over desktop access to news websites (Breaux 2015).

Dark social is a phrase coined by former Atlantic magazine deputy editor Alexis Madrigal to describe the large volume of traffic coming to his site from sources that he couldn't track. As Madrigal (2012) noted at the time, this problem exposed not only the range of sharing activities outside social platforms, but one of the great shifts that these platforms had visited on web media consumption—visibility:

> the social sites that arrived in the 2000s did not create the social web, but they did structure it. This is really, really significant. In large part, they made sharing on the Internet an act of publishing (!), with all the attendant changes that come with that switch. Publishing social interactions makes them more visible, searchable, and adds a lot of metadata to your simple link or photo post. (Madrigal 2012)

Social media has become the main way that we share news online, and are encouraged by news companies to share, because it makes our activity visible and measurable. There are several ways in which Facebook, for example, makes what you share more apparent. It first gives your post a permanent URL, so it is discoverable by search engines. It adds traffic referral data to any link you post, say to a news story. When someone clicks on your linked item, the metadata tells the publisher's server where your visit came from. Facebook's software also crawls the web to capture data about that site, and to auto-populate a preview image for that link, excerpting the content and making the share more attention grabbing. This last technique is designed to capitalise on the likelihood that visual material such as photos and videos is more engaging than text alone. Imagery makes your posts more shareworthy. Finally, social media provides a range of automated commendary tools so we can evaluate others' posts. As a whole, these algorithmic processes greatly elevate social media's role in promoting media sharing, and produce quantifiable data about the scale of post creation and engagement. In enabling news publishers to collect, aggregate and measure social sharing metadata, or referral data about visits coming from platforms to news sites, social media companies have constructed themselves as key players in the digital distribution of news.

As Madrigal also notes, social media platforms are only the latest in a long succession of computational systems for sharing information and news (see Fig. 2.1), each of which presented its own political and economic battles over how we could share information, what was and wasn't proper use of the system. To get a more complete understanding of these struggles to define the authorised boundaries of news sharing, it is instructive to traverse some of that history, starting with first popular distributed online system, PLATO.

Launched in 1960, the US educational computing platform PLATO connected display terminals at the University of Illinois to dozens of networked mainframe computers. The platform's development spawned many concepts now familiar in social computing including forums, message boards and chat rooms (Dear 2017) but also saw intense arguments over what was legitimate (coursework) and non-legitimate (gaming) use of the network (Jones and Latzko-Toth 2017). In a similar sense, France's successful Minitel videotex system, which delivered news, directory, gaming, ticketing and billpaying services to ordinary citizens across the country, as part of a government sponsored roll-out, was scandalised by the growth of 'messageries roses', adult oriented chat rooms (Mailland and

Driscoll 2017). US commercial service Prodigy offered news, email and bulletin board systems (BBS), but no chat, and alienated its subscriber base with over jealous censoring of content (Banks 2008). The UK's centralised Prestel service was simply too expensive and visually uninteresting for most subscribers (Lean 2016).

The most successful news sharing systems were those that democratised the hosting and exchange of news, like BBS, which allowed any computer hobbyist with a PC and modem to publish or connect with specialised networks via the telephone network (see Fig. 2.3).

Usenet, which was developed in 1979 at Duke University so that people could exchange public messages between connected computers, expanded this concept beyond the national. Over its first decade, Usenet gradually linked more and more research institutions, and became host to an extraordinary variety of specialist discussion or 'newsgroups'. There were struggles about the structural hierarchies, naming and control of these groups, and debates about what constituted permissible speech, all part of Usenet's evolution as a public access network. it is remarkable for being the first international scale decentralised news sharing initiative, with the user-led alt. newsgroups still being the largest section of the system. Sharing information with other systems however, like the defence research oriented ARPAnet was not easy, with technical and administrative hurdles to inter-mailing list communications (Hauben and Hauben 1997). In 1982, users dreamed of a World Net "that would tie all sorts of computers worldwide together" (ibid.), a vision that would be realised in 1993 with the World Wide Web, a graphical language, system of resource loca-

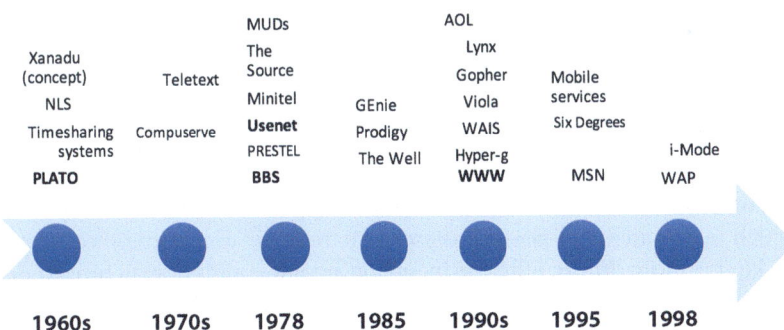

Fig. 2.3 Online news sharing systems development timeline, adapted from Weber (2017)

tors and open transmission software protocol that would enable any computer users to share information with another over existing telecommunications networks.

Internet historian Marc Weber (2017) argues that we lack a deep historical account of many of these early networks which might help us compare factors that are key to the effective distribution of information: the efficiency of different linking systems, and of strategies to reduce the incidence of misinformation. However, it is likely that the one core reason we chose to share news via privatised, controlled social media rather than the more openly owned and structured World Wide Web is automation.

The advent of the World Wide Web in 1993 gave every PC and modem owner the possibility of being an author-publisher, and with a graphical focus that brought a new, if low-resolution visuality to news sharing. Websites were the new way to share your interests, even if much of the content still consisted of URL lists pointing to interesting sites and documents, and blogrolls of favoured writers. Yet, while the web lowered the barriers to sharing information across the globe, beyond the territoriality of analogue media, it still required technical skill, and an understanding of computing and coding beyond the reach of most people (including the billion or so worldwide living without electricity).

Automating the web publishing process made it more accessible to more people. Geocities, the US-based webhosting service founded in 1996, lowered barriers to creating web pages with templates and neighbourhood directories, and later drag and drop publishing tools. Together with Angelfire, Tripod and much later MySpace, Geocities gave users a base from which to learn the principles of html coding and media uploading, but it was templating that simplified, expedited and fully democratised online news sharing. Publishing templates defined the layout and features of many blogging services from Blogger and Live Journal to WordPress, and the first social media services, Six Degrees in 1997, Lunar Storm in 2000 and Friendster in 2000.

In 2006, Facebook further revolutionised the automation of news sharing by enabling websites to install a share widget or button to their pages, which automated the posting of content to their accounts or contacts, making it more "more efficient by giving people a simple structure to do it" (Facebook 2006). In 2009, it then introduced its version of the like button, originally introduced by Friendfeed in 2007 before Facebook acquired that company. Liking enabled people to react to others' sharing activities, but only positively. Zuckerberg recognised the utility of this positive social reinforcement for encouraging interaction when he rejected calls for a 'dislike' button:

> The like button is really valuable because it's a way for you to very quickly express a positive emotion or sentiment when someone puts themselves out there and shares something. Some people have asked for a dislike button because they want to be able to say, "That thing isn't good." That's not something that we think is good. We're not going to build that, and I don't think there needs to be a voting mechanism on Facebook about whether posts are good or bad. I don't think that's socially very valuable or good for the community to help people share the important moments in their lives. (Zuckerberg in Lafferty 2016)

Share and react buttons are purposely designed technological affordances of Facebook that make acting on our impulses to pass on and respond to online information easy, quick and 'frictionless' (to use a term favoured in Silicon Valley). They encourage affective responses, but most obviously constructive ones as these are more likely to generate further interaction.

Facebook's resistance to automating critical signals is just one example of *affective regulation*, the process of controlling and directing expressive responses during social sharing. Another is Facebook's introduction during 2017 of a set of five new emoji reaction buttons—Love, Haha, Wow, Sad and Angry—to supplement the Like. These options were ostensibly introduced in order to reduce incidences of reaction avoidance, where users felt it was inappropriate to 'like' content that made them upset. However, Facebook also indicated it considered the new reactions 'stronger' signals of relevance than the original like, raising questions about how it weighs them in calculating post visibility, and what effect users might have on news feeds by choosing different types of emotional response.

How Users Affect What Is, and Can Be, Shared

Users have changed the way platforms can be used to share news. Software developer and designer Chris Messina (2007) came up with the idea to use keyword 'channel tags' as a way to signal that a group discussion was opening, but keeping the signal short enough to be embedded in the message. Hashtags are now used to organise and aggregate shared content on Facebook and Instagram, illustrating the normalisation of socio-technical standards for sharing online. Tumblr users also adopted the GIF or graphics interchange format to animate their personal reactions to posted content, drawing on an eclectic store of appropriated pop culture motifs. This playful convention was later adopted by digital-born news publishers like BuzzFeed, and GIFs are now being used by legacy media to give visual interest to stories and to animate simple infographics.

How we share news and what we share depends not only on a platform's affordances, but also its commendary culture. This becomes clear in contrasting Reddit and Twitter, the international platforms most clearly focused on news sharing. On Reddit, users take part in discussion groups, called subreddits, devoted to particular topics, and news sharing involves excerpting, explicating and debating, to some extent, stories from existing media sources. The top 5 subreddits in terms of subscribers were humour (funny) world news, and educational (AskReddit, todayilearned, science). Users come from the US, Canada and the UK primarily, and in the US are largely young, 18–29-year-old males (Barthel et al. 2016).

Twitter, on the other hand, is more cosmopolitan and gender balanced, with 57% male users and 42% females in total, although this ratio varies by country. 79% of Twitter users come from outside the US, including China, its biggest national market, and India its third largest, while many countries including the UK and Japan are heavier users than North Americans. While its users are diverse, Twitter operates mainly as a professional and expert communications network, with news sharing done primarily through images, video and hyperlinks, due to the messaging constraints (280 characters per post, double that of pre-2017 tweets). Links are used reciprocally to start conversations with followers and to signal an interest in locating similar information (Holton et al. 2014). More than half of the top most retweeted messages in 2017 were motivational, including three from Barack Obama, and two disaster appeals. While there is no recent global survey of account types on Twitter, an Australian study found that aspirational accounts were one of the top four concentrations, alongside teen culture (music and celebrity especially), sport and netizen/technologists (Bruns et al. 2017). That research also showed that user interests had changed over time, with technologists being a more important group in Twitter's early years, while teens and sports enthusiasts being later adopters.

Each evaluative system then demonstrates different politics of participation and recognition, based on its measures of social visibility, status and approval. On Reddit, which is a community of pseudonymous users, the title, visual content, placement and timing of a post will determine its visibility and popularity more than on Twitter, where real identities are more common and visibility is defined by numbers of followers and popularity of posts. A Twitter user's profile and status, or social authority, has a distinct positive effect on content sharing. In terms of approval, each Twitter post accumulates a register of signals, including retweets, favourites, replies, follower requests and the addition of the user to expert lists. By way of contrast, Reddit users, in a quasi-democratic gesture, use up and down-voting to register their approval or disapproval of posts. As pseudonymity and anonymity pose particular issues of recognition and behavioural control for Reddit, this service has developed an additional reputation strategy. Users accumulate 'karma' points (a Silicon Valley gesture towards the Buddhist concept of an individual's actions influencing their future), which then determine the degree of freedom they have to post information, the degree of attention paid to moderating their contributions, and their status within the system when users have low karma.

The sharing of politically contentious or illegal material can trigger internal or external regulation to control sharing behaviours, a subject we look at more closely in Chaps. 3 and 8. While the major social media platforms subscribe to the North American protection of speech freedoms, they nevertheless are obliged to control what we share, and how we speak about it in order to prevent the circulation of hate and discrimination, misinformation, propaganda and criminal activity. As Tarleton Gillespie argues in his investigation of content moderation online:

> Platforms must, in some form or another, moderate: both to protect one user from another, or one group from its antagonists, and to remove the offensive, vile, or illegal—as well as to present their best face to new users, to their advertisers and partners, and to the public at large. (Gillespie 2018: 124–125)

What we share and how it frames our relationship to the legal and political frameworks of nation state and platform revenues then affects what we care able to share. States, for example, routinely step in to regulate news sharing, showing they acknowledge its power to shape public opinions and political processes. Countries like China, Iran, Turkey, and Vietnam control to varying degrees both access to social media and activity on the platforms, usually to prevent political dissidence, and mobile internet access is sometimes restricted in areas dominated by religious and ethnic minorities. Governments will also restrict access to social sharing to further their own political agendas, as when the Ukrainian government blocked access to the popular Russian-owned VKontakte social platform on national security grounds (Kelly et al. 2017). As Chap. 3 will argue, these battles over access to news sharing systems represent a major front in struggles for freedom of expression and media freedom.

What we share is also, as this book argues, fundamentally reshaping the news business, its relationship to the social media platforms and its audiences, and the production of news. To understand its impact on news journalism, it's necessary to examine some of the factors that have affected social news sharing's integration into newsroom routines, and its part in influencing how news is constructed.

Reshaping the News: The Likeable Engine

In 2009, Richard Sambrook, then director of the BBC Global News Division, told the Oxford Social Media conference that he thought "the impact of social media was overestimated in the short term and underestimated in long term" (Bunz 2009). Unlike most media predictions, his was remarkably accurate. The legacy news media have not wholesale adopted BuzzFeed's social first approach to production, or, as Jonah Peretti's organisation did early on, tied wages to evidence of social impact, clicks, likes and shares. Yet, nearly a decade later, social media organisations and their users have had a profound influence on how news is identified, selected, produced, distributed, promoted and discussed.

At peak social sharing, before Google reasserted its dominance and Facebook changed its algorithm to demote news in favour of personal information from people's feeds, industry reports suggested anywhere from 7–50% of news traffic would come from social media referrals, depending on the site's business model and the story topic (Mitchell and Jurkowitz 2014; Parse.ly 2015). Those digital-born companies based on social first publishing strategies like BuzzFeed and Upworthy had referrals at the top of that scale. At this time, social media metrics were a proxy for digital news consumption. This conception drove the uptake of social analytics which we document in the next chapter, and a greater editorial focus on monitoring what was being shared online and why. Although there is now a healthy scepticism about the importance of social media for news making, and a move for news organisations to refocus on a more diversified approach to distribution (Cornia and Sehl 2018), it is worth remembering how and why newsrooms sought to integrate social media during this period.

The growth of commendary culture and the rise in social referrals to news sites saw news organisations become tightly bound into the social media ecology, investing in branded social media channels, advertising and revenue deals, hiring specialised social media teams, adopting digital workflows and analytics systems and exploring occasional partnerships with the platforms (Cherubini and Nielsen 2016). As Bruns (2018) suggests, journalists were under pressure to boost sharing and increase audience trust in news product via personal social media engagement with audiences. In turn, these social branding activities led to power inequities in the way some individual reporters could command public attention and mobilise audiences, and engendered a lesser hold by employers over the opinions and job mobility of those employees (Bruns, 222–223). So, news sharing affected production investment and innovation agendas, while destabilising (to some extent) existing labour models and relations.

From 2010 onwards, we were attempting to measure news sharing, first internal sharing of news across co-owned titles in Australia (Dwyer and Martin 2010) and then, together with our Share Wars colleagues, user-led sharing internationally. For the latter project, we used Share Wars' Likeable Engine, a homegrown news analytics tool. For four years from 2011, Likeable tracked social news sharing trends using data from 140–160 major news sites worldwide and information feeds from Facebook's and Twitter's public application programming interfaces (APIs). Like other later commercial analytics applications like Chartbeat, NewsWhip or Parse. ly, or the Guardian's in-house developed Ophan dashboard, Likeable enabled editors and journalists to monitor changing patterns of social media news distribution and consumption (including their own relative performance), to track trending stories and to strategise live editorial decision making in competitive online news markets.

Likeable was created by the Share Wars group, employees of one of Australia's top-rated online news sites Nine.com.au (formerly ninemsn). Share Wars was a start-up built by former news editor Hal Crawford, former Windows 8 editor Andrew Hunter and former Network Development Director Domagoj Filipovic. They sought to use its analytics capacity to discover "what makes stories shareable and how this new distribution force will change workflows, roles and resourcing" (Crawford et al. 2015). The project marked a period where company executives started to take an interest in the uses of computational intelligence in audience research via their creative agency Mi9, and as Nine Entertainment split with Microsoft Network. The founders have all moved on to senior executive positions in large news media organisations and Facebook, maintain a blog of the project findings at http://share-wars.com/.

The Likeable Engine had four core components:

1. News Feed Processor (extracting story URIs from news websites)
2. Database (storing story data and matching it with social media data)
3. Like Processor (extracting commendary data stats from FB and Twitter)
4. Live reporting Interface (graphing the mashed data)

Its architecture demonstrated the classic public/private nature of the social media ecology. It relied on public internet carriage and open standards web content (news sites), accessed public (but privatised) commendary information, formatted by proprietary social platform feeds, using bespoke scraping and querying algorithms and stored it using open source database software (see Fig. 2.4).

Until its decommissioning in 2016, the Likeable Engine scraped new news story URIs linked from its sample news homepages every 11–20 min-

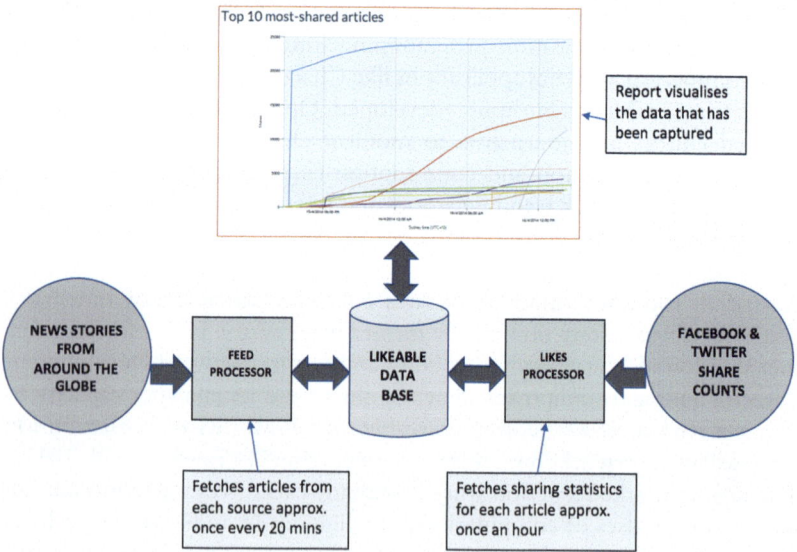

Fig. 2.4   Likeable Engine information model. Image: Fiona R Martin

utes and then queried Facebook and Twitter APIs for the share counts of those stories. It requested these counts hourly for the first 24 hours, then less frequently for 5 days. Where possible URIs were canonicalised to their Facebook IDs, to avoid the same story being differently counted on its mobile or web domain. The interface then displayed the top ten stories graphed over 22 hours, and listed the top 100 with their share counts. Users could filter by region (AU, UK, US), by date and by satire (with an eye already to post-truth news).

The journalists interviewed in the early days of the *Sharing News Online* project used Likeable as a complement to other paid analytics services such as Spike, Chartbeat, BuzzSumo, Omniture, and the in-built or native analytics provided by RedditInsight, YouTube and Google Analytics. Likeable users were primarily the ninemsn editorial staff, although users in several other workplaces, including Fairfax Media (which has since been taken over by Nine Entertainment), adopted the app. Interviews with five online journalists who used Likeable in two commercial newsrooms suggested that it played a useful and important role in their editorial routine when it was released, but had been overtaken by newer, more sophisticated analytics packages which they preferred.

The major insight from the interviews was the way in which analytics had become an important tool in editorial decision making. Interviewees said that they used analytics daily, and often throughout the day, to filter content, identify story ideas and trigger coverage, and to determine news scheduling and placement. Likeable was often consulted in the morning to identify story ideas based on what social media news was getting most user attention, where and when, to indicate whether journalists might need to produce reaction stories or explore new angles such as local perspectives. Two users regularly looked for 'pre-viral' stories or videos that were performing well on smaller news sites, and which had yet to be shared internationally. One sought news which "isn't prominently placed on the original website, or from sites that are not part of the normal news cycle".

Sharing analytics were also used to monitor the performance of competitor coverage of similar material. One news editor noted that Likeable helped him:

> to monitor sharing across the day and look at what's sharing well comparatively—also to think about domestically what might get a push from posting on social media.

Analytics also emphasised the temporal flows of sharing, with trends suggesting times when stories might be posted so they "move better" and are shared more. One user noted he always looked at the top videos and what time they were posted "live versus the number of shares they get".

Overall, the interviews suggested social analytics had five distinct uses in editorial decision making. They were regarded as:

- an evaluative system—to identify stories and topics that were sharing well, or which might go viral, and which stories should stay on the homepage
- a news filter—to identify what topics were getting most attention, where and when
- an alert system—to signal new stories that are sharing well on smaller sites, or the need for reaction stories to viral content
- a scheduling device—to suggest times when stories might be posted to attract more shares
- an audience filter—to indicate which on which publications and platform certain stories were being most often shared.

These interviews also suggested how traditional new values are being reinterpreted relative to social sharing metrics. A story's *timeliness*, which was once understood relative to the publication's production lead time, is now also determined by whether and how long it has had a presence on social media. The need to ensure optimal news sharing is also determining whether stories are posted to social media or the World Wide Web first. The audience *relevance* of a story is being assessed by where its sharing is initiated (from the article page or via social platforms) and on which platform/s people are posting about it. Controversial or polarising topics tend to be highly shared, suggesting *conflict* remains an important news value, but exploiting that interest demands journalists include provocative keywords in story straps, excerpts and headlines to attract searches and shares. Shareable items as a whole sit on either end of the *impact* spectrum: they must be either *novel* and pre-viral, or *ubiquitous*, that is, viral and otherwise newsworthy. These evolving ideas about what makes news significant shows just how subtly and comprehensively social sharing analytics are influencing journalists' normative interpretations and applications of news values.

While journalists were not asked if they understood how these figures were compiled, they did voice a range of concerns about the transparency of the metadata capture from Twitter and Facebook, particularly how analytics tools weighted views against shares or retweets, and how they should interpret differences in sharing relative to publication readership or audience size. One user requested better indexing of Australian news sites. The majority wanted better graphing of sharing in real time, one indicating that Omniture provided the best model.

These journalists' interest in tracking the rate at which news was shared was consistent with the news media's obsession with speed in news production and distribution. It also suggests that social virality is a central factor in the adoption of social analytics services such as Chartbeat, and a rationale quite distinct to measuring user attention to stories or journalistic engagement.

Our research was never intended to fully map journalistic responses to social news sharing—far better covered in reports like Caitlin Petre's *Traffic Factories* (2015) or Fedrica Cherubini and Rasmus Kleis Nielsen's *Editorial Analytics* (2016). Rather, we wished to trigger a critical enquiry into how social media news sharing is analysed, measured and valued. The next chapter takes up this story, particularly questions about the clarity and reliability of the data captured.

This newsroom encounter also highlighted the diversity of players in the social sharing ecology, with analytics companies based in Ireland, Israel and the US, and a distinct gap in the tracking of non-Western platforms like WeChat, Sina Weibo, LINE and Kakaotalk from our Asian region. This was a reminder that much news sharing knowledge still reflects the late twentieth-century cultural hegemony of transnational Western news domination. The deficiencies of this focus are obvious with the rise of BRICS countries. It was encouraging then to see, in December 2016, that NewsWhip recorded IndiaTimes.com as the most shared site internationally on Facebook, part of a shift to it acknowledging greater diversity in the publishers who are achieving high share counts (Corcoran 2017). In an increasingly globalised communications world, we need to understand how our news sharing is shaped by different local, national and extranational forces, and how commendary cultures might emerge in response to particular economic, political and social contexts.

The rise and fall of Likeable is one small part of that story. Likeable's shutdown was partly the result of transnational competition, from analytics start-ups with more venture funding, more viable business models and better designed products, and partly due to Facebook and Twitter's full commodification of what had previously been 'freemium' data subscription models. Likeable originally sampled data from the pre-2015 Facebook Developer API, which provided free access to separate counts of shares, likes, comments, and on-page comments—some of which were no longer available from the amended public API. It also drew on Twitter's public data feed. This had been narrowing for years as the company slowly withdrew users' permissions to access certain types of information, but it still provided tweet count data which was valuable to app developers and marketing services. Even if the free APIs had been somewhat unstable and subject to sudden change, they still enabled experimentation and innovation in the analytics space among a raft of small technology companies. The closure/commodification of both streams in 2015 undermined Likeable's already limited functionality, and as it didn't have a viable subscriber base, it was not a commercial proposition for Nine to buy that data from the platforms. Yet, Likeable had already fulfilled its ideological promise, introducing a group of journalists to the ground zero of analytics use, its incorporation into their news routines and the alteration of their production values and norms.

COMMENDING THE NEWS

Social media news sharing has become a powerful new force in digital news production, in its variety of commendary forms and practices, its everyday adoption, scale of interaction and integration with news media production, distribution and consumption. Platform designs and their affordances operate to enable audiences to make visible the news they value as shareworthy, to marshal attention to their judgements, and to enlist others in responding to their reactions. Their evaluations, when tracked, analysed and represented, affect not only platform advertising, but journalism practice. Commendary culture influences the reporting and editorial practices of journalists in ways that are both obvious and also difficult to quantify, especially given tech companies' relative lack of accountability for their calculus.

Social media platforms have, by promising informational and communicative agency, colonised the lifeworld of their users, and captured their commendary motivations and agency in ways and at a scale that have the potential to transform.

Read in light of this analysis, online sharing means much more than redistribution, communication or disclosure. It now encompasses the amplification of ideas, the speed and scale of reproduction, the ritual and affective nature of our acts and the differing levels of access we provide to our shared material. It also presages an era of machine learning and automated news discovery and redistribution.

There is little doubt that social sharing is reconfiguring news journalism, even where social referrals constitute a small percentage of traffic to a news site. That is because social media users now routinely influence what gets seen by others, and what is valued in the news selection process, in a circular and self-reinforcing logic, just by redistributing and evaluating news stories. Their sharing metrics feed the editorial algorithms of the platforms, influencing how news is made visible and prominent and generating the metrics that newsrooms will monitor for signs they are producing what the audience wants. It is this commendary dynamic, quite apart from the gravitation of advertising revenue to the platforms, that is reshaping the future of news and how it will reach audiences.

References

Allan, Stuart. 2013. *Citizen Witnessing: Revisioning Journalism Concepts.* Cambridge, MA: Polity Press.

Allan, Stuart, and Einar Thorsen, eds. 2009. *Citizen Journalism: Global Perspectives.* New York: Peter Lang.

Al-Rawi, Ahmed. 2017. Viral News on Social Media. *Digital Journalism* 7: 63–79. https://doi.org/10.1080/21670811.2017.1387062.

Alter, Adam. 2017. *Irresistible: The Rise of Addictive Technology and the Business of Keeping Us Hooked.* New York: Penguin.

Angus, Ian, and Sut Jhally. 1989. *Cultural Politics in Contemporary America.* New York: Routledge.

Aral, Sinan. 2018. Truth, Disrupted. The Big Idea. *Harvard Business Review.* July. https://hbr.org/cover-story/2018/07/truth-disrupted.

Banks, Michael. 2008. Prodigy: The Pre-Internet Online Service That Didn't Live up to Its Name. *techRepublic.* December 18. https://www.techrepublic.com/blog/classics-rock/prodigy-the-pre-internet-online-service-that-didnt-live-up-to-its-name/.

Barthel, Michael, Galen Stocking, Jesse Holcomb, and Amy Mitchell. 2016. *Nearly Eight-in-Ten Reddit Users Get News On the Site.* Pew Research Center. http://www.pewresearch.org/wp-content/uploads/sites/8/2016/02/PJ_2016.02.25_Reddit_FINAL.pdf.

Bastos, Marco Toledo. 2015. Shares, Pins, and Tweets. *Journalism Studies.* 16 (3): 305–325. https://doi.org/10.1080/1461670X.2014.891857.

Belk, Russell. 1988. Possessions and the Extended Self. *Journal of Consumer Research.* 15 (2): 139–168. https://www.jstor.org/stable/2489522.

————. 2010. Sharing. *Journal of Consumer Research* 36 (5): 715–734.

————. 2014. You Are What You Can Access: Sharing and Collaborative Consumption Online. *Journal of Business Research* 67 (8): 1595–1600.

Bell, Emily. 2016. The End of the News as We Know It: How Facebook Swallowed Journalism. *Medium.* March 7. https://medium.com/tow-center/the-end-of-the-news-as-we-know-it-how-facebook-swallowed-journalism-60344fa50962.

Bell, Emily, and Owen Taylor. 2017. *The Platform Press: How Silicon Valley Reengineered Journalism.* Tow Center for Digital Journalism. https://www.cjr.org/tow_center_reports/platform-press-how-silicon-valley-reengineered-journalism.php/.

Benkler, Yochai. 2004. Sharing Nicely: On Shareable Goods and the Emergence of Sharing as a Modality of Economic Production. *Yale Law Journal* 114 (2): 273–358.

Berger, Jonah. 2011. Arousal Increases Social Transmission of Information. *Psychological Science* 22 (7): 891–893.

————. 2013. *Contagious: Why Things Catch On.* New York, NY: Simon & Schuster.

Berger, Jonah, and Katherine L. Milkman. 2012. What Makes Online Content Viral? *Journal of Marketing Research* XLIX (April): 192–205.

Boczkowski, Pablo, Eugenia Mitchelstein, and Mora Matassi. 2017. *Incidental News: How Young People Consume News on Social Media.* Proceedings of the 50th Hawaii international conference on system sciences, Waikola, HI, 4–7 January 2017, 1785–1792.

Borschke, Margie. 2017. *This Is Not a Remix: Piracy, Authenticity and Popular Music.* New York: Bloomsbury Academic.

boyd, danah, Scott Golder, and Gilad Lotan. 2010. *Tweet, Tweet, Retweet: Conversational Aspects of Retweeting on Twitter.* HICSS-43. IEEE: Kauai, HI. January 6.

Breaux, Chris. 2015. The Evolution of Dark Social: Correcting Attribution in the Mobile App Age. *Chartbeat.* April 16. http://blog.chartbeat.com/2015/04/16/the-evolution-of-dark-social-correcting-attribution-in-the-mobile-app-age/.

Bruns, Axel. 2005. *Gatewatching: Collaborative Online News Production.* New York: Peter Lang.

————. 2008. *Blogs, Wikipedia, Second Life, and Beyond: From Production to Produsage.* New York: Peter Lang.

————. 2018. *Gatewatching and News Curation: Journalism, Social Media, and the Public Sphere.* New York: Digital Formations. Peter Lang.

Bruns, Axel, Brenda Moon, Felix Münch, and Troy Sadkowsky. 2017. The Australian Twittersphere in 2016: Mapping the Follower/Followee Network. *Social Media and Society* 3 (4). https://doi.org/10.1177/2056305117748162.

Bunz, M. 2009. How Social Networking Is Changing Journalism. *The Guardian.* September 18. https://www.theguardian.com/media/pda/2009/sep/18/oxford-social-media-convention-2009-journalism-blogs.

Chadwick, Andrew, and Christian Viccari. 2019. *News Sharing on UK Social Media: Misinformation, Disinformation, and Correction.* Online Civic Culture Centre. Loughborough University.

Cherubini, Federica, and Rasmus Kleis Nielsen. 2016. *Editorial Analytics: How News Media Are Developing and Using Audience Data and Metrics.* February 23. Oxford: Reuters Institute for the Study of Journalism.

Corcoran, Liam. 2017. The Most Engaged Sites on Facebook in December 2016 Newswhip. January 18. https://www.newswhip.com/2017/01/biggest-facebook-sites-december-2016/.

Cornia, Alessio, and Annika Sehl. 2018. Private Sector News, Social Media Distribution, and Algorithm Change. Reuters Institute for the Study of Journalism. http://www.digitalnewsreport.org/publications/2018/private-sector-news-social-media/.

Crawford, Hal, Andrew Hunter, and Domagoj Filipovic. 2015. *All Your Friends Like This: How Social Networks Took over News.* Sydney: HarperCollins.

Dean, Jodi. 2005. Communicative Capitalism: Circulation and the Foreclosure of Politics. *Cultural Politics* 1 (1): 51–74.

———. 2014. Communicative Capitalism and Class Struggle. *Spheres: Journal of Digital Culture.* November 1. http://spheres-journal.org/communicative-capitalism-and-class-struggle/.

Dear, Brian. 2017. *The Friendly Orange Glow: The Untold Story of the PLATO System and the Dawn of Cyberculture.* New York: Pantheon Books.

van Dijck, José, and Thomas Poell. 2013. Understanding Social Media Logic. *Media and Communication* 1 (1): 2–14. https://doi.org/10.12924/mac2013.01010002.

Dwyer, Tim, and Fiona Martin. 2010. Updating Diversity of Voice Arguments for Online News Media. *Global Media Journal: Australian Edition* 4 (1): 1–18.

Elizabeth, Jane. 2017. After a Decade, It's Time to Reinvent Social Media in Newsrooms. *American Press Institute.* November 14. https://www.american-pressinstitute.org/publications/reports/strategy-studies/reinventing-social-media/.

European Commission. 2016. *Code of Conduct on Countering Illegal Hate Speech Online.* Brussels: EC. https://ec.europa.eu/info/sites/info/files/code_of_conduct_on_countering_illegal_hate_speech_online_en.pdf.

Facebook. 2006. Facebook Enables Users to Share Video, Photos, News, Blogs and More from Anywhere on the Web. *Facebook Newsroom.* October 31. https://newsroom.fb.com/news/2006/10/facebook-enables-users-to-share-video-photos-news-blogs-and-more-from-anywhere-on-the-web/.

————. 2018. Bringing People Closer Together. Facebook Newsroom. January 11 https://newsroom.fb.com/news/2018/01/news-feed-fyi-bringing-people-closer-together/.

Fang, Anna, and Zina Ben-Miled. 2017. *Does Bad News Spread Faster?* 2017 International Conference on Computing, Networking and Communications (ICNC): Workshop. IEEE. https://doi.org/10.1109/ICCNC.2017.7876232.

Filloux, Frederik. 2018. Facebook Is Done with Quality Journalism. Deal with It. *Monday Note.* January 14. https://mondaynote.com/facebook-is-done-with-quality-journalism-deal-with-it-afc2475f1f84.

Flew, Terry, Fiona Martin, and Nic Suzor. 2019. Internet Regulation as Media Policy: Rethinking the Question of Digital Communication Platform Governance. *Journal of Digital Media Policy* 10 (1): 33–50.

Fuchs, Christian. 2014. Critique of the Political Economy of Informational Capitalism and Social Media. In *Critique, Social Media and the Information Society*, ed. Christian Fuchs and Marisol Sandoval, 51–65. New York: Routledge.

Fuchs, Christian. 2018. *Social Media: A Critical Introduction.* London: Sage.

Galtung, Johan, and Mari Ruge. 1965. The Structure of Foreign News: The Presentation of the Congo, Cuba and Cyprus Crises in Four Norwegian Newspapers. *Journal of Peace Research* 2 (1): 64–91.

German Law Archive. 2017. Network Enforcement Act (Netzdurchsetzunggesetz, NetzDG). September 1. https://germanlawarchive.iuscomp.org/?p=1245.

Gillespie, Tarleton. 2018. *Custodians of the Internet: Platforms, Content Moderation, and the Hidden Decisions That Shape Social Media.* Kindle ed. New Haven, CT: Yale University Press.

Glasgow University Media Group. 1980. *More Bad News.* London: Routledge & Paul Kegan.

Goggin, G., A. Vromen, K. Weatherall, F. Martin, A. Webb, L. Sunman, and F. Bailo. 2017. *Digital Rights in Australia.* Sydney: University of Sydney. http://digitalrightsusyd.net/research/digital-rights-in-australia-report/.

Goh, Debbie, Richard Ling, Liuyu Huang, and Doris Liew. 2017. News Sharing as Reciprocal Exchanges in Social Cohesion Maintenance. *Information, Communication & Society* 23. https://doi.org/10.1080/1369118X.2017.1406973.

Halpern, Daniel, Sebastián Valenzuela, and James E. Katz. 2017. We Face, I Tweet: How Different Social Media Influence Political Participation through Collective and Internal Efficacy. *Journal of Computer-Mediated Communication* 22 (6): 320–336.

Hansen, L.K., A. Arvidsson, F.Å. Nielsen, E. Colleoni, and M. Etter. 2011. Good Friends, Bad News: Affect and Virality in Twitter. In *Future Information Technology*, Part 1 in Communications in Computer and Information Science, vol. 185, 34–43. Berlin: Springer.

Hauben, Michael, and Ronda Hauben. 1997. *Netizens: On the History and Impact of Usenet and the Internet.* Los Alamitos, CA: IEEE Computer Society Press.

Hermida, Alfred. 2016. *Tell Everyone: Why We Share and Why It Matters*. Toronto, ON: DoubleDay.

Hern, Alex, Pamela Duncan, and Helena Bengtsson. 2017. Russian 'Troll Army' Tweets Cited More than 80 Times in UK Media. *The Guardian*. November 21. https://www.theguardian.com/media/2017/nov/20/russian-troll-army-tweets-cited-more-than-80-times-in-uk-media.

Hinton, Sam, and Larissa Hjorth. 2013. *Understanding Social Media*. London; Thousand Oaks: Sage.

Holton, Avery E., Kang Baek, Mark Coddington, and Carolyn Yaschur. 2014. Seeking and Sharing: Motivations for Linking on Twitter. *Communication Research Reports* 31 (1): 33–40.

Ihm, Jennifer, and Eun-mee Kim. 2018. The Hidden Side of News Diffusion: Understanding Online News Sharing as an Interpersonal Behavior. *New Media & Society* 20: 1–20. https://doi.org/10.1177/146144481877284.

Jenkins, Henry. 1992. *Textual Poachers: Television Fans & Participatory Culture*, Studies in Culture and Communication. New York: Routledge.

Jenkins, Henry, Sam Ford, and Joshua Green. 2013. *Spreadable Media: Creating Value and Meaning in a Networked Culture*. New York: New York University Press.

John, Nicholas A. 2017. *The Age of Sharing*. Cambridge; Malden: Polity Press.

Jones, Steve and Guillaume Latzko-Toth. 2017. Out from the PLATO Cave: Uncovering the Pre-Internet History of Social Computing. *Internet Histories* 1 (1–2): 60–69.

Kahne, Joseph, and Benjamin Bowyer. 2018. The Political Significance of Social Media Activity and Social Networks. *Political Communication* 35 (3): 470–493.

Kalogeropoulos, Antonis, and Nic Newman. 2017. 'I Saw the News on Facebook' Brand Attribution when Accessing News from Distributed Environments. *Digital News Project*. Reuters Institute for Journalism Studies. https://reutersinstitute.politics.ox.ac.uk/our-research/i-saw-news-facebook-brand-attribution-when-accessing-news-distributed-environments.

Kelly, Kevin. 1997. New Rules for the New Economy. *Wired*. September 1. https://www.wired.com/1997/09/newrules/.

Kelly, Sanja, Mai Truong, Adrian Shahbaz, Madeline Earp, and Jessica White. 2017. Freedom on the Net: Manipulating Social Media to Undermine Democracy. *Freedom House*. November.

Kennedy, Jenny. 2016. Conceptual Boundaries of Sharing. *Information, Communication & Society* 19 (4): 461–474. https://doi.org/10.1080/1369118X.2015.1046894.

Kümpel, Anna Sophie, Veronika Karnowski, and Till Keyling. 2015. News Sharing in Social Media: A Review of Current Research on News Sharing Users, Content, and Networks. *Social Media + Society* (July–December): 1–14. https://doi.org/10.1177/2056305115610141.

Lafferty, Justin. 2016. You Want a Dislike Button? Here's Why Facebook Isn't Giving You One. *Adweek.* February 26. https://www.adweek.com/digital/you-want-a-dislike-button-heres-why-facebook-isnt-giving-you-one/.

Lean, Tom. 2016. *Electronic Dreams: How 1980s Britain Learned to Love the Computer.* London; Oxford: Bloomsbury Sigma.

Lee, Sian, Long Ma, and Dion H. Goh. 2012. Why Do People Share News in Social Media? In *Active Media Technology, Proceedings of the 7th International Conference, AMT 2011 Lanzhou, China, September 7–9*, ed. N. Zhong, Vic Callaghan, Ali A. Ghorbani, and Bin Hu. Berlin; Heidelberg: Springer-Verlag.

Madrigal, Alexis C. 2012. Dark Social: We Have the Whole History of the Web Wrong. *The Atlantic.* October 12. http://www.theatlantic.com/technology/archive/2012/10/dark-social-we-have-the-whole-history-of-the-web-wrong/263523/.

Mailland, Julien, and Kevin Driscoll. 2017. *Minitel: Welcome to the Internet.* Cambridge, MA: MIT Press.

Martin, Fiona. 2015. The Case for Curatorial Journalism … Or, Can You Really Be an Ethical Aggregator? In *Ethics for Digital Journalists: Emerging Best Practices*, ed. David Craig Lawrie Zion, 87–102. New York: Routledge.

Media Insight Project. 2017. *'Who Shared It?': How Americans Decide What News to Trust on Social Media.* March. Associated Press NORC Center for Public Affairs Research and American Press Institute. https://www.americanpressinstitute.org/publications/reports/survey-research/trust-social-media/.

Meikle, Graham. 2016. *Social Media: Communication, Sharing and Visibility.* New York; Abingdon, Oxon: Routledge.

Messina, Chris. 2007. Groups for Twitter; or A Proposal for Twitter Tag Channels. Factory Joe. August 25. https://factoryjoe.com/2007/08/25/groups-for-twitter-or-a-proposal-for-twitter-tag-channels/.

Messing, S., and S.J. Westwood. 2014. Selective Exposure in the Age of Social Media: Endorsements Trump Partisan Source Affiliation When Selecting News Online. *Communication Research* 4 (8): 1042–1063.

Miller, Carlos. 2014. *The Citizen Journalist's Photography Handbook.* London: Ilex Press (Hatchette).

Mitchell, Amy, and Mark Jurkowitz. 2014. *Social, Search and Direct Pathways to Digital News.* Pew Research Center. March 13. http://www.journalism.org/2014/03/13/social-search-direct/.

New York Times. 2011. The Psychology of Sharing: Why Do People Share Online? Customer Insight Group. http://templatelab.com/the-psychology-of-sharing/.

Newman, Nic. 2018. *Digital News Project 2018. Journalism, Media, and Technology Trends and Predictions.* Oxford University: Reuters Institute for the Study of Journalism.

Oremus, Will. 2016. Who Controls Your Facebook Feed? *Slate.* January 3. http://www.slate.com/articles/technology/cover_story/2016/01/how_facebook_s_news_feed_algorithm_works.html.

Papacharissi, Zizi. 2015. *Affective Publics: Sentiment, Technology and Politics.* Oxford; New York: Oxford University Press.

Papacharissi, Zizi, and Maria de Fatima Oliveira. 2012. Affective News and Networked Publics: The Rhythms of News Storytelling on #Egypt. *Journal of Communication* 62: 266–282. https://doi.org/10.1111/j.1460-2466.2012.01630.x.

Parse.ly. 2015. *Understanding Traffic Patterns from the Top News Topics of 2015.* The Authority Report. http://learn.parsely.com/rs/314-EBB-255/images/authority-report-9.pdf.

Petre, Caitlin. 2015. *The Traffic Factories: Metrics at Chartbeat, Gawker Media, and The New York Times.* Tow Center for Digital Journalism.

Picone, Ike, Ralf De Wolf, and Sarie Robijt. 2016. Who Shares What with Whom and Why? *Digital Journalism* 4 (7): 921–932. https://doi.org/10.1080/21670811.2016.1168708.

PR Web. 2016. NewsWhip Inc. Announces the Issuance of a New Patent on Its Social Velocity Methodology. Wednesday, June 22. https://www.equities.com/news/newswhip-inc-announces-the-issuance-of-a-new-patent-on-its-social-velocity-methodology.

Reagan, Gillian. 2009. The Evolution of Facebook's Mission Statement. *Observer.* July 13. http://observer.com/2009/07/the-evolution-of-facebooks-mission-statement/.

Shaw, Frances, Jean Burgess, Kate Crawford, and Axel Bruns. 2013. Sharing News, Making Sense, Saying Thanks: Patterns of Talk on Twitter during the Queensland Floods. *Australian Journal of Communication* 40 (1): 23–40.

Singer, Jane B., David Domingo, Ari Heinonen, Alfred Hermida, Steve Paulussen, Thorsten Quandt, Zvi Reich, and Marina Vujnovic. 2011. *Participatory Journalism: Guarding Open Gates at Online Newspapers.* West Sussex: Wiley-Blackwell.

Swart, Joëlle, Chris Peters, and Marcel Broersma. 2018. Sharing and Discussing News in Private Social Media Groups. *Digital Journalism* 7: 187–205. https://doi.org/10.1080/21670811.2018.1465351.

Swartz, Aaron. 2015. Guerilla Open Access Manifesto. In *The Boy Who Could Change the World: The Writings of Aaron Swartz.* New York: The New Press.

Tandoc, Edson C. 2014. Journalism Is Twerking? How Web Analytics Is Changing the Process of Gatekeeping. *New Media & Society* 16 (4): 559–575.

Tharoor, Shashi. 2018. India's Social-Media Lynch Mobs. *Project Syndicate.* https://www.project-syndicate.org/commentary/india-social-media-bjp-trolls-attack-swaraj-by-shashi-tharoor-2018-07.

Trussler, Marc, and Stuart Soroka. 2014. Consumer Demand for Cynical and Negative News Frames. *International Journal of Press Politics* 19 (3): 360–379. https://doi.org/10.1177/1940161214524832.

Usher, Nikki. 2016. *Interactive Journalism: Hackers, Data and Code.* Urbana, IL: University of Illinois.

Vosoughi, Soroush, Deb Roy, and Sinan Aral. 2018. The Spread of True and False News Online. *Science* 359 (6380): 1146–1151.

Wadbring, Ingela, and Sarah Ödmark. 2016. Going Viral: News Sharing and Shared News in Social Media. *Observatorio (OBS*)* 10 (4): 132–149. http://www.scielo.mec.pt/pdf/obs/v10n4/v10n4a08.pdf.

Wardle, Claire. 2017. *Fake News. It's Complicated.* First Draft. February 16. https://firstdraftnews.org/fake-news-complicated/.

Wardle, Claire, and Hossein Derakhshan. 2017. Information Disorder: Toward an Interdisciplinary Framework for Research and Policymaking. September 27. Council of Europe and Harvard Shorenstein Center. https://firstdraftnews.org/wp-content/uploads/2017/10/Information_Disorder_FirstDraft-CoE_2018.pdf?x40896.

Weber, Marc. 2017. A Common Language. *Internet Histories* 1 (1–2): 26–38. https://doi.org/10.1080/24701475.2017.1317118.

Wittel, Andreas. 2011. Qualities of Sharing and their Transformations in the Digital Age. *International Review of Information Ethics* 15 (09/2011). http://www.i-r-i-e.net/inhalt/015/015-Wittel.pdf.

Zuckerberg, Mark. 2017. Bringing the World Closer Together. *Facebook.* June 23. https://www.facebook.com/zuck/posts/10154944663901634.

CHAPTER 3

The Numbers Game: Social News Analytics

Fiona Martin and Tim Dwyer

Early in the social media revolution, Gawker Media, the now defunct blog network, began to offer its writers traffic-based bonuses based on the popularity of its posts, a remuneration strategy which would change the way the worth of journalism was measured. According to an email from Nick Denton, the company's founder and owner, the aim was to encourage journalists to produce 'linkworthy' material, "a secret memo, a spy photo, a chart, a well-argued rant, a list, an exclusive piece of news, a well-packaged find" that would boost social sharing, increase pageviews and build audiences, "new readers who might discover it through Digg" or some other social sharing service (Boutin 2008). Gawker also developed a programme called Recruits, where new writers were paid $US5 for every 1000 unique visitors they attracted up to a threshold reward limit, and could land a job if they met traffic targets over three months. One of the results was that Gawker journalists would write to build their metrics, and as Denton would later reflect, "Editorial traffic was lifted but often by viral stories that we would rather mock. We—the freest journalists on the planet—were slaves to the Facebook algorithm" (Bloomgarden-Smoke 2014).

While Gawker later abandoned its bonuses scheme, as did other digital publishers (Bilton 2015) the idea of 'performance pay' or rewarding journalists for attracting online engagement became a subject of debate in newsrooms worldwide. Alongside the rise of social media news sharing, it was a factor in the rapid normalisation of social news analytics as a means to shape news production and distribution. Traffic bonuses were adopted

© The Author(s) 2019
F. Martin, T. Dwyer, *Sharing News Online*,
https://doi.org/10.1007/978-3-030-17906-9_3

at Forbes and other smaller publications (Carr 2014), and unsuccessfully proposed at the Trinity Mirror network in the UK, before collective bargaining prevented them from being introduced (Greenslade 2016). The concern raised then, which resonates now, was how would metrification affect the professional, public orientation and ethics of news reporting?

Attention metrics are now a key factor in the way editors value journalistic performance (Whipple and Shermak 2018) and, as Chap. 1 outlined, are central to the calculus of journalism value that is reshaping the news media's gatekeeping and distribution strategies. While much attention has been paid to the potential effect of this quantitative turn on journalism quality, in this chapter, we are more interested in what analytics can and can't measure about social media users' relationships with news journalism. In exploring this subject, we unmask the ambiguities of social signals and the difficulty of relying on them to determine the value of journalistic labour and products.

We start by examining how news was traditionally commodified and how social sharing has shifted the way in which that audience commodity is interpreted. We then explore how social analytics are created and what they purport to demonstrate, interrogating the factors that social platforms track in news use. In exploring the move of analytics away from simple measures of sharing to more complex calculation of social engagement, we traverse the new terrain of social media metadata, information that situates us in distinct social and cultural contexts, and allows the tracking of locative, temporal and networking trends. We introduce the concept of the metadata commodity, a new register of media commodification, which underpins the platform economy and its particular forms of capital accumulation, market organisation and competition. Finally, building on our Likeable example in Chap. 1, we consider how social media analytics are being used in the newsroom to accord journalism relevance, visibility and authority.

Crucially, rather than taking these measures as given, knowable assessments of what audiences think and do, we explore the ways in which sharing analytics are unaccountable and unstable. In particular, we question the robustness of mobile and cross-platform sharing measurements, given the complexity of monitoring users on the move and shifting between devices and commendary platforms. Where news consumption spans wearable devices, mobile phones, tablets, laptop and desktop computers, webpages and apps, just comparing measurements is a complicated process, made more difficult because definitions often differ between platforms, agencies and metrics companies (Ofcom 2014). This brings us back to the problem of *dark social*, news sharing that can't be easily tracked to its origin, and which indicates how little coordination there is between key actors in the news sharing ecology.

Our journey through the commercial vagaries and technical idiosyncrasies of social analytics will argue that we need to be taking a much closer look at the claims made by data brokers for their accuracy and comprehensiveness. In this, we join a robust critique of audience metrics in journalism studies (Anderson 2011; Nguyen 2013; Vu 2014; Carlson 2018). Our contribution is a historically grounded, systemic and ecologically informed view of how sharing metrics emerged from other news media measurement trajectories, how they fail to capture the complex meanings and motives we ascribe to news sharing and how platforms, their partners and audiences are shaping news agendas via the imaginary of more measurable, relevant and appealing approaches to news production.

THE NEWS NUMBERS GAME

News, like other commodities, historically has two forms of value—as information, and as a way of marshalling audiences. Marx famously explained the nature of this dualism in *Capital, Volume 1*:

> Commodities come into the world in the form of use-values or material goods, such as iron, linen, corn, etc. This is their plain, homely, natural form. However, they are only commodities because they have a dual nature, because they are at the same time objects of utility and bearers of value. Therefore they only appear as commodities, or have the form of commodities, in so far as they possess a double form, i.e. natural form and value form. (Marx 1867/1976/1990: 138)

Historically, in the geographically bounded markets of legacy media, news had natural or use value as timely, socially and culturally significant information which people needed to operate effectively in the world and to participate in society. It is true that news's exchange value was sometimes limited—its meanings could be "accidental, ephemeral and very often trivial", while those *faits divers* that no longer had novelty or immediacy could quickly become "garbage" (Lash 2002: 145). However, economic barriers to competition maintained the worth of news journalism to the public. Only wealthy, privileged publishers had the means and authority to create and distribute news media. In the social media age though, when any business or community group can issue its own news content, and the ability to publish, circulate and aggregate news has diversified, the exchange value of everyday, non-exclusive news is low and certainly far less than the platforms' aggregation of detailed online data about news consumers, their social network uses, preferences, attitudes and interests.

In this sense, the legacy news media's more durable value has been ideological, and derived from its capacity to marshal predictable, marketable audiences for persuasion and profit. Biltereyst and Meers remind us of Dallas Smythe's foundational observation that the key "commodity produced by the media industry is the audience itself, which is constructed and then sold to advertisers" (2011: 424). The use value of news audiences was in creating markets or symbolic legitimacy for mass media publishers, and their exchange value was based on the attention they offered, as measured by product exposure, in column inches or time on air. Generating the audience commodity also involved "labor power" (Smythe 2001: 233) both as people consumed media and in the statistical calculation of consumer capacities (Bolin 2010: 345–361). One of the most powerful means of calculating the electronic audience commodity was ratings, as Eileen Meehan's research into television audiences recognised. Ratings determined the value of particular demographic exposure categories that broadcast networks could sell to advertising agencies and media buyers, and networks then structured the delivery of content based on reaching these segments (Meehan 2005: 238–255). Ratings were not simply a measure of audience interest or attention, but a way of conducting an economic and political negotiation between broadcasters and advertisers.

Transposing this audience logic to the commercial internet meant finding a new quantification of exposure that was appropriate for an interactive medium. Web traffic, measured first as hits, then page accesses and page views, quickly became the preferred means of determining the kinds and scale of advertising that might cluster around websites (see Balnaves et al. 2011). This is not to say that the concept of traffic replicated the authority of television and radio ratings. Indeed, it more closely resembled the circulation figures of print media, where reach indicated cultural influence. However, over time, traffic was gradually correlated with information about the user IP addresses, domains and devices accessing these sites, to provide a more multi-faceted and potentially individuated picture of audience activity.

Indeed, the story of online media analytics is one of increasing complexity, as new tech players have entered the market and tried to track, analyse and commodify different forms of human behaviour. Google's history is important to this story as its original PageRank algorithm quantified the notions of page value and network significance that paralleled exposure in the old media. It then capitalised on this success by using search results to sell advertising. PageRank (Page et al. 1999) counted the quality and number of inbound links to a webpage as a measure of its importance, links being seen as endorsements from those doing the linking (Walker 2002). This early approach was slowly abandoned as link-farming and other means of gaming PageRank emerged, but it was enough to enable the company to dominate the search market and to develop other means of identifying informational relevance, salience and quality. Then through the aggregation and patterning of everyday searches, Google's engineers developed ways to commodify user search interests and preferences. Its keyword auctions and pay-per-click 'self-advertising service', AdWords, launched in 2000, had incorporated demographic targeting by 2006, personalised interest targeting by 2009, and physical location targeting by 2011 (Screaming Frog 2018). Its launch of Google News in early 2006 and purchase of YouTube in October of the same year then placed it as a central player in the commodification of both search and social news sharing.

Google's interlinked search and auction businesses generated a new register of audience commodity in the way that it exploited users' digital labour to generate revenues. Kang and McAllister argue that search extends and intensifies the commodification of user attention to the point where it constitutes cognitive labour, for instance, as we repetitively compile search strings and pursue relevant results (2011: 141–153). Those search terms are then indexed, analysed, valued and onsold to advertisers wishing to reach audiences using those terms. Google also sought to quantify user attention in other ways, after it bought YouTube in 2006. It introduced a video analytics suite that included calculations of visible attention and interaction: viewer retention duration, relative retention (compared to similar videos), user subscription rates and traffic referral sources. In developing these attention metrics, it is clear that Google was seeking to emulate (or surpass) the authority of traditional media ratings, and to establish a new order of social analytics that would capitalise on the desire of platform users to discover, explore and create information.

There is certainly much debate about whether our searches and social media activities constitute a form of work in the platform economy, or types of personal investment, self-satisfaction and creative realisation (see Jenkins et al. 2013 and Chap. 3). However, as Christian Fuchs (2014a; Fuchs and Sevignani, 2013) cogently argues, even if social media users derive a benefit—say, cultural recognition or status—from online news sharing, and do not feel they are working for, or being exploited by, the platforms they use, they are still unpaid for the time they spend generating capital benefit for those companies. The indirect benefits of cultural worth or social intimacy do not necessarily equate to monetary gain (although the manifest benefits of platform use clearly outweigh the creative investment in many users' minds). Centrally, however, our evaluative labour, in the search of social connection or self-promotion, generates more detailed information about our social lives, preferences and consumption patterns than traditional ratings measures, and so, when computationally analysed, is a more specific and valuable type of audience commodity. This data, when used to sell targeted advertising, is the material basis for platform revenues and the central pillar of the digital audience numbers game.

But even beyond the personal and evaluative data that platform users willingly provide, social media companies also collect data about every user who encounters their services on third-party sites. Both Google and Facebook track users of their services, and also those without accounts who visit websites that use their services. Facebook, for example, tracks non-members who browse websites that use Facebook's social plug-in, that is, its share and like buttons, or its log-in script, its ads, or measurement tools (Facebook 2018). Just visiting a website that uses Facebook services means your browser will be prompted to send Facebook your I.P. address, browser and operating system details, together with data about the site you visited (Baser 2018). As Baser notes. Twitter, Pinterest and Linked in have similar social sharing plug-ins, while Google and Twitter also offer log-in services. When people upload their phone contacts to Facebook, their contact data is added to their profile, or to a 'shadow profile' if they don't have a Facebook account.

The scale and scope of this type of tracking exceeds that of any earlier audience measurement system, representing what Trottier (2012) suggests is a "lateral and diffuse" regime of surveillance as much as a totalising approach. Calls to expose the extent and operation of this corporate scrutiny have come from all levels of public life, from US congressional politicians and EU bureaucrats to rights advocacy groups and human rights campaigners. This widespread concern recognises the capacity of analytics programs to correlate aspects of data and metadata to reveal intimate details that are not otherwise visible on public profiles. Gay and lesbian users, for instance, may be identifiable through their friend networks, or their consumption of certain types of media. A North American study of 58 thousand Facebook users found that their race, sexual orientation, personality and politics could be gauged reasonably accurately from their pattern of liking content (Kosinski et al. 2013). Given the potential for such detailed personal profiling it is critical for journalists to better understand not only how social media analytics deliver audience knowledge, but also their consequences for privacy and discrimination.

Social Media Analytics

By the 2000s, it was a remarkably complex job to track the cross-platform activities of individuals moving between wearable devices, mobile phones, tablets, laptop and desktop computers, webpages and apps, especially as audience metrics definitions often differed between platforms, agencies and measurement companies (Ofcom 2014). In contrast, social media analytics were presented as a solution to the problem of understanding audiences' indiscriminate, transplatform, transnational news referrals; a new order of meaning about where those audiences were, what they attended to and valued and how they arrived at a particular story.

The term 'social media analytics' refers to informatics tools, approaches and procedures designed to "collect, monitor, analyze, summarize, and visualize social media data" with a view to extracting information patterns that might provide useful intelligence into user behaviours or qualities for business, educational or other uses (Zeng et al. 2010: 14). Businesses have been keen, for example, to use analytics to identify opinion leaders or influencers in social media networks, to understand their reach and impact on their followers, and to co-opt them into promoting goods, services and ideas to their networks (Stieglitz et al. 2018). Platforms themselves have encouraged the development of analytics software and businesses to extend their own influence. In creating application programming interfaces (APIs) that allowed developers to access user data in order to create software or games for platform users, social media services provided information streams which also allowed the creation of tools that analysed and visualised user behaviour. In 2009, Trendsmap, the invention of a Melbourne-based web development company, Stateless Systems, brought together Twitter trending data from the platforms then public API, and mapped it onto Google Maps to provide real-time locational information about key conversations online. It gave journalists a way of discovering news as it happened and of following its impact around the globe. The same year, US tech investment company Betaworks, which also had stakes in the rise of Twitter, Tumblr and Bitly, launched Chartbeat, an analytics tool which was designed to track real-time web metrics. By 2011, Chartbeat had created a news focused web analytics service, Newsbeat and, the year after, released its first social media tracking tools to monitor sharing and conversations relevant to its clients, and to visualise the trends in consumption so publishers could tailor their output and publications strategy to specific audiences.

Social media analytics tools and services have promised media publishers more precise insights into audience behaviour than ratings in several respects:

- the real-time tracking, aggregation and patterning of individual user actions or the performance of single-story items,
- the aggregation of information about specific audiences, for certain genres of content
- the monitoring of consumption across digital platforms,
- the correlation and filtering of different data sources,
- the automated monitoring of consumption trends.

With access to relatively immediate information about how audiences are reacting to content, journalists have been able to change and test aspects of storytelling—tweaking headlines, excerpts, images and story structure, and then showing different versions to different slices of the audience in order to gauge which attracts the most social engagement. A/B testing, as it is called, allows newsrooms to maximise reach and audience engagement across its output, and to use optimisation algorithms to assess the best outcome for particular metrics (Hagar and Diakopoulos 2019). BuzzFeed undertakes a form of real-time affective regulation based on social analytics, where journalists practice 'sentiment control'—using analytics to select on which platform content should be posted, so as to attract the most favourable user reactions (Wang 2017). Analytics are also employed to determine when stories hit a trending measurement or meet performance goals. As a Nieman Lab report suggested, for BuzzFeed:

A published post, of course, is never just one post: Multiple versions of it—with different headlines, but also of different lengths and using different thumbnail art—are shown to BuzzFeed.com visitors until the winning combination emerges after a couple of hours. (Wang 2017)

Given that analytics can provide journalists with real time audience responses to content, and more types of data about the ways they interact with a page or move through a story, they give the sense of improved control over the complex task of editorial decision making. The numbers are concrete, and directly relatable to topics and presentational elements. For newsrooms facing the impacts of decreasing advertising revenues, increased competition, and constant corporate restructuring, social media analytics represent a degree of certainty in an otherwise highly uncertain mediascape.

Little wonder then that journalists have adopted them to gain greater insight into the variety of user behaviours within that broader, less knowable category of audience, and more understanding of individual reactions to stories. Alongside more conventional web traffic measures (volume metrics), and evidence of attention to reading, watching or listening to a story, such as duration on page, progression through file, keystrokes, cursor movement and scroll depth (attention metrics), real-time social media analytics represent a new way of understanding both user engagement with content and, through their commendary behaviours, more about the nature of the audiences to which they belong. At the same time, as the Likeable case in Chap. 1 indicated, analytics have and are being used editorially to gauge the worth of certain forms of content, and by proxy, of the journalists that produce it.

Some years ago, media audience scholar Philip Napoli predicted that the traditional value of media exposure would diminish as computational systems emerged for gauging users' interest in, and appreciation of, online cultural products and the workers that produce them (Napoli 2011). He foresaw precisely how the advent of news sharing measures would succeed old exposure metrics and pave the way for a new 'transactional analytics' based on user attention and engagement measures. In *Audience Evolution,* he argues that these alternative criteria which assess user interaction, appreciation and response give rise to two important consequences for media scholarship—they are a new frontier for digital audience research, and they herald conflicts between quantitative and qualitative approaches to understanding the meaning of media consumption (2011: 172).

We certainly agree with his first proposition. Indeed, we propose that social media news sharing has enabled the creation of a novel form of news value, based on information about the context in which online consumption takes place, which deserves much further study—the metadata commodity.

THE METADATA COMMODITY

As Canadian media economist Dwayne Winseck (2016: 100) notes, the old ideas of audience commodity (Meehan 2005) or, in its more recent guise, "Internet prosumer commodification" (Fuchs 2014b: 57), do not effectively explain the increasing influence of Facebook as a news source or publisher. Content creation and sharing themselves fail to generate significant value for social media platforms. Rather, by 2016, Facebook was the fifth largest media company in the world by revenues due to its aggregation and profiling of user knowledge and its application of this analysis to behaviourally targeted advertising (O'Reilly 2016; Garrahan 2016). Social media match registration, device and locational details, with viewing and sharing data as well as other metadata such as content keywords, in order to profile individual and aggregate user identities. Social media metrics attract ad buyers "since [they] are so visible, accessible, and seemingly such transparent markers of popularity and engagement" (Baym 2013). Profiling then offers the potential to enable automated or 'programmatic' placement of tailored, interactive ads that can extract even more consumer information (Garrahan 2016).

Social media datafication lays bare a new register of news commodification. Where the news media previously made money from both information distribution and audience attention, social media companies now effectively exploit information about audience relations with other people in their network, with the places they post from or mention, the devices they post from and services they use, with the time of posting and with specific conversations about ideas through hashtag phrases. Facebook invites you to tag your posts with details of who you're with and where you are, while Twitter can also track posts that are geo-located by mobile GPS positioning, or which mention geographical locations. All posts are time stamped, providing detailed information about our activities over the course of a day. The check-in data from posts and apps can be used to identify users' behaviours and their cultural backgrounds. Device data such as hardware statistics, system settings, and sensor setting can also be used to uniquely identify devices and users (Perez and Stringhini 2018).

3 THE NUMBERS GAME: SOCIAL NEWS ANALYTICS

This metadata, or data about data, records far more information about our relationships with media technologies and products than any preceding audience measurement regime. Metadata collection is automated, invisible and global, yet highly localised too, identifying us even when ostensibly anonymous by using internet protocol addresses and satellite positioning systems. The collection and analysis of this contextual information about our media consumption constitutes a new order of always-on industrial surveillance and capital accumulation, which sits alongside the old forms of extracting value from audiences.

In deploying the semiotic concept of 'double articulation', over two decades ago, media sociologist Roger Silverstone (1994, 2002) advocated the study of media consumption on two, integrated levels—where media acted as communicative technologies and as symbolic objects operating in particular socio-cultural contexts to connect people and structure their social worlds. In social media news sharing, we also see the metadata about the way we communicate and organise our social relations being used to restructure those social connections and contexts, and to shape our exposure to news on social media. This third level of meaning making creates a 'triple articulation' of commodification, which urgently requires scholarly investigation into its impacts on our cultural landscape and social relations.

What we call the *metadata commodity* refers to the value of information about our social relations in time and space, which can only be collated and interpreted as part of a 'machinic assemblage' (Celis 2015), the platform. It may involve information about the sender and the receiver of a shared message, and their times, places and frequency of communications, which are used to calculate various degrees and hierarchies of relatedness. What Maron and Carter (2017) call *referential* data about ourselves, our acts, locations, preferences and tastes, the information that we put in our social profiles, is correlated with this *transactional* data about who we correspond with, when, where, how and why. This metadata correlation then enables companies to identify the nature of our friend and family networks, our movements and activities. The social-spatial nature of this, as Courtois et al. (2014) note, is one of the key factors that can distinguish a new articulation of commodification, in this case as social media companies use their platforms and associated apps to track our presence across platforms, devices and places. Social media are not only communicative technologies and symbolic objects but also surveillance machines, gathering material about our lives and what we consume.

In 2010, software engineer Raffi Krikorian mapped the metadata provided by a tweet (see Fig. 3.1). His image lists around 20 distinct forms of

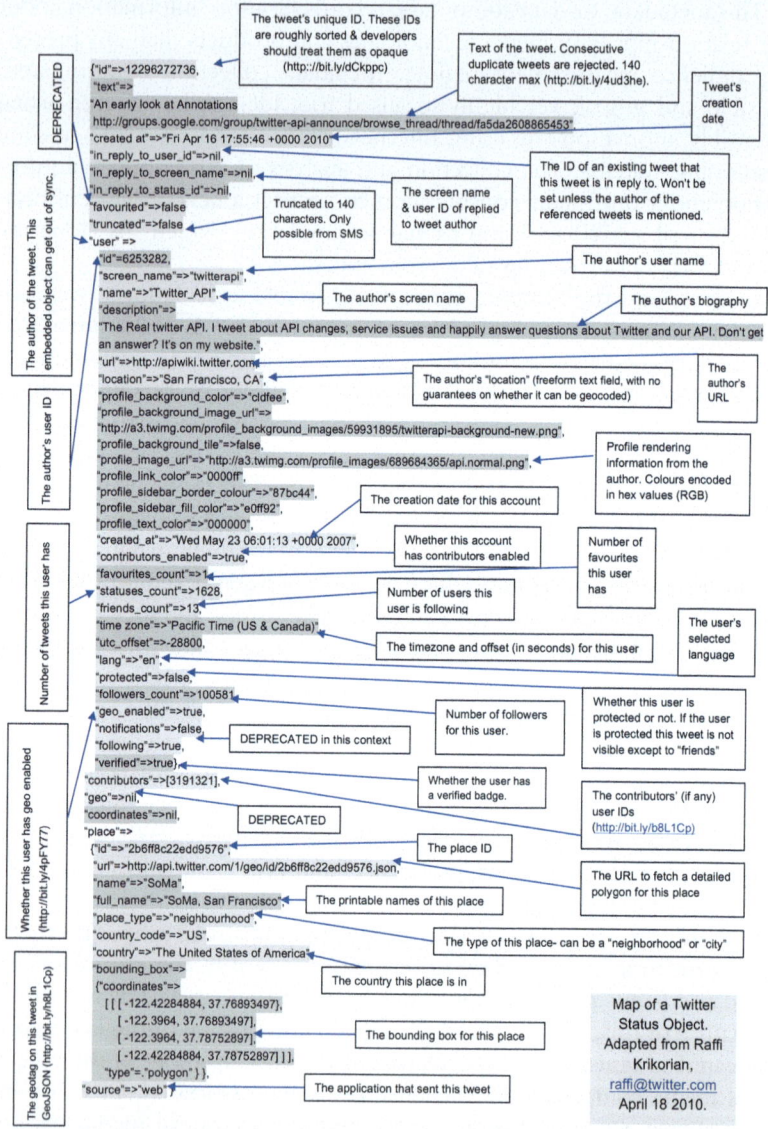

Fig. 3.1   The metadata of an early tweet, adapted from Krikorian, 2010

data encoded in the tweets alongside the content of the message, including the author's screen name, user name, biography, URL, location, place ID, time zone, language, followers, and number of people followed, verification detail, application and device used to post. It gives clear indication of the breadth of information that is relatively invisible to ordinary users of social media. A more recent study now estimates around 140 fields of metadata are associated with one tweet (Perez and Stringhini 2018).

Metadata is valuable transactional information as it allows social media companies to know more about where and when we share news, with whom and in what habitual patterns, than the substance of our commendary acts alone would convey. When matched with other consumption information, such as subscriber data on news items viewed and duration of session, companies could work out, for example, how long after viewing someone shared a story and roughly where they might have been when they did it. Correlating social and registration data could also help companies identify the super-sharers in their network, their routines and their characteristics. Aggregating the timing of similar news sharing allows news analytics companies like Chartbeat or Parse.ly to calculate the relative rate of sharing, or its 'social velocity'.

Metadata has underpinned the restructuring of the news media industry, spawning a whole new ecosystem of companies like Chartbeart which orbit the social media platforms, reliant on turning their data feeds into so-called 'actionable' insights for publishers, and bent on creating narratives about the significance of metrics for the survival of journalism in the digital age. However, as Napoli also suggested, as has Ien Ang (1991) and Silverstone before them, media research has long found use in questioning the certainties and assumptions of quantitative audience regimes. Indeed, it is more likely that the future of journalism depends on a deep critique of analytics programs and services, the social media data that underpins their calculus and the construction and meaning of the signals that platforms encourage us to register in our evaluation of news and information.

THE PROBLEMATIC OF LIKES

In news media terms, until recently, a Facebook or Instagram like, a retweet or a favourite of a news story published on a website signalled that the story being commended was attracting extended reach, beyond the platform of publication. Social media sharing was, for a time, a proxy for online consumption and networked engagement. Commendations, it was thought, equalled attention and approval, which in turn would trigger higher social news feed visibility and greater reach, leading in turn to even more interest and interaction.

However, digital audience studies eventually showed that sharing does not directly correlate with consumption or attention. Fifty-nine per cent of the links shared by news media, and retweeted on Twitter, are never clicked on and so the content is not seen—at least by that method of promotion (Gabielkov et al. 2016). Eighty-five per cent of Facebook users don't listen to the sound of the videos they watch (Patel 2016). Thus, while social sharing figures may indicate recognition of the masthead or news brand that is being shared, it is no substitute for more detailed analysis of how users consume the material or what they say about the value of it.

With major platforms slowly changing their algorithms to favour content from paid sponsors, communications commentators are now arguing the value of simple social signals such as favourites and likes has decreased. The only problem with this proposition is that it is difficult to argue that social sharing signals have ever had a stable, unequivocal currency. Rather, their meaning has always been in flux, modified and transformed during use, debated and dismissed as new forms of signalling worth emerge.

Due to its growing market power over the last decade, Facebook has had a unique ability to establish audience measurement standards for the differing forms of attention that users pay to digital media. Facebook's signature move in this regard was its iconic thumbs up 'like' button. In its early years, Facebook had measured user attention in comments on user-generated material and in shares of that content with other users. Reportedly, when the like button idea was floated in 2007, Mark Zuckerberg was initially lukewarm about introducing a simple approval signal, which he thought might distract people from making comments, and so diminish the platform's information gathering capacity (Speed 2015). This prediction was later disproved in user behaviour, but still, Facebook itself was not quite clear about the like button's meaning even at its soft launch, when it was described in a company blog post as the star rating to a restaurant review (Chan 2009)—a rating device without degrees of affection. Liking, as many commentators noted at the time, was an ambiguous social signal because it implied endorsement when that was not necessarily how users felt about the material they were viewing. They may have felt interested or concerned about a topic but ambivalent about the expression of the message. Some posts, such as those about deaths or tragedies, were not appropriate to like.

Even so, the like button, which was extended to third-party sites in 2010, became a durable feature, in part because of its capacity to generate simple, optimistic figures about user preferences. It helped Facebook to measure the popularity of content and so to rank and make it visible content in news feeds. It was also useful because one user's 'like' tended to attract further social approval from subsequent users, generating a cascade of supportive sentiment and demonstrated attention. But as many users and commentators complained, not all content was socially appropriate to like, particularly stories about deaths or tragedies.

The ambiguity of the like button saw it adopted for a variety of social uses—to indicate attention to a person's views or friendship with the poster, to cultivate favour with that person or maintain their relationship, to demonstrate that the person is aware of a debate or issue, or (in not liking) not willing to endorse a view or even to end a longer threaded conversation, as a signal that there is nothing more to say. As Eranti and Lonkila's (2015) survey research indicated, users show "imaginative abilities to use a single button to develop, maintain, and end social relationships and conversations, to get involved in social exchanges, to balance between sometimes contradictory expectations of their audience, and to build and maintain a face in front of their networked audiences". So, commendary signals, or 'interactions' as they're known in metrics parlance, can mean different things to different users, their meaning can change over time and they can be used to achieve various social ends.

Despite their inherent interpretative possibilities, commendary icons and reactive images like emojis and stickers have been designed to encourage more measurable social interaction, and to standardise and commodify user affect (Stark and Crawford 2015). By appropriating and elaborating simple Unicode emoticons, social media companies have used *reactive imagery* to calculate their users' emotional states, or to codify the depth of their social bonds, as when Snapchat introduced relationship status icons. Each image has a distinct numerical code in its metadata which enables it to be counted alongside related shared content. However, the range of emotions able to be associated with clicking the 'sad' Facebook button on a news post, makes the attempt at analysing users' communicative desires reductionist.

Social media analytics have various limitations of interpretation, compatibility, correlation and significance. At its most basic, news sharing data can be misleading because the story at the shared URL may never have been fully read, and reactions may be diverse or contradictory. Mentions, such as hashtags, direct messages and public comments present particular challenges for automated analysis due to semantic inconsistencies in the way users formulate their messages (Zeng et al. 2010). Interaction metrics are also unreliable because there is no general standard for comparing the worth of different types of commendation across different platforms. To return to the problem of dark social introduced in Chap. 1, there are also problems of tracking and correlating commendations across platforms and devices. Even once you have a set of figures to assess, you need a benchmark for establishing what success might look like, but this will vary depending on the publication, audience demographics, topic and genre. Social first publications like BuzzFeed, and those with younger audiences, will always score more highly on social sharing indicators. As the coming chapter will reveal, some polarising topics, like politics and sport are highly likely to attract commendation, as are opinion writing and novel scientific studies, but neither subject matter nor story type is a definite determinant of sharing behaviour. There are indicators of what topics share well, but no fool-proof formula for ensuring viral social sharing.

Commendary metrics—shares, interactions and mentions—make up a relatively small, but highly visible, part of the highly contested field of audience metrics. Cherubini and Kleis Nielsen (2016) note that while a share count is a clear measure of interest, if not attention, and interactions indicate what people do with news, it is harder to know what these measures say about the social meaning and significance of stories. Comments and hashtags can give a sense of that qualitative understanding, but only through sentiment analysis or deep dive textual analysis. Generally though, analytics packages represent mentions as raw numbers or binary estimates of positive and negative sentiment. As a whole, social sharing metrics are difficult to match definitively "to core interests like reach, engagement, loyalty, and impact" (Cherubini and Kleis Nielsen 2016: 37). Figure 3.2 shows where they are situated, and where they are absent, from the broader range of digital news metrics mapped in terms of the relative clarity of those measures and the types of issues they present for analysis.

Adapted from Cherubini and Kleis Nielsen, with permission. 2016

Caitlin Petre in her 'Traffic Factories' report gives another example of the difficulties of measuring commendation at Gawker, when management introduced comment interaction targets, with public shaming of those who failed to respond to at least 80% of user posts. As Petre observes the target conflicted with other performance metrics:

RELATIVELY CLEAR DEFINITIONS/MEASUREMENTS

LESS CLEAR DEFINITIONS/MEASUREMENTS

Interest	REACH	ENGAGEMENT	LOYALTY	IMPACT
Definition	The number of people exposed to content in a given time period	Time someone spends with content during a session or a given period of time	Frequency with which someone seeks out a given brand's site, app or social media content	Whether content made a difference in people's life (individual or societal)
Measurement	Unique users (<u>website)</u> User impressions (apps) Impressions (off-site social media use)	Session time (<u>website)</u> <u>Time</u> in apps (app) Engaged time (time spent actively interacting with content) Number of page visits	Return visits (website) User sessions (apps)	No agreed upon metrics
Data issues	De-duplication from devices to people App/browser proliferation Access to off-site data	Aggregation of individual users' engagement across devices, apps, and browser use integrating on-site/app engagement with off-site engagement	Aggregation across devices, apps, and browser use integrating on-site/app use with off-site use	No agreed upon sources of data

Fig. 3.2 A range of online metrics mapped in terms of relative clarity of definitions and measures

...there was no systematic way to measure or quantify the *quality* of these interactions, and some writers told me it was easy to hit the 80 percent target by responding to comments with, "great point!" or a similarly superficial contribution. To spend more time engaging with commenters, they said, would decrease their post count, which could, in turn, depress their number of unique visitors and their site's chance of getting a bonus. (Petre 2015)

Here, we see the task of interpreting commendary worth leading to confusion over what metrics are most meaningful, and best signify the value of journalistic labour.

Aside from the uncertainties of calculus presented by different types of audience analytics, and different analytics packages from competing platforms and third-party firms, the social media companies' own metrics formulations are constantly being tweaked and just as often questioned. Facebook has admitted misreporting sharing metrics on several occasions, for referral traffic, like and share counts and live video reactions (Peterson

2017). YouTube, Instagram and Twitter have all had purges to remove bogus, often machine generated subscriber and follower accounts and commendations. All platforms struggle with the widespread use of applications to generate fake followers and interactions. Yet, it is the platforms' promise of deeper audience insights than previous exposure regimes that have underpinned their market dominance.

On the whole, the field of digital audience metrics is one of ongoing change, unpredictability, competition and contest, with its dominance over an older order of exposure being based more on claims of individual surveillance, real-time aggregate analysis, big data and global scale than accuracy or reliability. There are certainly critics of the ways in which platforms have captured all aspects of the news commodity—as content hosts, audience analysts and advertising sales businesses. As Australian media lobby group Free TV has argued, part of the reason that Google and Facebook now command advertising revenues worldwide is "based on unsubstantiated and exaggerated claims around reach, viewability and effectiveness. They write their own standards and force advertisers to use their vertically integrated products to get access to their platforms" (Hickman 2018).

Yet, news sharing analysis also presents a familiar problematic for audience research—that of weighing factors of accessibility, scale and popularity against accuracy and deeper insight. For good reason then, a decade on from the adoption of social media metrics for editorial decision making, some newsrooms are starting to question how great a reliance they place on analytics, particularly for staff management and revenue generation.

THE DEVIL IS IN THE DETAIL

As Matt Carlson argues, understanding the implications of the 'measureable journalism' of the social media era involves "embracing complexity to avoid oversimplification" (2018: 408). In analysing how social sharing metrics are shaping news, researchers need to consider the forms and application of the material technologies (software, information infrastructure and external platforms) and the internal and external structural elements (organisations, labour, platform companies, third-party vendors, markets, regulators) as well as the aspects of agency (journalists' professional attitudes and aspirations, norms of practice, forms of consumption, cultural beliefs about news and public policy positions). Having considered materiality and structural issues so far, we now turn to look at the interaction of structure and agency—that is, the news media's moves to embrace social media metrics as part of audience knowledge tools for better serving their users and publics.

In the early days of social metrics, as they fundamentally shaped news production in BuzzFeed, Gawker, Huff Post and other digital-born publications, there was some journalistic resistance in traditional newsrooms to the idea of personalised audience monitoring driving professional news decision making. Journalists were reluctant to abandon notions of news sense and journalistic autonomy for measurements that only represented an online active section of their constituency. There were also concerns that so-called vanity metrics—numbers of likes and followers—were not as relevant as engagement metrics, including shares, comments, repeat visits and time spent on page. The quality debate or 'news gap' thesis (Boczkowski and Mitchelstein 2013), which argued that social media users favoured lifestyle and celebrity stories over more serious, professionally values hard news topics, also figured in opposition to too heavy an emphasis on social media analytics for editorial goal setting.

An additional problem with using news sharing analytics to guide news gatekeeping, which became obvious as journalism researchers began to examine exactly what was being shared, was that social sharing was sometimes a poor indicator of public good interests, being often motivated by personal and private interests, and organised using what Frank Pasquale (2015) calls the 'black box' of algorithmic processes. A Pew Research Center study of US social news sharing showed, for example, that user concerns about peer social judgments and corporate surveillance made them reluctant to share certain types of news with their social networks (Hampton et al. 2014). Its analysis of the social media talk around the Edward Snowden leak suggests that news which is politically polarising or confronting to discuss may be less likely to be talked about on social media channels than face-to-face. Further, it is impossible for journalist to gauge the reasons that any one story might become visible in a news feed, so sharing figures can only give a rough approximation of reach. As Facebook's senior policy executive Andy Connell said recently, there are "hundreds of thousands of signals" used to determine placement of items in news feeds (McDuling 2018), and newsrooms have access to little of that information.

Yet, as leading news organisations began to develop their own analytics dashboards, like the Guardian's Ophan (Woods 2015), and introduced roles like social media editors, community managers and audience development editors, journalists began to recognise that the business of distributing their work, calculating its impact and relating to audiences was changing. Ambivalence did not give way to acceptance as much as legacy news companies mandated new regimes of performance that would address competition by digital-born brands, using the digital competitor's forms of editorial calculus to rework their own strategies for attracting audience online. The strategy shift is well captured in Fredrica Cherubini and Rasmus Kleis Nielsen's guide to the growing uptake of editorial analytics, which argues that:

> Journalists today not only need analytics to navigate an ever-more competitive battle for attention. Many journalists also want analytics, as an earlier period of scepticism seems to have given way to interest in how data and metrics can help newsrooms reach their target audiences and do better journalism. (2016: 6)

Much of the early debate about the use of social media analytics in news production revolved around the so-called quality questions: would the news media create only what performs well in social engagement terms, and how might those fast-changing criteria affect what is produced and distributed? (Napoli 2011: 155). In his analysis of the rise of web metrics, An Nguyen put forward a common view about the negative consequences of chasing digital audience approval: "The problem is that the kind of news that can maximise audiences is often the so-called 'news you can use'—news that caters to the lowest common denominator of all tastes, addressing the most basic, least sophisticated and least sensitive level of lifestyles and attitudes" (Nguyen 2013: 152). The argument goes that so-called 'hard news'—dealing with serious public affairs of the day—that allows audiences to operate as well-informed citizens in a democracy demands greater 'cognitive effort', which ostensibly may trigger them to switch to another more popular metrics-driven news site.

We however see the news media's turn to analytics and 'calibrated' journalism as more of a labour or control concern than a quality issue. Across the globe newsrooms have adopted analytics as a tool to better guide audience response and development, a key factor in increasingly competitive, cross-border markets. However, while analytics have become a central tool in editorial decision making, they are generally still only used as one element in the editorial mix (Cherubini and Kleis Nielsen 2016). More worryingly, they have become a means of prioritising work time, and a contentious way of establishing targets and benchmarks for journalistic performance. Claire Petre's (2015) *Traffic Factories* report surveys the troubled integration of social media analytics into labour value and corporate status. As she notes, a newsroom's focus on performance metrics can have damaging effects on journalists' understanding of their worth. Online response metrics can "drown out" other forms of evaluation and exert a strong influence over journalists' emotions and morale. Metrification can also be a means of gamifying journalistic work, motivating staff to perform better and pitting journalists against each other in search of status rewards (Ferrer-Conill 2017). When used to manage news production or to discipline journalists, social media analytics function as techniques of control.

Performance metrics are now commonly used in newsrooms to set news-gathering agendas and to measure reach and digital exposure, and so to assess the worth of published articles, if not their authors. This means journalists wanting to meet their social engagement targets are subject to the ever-changing analytics agendas of social media platforms, and need to constantly reorient their content creation approaches to better ensure the visibility of their material in news feeds (Cohen 2018). As 75% of BuzzFeed content only appears on social media, not on its website, it has a special term for the constant process of re-evaluating what digital criteria should be prioritised in audience research and news production: "re-anchoring" (Ingram 2016). Poell and Nieborg (2018) situate this shift in cultural control to the platforms and their corporate agendas as the "platformization" of cultural production, whereby social media companies are taking an increasing role in dictating how and what news is produced, marginalising news companies as mere content suppliers, and assuming their traditional roles as news distributors and aggregators of audience.

We see another example of this platformization in the way that social media companies and software vendors have developed news research tools that help journalists 'discover' trending story material. Facebook, for example, developed Signal, a service which enables journalists to "surface relevant trends, photos, videos, and posts from Facebook and Instagram for use in their storytelling and reporting" (Mitchell 2015). Neil Thurman, in interviewing journalists about their social research practices, found they used SocialSensor and Spike for monitoring audience sentiment and news trends, Geofeedia for locative updates on breaking stories and for verifying the accuracy of content sources, and Twitter for its simplicity and familiarity of use in following and gauging the sentiment of conversations (Thurman 2018). Each tool was in a state of flux due to the continual updating of data gathering, processing and visualisation processes.

The uncertainty and, occasionally, mistrust that platform control can generate is evident in the fate of Facebook's Instant Articles (IA) project. IA is a Facebook content hosting scheme, launched in 2015, which offers partner publishers the chance to publish stories on Facebook servers that are promoted via its news feeds and optimised for mobile consumption. Facebook's initial pitch was quicker story-load times, reducing user bounce rates, together with integrated autoplay video, interactive functionality and tailored advertising. Publishers and Facebook were to share the mobile advertising revenue generated, and Facebook argued that news organisations would also benefit from improved ad placement, more effective targeting of user interests and better audience analytics. The lure of increased audience and ad revenues attracted major news outlets including *The Guardian*, *The New York Times*, NBC News, *National Geographic*, *The Atlantic*, BuzzFeed, BBC News, *Der Spiegel* and *Bild* (Mullin 2015). Publishers were, however, wary of IA's potential impact on traffic and audience relations, as users no longer needed to go to a news website to read articles, as they did when they followed conventional social referral links (Wolff 2015). On his retirement, the *Guardian's* veteran editor in chief, Alan Rusbridger, lamented that it was hard to predict whether the Facebook deal would be "the most brilliant, inspired thing to be doing or … a pact with the devil. We don't know at the moment" (Rusbridger 2015).

By 2017, the devil in the detail was apparent. IA stories were earning less for publishers than content hosted on their own sites. Facebook took 30% of ad revenue earned through its network placements and, although publishers could keep all the revenue from their own ads, they had limited placement and customisation possibilities. At that time, there was also no 'subscribe button' to convert visitors directly to subscribers, even though subscriptions were becoming a more important source of revenue than advertising. Some publishers complained that they were getting little audience information. By January 2018, a Columbia Journalism Review study found that more than half the original IA partners had not posted an article on a selected test day, suggesting that they had stopped using the service (Brown 2018). The quality of the content review also was questioned, when the Australian Broadcasting Corporation found ads for mainstream companies like BMW and Woolworths, a supermarket chain, running alongside articles with alt-right discriminatory content (Bogle 2018).

There is little doubt the gloss is wearing off from some of the news publishing partnerships that major platforms have brokered in recent years. Google's AMP, or accelerated mobile pages format, which makes similar claims to IA in providing fast-loading content, only increased traffic to 34% of the US publishers that used it and generated some difficulties in monetising content (Breaux and Doll 2018). The Apple News app too was boosting traffic to the client, but providing little in the way of revenue to clients. In her study of the economic relationship between four New Zealand news organisations and Facebook, Merja Myllylahti (2018) found that direct referrals, rather than social media referrals, drove most traffic to news sites, and the revenues from visits and shares were underwhelming, contributing little to their overall earnings. By correlating traffic sources and volume, numbers of Facebook referred visits and volumes of shares, with revenue from social shares, she established that visits from social media sites contributed 0.03%–0.14% to their parent companies' total revenue and social shares (not likes or comments) only 0.009%–0.2% of total revenue. Myllylahti is duly cautious about the accuracy and generalisability of her findings because, as she notes, there are no public models for calculating corporate social media incomes, however her findings tally with industry sources that have suggested the cost of servicing Facebook publishing can outweigh the revenue returns (WAN-IFRA 2017).

Issues of autonomy and control then are central to the new numbers game in news, which is being driven by the attention economy tactics of social media platforms and digital-born publications, and our wholesale adoption of commendary practices. When Facebook decided to downgrade publisher posts in its news feed at the beginning of 2018, there was great debate in the news media about the extent to which publishers needed to break away from a dependence of social media platforms (Bell and Taylor 2017). In a *New York Times* article called "The End of the Social News Era?", John Ridding, chief executive of the Financial Times was quoted as arguing that the rapid change in the terms of service with news publishers "is really bringing into focus just how powerful the platforms have become and how the infrastructure is a very difficult place for publishers to operate and navigate. That has big implications for how people receive news, where they find it and what the quality of their news is" (Masheswari and Ember 2018).

Algorithmic Shaping of News

A critical analysis of social media news sharing and its commodification is fundamental to understanding internet news economies and their impact on the business and normative social functions of journalism. But providing that analysis also requires attention to commendary culture and the ways in which the architectures of sociality (the platforms) and their users' pursuit of creative expression are mutually shaped and shaping (Allmer 2015; Postigo 2014).

There is little doubt that commendary culture is having a significant effect on how news is discovered, both by news consumers and journalists. For example, the structure of YouTube news videos feeds and subsequent search results is partly dependent on how uploading journalists and editors classify and tag news items, as well as the platforms' algorithmic structuring of indexing, searching and recommendations, and the evaluative interactions of downloading users. It is important to consider how this interdependence of annotation, search and evaluation then affects what content is made visible to news consumers, other journalists, aggregators and curators—and how in turn it might influence their ideas about what is new, significant or worth sharing. How likely is it, for example, that YouTube's algorithmic recommendation of top news videos increases the liking or sharing of these by users, and their redeployment on news sites?

Commendary metrics are also, as this chapter has argued, affecting the focus, conduct and outcomes of journalism, although more in combination with other types of news analytics than as a driving force, in the BuzzFeed mode. However, it is difficult to disentangle newsrooms' reliance on social media platforms for attention, engagement and redistribution from their other web-measurement regimes. This is particularly the case where companies are looking to automate social news discovery, and so tying gatekeeping processes to algorithmic approximations of what website audiences will find captivating and relevant on social media. Thus, the algorithmic turn in journalism is intimately tied to social news sharing, even where sharing itself and commendary signals more broadly provide a relatively small part of the overall audience development picture.

In their research on algorithmic culture, Hallinan and Ted Striphas ask two pertinent questions which have clear implications for the future of social media metrics-driven journalism:

> How do we contest computationally-intensive forms of identification and discrimination that may be operating in the deep background of people's lives, forms whose underlying mathematical principles far exceed a reasonable degree of technical competency? What is at stake in "optimizing" would-be cultural artifacts to ensure a more favorable reception, both by human audiences and by algorithms? (Hallinan and Striphas 2014)

Our first answer is that journalists, in order to avoid simply reflecting the social media order and its popularity-enforcing circuits, must become more critically literate about the construction, operation and uses of social media analytics, and so be able to effectively challenge their use in news production. This is most important as the novelty of metrification wears off and systems of quantifying journalism work fade into the background, becoming normalised means of organising labour relations.

Second, beyond the quality question, we argue that is it crucial for media researchers to study the types of alliances being made between platforms, news publishers and third-party application and service vendors to understand the longer-term consequences of promoting journalism on social media channels and striving to secure commendary activity. The evolution of that social sharing ecology is the subject of our next chapter.

References

Allmer, T. 2015. *Critical Theory and Social Media: Between Emancipation and Commodification*. Oxon, NY: Routledge.

Anderson, C.W. 2011. Between Creative and Quantified Audiences: Web Metrics and Changing Patterns of Newswork in Local US Newsrooms. *Journalism* 12 (5): 550–566. https://doi.org/10.1177/1464884911402451.

Ang, Ien. 1991. *Desperately Seeking the Audience*. London; New York: Routledge.

Balnaves, Mark, Tom O'Regan, and Ben Goldsmith. 2011. *Rating the Audience: The Business of Media*. London; New York: Bloomsbury Academic.

Baser, David. 2018. Hard Questions: What Data Does Facebook Collect When I'm Not Using Facebook, and Why? *Facebook Newsroom*. April 16. https://newsroom.fb.com/news/2018/04/data-off-facebook/.

Baym, N. 2013. Data Not Seen: The Uses and Shortcomings of Social Media Metrics. *First Monday*, 18, no. 10. October 7. http://firstmonday.org/ojs/index.php/fm/article/view/4873/3752.

Bell, Emily, and Owen Taylor. 2017. *The Platform Press: How Silicon Valley Reengineered Journalism*. Tow Center for Journalism. March 29. https://www.cjr.org/tow_center_reports/platform-press-how-silicon-valley-reengineered-journalism.php/.

Biltereyst, D., and P. Meers. 2011. The Political Economy of Audiences. In *The Handbook of Political Economy of Communications*, ed. J. Wasko, G. Murdock, and H. Sousa, 415–435. London: Wiley.

Bilton, Ricardo. 2015. Publishers Sour on Traffic-Based Bonuses. *Digiday.com*. January 26. http://digiday.com/publishers/publishers-sour-traffic-based-bonuses/.

Bloomgarden-Smoke, Kara. 2014. Nick Denton Announces Collective Leadership for Gawker Media. *Observer.com*. October 12. http://observer.com/2014/12/changes-at-gawker-media/.

Boczkowski, Pablo J., and Eugenia Mitchelstein, eds. 2013. *The News Gap: When the Information Preferences of the Media and the Public Diverge*. Cambridge, MA: MIT Press.

Bogle, Ariel. 2018. 'Facebook's Instant Articles Enabled Inflammatory Publishers to Profit from Big Brand Ads. *Australian Broadcasting Corporation*. March 29. https://www.abc.net.au/news/science/2018-03-29/facebook-advertising-fake-news-instant-articles-woolworths-bmw/9593948.

Bolin, Göran. 2010. Digitization, Multi-Platform Texts and Audience Reception. *Popular Communication* 8 (1): 72–83.

Boutin, Paul. 2008. Denton to Pay Bloggers Based on Traffic. *Gawker.* January 1. http://gawker.com/339271/denton-to-pay-bloggers-based-on-traffic.

Breaux, Chris, and Bradley Doll. 2018. Research Study: Only 1 in 3 Publishers See a Clear Traffic Boost from AMP. *Chartbeat*. August 23. http://blog.chartbeat.com/2018/08/23/research-study-1-3-publishers-see-clear-traffic-boost-amp/.

Brown, Pete. 2018. More than Half of Facebook Instant Articles Partners May Have Abandoned It. *Columbia Journalism Review*. February 2. https://www.cjr.org/tow_center/are-facebook-instant-articles-worth-it.php.

Carlson, Matt. 2018. Confronting Measurable Journalism. *Digital Journalism* 6 (4): 406–417. https://doi.org/10.1080/21670811.2018.1445003.

Carr, David. 2014. 'Risks Abound as Reporters Play in Traffic.' The Media Equation. *New York Times*. March 23. https://www.nytimes.com/2014/03/24/business/media/risks-abound-as-reporters-play-in-traffic.html.

Celis, Claudio. 2015. The Machinic Temporality of Metadata. *tripleC* 13 (1): 101–111.

Chan, Kathy. 2009. I Like This. *Facebook*. February 10. https://www.facebook.com/notes/facebook/i-like-this/53024537130.

Cherubini, Federica, and Rasmus Kleis Nielsen. 2016. *Editorial Analytics: How News Media are Developing and Using Audience Data and Metrics*. February 23. Oxford: Reuters Institute for the Study of Journalism.

Cohen, Nicole S. 2018. At Work in the Digital Newsroom. *Digital Journalism*. January 8. https://doi.org/10.1080/21670811.2017.1419821.

Courtois, C., P. Verdegem, and L. De Marez. 2014. The Triple Articulation of Media Technologies in Audiovisual Media Consumption. *Television & New Media* 14 (5): 421–439.

Eranti, Veikko, and Markku Lonkila. 2015. The Social Significance of the Facebook Like Button. *First Monday* 20, no. 6. https://firstmonday.org/ojs/index.php/fm/article/view/5505/4581. https://doi.org/10.5210/fm.v20i6.5505.

Facebook. 2018. Hard Questions: What Data Does Facebook Collect When I'm Not Using Facebook, and Why? *Facebook Newsroom*. April 16. https://newsroom.fb.com/news/2018/04/data-off-facebook/.

Ferrer-Conill, Raul. 2017. Quantifying Journalism? A Study on the Use of Data and Gamification to Motivate Journalists. *Television & New Media* 18 (8): 706–720. https://doi.org/10.1177/1527476417697271.

Fuchs, Christian. 2014a. *Social Media: A Critical Introduction*. London; Thousand Oaks; New Delhi: Sage.

———. 2014b. Critique of the Political Economy of Informational Capitalism and Social Media. In *Critique, Social Media and the Information Society*, ed. Christian Fuchs and Marisol Sandoval. London; New York: Routledge.

Fuchs, Christian, and Sebastian Sevignani. 2013. What Is Digital Labour? What Is Digital Work? What's Their Difference? And Why Do These Questions Matter for Understanding Social Media? *tripleC: Communication, Capitalism & Critique. Open Access Journal for a Global Sustainable Information Society* 11 (2): 237–293.

Gabielkov, Maksym, Arthi Ramachandran, Augustin Chaintreau, and Arnaud Legout. 2016. *Social Clicks: What and Who Gets Read on Twitter?* Proceedings of the 2016 ACM SIGMETRICS International Conference on Measurement and Modeling of Computer Science. 179–192. France: HAL archives-ouvertes. https://hal.inria.fr/hal-01281190/document.

Garrahan, Matthew. 2016. Advertising: Facebook and Google Build a Duopoly. *Financial Times*. June 24. https://www.ft.com/content/6c6b74a4-3920-11e6-9a05-82a9b15a8ee7.

Greenslade, Roy. 2016. Why Trinity Mirror Was Right to Abandon Individual Targets for Staff. *The Guardian*. January 5. https://www.theguardian.com/media/greenslade/2016/jan/05/why-trinity-mirror-was-right-to-abandon-individual-targets-for-staff.

Hagar, Nick, and Nicholas Diakopoulos. 2019. Optimizing Content with A/B Headline Testing: Changing Newsroom Practices. *Media and Communication* 7 (1): 117–127.

Hallinan, Blake, and Ted Striphas. 2014. Recommended for You: The Netflix Prize and the Production of Algorithmic Culture. *New Media & Society* 23: 1–2. https://doi.org/10.1177/1461444814538646.

Hampton, Keith N., Rainie Lee, Weixu Lu, Maria Dwyer, Inyoung Shin, and Kristen Purcell. 2014. *Social Media and the "Spiral of Silence"*. Washington, DC: Pew Research Center. http://www.pewinternet.org/2014/08/26/social-media-and-the-spiral-of-silence/.

Hickman, Arvind. 2018. TV Industry Calls for Mandatory Third-Party Measurement of Facebook and Google. *Ad News*. April 23. http://www.adnews.com.au/news/tv-industry-calls-for-mandatory-third-party-measure-ment-of-facebook-and-google#UZxsHkrDuUGdk8my.99.

Ingram, Matthew. 2016. BuzzFeed: Days of Counting Pageviews and Unique Visitors Are Over. *Fortune*. February 19. http://fortune.com/2016/02/19/buzzfeed-metrics/.

Jenkins, Henry, Sam Ford, and Joshua Green. 2013. *Spreadable Media: Creating Value and Meaning in a Networked Culture*. New York: New York University Press.

Kang, Hyunjin, and Matthew P. McAllister. 2011. Selling You and Your Clicks: Examining the Audience Commodification of Google. *tripleC* 9 (2): 141–153.

Kosinski, Michal, David Stillwell, and Thore Graepel. 2013. Private Traits and Attributes Are Predictable from Digital Records of Human Behavior. *Proceedings of the National Academy of Sciences* 110 (15): 5802–5805. https://doi.org/10.1073/pnas.1218772110.

Krikorian, Raffi. 2010. Map of a Twitter Status Object. *Wall Street Journal.* April 18. http://online.wsj.com/public/resources/documents/TweetMetadata.pdf.

Lash, Scott. 2002. *Critique of Information*, 145. London: Sage.

Maron, Deborah, and Erin Carter. (2017) *"More Than What It Seems": How Critical Theory, Popular Engagement and Apps Like Tinder Can Help Us Reframe Metadata and Its Consequences.* Proceedings of the International Conference on Dublin Core and Metadata Applications 2017. http://dcpapers.dublincore.org/pubs/article/view/3849.

Marx, K. (original 1867, trans. 1976). 1990. Penguin. In *Capital: A Critique of Political Economy*, vol. 1. London.

Masheswari, Sapna, and Sydney Ember. 2018. The End of the Social News Era? Journalists Brace for Facebook's Change. *New York Times.* January 11. https://www.nytimes.com/2018/01/11/business/media/facebook-news-feed-media.html.

McDuling, John. 2018. "Unworkable, Unnecessary and Unprecedented": Facebook Hits Back at ACCC. *Sydney Morning Herald.* December 13. https://www.smh.com.au/business/companies/unworkable-unnecessary-unprecedented-facebook-hits-back-at-accc-20181212-p50lvk.html.

Meehan, Elaine R. 2005. Watching Television: A Political Economic Approach. In *A Companion to Television*, ed. Janet Wasko, 238–255. Malden, MA: Blackwell.

Mitchell, Andy. 2015. Introducing Signal for Facebook and Instagram. *Facebook Media.* https://media.fb.com/2015/09/17/introducing-signal/.

Mullin, Benjamin. 2015. News Outlets to Ramp Up Publication of Instant Articles. *Poynter.* June 16. https://www.poynter.org/reporting-editing/2015/news-outlets-to-ramp-up-publication-of-instant-articles/.

Myllylahti, Merja. 2018. Attention Economy Trap. An Empirical Investigation into Four News Companies' Facebook Traffic and Social Media Revenue. *Journal of Media Business Studies* 15: 237–253. https://doi.org/10.1080/16522354.2018.152752.

Napoli, Philip. 2011. *Audience Evolution: New Technologies and the Transformation of Media Audiences.* New York: Columbia University Press.

Nguyen, An. 2013. Online News Audiences: The Challenges of Webmetrics. In *Journalism: New Challenges*, ed. Karen Fowler-Watt and Stuart Allan, 146–161. Bournemouth: Centre for Journalism & Communication Research Bournemouth University.

O'Reilly, Lara. 2016. The 30 Biggest Media Companies in the World. *Business Insider.* May 31. https://www.businessinsider.com/the-30-biggest-media-owners-in-the-world-2016-5/.

Ofcom. 2014. *Measuring Online News Consumption and Supply.* Roundtable Discussion, December 9th 2014. Reuters Institute for the Study of Journalism.

Page, Lawrence, Sergey Brin, Rajeev Motwani, and Terry Winograd. 1999. *The PageRank Citation Ranking: Bringing Order to the Web.* Technical Report. Stanford InfoLab. http://ilpubs.stanford.edu:8090/422/.

Pasquale, Frank. 2015. *The Black Box Society: The Secret Algorithms That Control Money and Information.* Harvard: Harvard University Press.

Patel, Sahil. 2016. 85 Percent of Facebook Video Is Watched Without Sound. *Digiday.* May 17. https://digiday.com/media/silent-world-facebook-video/.

Perez, Mirco Musolesi, and Gianluca Stringhini. 2018. *You Are Your Metadata: Identification and Obfuscation of Social Media Users Using Metadata Information Association for the Advancement of Artificial Intelligence.* Paper presented to 12th International AAAI Conference on Web And Social Media. University College London. https://www.ucl.ac.uk/~ucfamus/papers/icwsm18.pdf.

Peterson, Tim. 2017. FAQ: Everything Facebook Has Admitted about Its Measurement Errors. *Marketing Land.* May 17. https://marketingland.com/heres-itemized-list-facebooks-measurement-errors-date-200663.

Petre, Caitlin. 2015. *The Traffic Factories: Metrics at Chartbeat, Gawker Media, and The New York Times.* Tow Center for Digital Journalism.

Poell, Thomas, and David Nieborg. 2018. The Platformization of Cultural Production: Theorizing the Contingent Cultural Commodity. *New Media & Society* 20 (11): 4275–4292.

Postigo, Hector. 2014. The Socio-technical Architecture of Digital Labor: Converting Play into YouTube Money. *New Media & Society.* 18 (2): 332–349.

Rusbridger, A. 2015. The Future of Journalism. *Guardian Live.* May 22. http://www.theguardian.com/membership/video/2015/may/22/alan-rusbridger-on-the-future-of-journalism-video.

Screaming Frog. 2018. Adwords History. https://www.screamingfrog.co.uk/adwords-history/.

Silverstone, Roger. 1994. *Television and Everyday Life.* London: Routledge.

———. 2002. Complicity and Collusion in the Mediation of Everyday Life. *New Literary History* 33 (4): 761–780.

Smythe, D.W. 2001/1981. On the Audience Commodity and Its Work. In *Media and Cultural Studies: Key Works*, ed. M.G. Durham and D. Kellner, 253–279. Malden, MA: Blackwell.

Speed, Barbara. 2015. "A Cursed Project": A Short History of the Facebook "Like" Button. *New Statesman America.* October 9. https://www.newstatesman.com/science-tech/social-media/2015/10/cursed-project-short-history-facebook-button.

Stark, Luke, and Kate Crawford. 2015. The Conservatism of Emoji: Work, Affect, and Communication. *Social Media + Society* 1 (2). https://doi.org/10.1177/2056305115604853.

Stieglitz, Stefan, Milad Mirbabaie, Björn Ross, and Christoph Neuberger. 2018. Social Media Analytics – Challenges in Topic Discovery, Data Collection, and Data Preparation. *International Journal of Information Management* 39: 156–168.

Thurman, Neil. 2018. Social Media, Surveillance, and News Work: On the Apps Promising Journalists a "Crystal Ball". *Digital Journalism* 6 (1): 76–97. https://doi.org/10.1080/21670811.2017.1345318.

Trottier, Daniel. 2012. *Social Media as Surveillance: Rethinking Visibility in a Converging World*. Surrey: Ashgate Publishing.

Vu, Hong Tien. 2014. The Online Audience as Gatekeeper: The Influence of Reader Metrics on News Editorial Selection. *Journalism* 15 (8): 1094–1110.

Walker, J. 2002. *Links and Power: The Political Economy of Linking on the Web*. Proceedings of Hypertext 2002. 78–79. Baltimore: ACM Press. http://jilltxt.net/txt/linksandpower.html.

Wang, Shan. 2017. Adaptation, A/B Testing and Analytics: How BuzzFeed Optimizes the News for Its Audience. International Centre for Journalists. *IJnet*. September 19. https://ijnet.org/en/story/adaptation-ab-testing-and-analytics-how-buzzfeed-optimizes-news-its-audience.

WAN-IFRA. 2017. World Press Trends 2017. http://www.wan-ifra.org/reports/2017/10/10/world-press-trends-2017

Whipple, Kelsey N., and Jeremy L. Shermak. 2018. *Quality, Quantity and Policy: How Newspaper Journalists Use Digital Metrics to Evaluate Their Performance and Their Papers' Strategies*. International Symposium on Journalism. *#ISOJ Journal*, 8, no. 1. http://isoj.org/research/quality-quantity-and-policy-how-newspaper-journalists-use-digital-metrics-to-evaluate-their-performance-and-their-papers-strategies/.

Winseck, Dwayne. 2016. Reconstructing the Political Economy of Communication for the Digital Media Age. *The Political Economy of Communication* 4 (2): 73–114.

Wolff, R. 2015. Facebook Instant Articles Just Don't Add Up for Publishers. *Technology Review*. July 9. http://www.technologyreview.com/news/539066/facebook-instant-articles-just-dont-add-up-for-publishers/.

Woods, Ben. 2015. How the Guardian's Ophan Analytics Engine Helps Editors Make Better Decisions. *The Next Web*. April 13. https://thenextweb.com/media/2015/04/13/how-the-guardians-ophan-analytics-engine-helps-editors-make-better-decisions/.

Zeng, Daniel, Hsinchun Chen, Robert Lusch, and Shu-Hsing Li. 2010. Social Media Analytics and Intelligence. *IEEE Intelligent Systems* 25 (6): 13–16.

CHAPTER 4

The Business of News Sharing

Fiona Martin

In 2013, motivational news sharing site Upworthy was reported to be one of the fastest growing social start-ups in the world, with reports of it attracting between 50 and 80 million unique visitors at its peak (Dickey 2013; Klein 2013). Co-founded by Eli Pariser, a key figure in the creation of political platform Moveon, Upworthy was designed to identify and circulate uplifting stories that would change "hearts, minds and sometimes even, the world" (Upworthy 2018). Its emotive, curiosity provoking headlines ensured its posts were liked and shared exponentially more than its native born and legacy competitors. However, in December 2013, as Upworthy told National Public Radio, its monthly visitor numbers dropped suddenly and dramatically (Sanders 2017). By November 2014, it claimed its traffic was a quarter that of its best result—partly due to a change in Facebook's news feed algorithm. As Facebook engineers later told the New York Times, they had adjusted the algorithm to promote 'high-quality' journalism and minimise clickbait—articles which attracted lots of clicks, but little subsequent reading, sharing or liking, and which had teasing headlines like "you'll never believe what happened next" (Manjoo 2017). Upworthy suffered, as did its competitors ViralNova and Distractify (Barakat 2014).

Facebook has enormous power as a global redistributor of news. For nearly a decade it has been the key driver of traffic to news sites and a source of customer acquisition (Newman 2011). It is also well known for instituting sudden news feed changes, which have unexpected and occasionally unwelcome effects on the publishers which depend on its traffic.

© The Author(s) 2019
F. Martin, T. Dwyer, *Sharing News Online*,
https://Doi.org/10.1007/978-3-030-17906-9_4

91

However, in 2013, when it demoted the so-called 'viral publishers', tweaks to its algorithm, developed in collaboration with 29 unnamed media publishers, saw it announcing large traffic boosts to other news sites, including BuzzFeed:

> [W]e've found that on average referral traffic from Facebook to media sites has increased by over 170 per cent throughout the past year. In fact, from September 2012 to September 2013, TIME's referral traffic has increased 208 per cent. BuzzFeed is up 855 per cent. And Bleacher Report has increased 1081 per cent. (Osofsky 2013)

Adweek noted that the likely reason BuzzFeed didn't suffer in the click-bait purge was that it had established a team of investigative journalists to boost its serious news output, and it bought a lot of Facebook ads to drive traffic to its advertorials. As *Business Insider* argued:

> the message Facebook is sending isn't so much that it wants "high quality" content for its News Feed. It's that if you are a media company, and you depend on Facebook for your traffic, you better make sure Facebook is benefiting from your existence. (Carlson 2014)

As one of the key actors in the *social media ecology*, Facebook has what technology commentator Frederic Filloux (2010) calls a "gravitational effect". In its market dominance, it draws other smaller digital companies into various types of relationships with it that can underpin and boost their business, but simultaneously leave them vulnerable to tactical shifts in its policy and programming. In January 2018, when its response to the US 2016 fake news congressional inquiry was to downgrade news visibility in its feed at the expense of local information and family and friend posts, this move had potentially negative consequences for journalism globally. Many news publishers saw a decline in Facebook referrals (Gruen 2018; Cornia et al. 2018). A *Mediashift* comparison of Facebook news engagement for the top five news publishers in six markets internationally argued that this decline had been obvious for some time before Facebook's algorithm change, but that it would likely continue (Rantala 2018). Local news, which Facebook had tried to support, did little better. A Tow Center report found that the majority (11 of 13) of US regional metropolitan news publishers like the Boston Globe "averaged fewer interactions per [Facebook] post in the nine weeks following the pro-local algorithm change than in the two years before" (Brown 2018a), even though they were also participating in Facebook's Local News Subscription Accelerator (Owen 2018).

Yet, while Facebook has a significant effect on the news we see and share online, and significant market power, it is part of a broader shift in media where the command of audience attention no longer lies with news publishers, but with the platforms and news intermediaries that manage our social networking and commendary activities—almost all operating in the information technology sector, rather than traditional media industries.[1] This sector includes those companies providing the physical hardware that sustains our online communications, such as Apple, Microsoft, Samsung, Intel, AT&T, Cisco and Verizon, and those that provide the software systems or platforms to enable our everyday networking, like Alphabet, Facebook and Tencent—all of which belong to the top 40 companies by market capitalisation internationally (PriceWaterhouseCoopers 2018). In 2018 Tencent, the Chinese internet technologies and services corporation, had the second largest absolute increase in market value of these companies after Amazon.

The shift of economic power to IT companies can be seen as part of a longer trajectory of digital capitalism (Schiller 1999), informational capitalism (Fuchs 2011) or data capitalism (Mayer-Schönberger and Ramge 2018), which has seen the rapid commodification and appropriation of knowledge by transnational corporations using digital networked technologies, the integration of local, national and transnational markets, and the expansion of economic sectors that create informational goods and services. This trend includes the way in which our socialising and media making have been internetworked and commodified in new and diverse ways. As Mayer-Schönberger and Ramge (2018) argue, data is the new source of innovation and economic growth, and the future of business will depend on new organisational structures and the growth of automated means of tracking, managing and evaluating human behaviour.

This chapter analyses the networked political economics of news sharing by investigating the roles played by a constellation of social media companies and services in transforming online news production and distribution. We examine the business models, ownership patterns and market power of key global players, such as Google, Facebook and Microsoft, as well as smaller second tier players such as Twitter, and other *news intermediaries* such as Gigya, Outbrain, ICUC and NewsWhip. We also outline

---

[1] A point made initially by Nic Newman and his colleagues at the Reuters Institute (Newman et al. 2016), but without acknowledging the range of actors involved in consolidating platform power.

the topology of China's more closed internet ecology, where microblogging platform Sina Weibo had more active monthly users than Twitter worldwide, and WeChat reached the 1 billion user mark by early 2018.

There is an extraordinary diversity of corporations, companies and services, business strategies and models underpinning our everyday news sharing, some largely invisible except when we register for a new platform and sign the terms of service. Our first aim in this chapter is to systematise our understanding of our relationship with these actors, their competitive strategies and interrelationships, and the parts they play in restructuring the news media. In fact, by using the term platform, we are adopting another commonly used, polysemic concept that embraces the interrelatedness of digital media companies. When we talk about 'news sharing platforms', we erase layers of deeper meaning about the way different social media systems, their architectures and their enterprise connections manage news flows.

Platforms are digital information systems that provide content hosting, management and distribution services for their users, rather than producing most of that content, and which analyse that data for "customer service, advertising and profit" (Gillespie 2018: 18). The idea of a platform, as digital media scholar Tarleton Gillespie (2010: 35) argues, brings together the concept of computational infrastructure with the older meaning of an elevating architecture, which is the basis for "opportunity, action and insight", and from which one can assume a political position. A platform "suggests a progressive and egalitarian arrangement promising to support those who stand upon it" (p. 35)—the perfect third level signification for the intermediary hosts of user-generated content, who want to broker relationships with users, media companies, advertisers and analytics services, among others.

In information engineering, platforms are modular software architectures and within economics, they are the meeting place for double-sided markets, where two groups of users provide each other with benefits (Gawer 2014). Anabelle Gawer suggests that we bring the two concepts together in order to think of platforms as evolving organisations that create multi-sided markets. They:

1. federate and coordinate constitutive agents who can innovate and compete;
2. create value by generating and harnessing economies of scope in supply or/and in demand; and
3. entail a modular technological architecture composed of a core [*central stable components*] and a periphery [*loosely coupled changeable components*]. (Gawer 2014, editor's notes in italics)

For our purposes then, news sharing platforms are generally proprietary software systems which organise a variety of economic actors to create 'scalable, re-configurable, multisided markets' (Flew et al. 2019) for the information we share and the news we personally value, commend and discuss with each other. Most problematically, platforms bind users into a network of contractual relationships that we barely understand, which enable digital intermediaries to collect, analyse and commodify this intimate knowledge.

OUR SOCIAL SHARING CONTRACT

Social networking and social media companies offer individuals 'free' networking, content archiving and administration, messaging and publishing services, as well as access to entertainment content and services in exchange for the rights to collect, aggregate and analyse their data, and rights in the republication of their content. These rights are set out in the lengthy terms of service (ToS) we must accept when we register as a platform user. Unfortunately, ToS or conditions of use are so long and complex that very few people ever read them. One study of the time people take to read them indicates that "participants view policies as nuisance, ignoring them to pursue the ends of digital production, without being inhibited by the means" (Obar and Oeldorf-Hirsch 2018).[2]

This means that social media companies are largely free to pursue their ends in data surveillance, insofar as users are obligated to act to protect their own privacy or security. As José Van Dijck (2013: 46) argues the devil is not so much in the detail, but "in the default", meaning the default legal and usage settings that users are provided when registering. While a small percentage of users will read their contracts, and carefully structure the account setting to maximise their privacy and minimise disclosure, most people accept the default terms. Users' default contractual arrangements with social platforms support a state of constant and complete surveillance or, as Daniel Trottier (2012: 21) puts it, monitoring that is "totalizing and hierarchical" as well as "lateral and diffuse", including Facebook and Google's use of facial recognition technologies to tag user-generated or uploaded images. Platforms also capture the bulk of advertising revenues, rather than returning anything substantial to users.

[2] Deloitte (2017) found that 91% of users signing up to mobile app and service providers accepted but did not read terms of service before installing the app software.

As noted in the previous chapter, Marxist political economists see this arrangement as exploitative—they argue that social media users are doing unpaid work for the platforms, cognitive digital labour which produces the information that feeds corporate analytics and advertising process (Fuchs and Fisher 2015; Fuchs and Sevignani 2013; Terranova 2000).[3] Yet, the extent to which ordinary news sharing is work, or unrewarded labour, is unclear. Trevor Scholz's (2013) collection *Digital Labor: The Internet as Playground and Factory* provides differing accounts of how digital labour might be defined and the processes for 'monetising' cognitive capitalism. Several authors argue that our creative behaviours online are an intensification of traditional economies of unpaid work, with Jodi Dean's "work without work" (i.e. without pay or as fun) positioning social media production as the driver of "communicative capitalism" (Dean 2013). She talks about social media communication as a techno-connective fetishism, locking users into feedback loops of excitement and exhaustion, under the conditions of continual distraction. In this sense, her argument refers most to regular contributors or subscribers, who "constitute the basic unit of currency" (Postigo 2014: 13).

The market capitalisation of social media platforms, which is based on the capture and commodification of users commendary and other activities, indicates news sharing is a form of labour. Yet, it isn't wholly unrewarded. As Allmer (2015) recognises, users' positive experiences of social media are anchored by the social, informative and communicative use values of these technologies. Users can build and maintain extended, transnational sociality; amplify their ideas and promote their creativity to a networked audience; develop professional networks; harness affective relations in order to mobilise political and social activity; they can play, learn and do mischief through news sharing.

It is these communicative affordances which make users reluctant to abandon social media platforms even when they recognise that their data is being exploited or they are being manipulated. As Andrejevic (2009) puts it:

> ... the offer of a modicum of control over productive resources as well as the promise to resuscitate extended forms of community and to challenge centralised control over collective representations all gain their appeal against the background of the depredations of industrial capitalism.

---

[3] This is the expansion of an older argument about ratings measuring the work of attending to television (Meehan 2005).

Recent studies suggest social media users are often aware of the commodity transaction they undertake when they exchange personal information for corporate surveillance of their habits, activities and relationships and exposure to behavioural advertising (Rainie and Duggan 2016). Yet, they are not privy to the ways in which social media then might filter, curate and re-present their informational landscape, or how they may be manipulated in the service of corporate research. Facebook's emotional contagion research (Kramer et al. 2014), which sought to prove that users could be made unhappier by being exposed to more negative shared news, revealed how easily the company could capitalise on peoples' vulnerability to unauthorised uses of their information (Selinger and Hartzog 2016).

Indeed, as Nicholas John writes in his critique of the sharing economy (2017: 64–67), the notion of sharing adopted by social media companies actively obfuscates the actual commodity relations taking place. In both ToS and official communications, platforms talk about sharing information with third-party companies "rather than just selling it—or even transferring or sending it" (p. 66). Thus, our economic relations with social sharing systems are marked by asymmetrical power relations, with users having shared, complexly defined control over their information rights, informal labour exchange arrangements, little or no remuneration for their creative labour or personal data use and only basic information about the ways in which their information is commodified.

José Van Dijck's historically rich, critical cultural account of the rise of social media in *The Culture of Connectivity* (2013) unpacks the relational nature of the control that these news companies exert over their users. Aside from the *contractual* power they possess, these companies can also exploit the social meanings we have for sharing, and the influence we have over the uses of our information, the *connectedness* they offer, which directs "users to share information with other users through purposefully designed interfaces", and the industrial *connectivity* they enable, as they parse data out to third parties for analysis via their application programming interfaces (p. 47), quite often unbeknownst to their users.

Our sharing relations with social media platforms are also fundamentally shaped by the cultural origins and political allegiances of information technology companies. Most social media companies were founded in North America, in the information technology crucible of Silicon Valley, and so their foundation stories and mission statements reflect the free speech, free market traditions of liberal corporate North America. Barbrook and Cameron, for example, in their critique of the US new media industries, talk about this ethos as the Californian Ideology, "a contradictory mix of technological determinism and libertarian capitalism" (2007, online). This means what we choose to share is only regulated by what the companies determine as their 'community standards' or content policy. Such guidelines generally restrict people from sharing highly sexualised, violent, criminal and otherwise illegal material. However, it also leaves companies free to promote controversial, high traffic political extremism or to restrict the legitimate exchange of news about violent political persecution.[4]

Social media's rise to media market dominance is generally described as part of the neoliberal turn in world economics, in favour of free market organisation of all trade and positioning the individual as a competent, enterprising self-regulating actor. Yet, while Silicon Valley's innovators are very often described as libertarians, Stanford researchers have found that they hold a mix of strong social democratic views on welfare and social issues (pro-universal health care and immigration) and libertarian capitalist attitudes to regulation (Broockman et al. 2017). A survey of US technology entrepreneurs showed that they are overwhelming socially and culturally liberal, cosmopolitan and globally oriented in their outlooks. It is their views on the role of the state in regulating business that are more conservative. Tech entrepreneurs did not want their business, or online activities, to be trammelled by laws, agreements or codes, except to the extent these might protect them and their users from risk. Only ongoing legal and political pressure, exerted for example by a major trading bloc like the European Union, has seen regional regulation of platforms for collective privacy and rights protections.[5]

Aside from the US, there is also strong information technology and social media start-up culture in Israel, with two of the sharing intermediaries in this chapter, Gigya and Outbrain, founded there. With a highly educated population but few export commodities, in the 1990s the Israeli government saw an opportunity to focus on immaterial exports and made major investments in military research and IT venture capital that estab-

---

[4] For example, the United Nations accused Facebook of playing a determining role in the violence perpetrated against the Rohingya Muslim minority in Myanmar by not restraining the spread of ultra-nationalist hate speech (Meixler 2018). Facebook was also condemned for suspending Rohingya activist accounts and deleting posts describing their persecution (Wong et al. 2017).

[5] Here, we can note the General Data Protection Regulation of 2016, and also the European Commission's Code of Conduct for Countering Illegal Hate Speech Online 2016.

lished a basis for ongoing tech innovation (Senor and Singer 2009). However, most of the successful Israeli social start-ups have been bought out by larger US operations.

In the West at least then, the dominant corporate perspectives that have established commendary cultures are North America, championing strong free speech principles and individualism, with minimalist personal intellectual property and labour regulations, and maximal corporate protections. These ideas drive the ways social sharing companies do business and interact with each other and us. They explain the way that these companies can vigorously promote the idea of us building value through open, free social sharing, while simultaneously generating new orders of value from the largely unregulated commodification of data about our social activities and relationships.

The scale of data collection, processing, and analysis required to manage everyday news sharing, and sharing across multiple platforms and devices, has created new markets for data analytics services. Identity management companies such as Gigya and ForgeRock now administer the registration, personalisation of services and profiling of user activities, as they move between different publications and services. News analytics have also become an essential part of monitoring the sentiment of financial news, as ThomsonReuters does, to predict market movements and manage financial risk. Given the growth of the intermediary services needed to support, track and evaluate news sharing, it becomes important to study their interdependence with digital news businesses in order to understand how they work as an ecosystem to affect journalism's visibility, influence and authority.

THE SOCIAL MEDIA NEWS SHARING ECOSYSTEM

There are excellent recent studies of sharing in international digital news consumption (Newman et al. 2016; Pew Research Center 2016; Chadwick and Viccari 2019) and of news analytics use (Cherubini and Kleis Nielsen 2016) but few critical accounts of the emerging social news ecology, its data commodities or services, and impacts on industry restructuring. In Dwayne Winseck's proposal for a new political economy research agenda (2017: 98–100), he also points to several phenomena that deserve more attention for their importance in media industry transformation: media 'infrastructure' industries (to which we add service intermediaries); industry fragmentation and diversification; and the design of media to control, monitor or secure markets.

Our conception of *critical media ecology* signals our interest in the interrelationships and interactions between news producers, publishers, intermediaries and consumers that are transforming journalism, and after Nardi and O'Day (1999: 53), in the 'keystone species', the platforms whose presence is critical to the functioning of the greater news media ecosystem. Like the US schools of media ecology, after Innis, McLuhan and Ong, we are attentive to the evolution of media technologies and their effects on social organisation. Unlike that movement, rather than being interested in news sharing's impact on human cognition and behaviour, we are more focused on its political implications for media democracy, social inclusion and cultural diversity, all part of normative ideals about the role of journalism in society. We want to explore how platforms' reorganisation of news markets and labour might alter not only digital news commodities, but also who owns them, and how their production, consumption and redistribution is organised. We are particularly interested in the technologies of control used to manage and extract value from our news sharing. Finally, in the new institutionalist tradition we are concerned with the actions of institutions (government, regulatory and policy arrangements) to mediate and moderate the monopolistic tendencies of platforms.

By mapping the news sharing ecosystem, we can also see how sharing commodification has resulted in business models and services that reinforce the increasing industrial power of the social media giants, and lock journalists into their market innovation processes, affecting their work routines and rewards.

THE PLATFORM CORPORATIONS

There is now unprecedented global concentration of media publishing power in those behemoth digital corporations Alphabet/Google, Facebook, Apple and Microsoft, whose wealth is centred on platform operations. Together with Baidu, Tencent Holdings and other second tier new media companies such as Twitter and Yahoo, social media platforms are taking the lion's share of digital advertising globally (Bell 2016). According to Reuters, Google and Facebook alone were expected to capture half of all digital advertising and a fifth of all advertising revenue internationally in 2017 (Reuters 2017). In a 2018 international survey of news publishers, 44% said they were "more worried about the power and influence of the platforms than they were a year ago" (Newman 2018: 5) and often disappointed by the lack of revenues from content deals, and traffic referrals to their sites. The Tow Centre's ongoing study of platform-publisher relations found, however, that:

> despite negative rhetoric and sentiment in newsrooms toward technology companies, there is a rapid and ongoing merging in the functions of publishers and platforms, and an often surprisingly high level of involvement from platform companies in influencing news production. (Rashidian et al. 2018)

In their constant search for new market opportunities these tech companies also sponsor constant innovation in the news space: Facebook's Instant Articles and Google's 'Accelerated Mobile Pages', both designed to improve people's mobile news experience, the Apple News aggregator, Twitter's Periscope and Moments, and Facebook's Live. Snapchat's Discover is a small, newer player in the social news market, but one aiming its services at the valuable youth market. Facebook too is introducing the FBMessenger for Kids app, hoping to capture the under-13-year-old market segment, which is too young for Facebook accounts. All of these initiatives promote narratives about the benefits of mobility, connectedness (particularly audience/network growth) and control over information flows to lock both audiences and journalists into using these platforms as communicative infrastructure, and into providing data about their communications and contacts. Both Facebook and Google have launched multifaceted schemes to support public interest journalism, but the Google News Initiative and the Facebook Journalism Project are focused on training and collaboration that binds publishers more tightly to using their platforms.

According to a 2018 inquiry into platform influence in the media industries by Australia's Competition and Consumer Commission (ACCC), there are several distinct factors that underpin the rapid, widespread growth and market success of these companies including:

- the innovative, quality and popular products they supply to users
- the complementary benefits (e.g. social networking, publishing and promotion) that they provide to various groups of users
- the way that successful platforms can increase their value to users through marshalling the presence of other users ('network effects')
- their ability to harness information about their large user bases to successfully compete in advertising markets

- their acquisition of multiple digital platforms and related services which may provide them business efficiencies (i.e. vertical and horizontal integration). (ACCC 2018)

In terms of news distribution, Facebook is the most critical digital actor in the news sharing ecosystem (aside from the telecommunications companies that supply internet and mobile services). Apart from being the news media's direct competitor for advertising, it is an indirect and direct news distributor, a promotional platform and an innovation partner. It was the top social platform used to access news weekly for the four years to 2018 in 12 markets internationally, according to the Reuters Digital news survey, although its use dropped from 42% to 36% between 2016 and 2018. Despite downgrading news in its feeds, in mid-2018, it was still the major driver of social news sharing to publisher websites (Parse.ly 2018, and see Fig. 4.1), and in September of that year supplied between 25% and 30% overall of referrals to 2500 online media sites internationally (Radogna 2018). All major news publishers use the platform to expand their audience reach and share. Several major news publishers such as CNN, the New York Times, BuzzFeed and the Huff Post have been paid to create video content for its Facebook Live Service (Perlberg and Seetharaman 2016) and the company is negotiating with others about video news for its Facebook Watch channel.[6]

Facebook has had many forays into working with news publishers, the most substantial being its Instant Articles (IA) distribution service, which hosts news stories in full, uploaded by the publisher, and pushes them into news feeds, optimised for mobile platforms. The selling point for IA was that it would improve the loading times and visibility of articles on mobile devices. IA Articles initially attracted 72 major partners, including BBC News, The New York Times, BuzzFeed, and Der Spiegel, by also promising them more control over the look of articles, better advertisement placement and more detailed audience analytics, which would leverage Facebook's international influence and technical capacity. Publishers could sell ads and keep the revenue, or they could ask Facebook to 'monetise' them as part of a 70/30 revenue share deal. Yet, publishers were sceptical of the proposal from the start, worrying about giving Facebook control over their ad sales,

---

[6] In partnership with six telecommunications companies including Samsung, Nokia and Ericsson, it also tried to become the portal to the internet in developing countries, with internet.org later named its Facebook Basics app, and a range of internet provision experiments with drones and satellites (Hempel 2018).

and speculating that it might rapidly change strategic direction (McDermott 2014). By 2018, a Tow Centre study suggested that around 38 of the original partners had abandoned the format, and the proportion of IA articles to ordinary linked posts had not varied much (Brown 2018b). Industry commentators reported that IA offered few opportunities to insert ads in stories, no means of enforcing paywall conditions or enabling embedded subscription registrations, and publishers found they earned less from IA articles than those published on their own sites (Amditis 2017).

While Facebook argues that it is working to improve the business conditions for news sharing on IA, its multiple roles in the news sharing ecosystem raise concerns about the level of its control over news dissemination and revenue streams, and its opaque innovation agenda. Another recent experiment in six European countries, where news was moved from the news feed to a new 'explore' feed, saw some Slovakian publishers losing 400% of their interactions and two-third of their reach (Newman 2018).

There far is less industry concern about the impacts of Twitter on news distribution (Newman 2018). Twitter, the second most significant social news sharing service in the West, is a more active news destination than Facebook (Bruns 2018: 120), a factor it has encouraged through the purchase of live video streaming platform Periscope and the creation of the Moments tool, for creating stories from curated tweets. Twitter has shifted its aims and business model several times over the 12 years since it launched in 2006, transitioning from a status update service to a citizen journalism, promotional and business network that counts communications professionals among its core users. While it failed to make a profit until the last quarter of 2017, its growing stake in video advertising, slowly expanding user base and high-worth daily user figures have continued to attract venture funding, to a total of $1.5 billion by 2017. Targeted advertising, based on user profiles and activities is part of its advertising suite. While advertising made up 88% of Twitter revenues in the third quarter of 2016 (Yeung 2016), the rest was from licencing, via its ownership of reseller Gnip, and 'other' *data licencing services* such as analytics start-up Datamnr. It has also resold data for other social networks, such as Tumblr and Foursquare (Garside 2015).

Twitter's relationship with the news media is distinct from that of Facebook. Its referrals to news publishers are very small in comparison, at around 8.5% in 2016 (see also Fig. 4.1), but Twitter is a critical news source, verification and sharing network for journalists (Swasy 2016) and other information specialists. Its breaking news function drives major spikes in traffic to news sites during major events (Parse.ly 2016). Like Facebook, however, it has a problem with 'fake' news sharing. When the

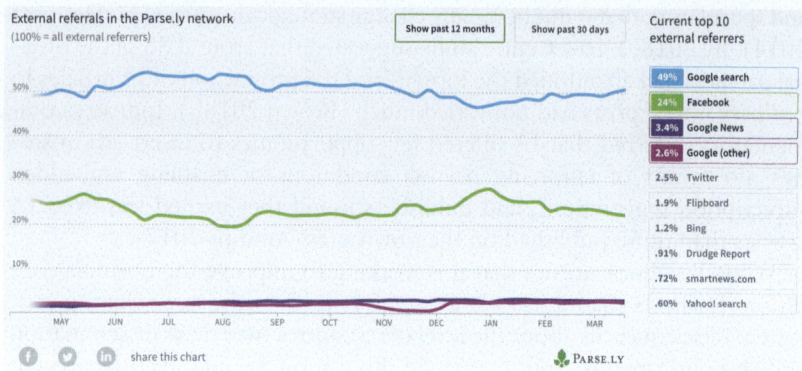

Fig. 4.1 Social media referrals for the 12 months to March 2019 to digital publishers tracked by Parse.ly analytics. Image and data courtesy of Parse.ly

2016 US election interference inquiry exposed Twitter's hosting of misinformation as a threat to its authority, it began purging malicious automated and other trolling accounts, deleting 70 million in May–June 2018 in order to change the ratio "between promoting public discourse and preserving safety" (Timberg and Dwoskin 2018).

Given the difficulties of hosting news sharing, news aggregator Apple News has taken a different, and seemingly less complicated path to commodifying commendary behaviour. With the slogan "News Worth Sharing", the Apple News app allows iphone, iPad and Mac desktop users in the US and the UK to construct a personalised news feed, with 'Spotlight' and 'Top Ten' content also selected by an editorial team based in New York. This team takes pitches for content to place in the feeds from news editors internationally via a dedicated Slack channel, but favours news from large news companies, investigative features and multi-part series (Dotan 2018). Editors have reported preferring this human interaction to the algorithmic lottery of Facebook placement (Brown 2018c). In addition, the app does not allow ad blockers, removing a key barrier to commodifying users' attention that has dogged news websites. The question now is whether Apple News will be better able to integrate advertising around its stories and generate significant advertising revenue for publishers. Early reports suggest publishers are unimpressed by the returns (Willens 2019).

User-generated news aggregation has become the core of the business model for other platforms like Reddit and Digg, the former which claims to be the front page of the internet, and the latter, what the internet is talking about. Both have relied on venture capital and advertising for revenue, although Reddit has a premium subscriber service, but their participatory ethos and Reddit users' preference for anonymity have made broader commercialisation difficult. Reddit, which web measurement company Alexa recently claimed to have become the third most visited website in the US, attracts longer duration visits than Facebook, but has not commodified social news sharing with the same degree of automation and evaluative design or behaviourally targeted advertising.

Where other platforms have sought to incorporate generalist news content, Microsoft has also sought to integrate its administrative software business with specialised corporate news sharing. In 2012, it acquired Yammer, an enterprise social networking platform designed for intracompany communications and later bought business networking platform LinkedIn in 2016, and the internet protocol video and phone call app Skype in 2017. Its strategy is clearly to build on its investment in enterprise software like Microsoft 365 and Sharepoint, and to offer freemium social services, that introduce news sharing users to its other business products and services and collect information on how they use and talk about its suite of offerings. With that aim in mind, in 2017, LinkedIn launched a section devoted to personalised business news, Trending Storylines, designed to keep its users on its site for longer periods. The initiative, which mimics Twitter's Moments, draws on its Pulse experience. It uses automated news curation and machine learning to compile stories based on keywords in user posts and the membership of their social networks, but is overseen by a team of 24 human editors.

In examining the major platform companies' pivot to news sharing, some common features emerge. These services are demographically segmented and/or highly personalised, with the widespread use of freemium pricing models that disguise the data value of user registration, content creation and social interaction. They are all attempting to generate revenue from advertising, on a scale and with scope that locally and nationally bound news media cannot hope to match.

The major platforms also engage in vertical integration that aids their news integration with, for example, Facebook owning Instagram, a photo and video sharing platform, WhatsApp, a mobile messaging platform and Crowdtangle, a publishing analytics platform. On one hand, this acquisition pattern expands revenue potential. On the other, it stands in contrast to another aspect of the multi-side platform market—the online news media's use of sharing intermediaries that have defined novel sectors of the news media business.

THE NEWS INTERMEDIARIES

As Fig. 4.2 suggests, the large platforms have supported the growth of a wide range of news intermediaries which handle different segments of the

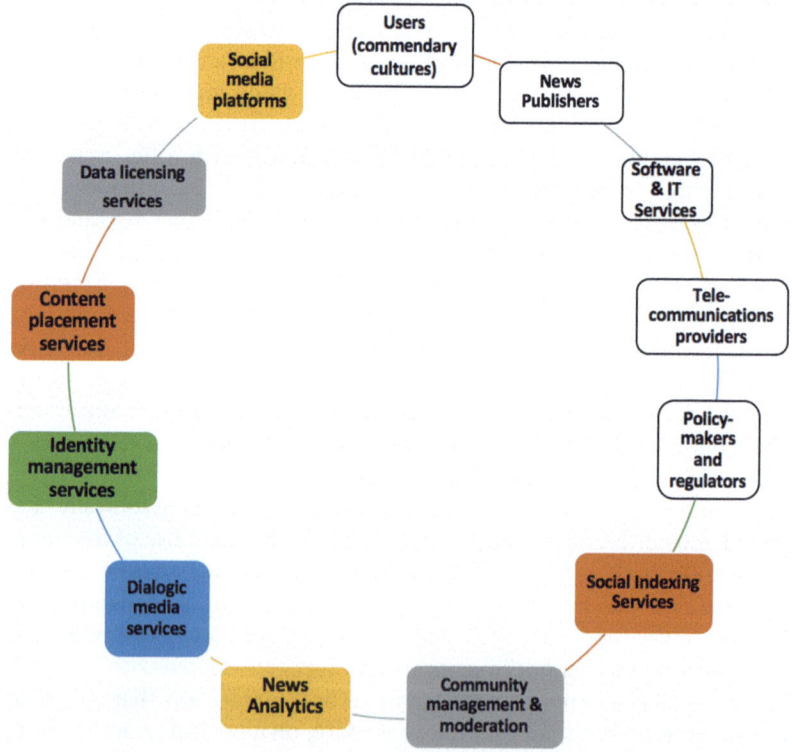

Fig. 4.2 The transnational social news sharing ecosystem. Image: Fiona R Martin

social sharing interaction from the collection, aggregation and profiling of data to the moderation of shared content. These platforms act as 'integrator' companies (Noam 2009: 437), generating market opportunities for many more small companies that facilitate our social media experience. Platforms have, for example, generated some income from application programming interfaces (APIs), which format their data streams for third-party analytics services. Data licensees, such as Chartbeat, Parse.ly and NewsWhip, then shape social streams into value-added services, which provide newsrooms with trending topic and story information based on variables such as user location, time of post, and social velocity or rate of sharing. This positions 'commendary culture'—the affective rituals and practices of gifting, recommending, reviewing and educating which sustain news sharing—as central to the rise of a new media industry sector and the growth of *social metadata* services (Fig. 4.2).

Metadata services span several categories. *News analytics* companies aggregate and re-present aspects of real-time news consumption in terms of source, location or impact, selling that information back to news companies to steer editorial decision making. The knowledge of how social media users get to a news story, what they choose to redistribute and how they amplify its consumption then influences newsroom resource allocation, coverage and story placement in a recursive loop.

While the market leaders were until recently Google Analytics and Adobe's Omniture, there are several services designed specifically to influence editorial decision making. New York-based Chartbeat, is a private, venture capital-funded competitor that has challenged the dominance of larger companies by providing tailored social media news monitoring. Chartbeat offers editorial subscribers a social tracking dashboard which allows them to follow social consumption and production trends based on the company's access to Facebook, Twitter, Reddit, YouTube and Instagram accounts. Chartbeat focuses on providing journalists and publishers new measures of 'engagement' based on the time and attention users give to content (Haile 2014). Irish competitor NewsWhip has raised $6.4 million from Japanese media giant Asahi Shimbun and The Associated Press, to develop its editorial strategy, which tracks social media news trends and digital influencers in real time (Lunden 2017b). Parse.ly, which launched its analytics platform in 2012, tracks audience data historically and in real time, as well as with predictive modelling that projects usage trends. All these services present aggregate data about news sharing behaviour in categorised streams, representing various forms of attention metrics.

Yet for news organisations, one of the major challenges to understanding how audiences are using its platforms is tracking individual users and profiling their behaviour over time so that this information can be interpreted against aggregate analytics on news use. *Identity management companies* such as Gigya and ForgeRock provide so-called 'frictionless' interfaces between news sites and social platforms, in turn collating the registration and activity data of users who log in this way. They also aggregate and profile audience data interests and activities, presenting yet more streams of audience knowledge.

Gigya, an Israeli start-up founded in 2006 and now based in Mountain View California, provides client identity services for social media interactions with over 700 major media brands, including international news companies Fox, Forbes, CNN, National Geographic, Direct TV and Times Publishing. Gigya keeps track of the news we share by providing intermediary log-ins to social media platforms from icons embedded in news articles. Gigya's behavioural data monitoring then captures our personal details, metadata about our origin site, destination platform and commendary activities, collating and profiling this information over time. Its application mediates user access to 35 social networking and media platforms. Gigya also offers publishers 'partnerships' with specialist infrastructure services that will enable them to data match registered user information with social media use information. As a sign of its growing industrial value, in 2017, it was acquired by the world's largest information logistics business, SAP, for a reported figure of $US350 million (Lunden 2017a). For SAP Gigya is a means of offering cloud-based customer profiling and 'conversion' services but, more broadly, it illustrates how user data acquired in one context, social news sharing, can be onsold and matched to other databases for more complete surveillance purposes.

News businesses are also using intermediary *content placement* services to manage the flows, commercialisation and regulation of social news sharing content. Outbrain, another Israeli company, handles native advertising for social sharing. It calls itself a 'discovery' platform that connects "marketers to their target audience through personalized recommendations on the world's leading publishers" (Outbrain 2018). The company supplies news publishers with recommended content links to articles that promote products or services, supposedly tailored to the user's interests. These recommendations appear as rows of hyperlinked image and headline excerpts at the end of a news article, under the heading 'promoted articles' or 'from the web'. Like Taboola and Revcontent, Outbrain has been criticised for curating low-quality, clickbait style material that devalues the journalism it is placed against. A 2016 analysis of recommended content on 50 major news sites found that less than half of the promoted links led to legitimate advertising content (ChangeAdvertising 2016). Yet, the majority of those brands used these services in an attempt to attract further advertising revenues from clickthroughs, regardless of the reputational issues.

In contrast to this disregard for the news user experience, *dialogic media services* are focused on encouraging users to comment on the news they share. Facebook, Disqus and Livefyre offer the most popular platforms for news commenting, acquiring data from publishers that use their plug-ins to manage social interactions. Livefyre, however, is a mercurial digital actor that exemplifies the constant search by information technology companies to develop new revenue stream from social sharing. Livefyre, which launched its commenting platform in 2012, quickly became News Corporations' service of choice. After working closely with News Corp in developing its software, Livefyre moved on, metamorphosing briefly into a social media aggregation and marketing tool, and then a social 'engagement' service. It bought Storify, a free social media curation service which citizen and professional journalists used to create and share stories, and converted it to a paid service. By 2015, having become large and diversified enough to attract $32 million in venture capital, Livefyre was acquired by Adobe. Adobe's interest in the service was transparent. It wanted to use Livefyre to create 'branded communities' and to learn how to make money from user-generated content.

An entirely new business sector, *community management*, has developed around encouraging, facilitating and 'moderating' user interaction of social platforms—that is, assessing comments and media contributions to see whether they meet publisher standards for public conversation and deleting or hiding them if they don't. Community managers have diverse roles, including:

- to assist in building audiences online for brands and public initiatives,
- to facilitate interaction between members of the community and the host,
- to ensure key information is communicated to community members
- to resolve conflict within the community, and
- to police the behaviour of members, suspending or banning accounts where individuals repeatedly breach participation guidelines or terms of service.

Moderation, the work of ensuring civil behaviour, is the most commonly recognised function of community managers, but is also carried out as a single focus, low-paid maintenance job. Increasingly though, automated moderation tools, such as language, image and video filters, are being employed to moderate content, in order to more quickly screen it for transgressive content. Artificial intelligence based filters now conduct first pass culls of illegal content, identifying some potentially 'violating' posts for human consideration. Users too are asked to report or flag posts that they feel are dangerous of offensive. Platforms use flagging as a way of co-opting users to perform complex acts of evaluation, further legitimating social media environments as publicly deliberative spaces (Crawford and Gillespie 2014).

In the early years of their development, social sharing platforms could rely on US 'safe harbour' provisions to protect them from prosecution for hosting dangerous or illegal content. As IT or tech companies, they were exempt from the content regulation constraints that applied to legacy media. However, they rapidly recognised the need to employ their own moderation strategies to ensure that they were not complicit in the sharing of child pornography, incitement to racist or sexual violence, and illegal business transactions (Gillespie 2018). In recent years, content moderation has become critical as national regulators act to reduce the posting and sharing of hate speech, misinformation, terrorist promotions and other forms of propaganda. Facebook, for example, maintains a global suite of internal human moderation teams, positioned largely in global south countries to take advantage of low wages. However, by 2019, around 8% of its 15,000 moderation staff worldwide worked in Berlin and Essen, in response to Germany's introduction of its Network Enforcement Act, which mandates removal of illegal speech within 24 hours.[7] Arguably, the safe harbour provisions of early internet regulation are no longer useful in a time when social media companies are some of the most important communications channels internationally (Flew et al. 2019).

News publishers have increasingly relied on social media platforms to host journalist and audience discussions about news content, both on branded channels and more widely, and so rely on platform moderation to prevent the excesses of user-generated content as a support to brand promotion and public deliberation. Formerly, in the heyday of participatory journalism, when Time magazine nominated 'You' as person of the year to acknowledge the scope of user contributions to knowledge (Time 2006)

---

[7] The number of moderation staff is based on a 2018 New York Times report (Fisher 2018). Most work with the Bertelsmann subsidiary Arvato, which claims to be the world's third largest business process outsourcing operation.

the news media had preferred in-house comments sections as a means of capturing audience feedback about the news they consumed (World Editor's Forum 2013). News commenting was celebrated as the most popular form of media participation (Reich 2011) even though it was only taken up by a small percentage of "highly motivated" audience members (Newman et al. 2016: 100). Yet, the media's enthusiasm for hosting this commendary activity was short lived. In response to bad behaviour in comments sections, and the additional production cost of policing this, many companies closed their sites to commenting, arguing social media channels were more accessible, less expensive and troublesome spaces for public deliberation (Martin forthcoming). Several difficulties have arisen as a result: publications have lost the traffic generated by commenter activity; it is harder to monitor and capture data about audience feedback where it is dispersed across several platforms; and branded news channels on social media still need moderation. Arguably, a social media news ecology that relies on encouraging commendary activity, and recognises comments as a rich qualitative measure of news value, will also need to acknowledge the central role that community management and moderation play in supporting civil, productive dialogic spaces.

In the communications field, community management is now seen as an essential aspect of running social sharing communities, whether they be branded news channels, retail marketplaces, workplace discussion boards or therapeutic self-help groups (Millington 2018). The market leader in moderation services for news media, Canadian headquartered ICUC, privately monitors branded social streams to police the legal and social propriety of comments made about shared story posts, to manage community development and to conduct 'social listening'—searching channels for key terms or discussions, cleaning the data for analysis, and gauging user sentiment using automated tools. ICUC, owned by Dentsu Aegis Network, the third largest marketing network in the world, offers 24-hour international moderation and community management services and is also positioning itself as a provider of social media content strategy. ICUC's transnational clients include the BBC and News Corp, and it has already swallowed UK competitor Tempero.

Moderation deserves closer study because of its key role in keeping social media users safe from nasty content and aggressive encounters, and focused on their commendary work. Moderators are charged with taking down instances of nudity and sexually explicit or violent content, as well as illegal speech such as material that promotes crime or animal abuse, or which constitutes harassment. Sarah T Roberts (2016) calls moderation "dirty work" because it exposes workers to abusive, illegal, threatening and offensive material at high volumes, is poorly paid and often outsourced or organised in call centres. Indeed, moderation has often been organised as virtual sweatshop labour because it handles material that is *not* shareworthy, and thus has little general value in analytical terms.

Roberts argues that moderation is not a new industry sector, but gig economy work. This claim needs closer analysis because the work is generally conducted under the umbrella of community management services, which are offered by several global companies including ModSquad, The Social Element, and Crisp, as well as thousands of smaller companies and the in-house teams employed by Facebook, Twitter, YouTube and other platforms. Pay and working conditions vary from site to site, and little if any comparative research has been done on these companies or their work organisation. Surveys conducted by the Australian Community Managers (ACM) network found this work was mainly done by women and was relatively poorly paid when compared to communication jobs of the same level (ACM 2016, 2018).

In contrast to the paid human labour usually involved in managing news commenting, *social indexing services* adopt the immaterial labour model of marshalling users to generate resource identifier information about the news they most value. Bookmarking services allow users to index and annotate lists of the universal resource locators (URLs) for news items they value, and to share these items with others in strategic ways. Diigo, the longest surviving company, operates a freemium model, with additional indexing options for subscribers. Pinterest is visually oriented, with a subscriber wall, and Start.me offers all content in a personalised page format. Digg's unstable business models for two older companies, Delicious and StumbleUpon, saw them both collapse in 2017.

The link shortening space however is more contested with Google, Twitter and Hootsuite all vying with start-ups like Bit.ly and TinyURL for access to data on social media information sharing trends. Link shortening services marshal data on social sharing of news commendations, by keeping a record of the long links people apply to reduce in size, for practical and aesthetic reasons. Twitter's character limit, for example, demands short links. Link shorteners can also be used to hide referral data in links, or to disguise blocked links. Most sell collated data on these activities to industry clients, who want information on who created and accessed these links. Some companies place ads on interstitial pages, which users land on before they get to their destination.

As a whole, social news sharing involves multiple, interconnected algo-rithmic transactions between social platforms, news publishers, their users and a range of metadata service providers, some of which are very little studied. While some of these intermediaries, like Gigya or NewsWhip, present to news publishers as tools for better audience knowledge or edi-torial decision making, as a whole, they comprise a co-evolving system of data brokers that have significant implications for what news is attended to, valued and exchanged. For users of these intermediaries, the critical concern is what data they keep on individuals, how this is aggregated with other datasets, and how it is sold to third parties or used by the platforms to develop new services or place personalised advertising.

China: A Closed, but Porous Ecosystem

By way of contrast to this deeply internetworked global ecosystem, China, with the world's largest number of internet users, has seen its ruling Communist Party nurture a few key social news sharing actors that coop-erate with its goals, including Sina Corporation (Sina Weibo) and Tencent (WeChat). It has done this by locking out most Western competitors, except for Microsoft's LinkedIn, which presented an essential interna-tional business networking tool for its capitalist ambitions, and a relatively risk-free dialogic environment, as users were presenting their professional profiles rather than personal views. Since the 20th anniversary of the Tiananmen Square massacre in July 2009, the nation's Golden Shield Project has comprehensively blocked mainland Chinese access to Facebook, YouTube, Twitter and most other major social media plat-forms, with the only way of reaching them being virtual private network (VPN) applications, which the government also tries to suppress. This censoring of the West has the dual effect of minimising the internal and international visibility of political dissidence and leaving the way clear for competition and innovation 'with Chinese characteristics'.

What began as a lively, diverse ecosystem of Western and Chinese mes-saging, networking and microblogging services in the mid-2000s was altered in 2009 after sweeping political intervention. In July of that year, not only did the CPC block access to Western platforms, but it also shut down all independent Chinese microblogs, blaming them for fomenting riots among the ethnic Uyghur people in Ürümqi, the capital city of their autonomous region (Bamman et al. 2012). Although popular services such as Renren, Kaixin001 and FanFou were relaunched and continued to compete for a slice of the emerging advertising and gaming markets

(Rabkin 2011), by August 2009, Sina Corporation, one of the country's major web publishing companies had stepped in to launch Sina Weibo, after agreeing to work with the CPC in monitoring and removing 'sensitive' content (Sullivan 2014). Within five years Sina, together with Tencent Weibo, had become critical public infrastructure for discussion, dissatisfaction and dissent—but only by collaborating with the CPC on its efforts to enforce political 'harmony' across the country, and its diaspora. In 2012, for example, CPC branches were set up inside company offices (Freedom House 2013) and a real name registration policy was introduced for all platforms.

Stockmann (2012) suggests that online media embody competing tendencies in China's authoritarian capitalism—with some moves towards political liberalisation countered by the persistent mechanism of surveillance and control. As King et al. (2013) note, the Chinese government has allowed online political expression to flourish, with the "full range of expression of negative and positive comments about the state, its policies, and its leaders" in order to maintain a hold on power. However, it moves to censor any news sharing, and suppress any social ties that promise to inform or mobilise collective political action. Further, in a parallel to Western social media's metadata commodity dynamics, market-based social media in China provide the government with "a source of public opinion that allows the state to obtain societal feedback about its policies and political goals" (Stockmann 2012: 255). The CPC also uses social news sharing to its own advantage, running counter-propaganda campaigns such as those conducted by the notorious Fifty-Cent party, and fabricating around 448 million social media comments a year (King et al. 2017).

There is significant competition between the major platforms which are "busy cannibalizing social networking firms, game developers, online video portals, logistics, and apps to strengthen their market position and compete with each other for the spoils of war" (Keane and Fung 2018: 49; Lashinsky 2018). Certainly there is also ongoing tension between the Communist Party and its vast bureaucracy and the platforms' powerful commercial interests. However there is ample evidence of close relationships between them. Pony Ma, owner of WeChat and chairman of Tencent Holdings, helped devise the government's e-commerce policy, while Alibaba, Jack Ma's company, handles around 80% of the country's online retailing. Early on in Alibaba's evolution Jack Ma's company reportedly partnered with the Hangzhou city government, in Zhejiang province, in order to grow its business. It also flourished under the provincial leadership of Xi Jingping, Zhejiang's Communist Party chief from 2002–2007 and now China's leader (Leng 2014). Ma, who has since travelled to South Korea on a trade mission with Jingping, has since been identified as a Communist Party member (Yuan 2018). Thus, while private ownership of social sharing platforms is more common than with China's legacy media, and they engage in overseas financing and share trading (Jia and Winseck 2018), there is little opposition to government control of content sharing.

Citizens and journalists, in contrast, have in the past tried to evade the real names policy, creating multiple, pseudonymous accounts, and used VPN apps to access the internet beyond the mainland. They share news using homophones and word play to substitute for banned terms and to express provocative ideas (Link and Qiang 2013). As Chap. 8 relates, they can also post spontaneously in response to major disasters in ways that can force the government to act on safety or environmental obligations.

However, under Xi Jinping's leadership, internet access and news sharing have become highly controlled and policed experiences. In 2016, Jinping's government began to tighten internet regulation to squash political opposition, first banning the sharing of 'unofficial' user-generated videos about current affairs or public events. WeChat stopped informing users of government interception of their messages and started censoring images of the Hong Kong protests. Users with registered mainland Chinese phone numbers could have their messages censored regardless of where they were in the world. In 2017, ahead of the 19th National Party Congress, the government set out to fully enforce its real names policy and to ban independent VPN applications which are used to circumvent China's 'Great Firewall' internet access controls. The country's largest telecommunications companies were required to block access to existing VPN services and government licences were introduced for any prospective VPN developers.

In an example of cross ecosystem cooperation, Apple's iTunes store, which is available in mainland China, withdrew VPN apps at the government's request. Google has similarly taken down YouTube material after complaints from the Chinese government, although far fewer items than were requested (Google 2018). The majority of these requests were lodged in 2017, as part of the roll-out of tighter speech restrictions in China. LinkedIn has cooperated with the government's policy in blocking unverified individuals from advertising jobs on its site (Mozur and Zhang

2017). Facebook too has worked on geo-locative censorship software, with a view to gaining access to Chinese markets (Isaac 2016).

Arguably, then, China's balance has tipped away from liberalisation in social media communications, and towards greater authoritarianism, with the support of the most powerful actors in its news sharing ecosystem, and following government negotiations with Western actors who want access to its markets. Even though China's social news ecology is relatively closed to the West, it is also 'porous', to use Margaret Roberts' (2018) description of the country's censorship regime, with data trading, finance and surveillance operating in and outside of the communist regime as an extension of Chinese soft power. Tencent, for example, has sought to increase its shareholding in Western platforms, buying a minority slice of teen platform Snap. This would suggest Chinese interest in accessing Western user data, with a view to expanding local products into diasporic use. Keane and Wu characterise the internationalisation of Chinese platforms as a proto-capitalist trend that nevertheless has to '"pay back" the government for its support' (2018: 61), by ensuring they stay within the bounds of its content regulation and surveillance regime. Thus, China's attempts to control its information space, and to extend this control overseas, are key concerns in the evolution of an international sharing economy.

The other major issue in the business of news sharing is the nature of information privacy and security, with increasing calls for transparency in data trading. While concerns about data privacy have been endemic to critical discussions of social media business models, the incident that raised it to popular global attention was Facebook's Cambridge Analytica scandal.

Social Media Data Trading

Facebook has always argued that it does not on-sell users' social sharing data. Rather, it has claimed, it uses data profiling as a way of selling targeted advertising opportunities to its clients. Mark Zuckerberg repeated this assertion several times at the 2018 US congressional inquiry into data privacy:

> There's a very common misperception about Facebook—that we sell data to advertisers. And we do not sell data to advertisers. We don't sell data to anyone. What we allow is for advertisers to tell us who they want to reach, and then we do the placement. (Zuckerberg in Rogers 2018)

This claim suggests a relatively closed and benign social sharing ecosystem. In truth, over the years, Facebook has provided social media data access to thousands of third-party app developers, including the Cambridge University psychologist Aleksandr Kogan. Back in 2014 and 2015, he collected personal profiles using a personality test app called 'This Is Your Digital Life' and then later onsold this information to Cambridge Analytica, a data analytics firm owned by billionaire Robert Mercer. From 320,000 app users, Kogan was able to extract the profile information of around 87 million Facebook users. Analytica then used this data in targeting messages at voters in Britain's Brexit referendum to decide if it would leave the European Union, and US voters in the 2016 election, won by Donald Trump. When this business was finally exposed by The Observer and the Guardian in a joint investigation (Cadwallader and Graham-Harrison 2018), international condemnation led to the US congressional inquiry, an inquiry by the UK Information Commissioner's Office, and influenced numerous other government investigations and data privacy regulations.

The scandal's relevance to digital journalism is in the way it focused attention on other attempts to influence those elections, which in turn led to the exposure of targeted political advertising and posts on social media platforms, and investigations into the broader landscape of automatically generated mis- and disinformation that was competing with news online. The European Commission's report on fake news and online disinformation proposes measures to "enhance transparency of online news, involving an adequate and privacy-compliant sharing of data about the systems that enable their circulation online" (European Commission 2018: 5), including requiring platforms to allow access to their data for inquiries into data authenticity (p. 20). UNESCO, acknowledging that social media platforms are the key to the spread of misleading news, has prepared a handbook to help educate journalists and others to identify and report questionable social media content (Ireton and Posetti 2018). Richard Fletcher and colleagues also built a 'truthmeter' app that assesses the journalistic credibility of social media contributors (Fletcher et al. 2017).

Alongside campaigns to reduce social sharing of 'fake news' have come moves to regulate information publishing on the social media platforms. The US has introduced controls on political advertising. Germany has introduced an anti-hate speech law, its Network Enforcement Act. France has passed laws against the spread of false information (Assemblée Nationale 2018). Internationally, there have been calls for national governments to introduce publishing and advertising transparency provisions to head off a wave of viral misinformation that is anticipated with the automation of "emotionally targeted news" (Bakir and McStay 2017). In Australia, the Competition Consumer Commission (ACCC), conducting the world's first inquiry into platform has already issued an interim report calling for an independent platform regulator, and a regulatory framework that recognises social platforms as media businesses and which:

> ... is able to effectively and consistently regulate the conduct of all entities which perform comparable functions in the production and delivery of content in Australia, including news and journalistic content, whether they are publishers, broadcasters, other media businesses, or digital platforms. (ACCC 2018: 12)

This recognition of social media platforms as media businesses, rather than IT companies, then raises further questions about the way they should comply with content regulation and privacy provisions, and what commitments they might need to make to address normative policy ideals like media freedom and pluralism.

MEDIA FREEDOM AND THE ALGORITHMIC TURN

Given the range of actors now involved in distributing and recirculating news online, and their consistent focus on commodifying social sharing activities, it is imperative that we re-examine the notion of press freedom through the lens of the metadata commodity. The concept of press freedom arose in the eighteenth century as a way to ensure citizens had the right to express their ideas without government interference or political retribution. It is now being recast by platform power and black boxed algorithms, in which everyday commendary experiences are tracked, measured, analysed and fed back to news media companies. This business model is primarily designed to construct more effective personalised advertising, and to deliver more of what we want to see, in order that we will feel comfortable and share more of ourselves in a circular cycle of commodification. It influences what we see and are motivated to share without its processes being visible or accountable.

What we should now be concerned about is not just overt political interference, but covert commercial intervention. What appears in our Facebook news feeds (or in Outbrain's recommendation tabs) goes well beyond what we commend to others. It is shaped by what the platform has learned about our tastes from tracking our online activities and what it knows will keep us glued to our news feeds: the news and opinions we approve of, the campaigns we support and the views that validate ours—or outrage us enough to engage. It is not necessarily accurate, truthful information, but news that is shareworthy. As Mark Pesce argues, Facebook's strategy of treating any and all information equally, and curating our news feeds to suit our interests and to confirm our social prejudices, is:

> creating a 'reality' that has very little to do with the facts on the ground. Someone who thinks Hillary is horrible will tend to see more of that in their Facebook feed, while someone who thinks Trump is horrible will see more of that. That's a serious problem in itself—leading to a collapse of consensus in the political sphere—and one now amplified by the direct economic interest Facebook has in providing a sticky newsfeed…
>
> That has created a 'reality trap' for Facebook: if it stops confirming user biases, its users will drift away. If a newsfeed angers users with 'fake news' contradicting [their] world view, those users will pay less attention to Facebook—meaning Facebook earns less revenue from its advertisers. This locks Facebook and its users into an accelerating cycle of untruth. (Pesce 2017: par. 26–27)

In using this alternate algorithmic or platform sphere to distribute news, journalism is constructing a new battle for press freedom—one in which it has to struggle to become more visible, more influential and more authoritative than misinformation and propaganda.

Despite its precarious economic and cultural position in the attention economy, the news media is and will remain a critical player in the business of social news sharing, and an essential information intermediary in the social media ecology. News journalism provides the professional storytelling ordinary citizens seek about the world, the research and verification procedures people rely on when they need truthful information about their societies and the privileged access to political and corporate life that enables monitoring of their actions. Rather than standing alone though, as the independent fourth estate, digital news companies now form part of a multifarious and interdependent business ecosystem in which they must struggle to capture value, and cooperate to survive.

REFERENCES

ACCC. 2018. Digital Platforms Inquiry: Interim Report. December 10. Australian Competition & Consumer Commission. https://www.accc.gov.au/focus-areas/inquiries/digital-platforms-inquiry/preliminary-report.

ACM. 2016. Australian Community Managers Career Survey 2015/2016 Australian Community Managers. http://www.acmsurvey.com/.

———. 2018. Australian Community Managers Career Survey 2017/2018. Australian Community Managers. https://www.australiancommunitymanagers.com.au/acm-survey-2018.

Allmer, T. 2015. Critical Theory and Social Media: Between Emancipation and Commodification. Oxon, NY: Routledge.

Amditis, Joe. 2017. Why Are Publishers Abandoning Facebook Instant Articles?

Andrejevic, Marc. 2009. Privacy, Exploitation, and the Digital Enclosure. Amsterdam Law Forum 1 (4): 47–62. http://amsterdamlawforum.org/article/view/94/168.

Assemblée Nationale. 2018. Proposition de loi relative à la lutte contre la manipulation de l'information, No. 799 [Proposed Bill on the Fight Against the Manipulation of Information, No. 799]. November 20. http://www.assemblee-nationale.fr/15/ta/tap0190.pdf.

Bakir, Vian, and Andrew McStay. 2017. Fake News and the Economy of Emotions: Problems, Causes, Solutions. Digital Journalism 6 (2): 154–175.

Bamman, David, Brendan O'Connor, and Noah A. Smith. 2012. Censorship and Deletion Practices in Chinese Social Media. First Monday 17 (3–5). March 2012. http://journals.uic.edu/ojs/index.php/fm/article/view/3943/3169.

Barakat, Christie. 2014. Facebook Killed the Viral Star: Upworthy's Traffic Plummets After News Feed Tweaks. Adweek. February 11. https://www.adweek.com/digital/facebook-killed-viral-star-upworthys-traffic-plummets-news-feed-tweaks/.

Barbrook, Richard, and Andy Cameron. 2007. The Californian Ideology. The Hypermedia Research Centre. http://www.hrc.wmin.ac.uk/theory-californianideology-main.html.

Bell, Emily. 2016. The End of the News as We Know It: How Facebook Swallowed Journalism. Humanitas Lecture, University of Cambridge. March. https://medium.com/tow-center/the-end-of-the-news-as-we-know-it-how-facebook-swallowed-journalism-60344fa50962.

Broockman, David E., Gregory Ferenstein, and Neil Malhotra. 2017. Predispositions, the Political Behavior of Wealthy Americans, and Implications for Economic Inequality: Evidence from Technology Entrepreneurs. Stanford University Graduate School of Business Research Paper No. 17-61. Updated June 1. https://papers.ssrn.com/sol3/papers.cfm?abstract_id=3032688.

Brown, Pete. 2018a. Facebook Struggles to Promote 'Meaningful Interactions' for Local Publishers, Data Shows. Columbia Journalism Review. Tow Centre. April 18. https://www.cjr.org/tow_center/facebook-local-news.php.

———. 2018b. Facebook Instant Articles Partners May Have Abandoned It. *Columbia Journalism Review.* Tow Center. February 2. https://www.cjr.org/tow_center/are-facebook-instant-articles-worth-it.php.

———. 2018c. Study: Apple News's Human Editors Prefer a Few Major Newsrooms. *Columbia Journalism Review.* Tow Center. June 5. https://www.cjr.org/tow_center/facebook-local-news.php.

Bruns, Axel. 2018. *Gatewatching and News Curation: Journalism, Social Media, and the Public Sphere.* New York: Peter Lang.

Cadwallader, Carole, and Emma Graham-Harrison. 2018. Revealed: 50 Million Facebook Profiles Harvested for Cambridge Analytica in Major Data Breach. *The Guardian.* March 17. https://www.theguardian.com/news/2018/mar/17/cambridge-analytica-facebook-influence-us-election.

Carlson, Nicholas. 2014. Facebook Changed How the News Feed Works – And Huge Website Upworthy Suddenly Shrank in Half. *Business Insider.* February 11. https://www.businessinsider.com.au/facebook-changed-how-the-news-feed-works-and-huge-website-upworthy-suddenly-shrank-in-half-2014-2.

Chadwick, Andrew, and Christian Viccari. 2019. *News Sharing on UK Social Media: Misinformation, Disinformation, and Correction.* Survey Report. Online Civic Culture Centre. Loughborough University. https://www.lboro.ac.uk/media/media/research/o3c/Chadwick%20Vaccari%20O3C-1%20News%20Sharing%20on%20UK%20Social%20Media.pdf.

ChangeAdvertising. 2016. The Clickbait Report. http://changeadvertising.org/the-clickbait-report/.

Cherubini, Federica, and Rasmus Kleis Nielsen. 2016. *Editorial Analytics: How News Media are Developing and Using Audience Data and Metrics.* February 23. Oxford: Reuters Institute for the Study of Journalism.

Cornia, Alessio, Annika Sehl, David A.L. Levy, and Rasmus Kleis Nielsen. 2018. *Private Sector News, Social Media Distribution, and Algorithm Change.* Reuters Institute for the Study of Journalism. https://reutersinstitute.politics.ox.ac.uk/sites/default/files/2018-10/Cornia_Private_Sector_News_FINAL.pdf.

Crawford, Kate, and Tarleton Gillespie. 2014. What Is a Flag For? Social Media Reporting Tools and the Vocabulary of Complaint. *New Media & Society* 18 (3): 410–428.

Dean, Jodi. 2013. Whatever Blogging. In *Digital Labour: The Internet as Playground and Factory,* ed. Trevor Scholz, 127–146. New York: Routledge.

Deloitte. 2017. *Global Mobile Consumer Survey: US edition.* The Dawn of the Next Era in Mobile. https://www2.deloitte.com/content/dam/Deloitte/us/Documents/technology-media-telecommunications/us-tmt-2017-global-mobile-consumer-survey-executive-summary.pdf.

Dickey, Megan Rose. 2013. Here's More Proof That Upworthy Is One of the Fastest-Growing Media Startups. *Business Insider.* November 12. https://www.businessinsider.com.au/upworthy-traffic-2013-11.

Dotan, Tom. 2018. Inside Apple's Courtship of News Publishers. *The Information.* February 14. https://www.theinformation.com/articles/inside-apples-courtship-of-news-publishers.

European Commission. 2018. *A Multi-dimensional Approach to Disinformation: Report of the Independent High Level Group on Fake News and Online Disinformation.* March 12. Directorate-General for Communication Networks, Content and Technology. https://ec.europa.eu/digital-single-market/en/news/final-report-high-level-expert-group-fake-news-and-online-disinformation.

Filloux, Frederic. 2010. The Facebook Gravitational Effect. *Monday Note.* August 1. https://mondaynote.com/the-facebook-gravitational-effect-2e898ea6623f.

Fisher, Max. 2018. Inside Facebook's Secret Rulebook for Global Political Speech. *New York Times.* December 27. https://www.nytimes.com/2018/12/27/world/facebook-moderators.html.

Fletcher, Richard, Steve Schifferes, and Neil Thurman. 2017. Building the 'Truthmeter': Training Algorithms to Help Journalists Assess the Credibility of Social Media Sources. *Convergence: The International Journal of Research into New Media Technologies.* Online. June 22. https://doi.org/10.1177/1354856517714955.

Flew, Terry, Fiona Martin, and Nic Suzor. 2019. Internet Regulation as Media Policy: Rethinking the Question of Digital Communication Platform Governance. *Journal of Digital Media and Policy* 10 (1): 33–50.

Freedom House. 2013. *Media Control in China: A Model of Complexity and Thoroughness.* May 6. https://freedomhouse.org/blog/media-control-china-model-complexity-and-thoroughness.

Fuchs, Christian. 2011. Cognitive Capitalism or Informational Capitalism? The Role of Class in the Information Economy. In *Cognitive Capitalism, Education and Digital Labor,* ed. Michael Peters and Ergin Bulut, 75–119. New York: Peter Lang.

Fuchs, Christian, and Eran Fisher, eds. 2015. *Reconsidering Value and Labour in the Digital Age.* Basingstoke: Palgrave Macmillan.

Fuchs, Christian, and Sebastian Sevignani. 2013. What Is Digital Labour? What Is Digital Work? What's Their Difference? And Why Do These Questions Matter for Understanding Social Media? *tripleC: Communication, Capitalism & Critique* 11 (2): 237–293.

Garside, Juliette. 2015. Twitter Puts Trillions of Tweets Up for Sale to Data Miners. *Guardian.com.* March 19. http://www.theguardian.com/technology/2015/mar/18/twitter-puts-trillions-tweets-for-sale-data-miners.

Gawer, Annabelle. 2014. Bridging Differing Perspectives on Technological Platforms: Toward an Integrative Framework. *Research Policy* 43: 1239–1249.

Gillespie, Tarleton. 2010. The Politics of 'Platforms'. *New Media & Society* 12 (3): 347–364.

————. 2018. *Custodians of the Internet: Platforms, Content Moderation, and the Hidden Decisions That Shape Social Media*. New Haven, CT: Yale University Press.

Google. 2018. *Transparency Report: China. Government Requests to Remove Content.* https://transparencyreport.google.com/government-removals/by-country/CN?hl=en.

Gruen, Andrew. 2018. *Yes, Facebook Referral Traffic Crashed and Burned — But not for These Nonprofit Publishers.* Nieman Lab. October 26. https://www.niemanlab.org/2018/10/yes-facebook-referral-traffic-crashed-and-burned-but-not-for-these-nonprofit-publishers/.

Haile, Tony. 2014. What You Think You Know About the Web Is Wrong. *Time.* March 10. http://time.com/12933/what-you-think-you-know-about-the-web-is-wrong/.

Hempel, Jesse. 2018. What Happened to Facebook's Grand Plan to Wire the World? Backchannel. *Wired.* May 17. https://Www.Wired.Com/Story/What-Happened-To-Facebooks-Grand-Plan-To-Wire-The-World/.

Ireton, Cherylin, and Julie Posetti, eds. 2018. *Journalism, 'Fake News' & Disinformation. Handbook for Journalism Education and Training*. Paris: United Nations Educational, Scientific and Cultural Organization.

Isaac, Mike. 2016. Facebook Said to Create Censorship Tool to Get Back into China. *New York Times.* November 22. https://www.nytimes.com/2016/11/22/technology/facebook-censorship-tool-china.html.

Jia, Lianrui, and Dwayne Winseck. 2018. The Political Economy of Chinese Internet Companies: Financialization, Concentration, and Capitalization. *International Communication Gazette* 80 (19): 30–59.

John, Nicholas A. 2017. *The Age of Sharing*. Cambridge; Malden: Polity Press.

Keane, Michael, and Anthony Fung. 2018. Digital Platforms: Exerting China's New Cultural Power in the Asia-Pacific. *Media Industries* 5 (1): 47–50.

Keane, Michael, and Huan Wu. 2018. Lofty Ambitions, New Territories, and Turf Battles: China's Platforms "Go Out". *Media Industries* 5 (1): 51–68.

King, Gary, Jennifer Pan, and Margaret E. Roberts. 2013. How Censorship in China Allows Government Criticism but Silences Collective Expression. *American Political Science Review* 107 (2): 1–18. https://doi.org/10.1017/S0003055413000014.

————. 2017. How the Chinese Government Fabricates Social Media Posts for Strategic Distraction, not Engaged Argument. *American Political Science Review* 111 (3): 484–501. https://doi.org/10.1017/S0003055417000144.

Klein, Ezra. 2013. Does Upworthy Prove Media Outlets Are Hurting Themselves by Publishing So Much Content? *Washington Post.* December 10. https://www.washingtonpost.com/news/wonk/wp/2013/12/10/does-upworthy-prove-media-outlets-are-hurting-themselves-by-publishing-so-much-content/.

Kramer, Adam D.I., Jamie E. Guillory, and Jeffrey T. Hancock. 2014. Experimental Evidence of Massive-Scale Emotional Contagion Through Social Networks. *Proceedings National Academy of Science* 111 (24): 8788–8790.

Lashinsky, Adam. 2018. Alibaba v. Tencent: The Battle for Supremacy in China. *Fortune.* June 21. http://fortune.com/longform/alibaba-tencent-china-internet/.

Leng, Shujie. 2014. Be in Love with Them, But Don't Marry Them. *Foreign Policy.* October 31. https://foreignpolicy.com/2014/10/31/be-in-love-with-them-but-dont-marry-them/.

Link, Perry, and Xiao Qiang. 2013. From "Fart People" to Citizens. *Journal of Democracy* 24 (1): 79–85.

Lunden, Ingrid. 2017a. SAP Buys Customer Identity Management firm Gigya for $350M. *Techcrunch.* September 24. https://techcrunch.com/2017/09/24/sap-is-buying-identity-management-firm-gigya-for-350m/.

———. 2017b. NewsWhip Nabs $6.4M from the AP, More to Shed Light on What's Trending. *Techcrunch.* February 14. https://techcrunch.com/2017/02/14/newswhip-nabs-6-4m-from-the-ap-more-to-shed-light-on-whats-trending/.

Manjoo, Farhad. 2017. Can Facebook Fix Its Own Worst Bug? *New York Times.* April 25. https://www.nytimes.com/2017/04/25/magazine/can-facebook-fix-its-own-worst-bug.html.

Martin, Fiona. forthcoming. *Mediating the Conversation: Governing Commenting on News Journalism.* New York; London: Routledge.

Mayer-Schönberger, Viktor, and Thomas Ramge. 2018. *Reinventing Capitalism in the Age of Big Data.* New York: Basic Books.

McDermott, John. 2014. Facebook Offers Publishers a Faustian Bargain. *Digiday.com.* October 28. http://digiday.com/platforms/publishers-dont-want-facebooks/.

Meehan, Elaine R. 2005. Watching Television: A Political Economic Approach. In *A Companion to Television,* ed. Janet Wasko, 238–255. Malden, MA: Blackwell.

Meixler, Eli. 2018. U.N. Fact Finders Say Facebook Played a 'Determining' Role in Violence Against the Rohingya. *Time.* March 13. http://time.com/5197039/un-facebook-myanmar-rohingya-violence/.

Millington, Richard. 2018. *The Indispensable Community: Why Some Brand Communities Thrive When Others Perish.* London: Feverbee.

Mozur, Paul, and Carolyn Zhang. 2017. LinkedIn Faces Setback in China as It Runs Afoul of New Rules. *New York Times.* November 10. https://www.nytimes.com/2017/11/10/business/linkedin-china.html.

Nardi, Bonnie A., and Vicki L. O'Day. 1999. *Information Ecologies.* Cambridge, MA: MIT Press.

Newman, Nic. 2011. *Mainstream Media and the Distribution of News in the Age of Social Discovery.* Oxford: Reuters Institute for the Study of Journalism.

———. 2018. *Journalism, Media, and Technology Trends and Predictions 2018.* Digital News Project. Oxford: Reuters Institute for the Study of Journalism. https://agency.reuters.com/content/dam/openweb/documents/pdf/news-agency/report/journalism-media-technology-trends-and-predictions-2018.pdf.

Newman, Nic, Richard Fletcher, David A. Levy, and Rasmus Klein Nielsen. 2016. *Digital News Report 2016*. Oxford: Reuters Institute for the Study of Journalism.

Noam, Eli. 2009. *Media Ownership and Concentration in America*. Oxford: Oxford University Press.

Obar, Jonathan A., and Oeldorf-Hirsch, Anne. 2018. *The Biggest Lie on the Internet: Ignoring the Privacy Policies and Terms of Service Policies of Social Networking Services*. TPRC 44: The 44th Research Conference on Communication, Information and Internet Policy, June 2018. https://doi.org/10.2139/ssrn.2757465.

Osofsky, Justin. 2013. More Ways to Drive Traffic to News and Publishing Site. *Facebook*. October 22. https://www.facebook.com/notes/facebook-media/more-ways-to-drive-traffic-to-news-and-publishing-sites/585971984771628.

Outbrain. 2018. https://www.outbrain.com/.

Owen, Laura H. 2018. Facebook's News Feed Changes Appear to Be Hurting—Not Helping—Local News. *Nieman Lab*. April 19. http://www.niemanlab.org/2018/04/facebooks-news-feed-changes-appear-to-be-hurting-not-helping-local-news/.

Parse.ly. 2016. *The Authority Report # 10*. January–March. http://learn.parsely.com/rs/314-EBB-255/images/authority-report-10.pdf.

———. 2018. *The Authority Report*. April–May. http://learn.parsely.com/rs/314-EBB-255/images/authority-report-15.pdf.

Perlberg, Steven, and Deepa Seetharaman. 2016. Facebook Signs Deals with Media Companies, Celebrities for Facebook Live. *Wall Street Journal*. June 22. https://www.wsj.com/articles/facebook-signs-deals-with-media-companies-celebrities-for-facebook-live-1466533472.

Pesce, Mark. 2017. The Last Days of Reality. *Meanjin Quarterly*. Summer. https://meanjin.com.au/essays/the-last-days-of-reality/.

Pew Research Center. 2016. *State of the News Media*. June 15. http://www.journalism.org/2016/06/15/state-of-the-news-media-2016/.

Postigo, Hector. 2014. The Socio-Technical Architecture of Digital Labor: Converting Play into YouTube Money. *New Media & Society* 18 (2): 332–349. https://doi.org/10.1177/1461444814541527.

PriceWaterhouseCoopers. 2018. Global Top 100 Companies by Market Capitalisation. Updated March 31. https://www.pwc.com/gx/en/audit-services/assets/pdf/global-top-100-companies-2018-report.pdf.

Rabkin, April. 2011. The Facebooks of China. *Fast Company*. January 12. https://www.fastcompany.com/1715041/facebooks-china.

Radogna, Megan. 2018. The Ultimate Referral Guide to Your Audience. Parse.ly. September 10. https://blog.parse.ly/post/1511/the-ultimate-referral-guide-to-your-audience/.

Rainie, Lee, and Maeve Duggan. 2016. *Privacy and Information Sharing*. Pew Research Centre. January 14. http://assets.pewresearch.org/wp-content/uploads/sites/14/2016/01/PI_2016.01.14_Privacy-and-Info-Sharing_FINAL.pdf.

Rantala, Varpa. 2018. Which Publishers Benefit Most from Facebook's News Feed Change? *Mediashift*. January 25. http://mediashift.org/2018/01/will-controversial-publishers-benefit-facebooks-news-feed-changes/.

Rashidian, Nushin, Pete Brown, and Elizabeth Hansen with Emily Bell, Jonathan Albright, and Abigail Hartstone. 2018. *Friend and Foe: The Platform Press at the Heart of Journalism*. Tow Center for Digital Journalism. June 14. https://www.cjr.org/tow_center_reports/the-platform-press-at-the-heart-of-journalism.php/.

Reich, Zvi. 2011. User Comments: The Transformation of Participatory Space. In *Participatory Journalism: Guarding Open Gates at Online Newspapers*, ed. Jane Singer, David Domingo, Ari Heinonen, Alfred Hermida, Steve Paulussen, Thorsten Quandt, Zvi Reich, and Marina Vujnovic. West Sussex: Wiley-Blackwell.

Reuters. 2017. Why Google and Facebook Prove the Digital Ad Market Is a Duopoly. Fortune. July 28. http://fortune.com/2017/07/28/google-facebook-digital-advertising/.

Roberts, Sarah T. 2016. Commercial Content Moderation: Digital Laborers' Dirty Work. In *The Intersectional Internet: Race, Sex, Class, and Culture Online*, ed. Safiya Umoja Noble and Brendesha M. Tynes, 147–159. New York: Peter Lang.

Roberts, Margaret E. 2018. *Censored: Distraction and Diversion Inside China's Great Firewall*. Princeton, NJ: Princeton University Press.

Rogers, Kaleigh. 2018. Let's Talk About Mark Zuckerberg's Claim that Facebook 'Doesn't Sell Data'. *Motherboard*. April 12. https://motherboard.vice.com/en_us/article/8xkdz4/does-facebook-sell-data.

Sanders, Sam. 2017. *Upworthy Was One of the Hottest Sites Ever. You Won't Believe What Happened Next*. All Tech Considered. National Public Radio. June 20. https://www.npr.org/sections/alltechconsidered/2017/06/20/533529538/upworthy-was-one-of-the-hottest-sites-ever-you-wont-believe-what-happened-next#.

Schiller, Dan. 1999. *Digital Capitalism: Networking the Global Market System*. Cambridge, MA: MIT Press.

Scholz, Trevor. 2013. *Digital Labour: The Internet as Playground and Factory*. New York: Routledge.

Selinger, Evan, and Woodrow Hartzog. 2016. Facebook's Emotional Contagion Study and the Ethical Problem of Co-opted Identity in Mediated Environments Where Users Lack Control. *Research Ethics* 12 (1): 35–43. https://doi.org/10.1177/1747016115579531.

Senor, Dan, and Paul Singer. 2009. *Start Up Nation: The Story of Israel's Economic Miracle*. New York: Hatchette Book Group.

Stockmann, Daniela. 2012. *Media Commercialization and Authoritarian Rule in China*. Cambridge: Cambridge University Press.

Sullivan, Jonathan. 2014. China's Weibo: Is Faster Different? *New Media & Society* 16 (1): 24–37. https://doi.org/10.1177/1461444812472966.

Swasy, Alecia. 2016. *How Journalists Use Twitter: The Changing Landscape of U.S. Newsroom*. London: Lexington Books.

Terranova, Tiziana. 2000. Free Labor: Producing Culture for the Digital Economy. *Social Text* 18 (2): 33–58.

Timberg, Craig, and Elizabeth Dwoskin. 2018. Twitter Is Sweeping Out Fake Accounts Like Never Before, Putting User Growth at Risk. *Washington Post*. July 6. https://www.washingtonpost.com/technology/2018/07/06/twitter-is-sweeping-out-fake-accounts-like-never-before-putting-user-growth-risk/.

Time. 2006. Person of the Year: You. Yes, You. You Control the Information Age. Welcome to Your World. *Time Magazine*. Saturday, December 16. p. 1.

Trottier, Daniel. 2012. *Social Media as Surveillance: Rethinking Visibility in a Converging World*. Surrey: Ashgate Publishing.

Upworthy. 2018. About Us. Our Story. https://www.upworthy.com/about.

Van Dijck, José. 2013. *The Culture of Connectivity. A Critical History of Social Media*. New York: Oxford University Press.

Willens, Max. 2019. 'Hard to back out': Publishers Grow Frustrated by the Lack of Revenue from Apple News. *Digiday*. February 25. https://digiday.com/media/hard-to-back-out-publishers-remain-frustrated-by-apple-news-monetization/.

Winseck, Dwayne. 2017. Reconstructing the Political Economy of Communication for the Digital Media Age. *The Political Economy of Communication* 4 (2): 73–114.

Wong, Julia Carrie, Michael Safi, and Shaikh Azizur Rahman. 2017. Facebook Bans Rohingya Group's Posts as Minority Faces 'Ethnic Cleansing'. *The Guardian*. September 20. https://www.theguardian.com/technology/2017/sep/20/facebook-rohingya-muslims-myanmar.

World Editors Forum. 2013. *Online Comment Moderation: Emerging Best Practices*. World Association of Newspapers, WAN-IFRA and Open Society Foundation. http://www.wan-ifra.org/reports/2013/10/04/online-comment-moderation-emerging-best-practices.

Yeung, Ken. 2016. Twitter Reports Q3 2016 Revenue of $616 Million, up 8 Per cent YoY; 317 Million MAU, up 3 Per cent YoY. *Venturebeat*. October 27. https://venturebeat.com/2016/10/27/twitter-q3-2016-earnings/.

Yuan, Li. 2018. Jack Ma, China's Richest Man, Belongs to the Communist Party. Of Course. *New York Times*. November 27. https://www.nytimes.com/2018/11/27/business/jack-ma-communist-party-alibaba.html.

CHAPTER 5

What We Share: Genre and Topicality on Facebook and Twitter

Fiona Martin

The following three chapters are based on empirical research conducted with the Share Wars group in 2015–2016, using news story URLs and Facebook and Twitter commentary data gathered by the Likeable Engine, matched with story content scraped from the websites of major news media organisations worldwide. The social media data was extracted from the then public APIs of Twitter and Facebook, and demonstrates the importance of researchers having ready access to information from these platforms in a transparent and ethical manner. Following the Cambridge Analytica scandal, Facebook shut down research access to its platform APIs, including for Netvizz, an application widely used to collect public page data (Bastos and Walker 2018; Hotham 2018). A global campaign ensued to persuade the platform to change its mind, emphasising the strict ethical controls of research institutions on social media studies (Bruns 2018). In response, Facebook has helped create a new initiative based in the US, Social Science One, which will give limited and highly controlled access to a small group of approved researchers to use its content to study misinformation in elections and democracy (Gonzalez 2018). We join the call for Facebook to broaden the terms of access to academic researchers, in the interests of future scientific inquiry.

Testing the News Gap Theory

In 2013, Pablo Boczkowski and Eugenia Mitchelstein's book *The News Gap* famously argued that news media audiences much preferred to read, comment on and share everyday stories about sport, crime, entertainment,

© The Author(s) 2019
F. Martin, T. Dwyer, *Sharing News Online*,
https://doi.org/10.1007/978-3-030-17906-9_5

and weather, rather than the public affairs-oriented stories that journalists value, about politics, international affairs and economics. So, they proposed that there was a supply-demand gap in journalism. This chapter tests that proposal, based on empirical research into the types of stories people have shared across the world, and what topics they preferred to share. The findings contradict the news gap thesis in some respects—suggesting, for example, that the stories we are most highly likely to commend to others are not about trivial celebrity gossip or polarised commentary, but about politics and include a good dose of public affairs focused summary news. We also argue that the nature of story sharing needs more careful classification and analysis to reveal the differences between significant and everyday sharing. Importantly, our study confronts the notion that social sharing is driving a clickbait culture that will dumb down news production.

In recent years, journalism scholars and policymakers have watched many news companies 'chasing clicks'—putting disproportionate emphasis on the production of shareable story topics and formats. The conventional wisdom has been that short formats, listicles and explainers, video and image-heavy stories will share better than conventional news and features. The rise of *Upworthy* and *Buzzfeed* has also generated industry speculation that short, positive lifestyle stories are more shared, and thus more socially valued, than complex, challenging public affairs reporting.

This chapter counters some of those suppositions. Our research is based on the results of a big data analysis of most shared news on Facebook and Twitter captured by the Share Wars Likeable Engine from 160 English language news sites internationally during 2014–2015. It explores which genres and styles of news journalism and which topics trigger high-volume sharing, and what constitutes everyday low-volume sharing. It also considers whether interactive, multimedia and participative features increase the likelihood that stories will be shared.

Importantly, the analysis suggests that politics and public affairs focused stories are shared more highly than non-public affairs-oriented stories (including celebrity and sports news) and more news and features are shared than opinion pieces. We also find that while visual material, comments and embedded links are all indicators of higher sharing, multimedia is not. This opens up new debates about the triggers for news sharing, and whether these include provocative comments and links to rich background or primary source material.

The chapter then gives a sense of the relative social value of the three normative forms of journalistic expression or sense making (news, features & opinion) allowing us to position our findings in existing debates about the political significance of news media: of news (agreed fact/truth) vis a vis opinion (personal belief/viewpoint); or of short form journalism versus longer, more descriptive and investigative work. This will allow us to interrogate the assumptions being made by journalists and editors about the most popular and profitable forms of storytelling. It will also contribute to our later discussion about how social media analytics might be used for media policy purposes in Chap. 7.

News Sharing and Journalistic Visibility

As we discussed in Chaps. 1 and 2, online news sharing has significant implications for the reach and visibility of online news journalism. Facebook's 2018 newsfeed algorithm change, in which it moved to re-prioritise family and friend posts over other types of content, saw a 1% reduction in branded news content appearing in newsfeeds worldwide, representing "a 20 per cent fall in reach for some news organisations" (Scott 2018). Its announcement then that branded news stories which generate significant interactions and comment threads, and those that include video (particularly live video) would be more likely to become visible in news feeds was important information for journalists hoping to counter the effects of the newsfeed shift.

Knowledge of what news shares well on different platforms is critical industry knowledge because the way in which news value is constructed and communicated has changed so radically in the last decade. As Boczkowski and Mitchelstein note, one dilemma facing news publishers in the digital age is that news has been unbundled from its packaged diet form (2013: 4). Search engines altered the economics of news publishing so that people no longer need to buy a newspaper, watch or listen to a whole bulletin in order to get the information they are seeking. Search makes any one item as visible as others, and lifts them out of their curated, brand context. This unbundling is compounded by the loss of advertising to the platforms. News media can no longer cross-subsidise costly public service investigations with display advertising, cheap and cheerful celebrity interviews, or restaurant reviews, or present us with a balanced diet of politically and economically important, and light entertainment. Thus, when every story can be consumed individually and its impact gauged from its response metrics, there is huge pressure on editors to favour the production of content which is likely to meet the approval of subscribers, and that demonstrates engagement to those advertisers that remain.

The visibility of news on social media also affects news organisations' agenda setting role. Professional news journalists claim relative political privilege to access parliament and other government bodies, courts and judicial processes such as specialist inquiries, for the purposes of producing news and analysis. While all forms of journalism have different forms of social value, news historically has been given special status because of its role in informing the public of significant public debates, enabling them to participate in political processes and to navigate their participation in business, education and other aspects of social life. As historical measures of public visibility or exposure such as circulation and ratings figures decline in importance, measuring what people view and commend online, as well as how and why they consume it, will be fundamental to establishing the news media's contemporary role in democracies.

As Boczkowski and Mitchelstein explain in their book, there are conflicting findings about the existence of a news gap between what users want and what the news media are providing. This makes revisiting the case interesting in light of the widespread shift to social analytics used in the newsroom, and growing interest in audience engagement. It is also a politically essential inquiry. If newsroom analytics consistently reveal a lack of citizen interest in public affairs content, this could lead to more lifestyle-oriented coverage, and a decline in the news media's incentive to perform its watchdog role by covering public affairs and conducting investigations. It may even, as the audience fragments across publications and platforms "undermine the position of the media in the circuit of public deliberation" (2013: 5). However, the news media's capacity to understand broader patterns of news consumption are hampered by the lack of access to competitor data. This makes studies like ours, which examine content shared from a variety of publications across the globe important to establishing benchmarks for news sharing behaviour.

Even so, while we have reasonable understanding of *why* people share news stories to their social networks and *how* they do it, as demonstrated in Chap. 1, we have less awareness of *what* they actually share. Studies to date present conflicting information about most shared topics and genres of news depending on the publications and platforms sampled. Bastos (2015), looking at items shared from *The Guardian* and *The New York Times* on five platforms, Facebook, Twitter, Google+, Delicious, Pinterest and StumbleUpon, found a type of news gap in the marked differences between the subject matter emphasis of articles published in news sections online, and those their users chose to commend. News users, he says, preferred to share opinion and local, national and world news, while editors tended to curate sport and economics, entertainment and celebrity stories on homepages above the fold. Users also preferred "hard news over soft and general news in a proportionally higher ratio than do newspaper editors" (Bastos 2015: 317).[1] Bright's study of sharing from BBC News, in contrast, found that news on politics and government was associated with lower sharing rates, although items about "space, science, and technology were shared at a much greater than average rate on all platforms" (Bright 2016: 354). Kalsnes and Larsson (2017), in studying four Norwegian publishers, also found editorial comment about soft news topics, particularly education, parenting and health, more often shared. Predictably, given what we know about commendary culture, each of these studies suggested that different platforms demonstrated different trends in the topic focus of news sharing. It is perhaps a given though, that business and economic news would be more shared on LinkedIn than Pinterest, where arts and culture news is the focus, and that Twitter shares would tend to promote public affairs and research news (Bastos 2015).

We also know that people's emotional state, and the sentiment or valence of stories affects the subject matter of stories that are shared. Again, there is conflicting information in these studies, with some claiming that positive, uplifting news is more likely to be shared than negative (Bakshy et al. 2011; Bright 2016) and our Share Wars partners and others finding the opposite (Crawford et al. 2015). Negative news attracts our attentions more than positive (Trussler and Soroka 2014), and is more useful to us. We take up the effect of affect on news sharing online in Chap. 6, and the news values in stories that contribute to people's news sharing choices.

Of all the news sharing research we have discussed so far, the largest study is the 2016 Reuters Institute Digital News Report (Newman et al. 2016), an international survey of 50,000 people in 26 countries. Despite its recognisable limits in terms of self-reported data about media consumption (see Boczkowski and Mitchelstein 2013: 10), its scope and focus on social sharing mean it can usefully inform our analysis of the potential news gap in socially shared news in several ways. First and fundamentally,

---

[1] In this characterisation, Bastos invokes traditional binary categorisations of news into 'hard', masculine topics, such as business, politics, economics and international relations and 'soft', more feminine topics such as entertainment, health, education and lifestyle.

it indicates that news sharing is now more common via social networks than on email, confirming our choice of social media as a more representative field from which to study shareworthiness.

Second, in terms of who shares news on social media platforms, the Reuters team found that controlling for other cultural and demographic variations among respondents, strong affiliations with the right- or left-wing politics are positively associated with sharing and commenting in social media networks, but not with sharing by email (p. 8). This would suggest that sharing of political content in a social media sharing study like ours, might be more prevalent than in a study like Boczkowski and Mitchelstein's, which did not look at social media commendation.

Third, the Reuters study found respondent interest in both hard news and commenting or sharing news was stronger than the relationship between respondent interest in soft news and commendary activity, with those people interested in hard news more likely to comment on both social media and news websites, while those interested soft news were less likely to comment on social media. This would suggest that, overall, a study like ours might expect to find a greater incidence of hard news than soft news sharing in our data set, as the data set is generated by commendary activity. We might also see a positive correlation between sharing of public affairs-oriented news and commenting in our data set, if those who share hard news are more likely to comment on the host site before or after they share it on social.

Indeed, we should also see a correlation between social media sharing and the overall level of comments on host news websites because the Reuters study found that "using social media for news as well as using many social media platforms will be positively associated with sharing and commenting activities outside social media environments" (p. 7) including posts on news websites.

At least some everyday sharing is based on "foraging and opportunism" (Purcell et al. 2010: 2), conducted when people have the time and motivation to read and share online news, or access their social news feeds. As Axel Bruns (2018) notes, there is a difference between everyday, serendipitous news sharing and the more viral sharing of 'acute' media events. In our study, we attend to this difference by distinguishing between everyday sharing and most highly shared articles, by setting a baseline for recognising what constitutes measurable sharing, and then taking slices of data at different thresholds of share counts to avoid focusing too much on the most highly shared or viral events.

THE QUESTIONS

This study uses social media analytics to examine what people commend on Twitter and Facebook—that is, what they value enough to recommend publicly by redistributing it to their friends, family and workmates. There are now several private companies that conduct this type of research, and which issue public reports about it as a way of attracting clients and media attention. NewsWhip, for example, issues regular reports on most viral content and an annual guide to social media publishing, which in 2018 looked at differences in the types of stories that were shared, liked and commented upon (Boland 2018). Buzzsumo does what the industry calls deep dive analysis, not only on most shared items, but also on content elements, such as what headline phrases were most and least engaging (Rayson 2017). Our work is less concerned with identifying what shares most for commercial purposes (although this was of definite interest to our Share Wars partners), but rather, to see if what we share can tell us anything about what news consumers want from journalistic endeavour, and how we might understand that elusive concept of the public interest through the operation of commentary culture.

Our study differs from Boczkowski and Mitchelstein's in a few respects. Theirs compared journalists' views of significant news, represented by the top-ranked news stories by placement on news homepages, with consumer choices, represented by data on most viewed, most emailed and most commented-on stories. We accept their proposition that professional news journalists tend to regard the production of public affairs stories more highly than softer human interest, lifestyle and entertainment stories, and so we are simply looking to see if the news gap is apparent in what people share socially. They included interviews with journalists and consumers, to get feedback on their analysis and to expand their knowledge of production/consumption contexts, where we have conducted a survey of ninemsn users to gather further details about what drives their sharing. That information is presented in Chap. 7. They systematically examined user behaviours during different periods of political activity, and while we have accepted their premise that political news consumption will change in response to events like elections, we did not factor this in as we were working with a random, multi-country sample of social media news sharing gathered across the seven months available to us for data gathering.

Our study undertakes a big data analysis of the most shared news on Facebook and Twitter from an international sample of English language news websites. Of the three social media platforms that are used most for sharing news, we chose to focus on Facebook and Twitter due to the automation on their sites, and their provision of public APIs, which meant data about URLs shared and share counts was readily available and comparable.[2] Reddit was not suitable for analysis because of the variable, idiosyncratic ways that people structure their information sharing, and the absence of a standardised data set for analysis.

It is possibly the last international academic study of social sharing performed while the social media companies were still making their APIs publicly accessible. Our key interest was in the identifying the most shared news story genres and topics. We wanted to see if social media users demonstrated a marked preference for a particular story form or narrative type, like features or opinion rather than traditional hard news. In order to test the news gap theory, we also wanted to know if users preferred 'softer' non-public affairs subjects, such as celebrity, sport or weather to 'hard' public affairs topics like politics, business or government, and what news topics they preferred sharing. We constructed four research questions alongside which we added two hypotheses, based on the news sharing literature.

RQ1: What are the most highly and most commonly shared news story genres?
RQ2: Is there a preference in social news sharing for 'softer' non-public affairs subjects over 'harder' subjects?
RQ3: What are the most highly and most commonly shared news story topics?
RQ4: How prevalent are the following forms of user engagement in these most shared stories: comments, links and multimedia?

Alongside RQ3, we propose H3, the hypothesis that the sharing of political content will be more prevalent in our study than in Boczkowski and Mitchelstein's, due to the greater likelihood of politically motivated individuals to share information on social media. In terms of RQ4, we also expect to find H4, a high correlation between social sharing and commenting on news websites, particularly on public affairs-oriented stories.

---

[2] The importance of these three sites is suggested by the Pew Research Center's report on social news use by North Americans, although we acknowledge the ethnocentric nature of that assumption (Matsa and Shearer 2018).

The broader aims of our broader study have been to establish a theoretically sound classification schema to enable better news sharing analysis and to document some of the challenges to investigating the nature of news sharing on digital platforms. These two aims emerged from the complex task of establishing how to collect this data, what limitations there were to our bespoke and novel process, and how we might clean and analyse our dataset for the purposes of obtaining rich qualitative information.

COLLECTING AND ANALYSING THE DATA

We began by gathering data from Facebook and Twitter APIs about the URLs and share counts of news shared by users of 116 news websites worldwide, a sample which like Boczkowski and Mitchelstein's study takes in publications of different sizes, with differing political orientations and from different media systems and cultures. The sample's eclectic mix, which was the result of earlier Share Wars projects, takes in mainstream international publications like New York Times, The Guardian, Wall Street Journal, CNN and BBC, regional publications like the South China Morning Post, nationals such as Zimbabwe's Sowetanlive or Canada's Globe and Mail, major metropolitan sources like The Washington Post and The Telegraph, market competitors like Times of India, The Hindu and India Today, and small local publications like New Zealand's Manawatu Standard and Otago Daily. It does not however, include Latin American publications. In terms of media origins, the sample includes newspapers, broadcasters and digital-born publications such as The Daily Beast, Huffington Post and Australia's Crikey.

The resulting analysis is based on a corpus of 20,000 universal resource locators (URLs) or web addresses for shared news stories gathered between August 2014–February 2015, together with the story content scraped from those addresses and their Facebook and Twitter share counts at a 5-day offset. Using this offset for share count collection was essential to ensure we captured the bulk of sharing of any one news item, which tends to peak at two days, and then tapers (Bastos 2015: 311). Rather than separating out interactions from each platform, and trying to match commendary activities that are likely not commensurate anyway, we work with Twitter's share count and Facebook's "total share count" incorporating the platform's weighted measurement of shares, likes and comments.

During the collection period, URLs were scraped from the sample publications' homepages roughly every 20 minutes using the Share Wars

'Likeable Engine' (see http://share-wars.com/).[3] The most prolific news publishing sites in the sample by number of unique URLs scraped were Huffington Post (125,070) and Yahoo7's The West Australian (78,864), while the smallest contribution was from the US magazine Entertainment Weekly (593), with all sites providing over 20,000 distinct URLs, some of which pointed to the same items.[4] These URLs were resolved to their 'canonical' addresses as used by Facebook when counting shares.[5] We discarded any URLs that we could not successfully download, including syndicated content that was only available for a brief period.[6]

The corpus analysed is illustrative of the most shared news for these publications for this period, rather than being a definitive set of the most shared stories overall internationally. This distinction is also grounded in two strategies taken to avoid sample bias.

First, there are differences in the editorial selection of homepage news. Some sites publish news on their homepages that doesn't get shared. This is particularly true of traditional news publishers that provide comprehensive coverage and whose breaking coverage is driven by syndicated newswires. Others such as BuzzFeed only publish their most shareable stories on their own website.

Second, while we sought to differentiate content that was highly shared from content that was barely shared, the baseline figure for a well-shared news story differs from site to site. If we had examined only those articles with the absolutely largest share count, our sample would have been biased

[3] Homepages may share content, or link to content on affiliate domains, such that content from these sites is not mutually exclusive.

[4] These may not correspond to distinct content, although the Likeable Engine applies heuristics to clean URL parameters that introduce spurious distinctions between identical URL targets.

[5] Multiple discovered URLs may correspond to a single shareable address on Facebook, because Facebook applies canonicalization:

- It follows any HTTP and "meta refresh" redirection that would be followed by a web browser.
- It uses the URL from metadata provided within a page, preferring the Open Graph URL (<meta property=og:url>) over the search engine-oriented <link rel=canonical> annotation.

URLs may be varied for user and campaign tracking, so this process ensures that spurious duplicates are often removed. In some cases, the same content presented in affiliated mastheads obtains a single canonical URL.

[6] A large portion of the content from yahoo.com was discarded for this reason.

towards sites with high market share (e.g. CNN), those with sharing-oriented editorial strategies (e.g. Huffington Post and BuzzFeed) and possibly towards particular topics and genres. So, instead, we took slices of the data from the top 25% and the lowest 25% of shared stories, where these percentiles were first calculated on a per-site basis. Each site thus contributed to the high or low sample in proportion with its URL frequency in the larger corpus after filtering. To produce a relevant baseline comparison of most shared content between sites, we only considered URLs with a total Facebook share count of at least three. This left us with a corpus of shared news articles.

Bias will remain in the sample, partly because some stories in the corpus are syndicated from other publications by the sample publication, and so are not automatically and directly attributable to the original publisher. We also acknowledge that story selection and placement on homepages will play a significant part in what users choose to share, while editorial agendas will vary from site to site, and between generalist news, and the arts and technology news sites, like TMZ and Entertainment Weekly, or Mashable and The Verge, that also form a part of our sample.

The remaining URLs, along with publisher details and Facebook headlines, were compiled in a spreadsheet, the stories called up and the content manually coded for genre and topicality. The final corpus consisted of 2000 URLs, half from the most highly shared quartile and half from the less shared quartile, which were then manually cleaned and coded by one coder, so an intercoder reliability check was not needed.

To code the news genre for each story item, we considered four factors: the *informational purpose* of the story, by story genre, and also using Boczkowski and Mitchelsteins' categories of *public affairs* and *non-public affairs* subject matter, to designate whether it fell into the hard or soft news basket. We also classified items by their *rhetorical organisation* and stylistic features of the narrative, and finally, by the publication's self-designated *section categorisation* of the story, information also relevant to classifying the story topicality. We also coded for the presence of *multimedia, embedded links* and *user comments*, all of which may trigger greater user involvement with the content, thereby possibly biasing the sample towards greater sharing.

To code our sample for the story informational purpose, we adopted broadly accepted legacy text genre categories, as much web content is also published in print or broadcast form, and the narrative structures are based on historic practices and conventions. We chose to use three established genre categories: news (conveying timely brief, factual information about socially significant events), features (conveying the background to, reasons for and psychological reactions to timely events and issues), and opinion editorial (persuasive commentary on newsworthy events and issues).

We then coded for the rhetorical or stylistic purpose of the story item. This classification was necessary because, while the stories may have had a clear informational purpose, they also usually had secondary specific purpose and specific stylistic characteristics, including voice and structure, that afforded them a rhetorical classification (see Bazerman 2004; Frow 2015). News stories were those articles under 500 words presented as *summary news, news analysis, research accounts,* based on a scientific study, or *human interest* accounts, presented with an anecdotal or experiential lead in what some news media call a 'readers first' style.

Feature stories proved to have many different stylistic forms including the *summary news* feature; the *backgrounder,* giving chronological context to a current affairs issue; the *explainer,* defining and explaining a particular news phenomenon; *reportage,* an extended reflection on an issue or question; *investigative,* involving the exploration of crimes, corruption or other wrongdoing; *human interest,* presenting everyday people's concerns in a manner designed to elicit empathy; *profile* of a celebrity or significant figure; *personal account,* a first persona experiential story; the *letter; advice column, obituary, research account,* and *satire,* the *listicle,* the *call-out,* asking for contributions to a story, the *repository page,* listing relevant definitions and stories for a given topic, and *specialist* fashion, food, sport and travel features. We also noted visual forms, with *photojournalism,* where the images were the primary content of the story, and the *infographic,* where a chart was the primary focus of the story.

With research accounts, we gave the same coding to news and features to get a better sense of how scientific research was valued across the two informational genres. There was also some blurring of rhetorical intention and form in the items we examined, such as a number of advice columns or reviews written as listicles. In those cases, the primary rhetorical intention was coded rather than the form. This means there are actually more listicles in the set than appears in the results by a small factor.

Opinion categories comprised *editorial,* the unbylined, 'voice of the paper' style position piece and other by-lined forms, including *analysis,* where a factual argument was pursued in a balanced manner, *commentary,* a polarised personally inflected argument, *review,* and *cartoon.*

This coding schema identified new narrative web genres: listicle, live blog, and photogallery, explainer and repository entry. We needed to construct these new categories of genre to describe the purpose of multimodal, hypertextual narratives (Askehave and Nielsen 2006; Caple 2009; Matheson 2004; Sjøvaag et al. 2011) and to respond to changes in narrative practice. For example, the listicle, a portmanteau term for list-article, is a common literary form online, exemplary of the attention economy in the way it distils key information to a list of points or images, the meaning of which is then briefly explained.

To address our hypothesis about the shareability of rich information, we then noted whether shared stories included audio-visual and multimedia material such as video, sound files, infographics, slideshows or games. We noted whether stories included social co-production factors, coding for the presence of *embedded hyperlinks*, which encourage users to search for other sources of information off-story page, and the provision of *user comments*, that is the invitation to participate in constructing story meaning. We then checked to see whether the story had attracted comments (as a binary yes/no proposition). We did try to code for other aspects of co-production, that is, whether the story was partly user generated by surveys, polls or other means, and how participation was indicated. However, we found little evidence of these forms in the sample.

In terms of coding for news topicality, we started by examining the ways the publications classified their stories, using section categorisations in the layout and indexing of the content. Where there was not a page tab or label to delineate this, it was determined from the URL or the section header at the top of the story page. Topicality coding was far more complex than any other factor, as we expected from the literature on automated topic tracking and keyword extraction (Allan 2002; Lee and Kim 2008), in terms of the work involved in examining the textual features to interpret the thematic specificity of stories. We initially designated two categories, primary and secondary topic, where the first would designate the main focus of the story based on the title tag of the page, the headline, any story precede, the prominence of topicality in the first paragraph of the article, and the overall focus of the story.[7] Only one primary topic was coded per article.

---

[7] The precede or standfirst is a sentence following the story headline that summarises or sells the story content, with details of its most central question or issue.

The primary topic categories were distilled from thematic studies of news online (Sjøvaag et al. 2011; Trümper and Neverla 2013). These topics were politics; business and industry; work; finance and economy; environment; crime, law and justice; disasters, accidents and deaths; health; education; religion; parenting; science and technology; social welfare; sports; media and communication; arts, culture and entertainment; history; natural history and animals. We chose to separate two of these categories into subfields. The first was arts and entertainment, where we wanted to gauge people's specific interest in celebrity, and avoid it distorting indications of more general interest in cultural production. The second was politics, where we added the sub-category war to distinguish war from the sharing of information about more unpredictable natural disasters.

We initially assumed that secondary categories were necessary as topicality is contextually variable, always in flux and not exclusive. This category often added specificity to the nature of the primary topic, for example, health/ malaria. However, we found that the sheer diversity of secondary topicality made the second category redundant for any analytical purposes. Once the coding was completed, we loaded the spreadsheet data into SPSS and then generated the findings relevant to each research question and hypothesis.

WHAT WE FOUND

Overall, in response to RQ1, news was by far the most highly shared and most commonly shared story genre, making up 57.7% of the top quartile shares, and 62.1% of the bottom quartile shares—so overall 59.9% of the data set. Feature shares made up significant proportions of the top and bottom quartiles though were more highly shared than commonly shared (30.1% and 25.4%). Opinion shares made up only 12.2% and 12.5% respectively of the sample.

In terms of style, Fig. 5.1 shows that summary news was overwhelmingly the most shared informational purpose or genre category across both quartiles, and more so in everyday sharing even than among more highly shared stories.

Looking more closely at the rhetorical intention of stories, we find again, sharing predominantly of factual news genres, in particular, summary news, which is more favoured in everyday sharing than in more highly shared contexts (Fig. 5.2). Summary news style stories make up 48% of most highly shared news and more than half (56%) of everyday news sharing. Backgrounders and reportage also demonstrate shareworthiness in the top quartile story sample (7.8% and 6.3%), although less so in the bottom quartile (6.3% and 3.1).

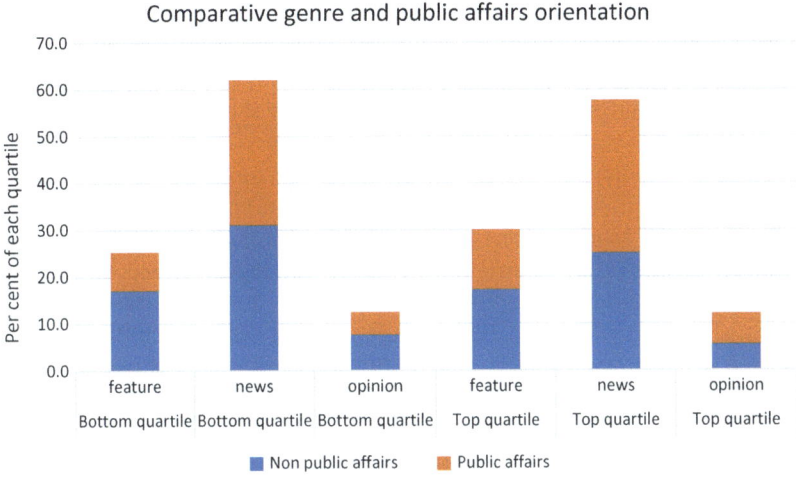

Fig. 5.1 Comparative story genre and public affairs orientation in most highly shared news on Facebook and Twitter August 2014–February 2015. Image: Fiona R Martin

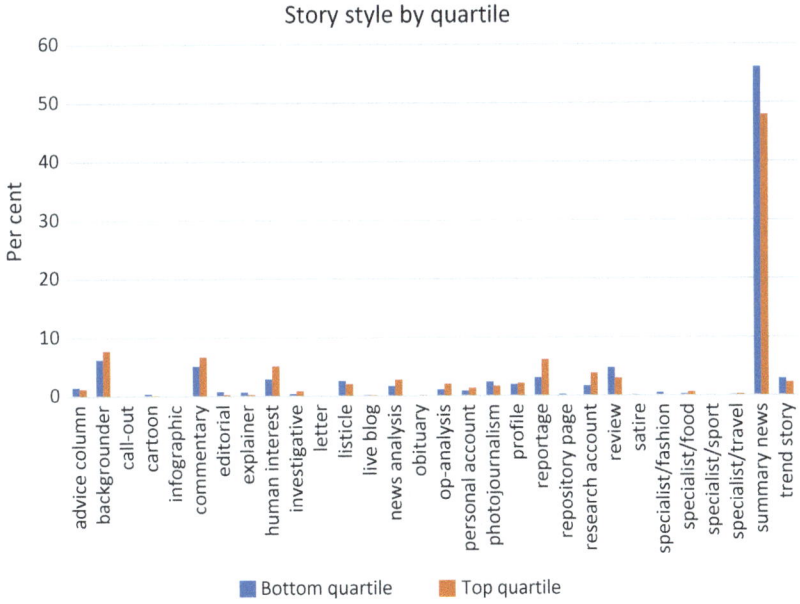

Fig. 5.2 Preferred story style in most highly shared news on Facebook and Twitter August 2014–February 2015. Image: Fiona R Martin

Opinion did figure relatively strongly in comparison to other factual news genres, with commentary occupying 6.8% of the most highly shared stories and 5.2% of everyday sharing while reviews, which constitute valuable consumer advice, made up 4.8% of ordinary sharing and 3% of most high-shared stories. As the more popular forms of opinion, they do confirm that audiences are more captivated by techniques of personal persuasion and critique, than the more detached, rational argument of analysis or editorial. Human interest news, with its emotional orientation, also attracted marked sharing attention. It was more highly shared than commonly shared though, suggesting the special or unusual nature of some personally oriented stories. Interestingly, even though research accounts figured in both feature and news genre categories, this was not an overwhelmingly popular sharing genre—although at 3.9%, research accounts were more often highly shared than reviews.

The news gap theory is challenged by the fact that there was a balance of both public affairs (281) and non-public affairs oriented (280) summary news items shared in the bottom, everyday sharing sample, and slightly more PA summary news items (280) in the highly shared sample, than NPA (200). Further, in the bottom quartile of everyday sharing, there was relatively more PA content in all categories of 'hard' news-related feature genres (backgrounder, reportage, research account, and investigative) and all opinion content categories except reviews.

In respect to RQ2, overall, public affairs (PA) oriented content was more highly shared than softer news in both news and opinion genres (see Fig. 5.1 and Table 5.1). Overall, PA stories dominate the top quartile set

Table 5.1 Public affairs orientation percentages, by news genre shared on Facebook and Twitter August 2014–February 2015

	Bottom quartile	Bottom quartile	Bottom quartile	Bottom quartile	Top quartile	Top quartile	Top quartile	Top quartile
	Feature	News	Opinion	Total	Feature	News	Opinion	Total
Non-public affairs	17.2	31.2	7.7	56.1	17.4	25.2	5.6	48.2
Public affairs	8.2	30.9	4.8	43.9	12.7	32.5	6.6	51.8
Total	25.4	62.1	12.5	100.0	30.1	57.7	12.2	100.0

Image: Fiona R Martin

(PA 518 vs NPA 482). The figures from the top quartile show a small but statistically significant positive difference in news (32.5% versus 25.2%) and opinion (6.6 versus 5.6%) categories. Even the everyday sharing figures suggest little difference in preference for hard or soft news.

With features, however, the situation is reversed, as it is more generally with everyday sharing, where non-public affairs stories are preferred (overall NPA 561 to PA 439). Among the most commonly shared, non-public affairs content is more than twice as popular as more politically and economically significant material. In the top quartile, however, NPA features are only 4.7% more shared than harder subject matter.

There were more surprising findings with respect to RQ3: what are the most highly and most commonly shared news story topics? As Table 5.2

Table 5.2 Most commonly and most highly shared story topics on Facebook and Twitter August 2014–February 2015

Topic	Bottom Q		Top Q	
	Count	Column N %	Count	Column N %
Accidents and deaths	36	3.60%	43	4.30%
Arts, culture and entertainment	109	10.90%	111	11.10%
Arts, culture and entertainment	127	12.70%	77	7.70%
Business and industry	79	7.90%	49	4.90%
Crime, law and justice	125	12.50%	133	13.30%
Disasters	15	1.50%	8	0.80%
Education	7	0.70%	20	2.00%
Environment	13	1.30%	13	1.30%
Environment/weather	8	0.80%	11	1.10%
Finance and economy	40	4.00%	23	2.30%
Health	41	4.10%	46	4.60%
History	5	0.50%	9	0.90%
Media and communication	15	1.50%	20	2.00%
Natural history and animals	5	0.50%	22	2.20%
Parenting and family relation	12	1.20%	19	1.90%
Politics	106	10.60%	147	14.70%
Politics/war	31	3.10%	46	4.60%
Public works and administrât	24	2.40%	42	4.20%
Religion	2	0.20%	10	1.00%
Science and technology	28	2.80%	41	4.10%
Social welfare	9	0.90%	11	1.10%
Sport	157	15.70%	80	8.00%
Work	6	0.60%	19	1.90%
Total	1000	100.00%	1000	100.00%

Image: Fiona R Martin

(over page) shows, the most highly shared primary story topic, listed in the top quartile column on the right, was general politics at 147 relative shares, with crime, law and justice, the second at 133 relative shares, and only then arts, culture and entertainment generally (111). When we add the total number of politics/war shared items to those from the general politics category (193), and combine both general arts and celebrity categories (188), we find politics is still the most shared topic from our most highly shared story corpus. In this top quartile, sport stories were only a little more likely to be shared as celebrity stories. Health, business and industry, education, science and technology and death and accidents appear as second tier sharing, with around 4% of the most highly shared corpus.

In the bottom quartile, the everyday sharing slice of our dataset, the results look a little more like the news gap thesis, with sport the most commonly shared topic (15.7%), followed by celebrity (12.7%), general arts and entertainment (10.9%), and only then politics (10.6%). However, the difference between the overall percentages of the most shareable topics is fairly small, particularly when war is added to politics, taking this topic to the second highest share count. This suggests that the news gap is not significant even in terms of the topics we share every day on social media platforms. The clear difference with Boczkowski and Mitchelstein's findings is the very low sharing of environment/weather stories. However, given that some of this data was collected during the lead-up to the Paris United Nations Climate Change Conference, a number of climate change stories were primarily about the politics of the negotiations, and so coded as political.

In terms of H3, the hypothesis that the sharing of political content will be more prevalent in our study than in Boczkowski and Mitchelstein's, we can see that evidenced in the most highly shared stories sample, which tallies with the proposal that more politically invested individuals from both ends of the right-left spectrum would be inclined to share widely within their interest networks.

Turning to RQ4, factors associated with sharing engagement or commendary activities, we found that the presence or capacity for comments is associated with higher sharing, and links with sharing in the top quartile.

In terms of online engagement, we found that stories that had comments registered on the news website or even the capacity for commenting, but no comments posted, were positively associated with sharing in contrast to stories without that participative option. Over half of the most shared stories (54.7%) had comments posted on the news website, suggesting some conversational investment by news consumers, as had nearly a third of everyday shares. Even stories that had commenting enabled, but had accrued no user response, were shared more than those without commenting. Nearly a third (32.1%) of the most shared stories were open for comment, and close to a half of the commonly shared stories (46.8%). These outcomes tally with our hypothesis H4 that we would find a correlation between social media sharing and the overall level of comments on host news websites, based on the Reuters study findings (see Fig. 5.3).

The presence of embedded links was also slightly positively associated with the most highly shared stories, although not clearly with the commonly shared items.

The majority of most highly shared stories contained links (54.1%) and most commonly in news and feature stories, rather than opinion. Conversely, in more commonly shared stories, links were less prevalent, although present in similar story proportions to the top quartile (Fig. 5.4).

Curiously, in investigating RQ4, the presence of multimedia in news seemed to have less bearing on whether stories were shared or not than we might have expected. Less than half of the most highly shared stories had some form of multimedia content (42.1%) and just over a third of the everyday shares (36.5%) (Table 5.3).

Given the cost of producing rich media content, we thought it important to analyse what types of multimedia were actually shared, and in what informational types of stories, to get a better sense of where the invest-

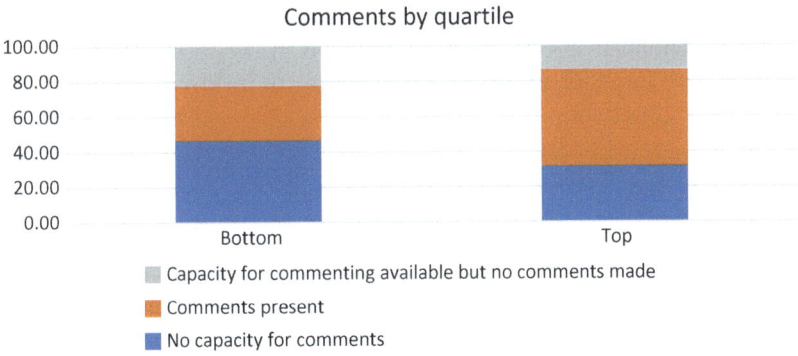

Fig. 5.3 Website comments on the most shared news stories on Facebook and Twitter August 2014–February 2015. Image: Fiona R Martin

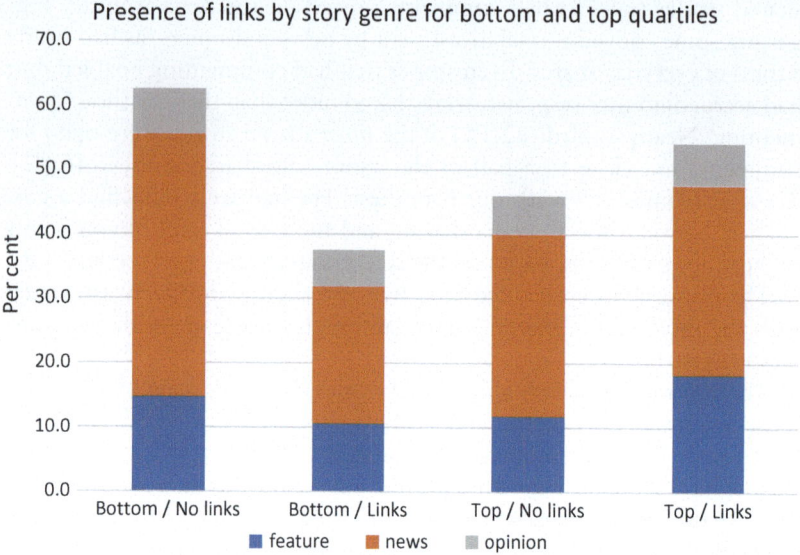

Fig. 5.4 Presence of links by story genre in the most shared news stories on Facebook and Twitter August 2014–February 2015. Image: Fiona R Martin

ment was justified. Overwhelmingly, the most highly shared and most commonly shared stories included video, followed by photogalleries, slideshows and tweets. This content was situated mostly in opinion and feature stories shared in the top quartile, probably because of the longer production lead times for those genres of news media. That video and slideshow enriched stories are more apparent in the most highly shared quartile bodes well for the production investment involved, as it indicates greater shareworthiness (Fig. 5.5).

WHAT THIS MEANS

This research has a range of new insights for digital journalism studies in the analytics moment. First, we distinguish between what we commonly share and what we share to a high degree, suggesting we can begin to explore different degrees of sharing activity and with which subject matter they are concerned. Rather than just focussing on the nature of 'viral' outliers in sharing, we can now consider the material we value more highly on social platforms, alongside that which drives ordinary, low-level sharing exchanges.

Table 5.3 Multimedia in the most shared news stories on Facebook and Twitter August 2014–February 2015

Multimedia	Bottom Q		Top Q	
	Count	Column N %	Count	Column N %
Animation	1	0.1%	0	0.0%
Audio	0	0.0%	3	0.3%
Charts	0	0.0%	1	0.1%
Documents	0	0.0%	1	0.1%
Facebook	0	0.0%	3	0.3%
Form	1	0.1%	0	0.0%
GIF	5	0.5%	6	0.6%
Infographic	13	1.3%	11	1.1%
Instagram	8	0.8%	8	0.8%
Map	1	0.1%	9	0.9%
Photogallery	102	10.2%	70	7.0%
Podcast	4	0.4%	8	0.8%
Report	1	0.1%	0	0.0%
Slideshow	20	2.0%	66	6.6%
Table	0	0.0%	1	0.1%
Tinder	0	0.0%	1	0.1%
Twitter	43	4.3%	50	5.0%
Video	226	22.6%	305	30.5%
Vine	0	0.0%	1	0.1%
Inc.multimedia	365	36.5%	421	42.1%

Image: Fiona R Martin

Second, our work suggests the news gap on the two largest social media platforms is not as great as we might have assumed. This proposal is supported in part by the popularity of news as an informational form. Despite widespread concerns about the polarisation of the news media, opinion made up a low percentage of both high level and everyday social shares, suggesting it is less valued or useful than news as a way of brokering social connections. Features, which require more research investment than news, are also demonstrably shareworthy in the everyday and more uncommonly highly shared categories. This is good news for journalists, who value this more creative and diverse type of production and for audiences, as features can convey more complex contextual details than news.

The absence of a pronounced news gap was also suggested by both the balance of PA and NPA summary news in the bottom and top quartiles, the overall dominance of PA content in the most highly shared news sam-

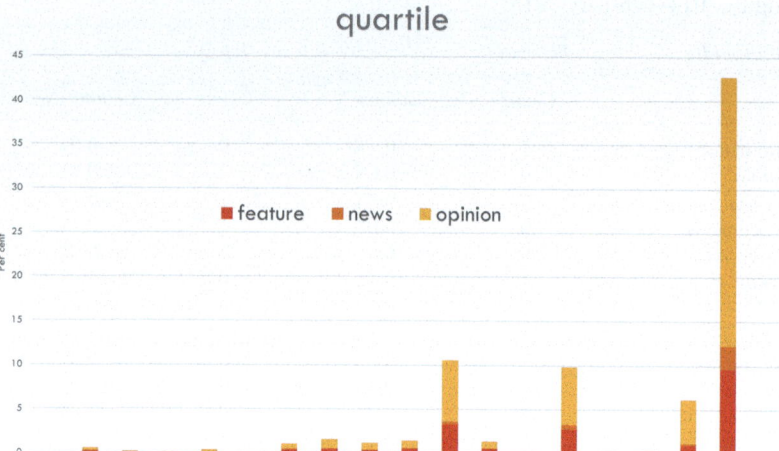

Fig. 5.5 Multimedia types by story genre in the most shared news stories on Facebook and Twitter August 2014–February 2015. Image: Fiona R Martin

ple and the predominance of PA content in both news and opinion categories in that sample. Certainly, there is, overall, a greater tendency to soft stories in everyday news sharing, but this type of sharing activity has a lesser engagement and reach than the top quartile sharing, so is not as publicly visible. Further, when people are doing ordinary low-level commendation, they are more likely to exchange PA-oriented news feature and opinion content, suggesting they are regularly engaged in conversations about socially significant issues.

The third form of evidence against a significant news gap in online news sharing comes from an analysis of the most shared topics. Here, politics tops arts, culture and entertainment to be the most highly shared subject matter, as predicted by our hypothesis. This may be because those who are most likely to share content are politically motivated, as suggested by H3, or because politics arouses strong emotions, which, as Chap. 7 will detail, are key to motivating commendary activity. Either way, it suggests good citizen engagement with public affairs—as does the second tier sharing of business and industry, education, and science and technology stories.

Sport and celebrity, two of the other 'soft' topics that Boczkowski and Mitchelstein attributed to the news gap, were much less highly shared than politics and the arts, suggesting that while they may be important in the everyday, they have lesser significance for users' broad social networks.

Everyday social news sharing does follow the news gap profile to some extent, but politics is far from absent, especially when warfare is part of the commendary circuit. The relatively low incidence of non-political environment and weather stories was intriguing, and deserves further study. It is possible that the proximity of the Paris Climate Change Accord impacted the framing of these types of stories, so they were more likely to be coded public affairs. Further, the frequency and significance of weather stories depends on irregular factors that might not be captured in even a one-year survey period. Perhaps the loss of science and environment reporters worldwide has reduced the amount of creative coverage given to this field, or the coverage that exists is not constructed to engage people in commendary acts. Alternatively, even though weather is a good conversation starter between strangers, perhaps it is not a topic that people feel strongly enough about to share. Finally, it is also possible that environmental issues and climate change may be topics that people feel uneasy commending to others, and which engender polarised debate on social media that people would prefer to avoid.

In terms of future research around news topicality, the fact that political affiliation may influence people's rate of sharing needs consideration. It certainly needs investigation in relation to commendary acts more widely, to see just how it influences different types of information co-production, including link clicking, commenting, voting and tagging of content. There is a low incidence of shared content with embedded forms of co-production such as polls, surveys and call-outs, but the level of everyday commendation possible on most stories raises questions about the extent to which audiences value those opportunities for interaction with political subject matter.

Certainly commenting, which is positively correlated with news sharing, is a rich area for further study, particularly given the need for news media to build engagement and audience loyalty. We would like to know, for example, whether those that commend stories also comment on news websites, and if so, which comes first—the act of commending a story on social media, or the conversation on a news website? If those who commend are not those who comment on news websites, what impact, if any, does an active conversational thread have on the decision to share. Or is it simply the case that stories likely to inspire or provoke users to comment are also those that motivate their commendary impulses?

Similarly, is there a case in the sharing data to justify the effort journalists might put into adding hyperlinks to a story? Linking can add illustrative, evidential and contextual details, giving a story additional informational and educative value. The highly shared sample's slight positive association with linking in news does not provide strong evidence that links matter in the decision to share, but this could be a question for future audience research that would establish to what extent journalism innovation increases engagement, and in what ways.

Such a study must include multimedia given the uneven findings about whether the presence of multimedia content in a news story is correlated with social sharing of that content. It is well established in industry studies that images and video are key to higher sharing and retweeting, although Facebook's inflated video viewing statistics, which drove the media's so-called 'pivot to video', have now been exposed (Lapowsky 2018). Video appeared as the most shared form of multimedia, but the attention given to photogalleries and slideshow material also needs exploration, particularly to see if there is a longer duration of sharing of these media rich resources, beyond the initial two-day peak.

The final key aspect of any study into the relationship between digital journalism innovation and online news sharing would have to be understanding whether, if at all, co-production opportunities shaping commendary decisions. The low incidence of co-produced or participatory content which is shared in either quartile of our corpus suggests, as Boczkowski and Mitchelstein's study found, that this material is not necessarily popular, at least in its exchange. This indicates that further research is needed to establish whether its value is more in the making, than in commendary terms, and to expand our understanding of what audiences value in engagement strategies.

Our study has provided a robust schema for assessing the genre and topicality content of social news sharing, which takes into account stylistic factors that might influence social sharing, and acknowledges the rise of digital genres that are shaping commendary choices and attention metrics. The listicle's use in a variety of rhetorical categories including advice columns and reviews certainly deserves further study as a device to focus consumer attention, and to more quickly deliver news information, as does the emergence of the photogallery and the slideshow as tools for visual storytelling.

As a whole, our investigation counters concerns about analytics-driven newsrooms being locked in a race to the bottom, driven by the audience's turn to light entertainment and quick reads, or opinionated rants. Rather, we find audience interest in traditional aspects of journalism—its summary news function, public interest orientation and provision of socially significant ideas. Longer form story styles are also well shared and, more than lists and live blogs indicating the journalistic effort put into those articles, are worth recirculating widely. This is not to say that people do not appreciate all the soft stories that Boczkowski and Mitchelstein's earlier work identified—it's just that these do not tell the full story of what we share on social platforms, where our identity construction and social relationship maintenance play a strong part in what we choose to commend, and so shape sharing agendas that are very different to what we might view online.

Expanding User Horizons

With journalism increasingly invested in social media analytics to take the pulse of its relationships with audiences, it is imperative that, occasionally, those doing the measuring look beyond the results streaming to their desktop and try to access comparative data about what audiences like, share, tag and otherwise commend. This is going to be increasingly hard for researchers to access without special funding and permissions, as the platforms lock down their APIs and use them to extract further commodity value from user data.

Our research has provided a significant insight into the heterogeny of social news sharing, and the possibility that it is indeed expanding, rather than contracting user horizons. It dismisses concerns that social media users aren't interested in politics or civics and have been captured by celebrity gossip and 'what happens next'-style clickbait. It also demonstrates the uses of data analytics alongside traditional content analysis for producing substantial insight into news consumption beyond single story and masthead engagement.

There are many further aspects of news sharing that need studying in order to support the development of digital news journalism, including our finding that multimedia content is not always directly associated with sharing. Our work illustrates most clearly, though, that industry could stop obsessing over 'viral' news, with its unusually high levels of recirculation. Instead they might focus on a larger slice of highly shared and ordinarily shared stories to understand what audiences value enough to commend regularly to large numbers of their contacts, and what they are likely to take note of day-to-day.

The next chapter takes another approach to investigating part of the Likeable dataset in order to understand what part news language might play in the decision to commend a story. Using a different type of data analytics, linguistic Monika Bednarek undertakes an automated investigation of the words and phrases that characterise news sharing from mainstream news publications.

REFERENCES

Allan, James W. 2002. *Topic Detection and Tracking: Event-Based Information Organization*. Norwell, MA: Kluwer Academic Publishers.

Askehave, Inger, and Anne Ellerup Nielsen. 2006. Digital Genres: A Challenge to Traditional Genre Theory. *Information Technology & People* 18 (2): 120–141.

Bakshy, E., J.M. Hofman, W.A. Mason, and D.J. Watts. 2011. Everyone's an Influencer: Quantifying Influence on Twitter. In *Proceedings of the Fourth ACM International Conference on Web Search and Data Mining*, 65–74. New York, NY: Association for Computing Machinery. https://doi.org/10.1145/1935826.1935845.

Bastos, Marco Toledo. 2015. Shares, Pins, and Tweets. *Journalism Studies* 16 (3): 305–325. https://doi.org/10.1080/1461670X.2014.891857.

Bastos, Marco, and Shawn Walker. 2018. Facebook's Data Lockdown Is a Disaster for Academic Researchers. *The Conversation*. April 11. https://theconversation.com/facebooks-data-lockdown-is-a-disaster-for-academic-researchers-94533.

Bazerman, Charles. 2004. Speech Acts, Genres, and Activity Systems: How Texts Organize Activity and People. In *What Writing Does and How It Does It: An Introduction to Analyzing Texts and Textual Practices*, ed. Charles Bazerman and Paul Prior, 309–339. Mahwah, NJ: Erlbaum.

Boczkowski, Pablo J., and Eugenia Mitchelstein, eds. 2013. *The News Gap: When the Information Preferences of the Media and the Public Diverge*. Cambridge, MA: MIT Press.

Boland, Gabriele. 2018. Trends in Social Media Analytics. *Newswhip*. August 20. https://www.newswhip.com/2018/08/trends-in-social-media-analytics/.

Bright, Jonathon. 2016. The Social News Gap: How News Reading and News Sharing Diverge. *Journal of Communication* 66: 343–365. https://doi.org/10.1111/jcom.12232.

Bruns, Axel. 2018. Facebook Shuts the Gate after the Horse Has Bolted, and Hurts Real Research in the Process. *Medium*. April 25. https://medium.com/@Snurb/facebook-research-data-18662cf2cacb.

Caple, Helen. 2009. Multi-semiotic Communication in an Australian Broadsheet: A New News Story Genre. In *Genre in A Changing World, Perspectives on*

Writing, ed. C. Bazerman, A. Bonini, and D. Figueiredo, 243–254. Fort Collins, CO: The WAC Clearinghouse and Parlor Press.

Crawford, Hal, Andrew Hunter, and Domagoj Filipovic. 2015. *All Your Friends Like This: How Social Networks Took over News*. Sydney: HarperCollins.

Frow, John. 2015. *Genre: The New Critical Idiom*. London: Routledge.

Gonzalez, Robbie. 2018. Facebook Is Giving Scientists Its Data to Fight Misinformation. *Wired*. May 29. https://www.wired.com/story/facebook-is-giving-scientists-its-data-to-fight-misinformation/.

Hotham, Tristan. 2018. Facebook Risks Starting a War on Knowledge. *The Conversation*. August 17. https://theconversation.com/facebook-risks-starting-a-war-on-knowledge-101646.

Kalsnes, Bente, and Anders Olof Larsson. 2017. Understanding News Sharing across Social Media: Detailing Distribution on Facebook and Twitter. *Journalism Studies* 19 (11): 1669–1688.

Lapowsky, Issie. 2018. A New Facebook Lawsuit Makes 'Pivot to Video' Seem Even More Shortsighted. *Wired*. October 17. https://www.wired.com/story/facebook-lawsuit-pivot-to-video-mistake/.

Lee, Sungjick, and Han-Joon Kim. 2008. *News Keyword Extraction for Topic Tracking*. Proceedings of Fourth International Conference on Networked Computing and Advanced Information Management, Gyeongju, South Korea. IEEE. https://doi.org/10.1109/NCM.2008.199.

Matheson, Donald. 2004. Negotiating Claims to Journalism: Webloggers' Orientation to News Genres. *Convergence* 10 (4): 33–54.

Matsa, Katerina, and Elisa Shearer. 2018. *News Use Across Social Media Platforms 2018*. Pew Research Center. September 10. http://www.journalism.org/2018/09/10/news-use-across-social-media-platforms-2018/.

Newman, Nic, Richard Fletcher, David A.L. Levy, and Rasmus Kleis Nielsen. 2016. *Digital News Report 2016*. Oxford: Reuters Institute for the Study of Journalism.

Purcell, Kristen, Lee Rainie, Amy Mitchell, Tom Rosenstiel, and Kenny Olmstead. 2010. *Understanding the Participatory News Consumer: How Internet and Cell Phone Users Have Turned News into a Social Experience*. Pew Research Center. March 1.

Rayson, Steve. 2017. We Analyzed 100 Million Headlines. Here's What We Learned (New Research). *Buzzsumo*. June 26. http://buzzsumo.com/blog/most-shared-headlines-study/.

Scott, Caroline. 2018. Advice from Facebook for Reaching Wider Audiences after the Latest Newsfeed Updates. *Journalism.co.uk*. April 12. https://www.journalism.co.uk/news/facebook-newsfeed-updates-drive-meaningful-social-interactions-to-reach-wider-audiences/s2/a720323/.

Sjøvaag, Helle, Hallvard Moe, and Eirik Stavelin. 2011. Public Service News on the Web. *Journalism Studies* 13 (1): 90–106.

Trümper, Stefanie, and Irene Neverla. 2013. Sustainable Memory: How Journalism Keeps the Attention for Past Disasters Alive. *Studies in Communication Media* 2 (1): 1–37.

Trussler, Marc, and Stuart Soroka. 2014. Consumer Demand for Cynical and Negative News Frames. *The International Journal of Press/Politics* 19 (3): 360–379. https://doi.org/10.1177/1940161214524832.

The Language and News Values of 'Most Highly Shared' News

Monika Bednarek

Studying the uses of language in social media news sharing is central to understanding how its industrial ecology operates, and how its actors and processes might influence the production of news journalism. Google and Facebook have built empires on the acquisition of user-generated text, and the identification, patterning and commodification of keywords in our searches, conversations and annotations. In those cases, the words we most often search for or discuss have intrinsic value to advertisers, based on their capacity to capture our browsing attention. News, too, has historically been shaped by particular rhetorical strategies, packaged with compelling headlines, summary leads and concise, active language that demands the reader's attention.

Yet, little public research has been done on the language of most shared news. For our Share Wars partners, it was critical to explore what linguistic factors people value in the communication of news—and whether these conform to, or diverge from, the contemporary language of news and the traditional 'news values' that guide journalists in filtering and selecting information that will be newsworthy—that is, timely, relevant and interesting in other ways to their audience. From an industry perspective, if the words we share online most often emphasise particular criteria, like the unusual aspects of an event or positive emotional reactions, then these may be indicators as to how journalists could shape their stories for greater shareability.

F. Martin, T. Dwyer, *Sharing News Online*,
https://doi.org/10.1007/978-3-030-17906-9_6

Here linguist Monika Bednarek, a co-investigator on the Sharing News Online team, uses computational techniques to examine how the language of a set of most highly shared stories constructs newsworthiness, providing insights into how news might be packaged for an era of social sharing.

INTRODUCTION

This chapter shifts our focus to the language of most shared news stories. In it I analyse how language contributes to constructing such items as newsworthy. That is, the chapter asks a series of questions: What news values are construed in shared news and how? What linguistic patterns can be found? (Bednarek 2006; 2015a) What can these factors tell us about the shareability of news on social media?

A considerable amount of non-linguistic research has explored the use of social media by audiences for news consumption and exchange within social networks (e.g. Olmstead et al. 2011; Hermida et al. 2012; Bruns et al. 2013), with many studies seeking predictors of, reasons for and causes of information sharing (such as status seeking, socialising, entertainment, physiological arousal)—which may include the sharing of news items (e.g. Berger 2011; Lee and Ma 2012; Weeks and Holbert 2013).

However, little research is available on the linguistic characteristics of viral online news (an exception being Blom and Hansen 2015 on 'clickbait'). Nevertheless, some non-linguistic research has examined characteristics of the content of shared news. In their study of 'most emailed' *New York Times* articles, Jonah Berger and Katherine Milkman (2011: 5–6) coded articles into positive/negative and evoked emotions (anxiety, anger, awe, sadness) and argued that affect-laden content is more viral, or likely to be highly shared, than non-affective content, while positive articles are more viral than negative articles. However, what they called "high-arousal" emotions are more viral than others, regardless of positivity/negativity. They claimed that content that evokes positive high-arousal emotions (including awe and high amusement), and negative high-arousal emotions (including anger and anxiety), is more viral than content that evokes "more of a deactivating emotion (i.e., sadness)" (Berger and Milkman 2011: 10). In addition, articles that are interesting/surprising and practically useful (informative) are more likely to be 'most emailed'. In contrast to this study, Lars Kai Hansen and his co-authors' (2011: 12) study of tweets suggested that "negative news is more retweeted than positive news", and they concluded that negativity promotes retweeting and virality in news items, but not in non-news. To explain their differing result, these scholars argued that there might be differences between shared stories on email networks and Twitter networks.

In an analysis of most shared UK news stories on Twitter (from BBC, Channel 4, *Guardian*, Sky, *Telegraph*), Nic Newman (2011: 22–24) proposed that the items that tend to do well are breaking news and original, distinctive content. In relation to topic, style and genre, he identified items relating to disasters/deaths, quirky/funny items, and provocative comment/analysis as more shareable. In addition, his analysis of 'mood' factors suggested that most shared stories involve shock/surprise or are funny/weird. Tony Harcup and Deirdre O'Neill's (2017) content analysis of news values in top 10 Facebook stories and the top 15 most tweeted stories also suggests bad, surprising or entertaining news was most frequently shared.

Finally, in Crawford et al. (2015), the industry partners to the Sharing News Online project provided a practice-based perspective on the four qualities that make news shareable, arguing it should be simple, emotional, new/unexpected and triggered (prompted by something).

These and similar analyses tended not to report closely on linguistic features of shared news, as they were focused on other objectives in coding story content, sometimes automated via tools such as sentiment analysis, or on identifying the significance of these changing practices for the media industry and their attendant policy debates. This chapter thus adds a specific *linguistic* focus to investigating 'most highly shared' news.

A LINGUISTIC APPROACH TO NEWS VALUES ANALYSIS

This chapter examines the linguistic indicators of news values (Galtung and Ruge 1965) in the most highly shared news on Facebook. In much of the relevant literature it is assumed that journalists measure and judge the perceived newsworthiness of events according to a set of values such as Proximity, Negativity and Unexpectedness (see Caple and Bednarek 2013). News values are then discursively constructed in writing (Bednarek and Caple 2012), and play a role in story placement, and distribution prioritisation. In this way they make up a professional value system which reflects and reinforces dominant societal ideologies (Bell 1991: 156).

Surprisingly, given their centrality to contemporary journalism, there was little analysis of news values and social media networks or news sharing at the time these analyses were undertaken. In his study of news framing on Twitter, Ben Wasike (2013: 11, 20) claimed that to that point "no studies have looked specifically at [...] news values vis-à-vis media format as pertaining to social media". While Zizi Papacharissi and Maria de Fatima Oliveira's (2012) Arab Spring study analysed tweets around the #egypt hashtag using a combination of content and discourse analysis, their conceptualisation of news values was very broad—they applied 'news values' analysis to all tweets, regardless of type and origin, including expressions of opinion by bloggers and activists. Tony Harcup and Deirdre O'Neill's (2017) recent study of news values in the top socially shared UK stories of 2014, which postdates this analysis, only generally defines the way content was identified with certain values and relied on journalists who had internalised those values to identify them in the texts.

To provide a deeper understanding of the news values encoded in the most highly shared items on Facebook, this chapter employs a new framework—discursive news values analysis (DNVA), developed by myself and linguist Helen Caple (Bednarek and Caple 2017, and previous publications). While it is beyond the scope of this chapter to give a detailed outline of DNVA (see www.newsvaluesanalysis.com), these are the three basic tenets:

- News values are defined as the 'newsworthy' aspects of events (including news actors): Eliteness, Impact, Negativity, Personalisation, Proximity, Timeliness, Superlativeness, Consonance and Unexpectedness (Table 6.1). This list is based on a review of the literature on news values.
- These news values are linked systematically to semiotic resources. See Table 6.1 for a summary and Bednarek and Caple (2017) for a more complete version.
- This provides a framework for analysis—for instance, it becomes possible to identify words and expressions in a text or dataset that may potentially establish newsworthiness. Such forms are labelled 'pointers' to newsworthiness (Bednarek and Caple 2014: 145). However, close attention needs to be paid to the meaning potential of the linguistic resource as used in a news story, as well as to the target audience and time/place of publication.

As Table 6.1 indicates, news values are constructed through a variety of linguistic resources, including place and time references and evaluations of importance, significance or unexpectedness. While Positivity is not included, because it is recognised by some scholars only as a news value

Table 6.1 Linguistic resources for construing newsworthiness

News value	The event is constructed as...	Linguistic resources
Eliteness	Of high status or fame (including news actors, organisations, etc.)	various status markers, including labels, recognised names, evaluations of importance, descriptions of achievement (*experts at Harvard university, a high-profile arrest, Barack Obama, the Oscars, a key federal government minister, top diplomats, were selling millions of records a year...*).
Impact	Having significant effects or consequences (not limited to impact on the target audience)	evaluations of significance (*momentous, historic, crucial...*); reference to real or hypothetical important or relevant consequences (*note that will stun the world, Australia could be left with no policy, leaving scenes of destruction...*)
Negativity	Negative	negative evaluations (*terrible, dangerous, slaughter...*); reference to negative emotion and attitude (*distraught, worried; condemn, criticise...*); negative lexis (*conflict, damage, death, crisis, abuse, controversial, row...*), other references to negative happenings (e.g. the breaching of socially approved behaviour/norms)
Personalisation	Having a personal or 'human' face (involving non-elite actors)	references to 'ordinary' people, their emotions, experiences (*Charissa Benjamin and her Serbian husband; 'It was pretty bloody scary'; But one of his victims [...] sobbed; Deborah ... said afterwards: 'My sentence has only just begun'...*).
Proximity	Geographically or culturally near	explicit references to place or nationality near the target audience (*an Australian; Australia, Canberra woman...*); references to the nation/community (*the **nation**'s capital; home-grown...*); inclusive first person plural pronouns (***our** nation's leaders...*); cultural references (e.g. *prom, haka*)
Timeliness	Timely in relation to the publication date: new, recent, ongoing, about to happen, current or seasonal	indications of newness or change (*fresh, new, latest, for the first time...*); explicit time references (*today, yesterday, within days, now...*); implicit time references (*continues, ongoing, have begun to...*), selected verb tense and aspect (*have been trying, is preparing, is about...*); references to seasonal or current happenings/trends

(*continued*)

Table 6.1 (continued)

News value	The event is constructed as...	Linguistic resources
Superlativeness	Of high intensity or large scope/scale	quantifiers (*many, all, thousands...*); intensifiers (*sensational, dramatically, super, severe, extreme...*), including intensified lexis (*epidemic, smashed, stun, wreck...*); references to growth/escalation (*growing, raised...*), repetition (*building after building...*); some instances of metaphor/personification/simile (*a tsunami of crime; epidemic swallowing Sydney, looked like the apocalypse...*); comparison (*biggest counter-terrorism raid, most shocking child abuse case...*).
Consonance	Stereotypical	constructions of stereotypes, for example through evaluations of expectedness (*notorious, famed for...*) or similarity with past (*typical style, once again...*)
Unexpectedness	Unexpected	evaluations of unexpectedness (*different, astonishing, strange...*), comparisons that indicate unusuality (*the first time since 1958, Sydney's wettest August in 16 years*); references to surprise (**shock at North Cottesloe quiz night; people just really can't believe it...**); references to unusual happenings (**British man survives 15-storey plummet...**).

Image: Monika Bednarek

and may play a role only in the creation of some types of news, this chapter will consider both Negativity and Positivity in order to explore if stories with one or the other valence are shared more by users.

In the rest of the chapter DNVA is used to analyse how news values are constructed in 'most highly shared' news items. It only reports on analysis of language, while images—and their interaction with language—are analysed in Bednarek and Caple (2017).

DATASET

This case study analyses a dataset (corpus) of 99 online news items whose URLs were widely shared among Facebook users. The decision to start with a small corpus was deliberate, as it allowed a combination of quantitative and qualitative analysis. The corpus is limited to English-language items originating with print and broadcast 'heritage' news media organisations, both 'popular' (e.g. *Daily Mail*) and 'quality' (e.g. *The New York Times*).[1] Items from other media organisations were excluded (including 'digital natives' such as *Buzzfeed*, magazines such as *Time* and specialist publications such as *Hollywood Reporter*) due to their social sharing bias or specialist content focus. The business model of *Buzzfeed*, for example, centres on promoting sharing and it publishes much content that would not traditionally be called 'news', such as funny cat videos. Facebook sharing was the focus because Facebook is the top social media platform for news internationally (Newman et al. 2017) and has been called the 'news powerhouse among the social media sites' (Anderson and Caumont 2014).

To compile the corpus, Share War's Likeable Engine analytics software was used to extract the top 200 items by total Facebook share count as at early September 2014. From these, only items that could be considered as traditional written news stories were collected, excluding any visual-centric items (e.g. photo essay, image gallery, video), opinion and analysis (e.g. advice, explainers, commentary), interactives (e.g. quiz, test), features, obituaries, interviews and so on. This was done to exclude any items that did not lend themselves to DNVA, as their communicative function was not necessarily to construct events as newsworthy. Items were included in the corpus if they described an event, happening or issue concerning other participants and if the reported event was either new or a new development. The selection decisions were made on the basis of visiting each of the 200 URLs and assessing each item manually in turn (see Bednarek 2016). The resulting dataset includes mainly hard news, soft news and research news.

All items in this Shared News Corpus (SNC) come from English-language news media organisations across four different national cultures (the UK, US, Australia, New Zealand). The corpus is US-centric, and contains 69 items from ten US news outlets, 24 items from six UK news outlets, five items from three Australian news outlets and one item from a New Zealand news outlet. The three organisations represented with most items are CNN (23) and Fox News (20) from the US, and *the Daily Mail* (13) from the UK.

[1] News Corp Australia's site news.com.au was also included, bringing together reporting from their print newspapers such as *The Daily Telegraph*, *The Courier-Mail* and *Herald Sun*.

METHODOLOGY

This study combines corpus linguistic techniques with manual, computer-aided annotation. Corpus linguistics is an empirical approach to the analysis of linguistic data that makes use of computer technologies to analyse computerised collections of text (corpora). A corpus linguistic investigation usually focuses on language use and typicality (repeated patterns), and may combine quantitative with qualitative analysis. Quantitative information includes the analysis of frequent words or combinations of words, while qualitative analysis usually proceeds via concordancing. This technique produces all occurrences for a particular search term, together with its surrounding text/co-text (see Fig. 6.1 below). Concordancing is useful for qualitative analysis, as the co-text can be expanded, and because concordances can automatically be sorted in different ways. Corpus linguists may also tag their corpus, which adds information to particular words, for example in relation to their likely meaning (semantic tagging).

Accordingly, the SNC was tagged using the UCREL Semantic Analysis System: USAS (Archer et al. 2002). Each semantic tag denotes the correspondence of an item to one of 21 discourse fields, such as 'Emotional Actions, States & Processes' or 'Time' with 232 subdivisions such as 'Happy/sad: Happy' or 'Time: General: Future'. In other words, the tagging is based on 'semantic fields which group together word senses that are related by virtue of their being connected at some level of generality'

's Ural mountains has injured at least 950 people, as the sho

es were dead. It looked to us at least 70 per cent of the imag

top, inspect minutely and ask at least 6 questions about ever

th's atmosphere at a speed of at least 54,000 km/h (33,000m

en Repeat everything you say at least 5 times. Test 8: Grocer

nothing else on television for at least 5 years. Test 11: Mess

suffered cuts and bruises but at least 46 remain in hospital. /

dicted path. The quake killed at least 222 people, injured nea

mployees, provided they work at least 20 hours a week and hi

cation is anathema, has killed at least 2,300 people since 201

Fig. 6.1   Some concordance lines for *at least*. Image: Monika Bednarek

(Archer et al. 2002: 1). For example, the items *recent, latest, new* all belong to the semantic field labelled 'Time: Old, new and young; age' and are tagged as such. Using a corpus of American newspaper texts, corpus linguist Amanda Potts (2013) found that in approximately 85% of cases the semantic tag listed first in the string of candidates and deemed 'most likely' by the USAS tagger was appropriate. I worked with a list of the most frequent semantic tags, based on the first sense tag and the first domain when multiple tags/domains were assigned and treating multi-word expressions as single tokens. Analysis was restricted to the top 100 most frequent tags.

Further, various frequency lists were extracted from the SNC using the corpus linguistic software programme WordSmith (Scott 2015): a list of word forms, lemmas and n-grams (2-grams, 3-grams and 4-grams). *Lemma* is a term for a 'word' that includes all its respective forms and is reproduced in all caps (e.g. the lemma BE includes the word forms *am, be, was, is,* etc.), while *n-gram* refers to the repeated combination of *n* words (e.g. *of the; at the end*). The lists of word forms and n-grams were sorted according to *range* (the number of items/stories that a word form occurs in), and the lemma list was sorted according to frequency (because sorting according to range was not available). For reasons of scope, analysis of word forms, lemmas and n-grams was then restricted to those occurring across at least 20 (of 99) items. This limit is important as we need to consider occurrences across a range of shared news texts, rather than those occurring in only one or a few items.

Following a similar procedure as that suggested in Bednarek and Caple (2014) and Potts et al. (2015), all lists (word forms, lemmas, n-grams, semantic tags) were examined to identify items and tags that might be 'pointers' to a specific news value, based on their meaning potential (but not their actual use, as comprehensive concordancing was only undertaken if explicitly mentioned below). To identify pointers I consulted the linguistic framework for DNVA introduced above as well as the USAS manual (Archer et al. 2002). Bednarek (2016) provides further information on this process.

In addition to the corpus linguistic techniques (semantic tagging, frequency analysis, concordancing), computer-aided manual annotation was used for the purpose of triangulation. For each of the 99 corpus texts the headline (H) and the lead or opening paragraph (OP) were read and then coded for each news value using UAM Corpus Tool (O'Donnell 2015), a software program that can be used to annotate text manually, with the software then providing the researcher with patterns. Analysis was limited to headlines and opening paragraphs, because in traditional news stories these act as *summary* (van Dijk 1988), *abstract* (Bell 1991) or *nucleus* (Iedema et al. 1994), and contain language that represents the topic as newsworthy (White 1997; Mahlberg and O'Donnell 2008). Often, the lead establishes the 'news values angle', although this is not necessarily the case with all SNC items. Three coding choices were used in annotating headlines and opening paragraphs: 'yes' (the news value is constructed), 'no' (the news value is not constructed), 'possible' (for debatable, unclear, uncertain or special cases—see examples in Bednarek and Caple 2017: 200–203). The coding manual is available online (Bednarek 2015b).[2] In reporting results for each news value below, I will first comment on findings from the identification of pointers in the frequency and tag lists, before providing results from this manual analysis of opening paragraphs and headlines.

RESULTS

Eliteness

Eliteness is signalled in news by references to powerful and prominent figures, and is likely a factor in social sharing although this was not clear from the initial computational analysis. Several items from the frequency lists clearly point to Eliteness, including OFFICIAL, UNIVERSITY, GOVERNMENT, PRESIDENT and US/UNITED STATES, STATE (noun), AMERICAN (the US as elite country/nationality), while the lemmas CITY, AREA, COUNTRY and GROUP would need further investigation as to whether they refer to an elite place or group (e.g. as part of a high-status role label such as *business groups*). Promising semantic tag candidates that would deserve further qualitative investigation are listed in Table 6.2.

Even without concordancing, however, it was clear that not all instances constructed Eliteness—for example, *Afghanistan* would not be considered an elite place in this dataset, and personal names such as *Kathryn* may refer to ordinary people rather than elites. In addition, the semantic field S7.1+ comprises items relevant to the establishment of Eliteness (*leading, chief*), as well as items which are less likely to construe this news value

---

[2] In addition to the manual annotation, Hs and OPs were also analysed using corpus linguistic software, as reported in Bednarek and Caple (2017).

Table 6.2   Semantic tag candidates for Eliteness

Semantic tag and paraphrase	Some instances from the corpus
G1.1 tags (e.g. Government)	Authorities, parliament, congressional, officially, federally, governmental...
S7.1+ (Terms depicting power/authority/influence and organisation/administration)	Leading, lead, managing, leadership, chief, forced, ruled, won...
G2.1 (Law & order)	Rules, police, law, court, regulations, legal, judge...
Z2 (Geographical names)	Washington, Salzburg, Afghanistan, American, Irish, Israeli...
M7 (Places)	Place, country, town, area, region, district, province, hometown...
S5 tags (Groups and affiliation)	Crowd, group, member, team, network, mob, federal, independent, affiliate...
Z3c (Other proper names)	Starbucks, Pepsi, UN, Yale, RSPCA...
Z1 tags (Personal names)	Jim, George, Amy, Kathryn...

Image: Monika Bednarek

(*won*). Thus, it is not currently possible to use a semantic tagger as a news values tagger. At the same time, it was too time-consuming to examine each instance of each tagged item qualitatively.

Manual analysis of headlines and opening paragraphs (based on reading each headline and opening paragraph and using three coding choices, as explained above), however, suggests that 44 Hs and 49 OPs construct Eliteness, while 20 Hs and 16 OPs 'possibly' do so. For instance, words such as *officials, federal, world leaders* and *state* (e.g. *The South Carolina State House*) co-textually construct Eliteness in relation to both news actors and sources (see Bednarek and Caple 2017: 206–207). Where the headline constructs Eliteness, but the opening paragraph does not, the latter tends not to be a typical summary 'hard news' lead, for example:

- Emily Kraus was psyched.
- Let's get ready to … mumble.
- An e. You can write it with one fluid swoop of a pen or one tap of the keyboard. The most commonly used letter in the English dictionary. Simple, right?
- Are you prepared for the impending zombie invasion?
- It was a scene as creepy as a Hannibal Lecter movie.

In such leads, we can see that it is only partially through the construction of news values (e.g. Personalisation: *Emily Kraus was psyched*; or Superlativeness: *as creepy as a Hannibal Lecter movie*) that readers are attracted to the story. Rather, stylistic aspects of language such as direct audience address and rhetorical questions attract audiences to these items, inviting them to engage with the content.

Impact

Impact relates to the significant outcomes and effects of a reported event, which the audience may see as shareworthy. Pointers to Impact in the corpus consist of the noun RESULT and the verbs LEAVE, CAUSE, BECOME, FOLLOW and HELP. While HELP may point to positive impact (if something/someone has helped to achieve a desirable outcome), the other lemmas seem to be lexical markers of causality which establish Impact only if they construct the news event as having significant effects or consequences. With all of the Impact pointers, the co-text would therefore need to be examined. This is also the case with the related semantic tag candidates A2.2 (Affect: Cause/Connected, e.g. *result, cause, factor, causal, link, induced, responsible, consequences...*), A2.1+ (General/abstract terms denoting [propensity for] change, e.g. *transforming, became, occurrence, changed, make a difference, affected, happened...*) and S8+ (Helping, e.g. *rescue, supporting, welfare, blessing, promoting, helps, benefit, aid...*). However, A11.1+ (Abstract terms denoting importance/significance) may be a more promising candidate, as words tagged as such do seem to point more clearly to significance, including: *major, serious, significant, priority, fundamental, important, emergency, crucially, decisive, central*.

The manual analysis of headlines and opening paragraphs suggests that Impact tends not to be explicitly constructed in either, with only 12 Hs and 18 OPs clearly doing so. Modal verbs like *will* or *could* act as important cues to the establishment of Impact in surrounding text. Sometimes the lead makes the impact explicit where the headline does not, as in examples (1–3):

(1) Arizona lawmakers pass controversial anti-gay bill (H)
    Arizona's Legislature has passed a controversial bill **that would allow business owners, as long as they assert their religious beliefs, to deny service to gay and lesbian customers**. (OP)

(2) Federal judge rules DC ban on gun carry rights unconsti-
tutional (H)
A federal judge in the District of Columbia on Saturday overturned
the city's total ban on residents being allowed to carry firearms
outside their home **in a landmark decision for gun-rights
activists.** (OP)

(3) In Medical First, a Baby With HIV Is Deemed Cured (H) Doctors
announced on Sunday that a baby had been cured of an HIV infec-
tion for the first time, a startling development **that could change
how infected newborns are treated and sharply reduce the
number of children living with the virus that causes AIDS.** (OP)

Descriptions of social media impact are an interesting sub-category
where both Impact and Superlativeness are constructed:

(4) A video of the passionate haka performed by the comrades of three
fallen New Zealand soldiers <u>has gone</u> <u>viral</u>, with **tens of thousands
of people around the world watching the clip.**

(5) Stephen Hawking's decision to boycott the Israeli president's conference <u>has gone</u> <u>viral</u>. **Over 100,000 Facebook shares** of the
Guardian report at last count.

Impact here relates to uptake by social media. The answer to the always
present putative audience query *why is this newsworthy?* is here that this
item has already captured massive global audience attention. The presence
of such stories in the SNC (often using the phrase *go viral*) indicates that
heritage news organisations seem to 'piggy-back' on the social media.
They do this by posting news stories about content that has already gone
viral—stories which then become widely shared themselves and which are
not necessarily 'news' in the traditional sense.

Negativity/Positivity

In line with earlier studies of shared news, this corpus suggests Negativity
is a more important news value than Positivity, based on both automatic
and manual analysis. Pointers to Negativity from the frequency lists include
lexis relating to crime and death such as the noun POLICE and the verbs
KILL and DIE. The verb HELP can also construct Negativity when it is
used in connection with human suffering (where help is needed), but as

suggested above it can also construct positive Impact. GROUP may establish Negativity if it accompanies negative words (e.g. *extremist groups*).

The word form *good*, which occurs across 21 different news items, may at first glance appear to construct an event as positive. However, of the 25 instances, many have other meanings (e.g. *a good number of, good morning, good food, good-natured, be a good student, has any good idea about*), and in some instances positivity is negated, contrasted with alternative views or counter-factual:

(6) [Item about prison inmates put on bread and water for destroying US flag]
   'It's just another vindictive policy that has <u>nothing to do with running a **good** jail system.</u>'

(7) [Item about planned ban on large sugary drinks]
   'I think it's a **good** idea,' said Sara Gochenauer, 21, a personal assistant from the Upper West Side. [...] <u>But others said consumers should be free to choose.</u>

(8) [Item about review of animals and plants]
   'This update offers both **good** and <u>bad news</u> on the status of many species around the world.'

(9) [Item about survey that shows that public opinion often deviates from facts]
   How can you develop **good** policy when public perceptions can be so out of kilter with the evidence?

The word *good* also occurs in research contexts in relation to benefits, where the research news itself is evaluated neutrally or positively/negatively, for example:

(10) <u>It sounds too</u> **good** <u>to be true but</u> new research says having dessert—along with the traditional fry up—burns off the pounds. [research news presented as positive]

(11) <u>Bad</u> news for dads: Babies 'should share mother's bed until age three' because it's **good** for their hearts [...] The <u>controversial</u> advice comes from [...] [research news presented as controversial/negative]

In sum, there are only few instances where the word *good* clearly seems to contribute to constructing Positivity, for instance in an item about teenagers saving a five-year-old girl from a kidnapper:

Table 6.3   Semantic tag candidates for Negativity/Positivity

Negativity	B2- (Disease)	*injuries, wounds, disease, hurt, disabilities, diabetes, coma, stroke, cancer, leukaemia...*
	G2.1- (Terms relating to crime/criminal activities)	*terrorism, criminal, fraud, kidnapping, illegal, guilty, crimes...*
	L1- (Terms relating to death)	*death, murder, suicide, killed, died, dead, executed, assassinated, slaughtered...*
	G3 (Warfare, defence and the army; weapons)	*shooting, gun, firearm, weapon, rocket, shot, rifle, military, invasion, war, missiles, ceasefire...*
	E3- (Violent/Angry)	*hit, wallop, angry, violently, assault, furious, attack, cruel, riot, violence...*
	A1.1.2 (Damaging and destroying)	*accident, destroyed, damages, violated, damaged, wreaked, harm, ruins, wreckage, break, crash, slash...*
	W4 (Weather)	*hurricane, snowstorm, flood, tornado, storm, breezy, monsoon, rains, wind, flooding...*
	G2.1 (Law & order)	*rules, police, law, court, regulations, legal, judge...*
Negativity or Positivity	S8+ (Helping)	*rescue, supporting, welfare, blessing, promoting, helps, benefit, aid...*
Positivity	A5.1+ (Evaluation: Good)	*great, good, super, wonderful, OK, well, positive, fine, fantastic...*

Image: Monika Bednarek

(12) Although the suspect remains at large, Temar feels **good** about finding Jocelyn. 'I just feel like I did something very accomplishing today,' the teen said. The girl's family couldn't agree more.

Table 6.3 lists semantic tags that may be associated with Negativity (e.g. disease, crime, death, warfare, violence, damage and bad weather) and those that USAS calls Evaluation: Good.[3] However, the sheer wealth of negative tags indicates that Negativity is a more important news value than Positivity.

---

[3] The USAS category of Evaluation includes 'evaluative terms' depicting quality, truth, accuracy and authenticity (Archer et al. 2002: 5–6), but is not further explained. The difference between negative evaluative language, reference to negative emotion/attitude and negative lexis in Table 6.1 is that evaluative language expresses opinion, while emotion references label emotional experiences, and negative lexis concerns the use of vocabulary to describe negative events without automatically indicating writer dis/approval (see further Bednarek and Caple 2012, 2017).

This assumption is confirmed by the manual analysis. Only 17 headlines and 21 opening paragraphs construct Positivity, while 55 Hs and 51 OPs establish Negativity, and 27 headlines and OPs have unclear or no valence. Positivity is established in a variety of contexts, including in research news and in descriptions of positive acts of heroism, wit, tenacity or kindness (see examples in Bednarek and Caple 2017: 213).

Interestingly, a few instances of Negativity simultaneously establish Unexpectedness, in cases of situational irony:

(13) A Kentucky pastor who starred in a reality show about snake-handling in church has died—of a snakebite.

(14) Suicide Bomb Trainer in Iraq Accidentally Blows Up His Class.

It seems likely that situational irony is a subset of viral news more generally.

Personalisation

The news value of Personalisation is discursively constructed when an event has a personal or 'human' face (involving non-elite actors, including eyewitnesses). From the frequency lists, the nouns CHILD, MAN, WOMAN, FAMILY, PARENT may be classified as pointers to Personalisation, if we assume that they are used to refer to ordinary people rather than elites. The frequency of lemmas pointing to children and families (CHILD, FAMILY, PARENT) is noteworthy here. The relevant semantic tags in the top 100 associated with Personalisation are S4f (Kin, female, e.g. *mother, mummy, bride, wives, mothers, sister, niece*), S2 tags (People, e.g. *people, children, females, man, child, woman, boy, girl*) and Z1 tags (Personal names, e.g. *Jim, George, Amy, Kathryn*). However, if these lemmas and word forms are used in a generic sense or to refer to groups, it is debatable whether Personalisation is constructed. One could argue that any reference to ordinary humans—as in the headline of example 15—is less abstract and more personalised than text where they are not mentioned at all. However, a stronger form of Personalisation is expressed in the opening paragraph of example 15, which focuses on the anxiety of one individual about his family.

(15) Hundreds of kidnapped **Nigerian school girls** reportedly sold as brides to militants for $12, **relatives** say (H)

Samson Dawah was nervous. For two weeks, he had waited for any bit of information regarding his niece, who was among the 234 Nigerian school girls likely kidnapped by the terrorist group Boko Haram. This week, he gathered his extended family. He had news but also an unusual request. He asked that the elderly not attend. He wasn't sure they could bear what he had to say. (OP)

There are also instances where non-elite people are described as engaging in criminal activity (e.g. *Drug addict parents gave 23-month-old son methadone 'like Calpol' before he died of overdose*), which makes them less 'ordinary' and more like 'criminals'. In other words, the news actors are constructed as 'Other' rather than as 'Us'. Both generic/group references and references to the criminal activities of non-elites could therefore be considered as constructing only weak Personalisation (if at all), but make up a considerable amount of the references to non-elites in Hs and OPs (Table 6.4).

Manual analysis shows that reference to ordinary news actors occurs when they are described as agents or patients of negative activities or as otherwise suffering, and also in the context of positive or unexpected events/actions or significant social media impact (Bednarek and Caple 2017: 212–213).

Proximity

Proximity, which refers to the construction of geographical or cultural closeness in relation to the audience, is not clearly relatable to shareability without greater understanding of who is reading the story. Semantic tags

Table 6.4 Personalisation

News value	Sub-category	Headlines	OPs
Personalisation	adults/mix/unspecified	12	14
	Children	10	5
	Total	22	19
Possible or 'weak' Personalisation	Generic or group	20	33
	Engaged in criminal activity	3	3
	Total	23	36
No Personalisation	N/A	54	44

Image: Monika Bednarek

and lemmas that point to the construction of Proximity include the tags Z2 (Geographical names, e.g. *Washington, Salzburg, Afghanistan, American, Irish, Israeli*), M7 (Places, e.g. *place, country, town, area, region, district, province, hometown*) and the lemmas US/UNITED STATES, AMERICAN, STATE (noun), CITY, AREA, COUNTRY. They construe Proximity if they are used to refer to a location close to the news audience. For example, US/UNITED STATES and AMERICAN would construct nearness for North American readers. With the nouns STATE, CITY, AREA and COUNTRY, the co-text and context would show whether or not they refer to locations near the target audience. Similarly, it would be necessary to align geographical references tagged as Z2 and M7 with the news publication in which they occur to gain insights into the construction of Proximity for the original target audience.

However, the manual analysis of headlines/OPs suggests that while 15 headlines and 31 OPs construct Proximity for the original target audience by referring to the country or nationality of the news outlet, the majority (34 Hs/40 OPs) do not. US news outlets do, however, tend to refer to Americans, American locations, institutions and aspects of American culture (Bednarek and Caple 2017: 208–209). An additional 50 headlines and 28 OPs possibly construct Proximity, since they refer to a country that is either geographically or culturally close to the target audience or contain a cultural reference of some kind—such as *prom, Obama, gun-rights, haka*. Note that this analysis of the construction of Proximity for the *original* target audience ignores the audience of Facebook users who *shared* these items, for which Proximity may or may not be established.

Timeliness

It was expected that the news value of Timeliness would be present in most of the shared stories, since the working definition of corpus 'news' items required that the reported event had to be new or a new development. This meant that it wasn't possible to independently explore whether news stories constructed as 'timely' are shared more than news stories not constructed as timely.

Several items from the frequency lists could be used to establish Timeliness (including newness): This includes lemmas that point to constructions of events as recent (LAST, WEEK),[4] immediate (NOW, LATE [includes *latest*]), about to happen (*soon*), continuing (STILL) or starting

---

[4] I categorised WEEK as a pointer to Timeliness but not YEAR or MONTH, on the assumption that references to *last/this year/month*, for example, would in most cases refer to

(the verb START), or as the first (FIRST; *the first*) or otherwise new (NEW, NEWS). In fact, when considering the lemmas NEW and NEWS, the former is a much better predictor of Timeliness than the latter, unless it is part of a proper noun (*New York*). One clear subset of items in the SNC shows that 'newness' is constructed in relation to research—thus, the adjective *new* co-occurs significantly with *study* and *research*.

Semantic tags that seem like potential candidates include:

- T1.3 (Time: Period, e.g. *days, hours, years, months, night, week, period, evening, Monday, May*),
- T 1.1.2 (Time: General: Present; simultaneous, e.g. *now, today, yet, instant, present, updates, meanwhile, instantaneous, currently, tonight, daily, coincides with*),
- T1.1.3 (Time: General: Future, e.g. *will, future, tomorrow, impending, coming, shall, soon*),
- T2 tags (Time: Beginning and ending, e.g. *start, remain, continue, former, beginning, source, remain, established, initial, stopped, still, going on*),
- T3 tags (Time: Old, new and young; age, e.g. *adult/s, x-old, young, baby, recent, latest, original, of this age, middle-aged, new, over the age of, death*), and
- A10+ (Finding, showing, e.g. *revelation, finding, showing, exposed, revealed, traced, indicated, found, debunked*).

Again, it is apparent that semantic tags are too broad for DNVA. For example, 'Time: Old, new and young; age' includes items relevant to the construction of Timeliness such as *recent, latest, new* and irrelevant items such as *years old, age group*.

The manual analysis of headlines and leads suggests that about 70–80% of Hs/OPs construct Timeliness, and the numbers are even higher, especially in the Hs, if 'possible' instances are included.

Superlativeness

The news value of Superlativeness is constructed through language that establishes large scale and scope or high intensity, emphasising the magnitude of news. This study found many pointers to Superlativeness, but it was difficult to argue a simple correlation between that value and

a point in time too far removed from the time of publication to emphasise the Timeliness of the constructed event.

Table 6.5   Semantic tag candidates for Superlativeness

Lemmas, word forms, n-grams	Semantic tag and paraphrase	Some instances from the corpus
GROUP	S5 tags (Groups and affiliation)	Crowd, group, member, team, network, mob, federal, independent, affiliate...
#, MORE, ONE, ALL, TWO, JUST, THAN, SO,	N1 (Numbers)	Two, thousands, 2004, million, 1974, 45...
ONLY, THREE, LIKE, WORLD, EVEN, FOUR,	N5 tags (Quantities, including N5+, N5++)	Percent, handful, dose, set, dozen, several, Some, both, any, amount,
MANY, HIGH, VERY,		number...
SUCH, LEAST, EVERY,		Many, dozens, onslaught, hundreds,
MUCH, LARGE,		multiple, enough, much...
LONG, NUMBER, five,		Increased, more, most, a lot, as well
six, really, several, second,		as, extra, added...
various n-grams with	N5.1+ (Terms depicting	All, any, every, each, full, total...
numbers (# symbol);	maximal/maximum	
more than; at least; the	quantities)	
world	A13.3 (Degree:	Very, highly, helluva, really,
	BoostersIntensifiers that	particularly, increasingly, greatly,
	amplify to a high degree)	extremely, considerably...
	A14 (Focusing subjuncts	Just, only, solely, alone, especially,
	that draw attention to/	exclusively...
	focus upon X.)	
	A13.2 (Intensifiers that	Most, fully, absolutely, literally,
	amplify to the upper	perfectly, absolutely, totally...
	extreme)	

shareability. Table 6.5 summarises semantic tag candidates and items from the frequency lists that point to Superlativeness.[5]

The lemma GROUP can co-textually establish Superlativeness when used to emphasise quantity (e.g. *a huge group of volunteers*). LEAST, *at least* and *more than* are also included on the assumption that they can construct an ensuing number as high. Concordancing of the lemma LEAST shows that of 42 occurrences, 39 are instances of *at least* and most of these are followed by a number, with many constructing the reported event as of high intensity or large scope/scale (see Fig. 6.1). Sometimes Superlativeness is combined with Impact and Negativity in references to

---

[5] In including all these items here (various intensifiers, quantifiers [including numerals], focusing subjuncts, comparison, the noun WORLD and the bigram *the world*), I have been less conservative than with other news values, as some of these can function in different ways (e.g. *so* can be a conjunction as well as an intensifier).

the negative consequences for a large amount of people (... *has injured at least 950 people; killed at least 222 people*).

However, the manual analysis of headlines and leads shows that not all of these construct Superlativeness: 59 headlines and 42 opening paragraphs do not, while 40 H and 54 OPs do. As with most other pointers, further qualitative investigation of Superlativeness indicators would be necessary. While it is not possible to do so for the whole corpus, we can have a brief look at some pointers that occur across at least four opening paragraphs: numbers, word forms and phraseologies. Examination of all 35 occurrences of numbers (#) in the OPs shows that some of them do construct Superlativeness (especially those expressing large amount), while others refer to date and time, the age of news actors, or other aspects (*.22-calibre rifle*). The word forms *world, thousands* and *most* construe Superlativeness in several OPs (with exceptions, e.g. *planned to travel the world*), while the word *one* does so only on occasion. Different modes of expression can be identified:

- vague large number (e.g. *thousands of*) + [ordinary] NEWS ACTOR;
- [ordinary] NEWS ACTOR *around the **world***
- superlative ADJ [+SCOPE] (*our embattled PM's **most** embarrassing moments;... in the **most** ambitious effort yet; **the oldest in the world**; one of the **strongest** storms recorded **on the planet**).

Such and other expressions are used to construct the uniqueness of a news actor (*the oldest in the world*), emphasise the large amount of non-elite news actors involved (*thousands of NEWS ACTOR; NEWS ACTOR around the world*), the degree of an event or action (*one of the strongest storms recorded on the planet; our embattled PM's **most** embarrassing moments*), or the scope of a discovery (*a whole new **world** of ... has come to light*). The pattern superlative ADJ *in the world* seems to be a highly conventionalised strategy, similar to a journalistic practice where *world's* co-occurs with comparative and superlative adjectives and has the meaning 'of the highest measure' (Duguid 2010: 120).

Consonance

Consonance relates to the (stereo-)typical construction of an event (its news actors, social groups, organisations, nations). No potential pointers to Consonance can be identified from the frequency lists (word forms, lemmas, n-grams), while the semantic tag A6.2+ (Comparing: Usual) may indicate instances where Consonance is established in the corpus (including *common, commonly, trend, usual, natural, typical, regular, routinely, standard, normal, average...*), although concordancing would need to confirm this. Generally, it may well be the case that it is rarely individual word forms that are used to establish this news value, but rather that Consonance is construed more implicitly. This hypothesis is confirmed by the results of a previous large-scale corpus study of news (Potts et al. 2015: 170).

The manual, computer-aided annotation of Hs/OPs suggests that 20 headlines and 27 OPs 'possibly' construct Consonance.[6] OPs may provide more information than the headlines, for instance a news actor's national or regional origin, as in (16):

(16) Sheriff: Father kills man sexually abusing his daughter (H)
A **Texas** father caught a man sexually assaulting his 4-year-old daughter and punched him in the head repeatedly, killing him, authorities said. (OP)

In this case, the headline does not indicate where the event took place, whereas the opening paragraph identifies the location as Texas, which may conform to a potential stereotype that some members of the target audience hold about Texans—that they like to take the law in their own hands. The manual analysis also identified some potential co-textual cues to Consonance, such as place and nationality names (e.g. *Texas, Ireland, German*), proper nouns (e.g. *George Zimmerman, Aldi*) and references to professions or roles (e.g. *UKIP candidate, artist, D-day vet*) as well as explicit and implicit evaluation (e.g. *drug addict parents, wacky piano*) and characteristics attributed to a group (*many animal lovers find, most broody mothers see*).

Unexpectedness

No semantic tags were identified that point to Unexpectedness, although the lemma FIRST and the bigram *the first* do—when they construct an

---

[6] Consonance concerns the construction of stereotypes, but it is difficult for the analyst to know the stereotypes held by the target audience of any particular publication. Therefore, a very conservative approach was adopted to the coding of this news value, in that the 'possible' option was always chosen.

event as unusual (e.g. *the first time since*) rather than new (=Timeliness). In fact, the manual analysis of Hs and OPs shows that although some explicit evaluations occur (e.g. *unusual, bizarre, rare, miracle, startling*) Unexpectedness is often constructed by relatively factual descriptions of events that many would evaluate as unusual, as in (17).

(17) The Penguin foundation has a global callout for knitters to make pullovers for penguins in rehab.

It is a reasonable assumption that most readers would be surprised that a) penguins can be in 'rehab' and b) that they would need or wear pullovers. Unexpected research findings are an important sub-category here (examples 18–22):

(18) Researchers at Granada University in Spain have found that beer can help the body rehydrate better after a workout than water or Gatorade.
(19) Tequila shots may do more than lighten the mood at a party; the drink may be beneficial for your health as well.
(20) Logically it may be assumed that the more children a mother has, the more stressed out she will be, but a new study has revealed that this is not the case.
(21) Chocolate cake breakfast could help you lose weight
(22) Semen is 'good for women's health and helps fight depression'

Here the findings are constructed as counter-intuitive—for instance, that consumables with a reputation of being harmful are beneficial or that more children do not mean more parental stress. It appears that research findings that are shared widely tend to be constructed as both new and unexpected. This is a useful insight for different user groups who desire a wider impact (health sector, NGOs, academics).

In total, the construction of Unexpectedness is a feature of 41 headlines and 26 OPs and possibly of a further 48 OPs and 41 Hs, so is the fourth most common news value identified in these elements of the news story.

Quantitative Summary of Results

Tables 6.6 and 6.7 provide a quantitative summary of the results. These numbers represent trends rather than facts, since researcher subjectivity in

Table 6.6 Quantitative trends and potential pointers to news values

News values	'Yes'		'No'		'Possible'		Potential pointers (word forms, lemmas and n-grams with a range of at least 20)	Potential pointers (among top 100 most frequent tags)
	H	OP	H	OP	H	OP	Full text corpus	Full text corpus
Eliteness	44	49	35	34	20	16	OFFICIAL, UNIVERSITY, GOVERNMENT, PRESIDENT, US/UNITED STATES, STATE (noun), AMERICAN (CITY, AREA, COUNTRY, GROUP)	G1.1 tags (e.g. Government); S7.1+ (Terms depicting power/authority/influence and organisation/administration); G2.1 (Law & order); Z2 (Geographical names); M7 (Places); S5 tags (Groups and affiliation); Z3c (Other proper names); Z1 tags (Personal names)
Impact	12	18	86	78	1	3	RESULT, LEAVE, CAUSE, BECOME, FOLLOW, HELP	A11.1+ (Abstract terms denoting importance/significance); A2.2 (Affect: Cause/Connected); A2.1+ (General/abstract terms denoting [propensity for] change); S8+ (Helping)
Personalisation	22	19	54	44	23	36	PEOPLE, CHILD, MAN, WOMAN, FAMILY, PARENT	S4f (Kin, female); S2 tags (People); Z1 tags (Personal names)
Proximity	15	31	34	40	50	28	US/UNITED STATES, AMERICAN (STATE, CITY, AREA, COUNTRY)	Z2 (Geographical names); M7 (Places)

(continued)

Table 6.6 (continued)

News values	'Yes'		'No'		'Possible'		Potential pointers (word forms, lemmas and n-grams with a range of at least 20) — Full text corpus	Potential pointers (among top 100 most frequent tags) — Full text corpus
	H	OP	H	OP	H	OP		
Superlativeness	40	54	59	42	–	3	#, MORE, ONE, ALL, TWO, JUST, THAN, SO, ONLY, THREE, LIKE, WORLD, EVEN, FOUR, MANY, HIGH, VERY, SUCH, LEAST, EVERY, MUCH, LARGE, LONG, NUMBER, *five, six, really, several, second,* various n-grams with numbers (# symbol); *more than; at least; the world* (GROUP)	N1 (Numbers; N5 tags (Quantities); N5.1+ (maximal/maximum quantities); A13.3 (Degree: Boosters); A14 (Focusing subjuncts); A13.2 (Intensifiers); S5 tags (Groups and affiliation)
Timeliness	69	78	8 (+16 N/A)	17 (+4 N/A)	6	–	LAST, WEEK, NOW, LATE [incl. *latest*]), *soon,* STILL, START (V), FIRST, *the first,* NEW (NEWS)	T1.3 (Time: Period); T 1.1.2 (Time: General: Present; simultaneous); T1.1.3 (Time: General: Future); T2 tags (Time: Beginning and ending); T3 tags (Time: Old, new and young); A10+ (Finding, showing)
Consonance	–	–	79	72	20	27	no potential pointers	A6.2+ (Comparing: Usual)
Unexpectedness	41	26	17	25	41	48	FIRST, the first	–

Image: Monika Bednarek

Table 6.7   Quantitative trends and potential pointers to Negativity and Positivity

	H	OP	Full text corpus: Potential pointers (word forms, lemmas and n-grams with a range of at least 20)	Full text corpus: Potential pointers (among top 100 most frequent tags)
Negativity	55	51	POLICE; KILL; DIE (GROUP)	B2- (Disease); G2.1- (Terms relating to crime/criminal activities); L1- (Terms relating to death); G3 (Warfare, defence and the army; weapons); E3- (Violent/Angry); A1.1.2 (Damaging and destroying); W4 (Weather); G2.1 (Law & order)
Positivity	17	21	(*good*)	A5.1+ (Evaluation: Good)
Unclear or no valence	27	27	(HELP)	S8+ (Helping)

Image: Monika Bednarek

coding plays a role. With respect to the potential 'pointers' in the frequency lists and tags, their identification was based on meaning potential rather than actual use, as comprehensive concordancing could only be undertaken in some cases.[7] As these tables illustrate, there is no unequivocal correlation between the frequency of Hs/OPs that construct a specific news value and the frequency of potential pointers. For instance, there are few potential pointers to Unexpectedness, yet this news value is constructed in at least 41 (of 99) corpus items. My hypothesis is that some news values, such as Unexpectedness and Consonance, are perhaps more frequently established through implicit means, including relatively factual descriptions of events—as we have seen with Unexpectedness. The frequency of pointers also depends on differences between linguistic resources. For example, the fact that more items are included under Superlativeness does not in itself tell us that this news value is more important than others in shared news—grammatical items such as intensifiers and quantifiers are simply more frequent in language.

---

[7] Brackets have been used in the 'word form/lemma/n-grams' column to identify questionable pointers, which certainly only construe the respective news value in certain co-texts.

Eliteness, Superlativeness, Unexpectedness and Negativity do seem especially important in the language of shared news.[8] However in general, all 'traditional' news values appear and there is a fair amount of variety in the range of values represented. For instance, it is not the case that Facebook users *only* share items about news actors constructed as 'elite' (e.g. Hollywood stars) or about news constructed as 'positive' (e.g. 'feel-good' stories). This variety might reflect the fact that Facebook users, like other online news consumers, have varying backgrounds, interests and behaviours (see e.g. Olmstead et al. 2011).

As far as the corpus techniques of word lists and semantic tagging are concerned, some key limitations have emerged, particularly in the computational approach adopted. First, further qualitative analysis is required for a comprehensive picture, because not all lemmas/word forms are good predictors for newsworthiness construction (compare the analysis of *good*) and a semantic tagger cannot be used as a news values tagger since the semantic fields are often too broad. Second, news values are not necessarily established by frequently recurring word forms or words from the same semantic field (see Consonance). Unless a specific news values tagger is developed for this purpose, qualitative analysis is crucial.

Further, while I have not commented on this above, at least one of the news items in the SNC ('Historian believes bodies of 800 babies, long-dead, are in a tank at Irish home for unwed mothers') was identified as containing inaccuracies (Walsh 2014). The virality of false, fake or hoax news on social media platforms is clearly a problem for the public and researchers (Lazer et al. 2017). There has been a deluge of misinformation and propaganda on social media channels since 2014, with the emergence of a new industry which aims to design such items to be shared (Allcott and Gentzkow 2017).

CONCLUSION

This linguistic analysis of shared news from heritage news sources suggests the 'traditional' news values of Eliteness, Negativity, Personalisation and Proximity, Superlativeness, Timeliness, and Unexpectedness remain important to social media users. Are surprising/unexpected, positive, and affective/emotional news items shared more, as some studies have sug-

---

[8] Proximity also emerges as important if cultural references are included (see Bednarek and Caple 2017).

gested? This study indicates that unexpected news is an important sub-category of socially shared news, including in relation to research news. It also seems that while Facebook users redistribute a mix of positive and negative items from heritage news media, negativity is a more important news value than positivity, in line with earlier studies of socially shared news. Some of these negative items concern controversial topics (e.g. gun rights, Israel) and some construct the event as high in negative impact (e.g. killing or injuring many people). Together with the fact that children are often mentioned and that surprising news is important, it is also likely that affective news is shared more, since these sub-categories are likely to evoke strong audience emotions. This hypothesis is taken up in the next chapter, where research with a group of news consumers reveals the contours of those affective relations.

The SNC analysis also suggests that there is ground for concern about the type of research news that is widely redistributed—namely, 'unexpected' results of the kind *Chocolate cake breakfast could help you lose weight*. The audience interest in sharing such research news might be to the detriment of other research that is equally, if not more, important, but cannot easily be easily constructed as unexpected, and therefore tends not to be as widely shared. Another concerning finding from a public interest position is the way in which news organisations 'piggy-back' on social media by creating or re-publishing items about viral content (see Chap. 9). Social media platform companies can thus be seen to have a clear impact on the heritage news media agenda, and this is doubly problematic when the socially shared content is inaccurate or deliberately misleading.

From a linguistic perspective, there is considerable variety in the news items that are widely shared, ranging from stories about elites and ordinary people to negative items about deaths, positive acts of heroism or kindness, or items with significant social media impact, to name but a few. The news values constructed in shared news thus represent a range of different societal ideologies and priorities, partly because the individuals who share such news are not a uniform group. This is supported by research into news sharing communities which suggests that there are different clusters or types of online news consumers (Herdağdelen et al. 2013; Zeller et al. 2013), "each of which behaves differently" (Olmstead et al. 2011: 1).[9] If "users are more likely to share news stories that they like and

[9] Further, surveys where respondents identify to what extent they are interested in or consume different types of news (such as science/technology, health/education,

find relevant" (Ma et al. 2014: 612), and, if they differ in their likes and interests, it follows that the content that is shared is also varied. Ultimately, then, this case study has also shown that the type of news that is shared depends at least to some extent on the user who shares it within their specific social networks.

This case study focused quite deliberately on stories shared from the heritage news media. Future studies could replicate this study with non-heritage news media for comparison, and could broaden the dataset to reflect more national diversity in the sampling of most highly shared stories. Likewise, this case study could provide a useful reference point for research in 10 or 20 years' time to explore if and how the heritage media cope with continual digital disruption and if any shifts in newsworthiness have occurred.

References

Allcott, H., and M. Gentzkow. 2017. Social Media and Fake News in the 2016 Election. *Journal of Economic Perspectives* 31 (2): 211–236.

Anderson, M., and A. Caumont. 2014. How Social Media Is Reshaping News. *Pew Research Center Fact Tank*, September 24. http://www.pewresearch.org/fact-tank/2014/09/24/how-social-media-is-reshaping-news/. Accessed 10 April 2015.

Archer, D., A. Wilson, and P. Rayson. 2002. Introduction to the USAS Category System. http://ucrel.lancs.ac.uk/usas/usas guide.pdf.

Bednarek, M. 2006. *Evaluation in Media Discourse. Analysis of a Newspaper Corpus*. London/New York: Continuum.

———. 2015a. Voices and Values in the News: News Media Talk, News Values and Attribution. *Discourse, Context, Media*.

———. 2015b. Coding Manual. https://www.newsvaluesanalysis.com/our-book/.

———. 2016. Investigating Evaluation and News Values in News Items That Are Shared Via Social Media. *Corpora* 11 (2): 227–257.

Bednarek, M., and H. Caple. 2012. *News Discourse*. London/New York: Continuum.

entertainment/celebrity) clearly show variation, with some influence of age and gender (Levy and Newman 2014; Anderson and Caumont 2014). However, what respondents **say** they are interested in may not be identical to the types of news they actually view or share, and results may be different if only social media users are questioned (see Anderson and Caumont 2014 on what types of news Facebook users regularly see, and Bruns et al. 2013 on Australian news topics that receive attention from Twitter users).

———. 2014. Why Do News Values Matter? Towards a New Methodological Framework for Analyzing News Discourse in Critical Discourse Analysis and Beyond. *Discourse & Society* 25 (2): 135–158.

———. 2017. *The Discourse of News Values: How News Organisations Create Newsworthiness*. Oxford: Oxford University Press.

Bell, A. 1991. *The Language of News Media*. Oxford: Blackwell.

Berger, J. 2011. Arousal Increases Social Transmission of Information. *Psychological Science* 22 (7): 891–893.

Berger, J., and K.L. Milkman. 2011. What Makes Online Content Viral. *Journal of Marketing Research*, Ahead of Print, pp. 1–17. https://doi.org/10.1509/jmr.10.0353.

Blom, J.N., and K.R. Hansen. 2015. Click Bait: Forward-Reference as Lure in Online News Headlines. *Journal of Pragmatics* 76: 87–100.

Bruns, A., T. Highfield, and S. Harrington. 2013. Sharing the News: Dissemination of Links to Australian News Sites on Twitter. In *Br(e)aking the News. Journalism, Politics and New Media*, ed. J. Gordon, P. Rowinski, and G. Stewart, 181–209. Bern/New York: Peter Lang.

Caple, H., and M. Bednarek. 2013. Delving into the Discourse: Approaches to News Values in Journalism Studies and Beyond. *Oxford: Reuters Institute for the Study of Journalism*. The University of Oxford. https://reutersinstitute.politics.ox.ac.uk/sites/default/files/Delving%20into%20the%20Discourse_0.pdf.

Crawford, H., D. Filipovic, and A. Hunter. 2015. *All Your Friends Like This: How Social Networks Took Over News*. Sydney: Harper Collins.

Duguid, A. 2010. Newspaper Discourse Informalisation: A Diachronic Comparison from Keywords. *Corpora* 5 (2): 109–138.

Galtung, J., and M.H. Ruge. 1965. The Structure of Foreign News: The Presentation of the Congo, Cuba and Cyprus Crises in Four Norwegian Newspapers. *Journal of Peace Research* 2 (1): 64–91.

Hansen, L.K., A. Arvidsson, F. Å. Nielsen, E. Colleoni, M. Etter. 2011. Good Friends, Bad News: Affect and Virality in Twitter. Paper Presented at The 2011 *International Workshop on Social Computing, Network, and Services (SocialComNet 2011)*, Loutraki, Crete, Greece.

Harcup, T., and D. O'Neill. 2017. What Is News? News Values Revisited (Again). *Journalism Studies* 18 (12): 1470–1488.

Herdağdelen, Amaç, Wenyun Zuo, Alexander Gard-Murray, and Yaneer Bar-Yam. 2013. An Exploration of Social Identity: The Geography and Politics of News-Sharing Communities in Twitter. *Complexity* 19 (2): 10–20.

Hermida, Alfred, Fred Fletcher, Darryl Korell, and Donna Logan. 2012. Share, Like, Recommend. *Journalism Studies* 13 (5): 815–824.

Iedema, R., S. Feez, and P. White. 1994. *Media Literacy*. Sydney: Disadvantaged Schools Program, N.S.W. Department of School Education.

Lazer, D., Baum, M., Grinber, N., Friedland, L., Joseph, K., Hobbs, W., and Mattsson, C. 2017, May. Combating Fake News: An Agenda for Research and

Action. Harvard Kennedy School Shorenstein Center. https://shorensteincenter.org/wp-content/uploads/2017/05/Combating-Fake-News-Agenda-for-Research-1.pdf.

Lee, C.S., and L. Ma. 2012. News Sharing in Social Media: The Effect of Gratifications and Prior Experience. *Computers in Human Behavior* 28 (2): 331–339.

Levy, David, and Nic Newman. 2014. *Reuters Institute Digital News Report 2014.* Oxford: Reuters Institute for the Study of Journalism.

Ma, Long, Chei Sian Lee, and Dion Hoe-Lian Goh. 2014. Understanding News Sharing in Social Media. *Online Information Review* 38 (5): 598–615.

Mahlberg, M., and O'Donnell, M.B. 2008. A Fresh View of the Structure of Hard News Stories. In S. Neumann and E. Steiner (eds.). *Online Proceedings of the 19th European Systemic Functional Linguistics Conference and Workshop,* Saarbrücken, 23–25 July 2007. http://scidok.sulb.uni-saarland.de/volltexte/2008/1700.

Newman, N. 2011. *Mainstream Media and the Distribution of News in the Age of Social Discovery.* University of Oxford: Reuters Institute for the Study of Journalism, September 2011. https://reutersinstitute.politics.ox.ac.uk/sites/default/files/Mainstream%20media%20and%20the%20distribution%20of%20news%20in%20the%20age%20of%20social%20discovery.pdf.

Newman, N., R. Fletcher A. Kalogeropoulos, D.A. Levy, and R. Kleis Nielsen. 2017. *Digital News Report 2017.* University of Oxford: Reuters Institute for the Study of Journalism. http://www.digitalnewsreport.org/.

O'Donnell, M. 2015. UAM Corpus Tool. Version 3.2. http://www.wagsoft.com/CorpusTool/download.html.

Olmstead, Kenny, Amy Mitchell, and Tom Rosenstiel. 2011. Navigating News Online: Where People Go, How They Get There and What Lures Them Away. *Pew's Research Center's Project for Excellence in Journalism.* http://www.journalism.org/analysis_report/navigating_news_online. Accessed 25 August 2013.

Papacharissi, Zizi, and Maria de Fatima Oliveira. 2012. Affective News and Networked Publics: The Rhythms of News Storytelling on #Egypt. *Journal of Communication* 62 (2): 266–282.

Potts, A. 2013. *At Arm's Length: Methods of Investigating Constructions of the 'Other' in American Disaster and Disease Reporting.* Ph.D. Thesis, Lancaster University, UK.

Potts, A., M. Bednarek, and H. Caple. 2015. How Can Computer-Based Methods Help Researchers to Investigate News Values in Large Datasets? A Corpus Linguistic Study of the Construction of Newsworthiness in the Reporting on Hurricane Katrina. *Discourse & Communication* 9 (2): 149–172.

Scott, M. (2015). *Wordsmith* (Version 6.0.0.235 – 2/08/2015). [Computer Software]. http://www.lexically.net/wordsmith/.

van Dijk, T. 1988. *News as Discourse.* Hillsdale, NJ: Erlbaum.

Walsh, J. (2014). That Story About Irish Babies Buried in a Septic Tank Was Shocking. It Also Wasn't Entirely True. *New Republic*, June 24. https://newrepublic.com/article/118316/800-irish-babies-buried-septic-tank-was-partly-bogus-story. Accessed 2 January 2017.

Wasike, B.S. 2013. Framing News in 140 Characters: How Social Media Editors Frame the News and Interact with Audiences Via Twitter. *Global Media Journal – Canadian Edition* 6 (1): 5–23.

Weeks, B.E., and R.L. Holbert. 2013. Predicting Dissemination of News Content in Social Media: A Focus on Reception, Friending and Partisanship. *Journalism & Mass Communication Quarterly* 90 (2): 212–232.

White, P.R.R. 1997. Death, Disruption and the Moral Order: The Narrative Impulse in Mass Media "Hard News" Reporting. In *Genres and Institutions: Social Processes in the Workplace and School*, ed. F. Christie and J.R. Martin, 101–133. London: Cassell.

Zeller, Frauke, Joshua O'Kane, Elizabeth Godo, and Abby Goodrum. 2013. A Subjective User-Typology of Online News Consumption. *Digital Journalism* 2: 214–231. https://doi.org/10.1080/21670811.2013.801686.

CHAPTER 7

Affect and the Motivation to Share News

Fiona Martin and Virginia Nightingale

In mid-2014, there was a global outcry when a Facebook research team was revealed to have experimented on 689,003 of the platform's users, trying to manipulate their emotional states by changing the content of their news feeds, without their explicit consent for the research.[1] The finding of its 'emotional contagion' study (Kramer et al. 2014) argued that people's moods, and their subsequent news sharing, can be affected by the content they view on their news feeds—or, as the abstract rather naively indicated (given decades of media effects studies), feelings can be transferred from one person to another "without direct interaction between people (exposure to a friend expressing an emotion is sufficient), and in the complete absence of nonverbal cues" (ibid.). Despite the flaws in that research, which we'll explore shortly, this study exemplifies a particular fetish of social media research, which has been to explore for commercial gain how emotions and feelings impact on what we share online.

Corporate interest in exploiting our visceral reactions for persuasion and profit has given rise to theories of 'affective capitalism'. To affect is to act, or have an impact, on something; to touch or move someone emotionally. Affective capitalism encapsulates all the ways in which our body/brain reactions and intuitive ties to people, places and things are monitored, patterned and analysed in order to create goods and services that will

---

[1] The team consisted of Adam Kramer, then head of Facebook's Data Science section, and two academics from Cornell University, then graduate student, Jamie Guillory and Professor Jeffrey T. Hancock, now at Stanford.

© The Author(s) 2019
F. Martin, T. Dwyer, *Sharing News Online*,
https://doi.org/10.1007/978-3-030-17906-9_7

exploit those instinctive responses. It is the commodification of expressive thought and action, the push for us to put moods and 'gut feeling' before reflection in our response to marketing strategies (Karppi et al. 2016). Affective capitalism is apparent in concepts like neuromarketing, sensory branding and emotional design and in the expansion of notification systems. It also binds news, and older affective regimes, to the commendary circuits of social media, which act to encourage our spontaneous but regularised contributions to platform datasets. Further as McStay (2016) argues we are seeing greater commercial use of capture, biofeedback and analysis technologies, or what he terms "empathic media", to understand our feelings, moods and emotions.

News is replete with emotion (Peters 2011), a vehicle for affective relations that triggers our desire to articulate and share our feelings, and to seek out others who will value and validate them. On social media we can do that instantly, amplifying not only the message but the intensity of the feeling attached to it. This chapter addresses two key sociological questions—what motivates people to share news they find online, and what feelings are involved in their decision to commend a story?—with an interest in the ways that culture and its intersection with the politics of news making inflect the answers. In our study we explored the answers via a survey of our industry partner's audience, the users of what was then ninemsn, an online co-production of Australia's Nine News Network and Microsoft Network (see Appendix). In surveying the literature for this work, we recognised that not enough public research investigates why people share in a specific cultural context, with attention to audience demographics. So, we took the opportunity to involve a group of commercial news users in sharing activities and to document their choices and rationales for action in real time. Here we present the findings of that research, comparing them to the results of existing sharing studies and Share Wars' own theories about why people share news on social media.

We begin by revisiting the key propositions about news sharing motivation—that it is triggered by emotional arousal, that it is status seeking, politically motivated and informational. We look at the strong evidence for sharing being influenced by people's immediate feelings about an event or issue, and discuss why we are interested in research that explores the broader nuances of people's emotional investments in story sharing and their *affective relations* with their social networks. We also examine why the concept of *affect* is critical to understanding people's decisions to share social media content, and why Facebook's contagion study represents far less interesting avenues for investigating sharing behaviours than those attuned to culture and politics.

The chapter then explores six facets of our audience research with the ninemsn audience: the cultural context for news sharing, the nature of the cohort (including gender, location and age), the emotional trigger for sharing, the factors that made stories shareworthy, the feelings the stories evoked and the expectation of a response from people's sharing networks and considers how these map onto traditional news values.

This study reveals the majority of the sample participants shared stories to inform/educate or to show they cared, rather than to amuse, inspire or amaze, although there were marked gender and age differences in sharing motivation. The aspect of the story that triggered sharing also varied by age and by gender. We found, for example, that women more often shared stories that made them feel sad or heartwarmed, while the men shared stories about which they felt angry. Overall the findings suggest that emerging social media editorial strategies need to closely consider cultural differences in user interests, and less sensationalist motivations for sharing than might be signalled by click-driven metrics.

REVISITING THE QUESTION OF MOTIVATION

In Chap. 2 we established that online news sharing is motivated by the desire for different kinds of social connectedness and triggered by a strong reaction to the act of viewing shareable content. There are, of course, many factors that contribute to the reasons people share news online: their interest in the topic, content visibility or prominence in the news feed, and the viewer's bond with the person or company that posted it. Early uses and gratifications studies propose people share YouTube videos for inter-personal expression, that is, to communicate about oneself and to "have a voice in the marketplace of information" (Hanson and Haridakis 2008); while students sharing news on Facebook, Twitter, RenRen and YouTube did so primarily in order to access information, to socialise with others, and to build status in their social network (Lee et al. 2011).

However these types of studies give an instrumental understanding of sharing, with little discussion of the social or cultural context underpinning sharing behaviour. As Macskassy and Michelson (2011) argue in their study of retweeting, context is critical to understanding why someone might share content. They put forward four models which explain Twitter sharing, and which sometimes operate concurrently: the general model, where people retweet recently seen news of interest; the recent communication model, where people retweet something from a person they've recently been in contact with; the on-topic model, where the content is relevant to the retweeter's ongoing interests; and the homophily model, where someone retweets content from a user with a similar profile. Commendary activity is also driven by historic and politically inflected rationales for social connectedness, such as we see in the #BlackLivesMatter or #MeToo social media movements.

Yet the embodied impetus tying our desire to share with the act of selection and exchange is affective. It is based on our immediate reactions to media representations, the feelings these generate, the intensity of those sentiments and their impact on our actions. Affect, feeling and emotion are as important to mobilising civic engagement as reason or ideology (Papacharissi 2015). They are also critical factors for journalism studies to explore as media use becomes more mobile, personalised, and surveilled for evidence of our taste and preferences.

Affect in socio-psychological terms refers to the study of emotions and the physiological responses that accompany them. In cultural studies, however, it refers to the intriguing pre- or proto-conceptual gap between content and effect, the various forces that pass through and between bodies in the moment before acting, the influence and intensity of emotional encounters (Massumi 1995; Steigworth and Gregg 2010). Affect, as Massumi says, is related to the exercise of power but it is "proto-political. It concerns the first stirrings of the political, flush with the felt intensities of life. Its politics must be bought out" (2015: 5). There is a vast literature that demonstrates some of the politics of affect, with major debates between cultural studies scholars, social scientists, computing science and the neurosciences about its nature, location, operation, relationship to intentionality and meaning (Cromby and Lewis 2016; Leys 2012; Wetherell 2012; Serrano-Puche 2015). In particular, recent research into how machines might replicate and demonstrate affect may be key to our future relationships with artificial intelligence (Norman et al. 2003) and the new orders of automation and wealth creation emerging from Silicon Valley.

Our interest is not to intervene in these debates, but to explore the ways in which audiences interpret their own affective relationships to news sharing, and what this might mean for future studies of digital media sociality and cultural connectedness.

For more than 30 years, psychologists, sociologists and creative industries researchers have explored the different ways in which our emotions, feelings and immediate reactions to representational stimuli like online media are related to, and influence, our cognitive processes and actions (Norman 1988, 2004; Wetherell 2012; Benski and Fisher 2014). In prosaic terms, marketing psychology research has established that physiological and emotional arousal increases the likelihood of information sharing (Berger 2011, 2013, 2016; Berger and Milkman 2012; Nikolinakou and Whitehill King 2018). However, there is a deal of conflict about the extent to which particular emotions sponsor news sharing behaviour. According to Berger and Milkman (2012: 1) news that is "high-arousal positive (awe) or negative (anger or anxiety)" will be more 'viral' than that which "evokes low-arousal, or deactivating, emotions (e.g., sadness)". Hansen et al. (2011) add nuance, showing newsy tweets with negative sentiment were more likely to be shared than those with positive sentiment. Yet Song (2016) argues bad news is more likely to be shared than uplifting news, "because negative information draws more attention than positive information", a claim we noted in Chap. 4 that focuses us on the context for sharing.

Context was not a particular concern of Facebook's emotional contagion research, which, aside from demonstrating very small effects, fails to consider the complexity of emotional expressions used on social media (Van Ryn and Fordyce 2014) and in doing so ignores the interpretive issues with sentiment expressed as sarcasm and other forms of humour. It also failed to consider the affective impact of different forms of expression in posts—photographs, GIFs and video, focussing on the text rather than the representational qualities of commendation. Certainly, these types of studies are driven by the data analytics and engineering science approaches used to manage and monitor platform activity. We, in contrast, wanted to know what news sharing means to the people who do it.

Working out why users might share any given news story is complicated by the opacity of the algorithmic factors that govern news placement and promotion on social media platforms. The composition of news feeds is personalised and time variable, making large-scale comparative studies of how story presence impacts commendation a significant investment in audience recruitment, data capture and analytics. However, in the case of our study, we had access to a group of dedicated news sharers via our industry partner ninemsn, and the chance to interrogate their commendary decision making in real time via an online survey.

The Sharing News Online Survey

Ninemsn users are a distinct and valuable type of commercial news audience online. At the time we conducted our survey, the Nine News website was one of the leading news services in Australia and still is in, or near, the top ten depending on the measurement system used (Roy Morgan 2018; Nielsen 2019). It was also partnered with Microsoft Network at the time we started our research, and so was intimately linked in socio-technological terms to the platform ecosystem driving change in news media. Finally, Nine News has long been associated with a populist news agenda, exemplified by its tabloid current affairs television (Rowe 2000), in which techniques of affect are extensively used to capture audience attention. Thus, we can assume most of our respondents will have been primed to affective engagement with online news by their regular exposure to ninemsn's output.

We set out to survey ninemsn users at the moment that they shared content from the website to Facebook in order to capture their immediate affective responses to the stories they'd selected for commendation. Their sharing action triggered an online survey invitation, formulated according to research ethics approved at the University of Sydney, and was also meant to trigger the capture of the shared URL. Due to technical issues with the captured script, we were unable to match survey answers to the shared stories for most of the cohort, limiting the scope of our planned analysis. However, we received a strong response to the survey, which was offered to each person who shared a story online from the ninemsn news site from 8 March 2016 to 18 April 2016, and was completed by 4446 respondents.

The survey explored two main questions. First, what motivates people to share news stories they find online? Second, what emotions are involved in the decision to share a story? We explored the issue of motivation by asking participants the reason for their sharing and what it was about the story that made the respondent decide to share it. To gauge the emotions involved in sharing news stories online, we asked firstly how the story they shared had made them feel, and secondly how they felt (in general) when others 'liked' or responded negatively to their shared stories.

The survey was constructed in collaboration with our partners, and its final version reflects their preference for brevity in the light of potential survey fatigue. It also reflects the emotive responses they were foregrounding in their model for news sharing (Crawford et al. 2015: 116–158). The survey consisted of five multiple choice questions:

RQ 1. Why did you share this news story?
RQ 2. What was it about this story that prompted you to share it?
RQ 3. How did this article make you feel?
RQ 4. When others 'like' and comment positively on your posts, do you feel...? (choose one of options offered)
RQ 5. When others comment negatively on your posts are you...? (choose one of options offered)

The survey, which can be found at the end of this chapter, included the opportunity for respondents to provide comments in the 'other' option, in response to Questions 1 and 3, so we gathered some qualitative data to support the quantitative analysis. In addition to the main survey questions, respondents were asked to volunteer their gender and age information, along with their postcode. The age categories reflect audience measurement conventions rather than Australian Bureau of Statistics standard groupings which use multiples of five years.

OUR SURVEY RESPONDENTS

When we compared the age and gender breakdown of our sample with both the Australian national population data and the ninemsn audience profile, it was obvious that older men and women had been more likely to respond than other age groups. Women 46 years and over were significantly more likely complete the survey than other ninemsn users (Tables 7.1 and 7.2).

Table 7.1 Sharing News Online audience survey demographics, April 2016

Age	Gender		Total
	Female	Male	
18–24	67	28	95
25–30	163	35	198
31–35	180	66	246
36–45	573	246	819
Over 46	1997	1091	3088
Total	2980	1466	4446

Image: Fiona R Martin

Table 7.2   Sharing News Online audience survey demographics comparison, April 2016

Age	Female %			Male %			Totals %		
	Survey	Ninemsn	Pop	Survey	Ninemsn	Pop	Survey	Ninemsn	Pop
18–24	2	3	6	1	3	6	2	6	12
25–30	4	3	9	1	9	10	4	12	19
31–35	4	11	9	1	9	9	5	20	18
36–45	13	15	9	6	9	8	19	24	17
46+	45	20	18	25	18	16	70	38	34
Totals	67	52	51	33	48	49	100	100	100

Image: Fiona R Martin

Given the nature of our sample, we have been cautious in drawing con-clusions about the younger respondents compared to other age groups. Nevertheless, we believe that the information our survey provides is an interesting indication of motivations and emotions associated with online sharing news, and particularly of the views held by older women (1997 respondents) and men (1091 respondents).

A bonus for our survey came in the form of respondents' qualitative comments in the 'other' options included for Questions 1 and 3. For Question One 1912 respondents (20.5%) chose to comment on what it was about the story that prompted them to share it, and for Question Three 2684 (15% of survey respondents) commented on how the story made them feel. Some respondents used these comments fields to create a sort of mini-dialogue about their story sharing:

> #75219851   9/04/2016   Female, 46+
> *Q 1: What prompted you to share this story?*
> A. To help find this little girl alive and unharmed. I am hoping others will share it also so that it is seen by as many people as possible.
> *Q 3: How did this article make you feel?*
> A. Scared for the life of this toddler and extreme sadness for the par-ents, friends and families. Anxious to get the public to stop what they are doing and, actively and urgently, help find this little child.

WHY DID YOU SHARE THIS PARTICULAR NEWS STORY?

For RQ 1, respondents were asked to choose one only of the answer options. However, 1126 of the survey respondents chose more than one option, and for this reason their answers could not be included in the statistical analysis, leaving a total of 2799 respondents as the sample size for this question. Significantly 83% of the 2799 respondents selected 'to show I care about the topic' or 'to educate/inform others' (Table 7.3).

There was a marked gender difference between men and women, especially in the older age categories. Overall men were more likely to choose the pedagogical rationale over the caring one, while women were fairly evenly split between the two. While no significant statistical differences were demonstrated among the options chosen by the younger members of our sample, differences were shown to be significant for the 36+ and the 46+ groups. Women in these age ranges favoured "to show I care" as a sharing motivation, where men 36–45 were more likely than women in their age range to choose to share to "shock and surprise" or "for a laugh" (Fig. 7.1). A significant number of men 46+ also selected "for a laugh", and also "to educate and inform" compared with others in their age category. Overall, though, these results indicate the majority of respondents were concerned about the people around them and the world they live in.

Just over 20% of our sample responded to RQ1 by choosing the 'other' option. Their comments reveal something of the multiple social roles news sharing plays in everyday life, linking individuals with each other, with their society and culture and with the economic, judicial and governmental institutions that structure their work, education and political worlds. For our respondents, there are three main motivators for sharing a story:

Table 7.3 Motivation for sharing news from ninemsn, Sharing News Online audience survey

Why did you share this particular news story	F	%	M	%	Total %
To shock/surprise my friends	95	4	65	6	5
For a bit of a laugh	137	6	103	9	7
To show I care about the topic	773	43	310	34	40
To educate/inform others	759	41	419	47	43
To inspire my friends	91	5	47	4	5
Totals	1855		944		100

Image: Fiona R Martin

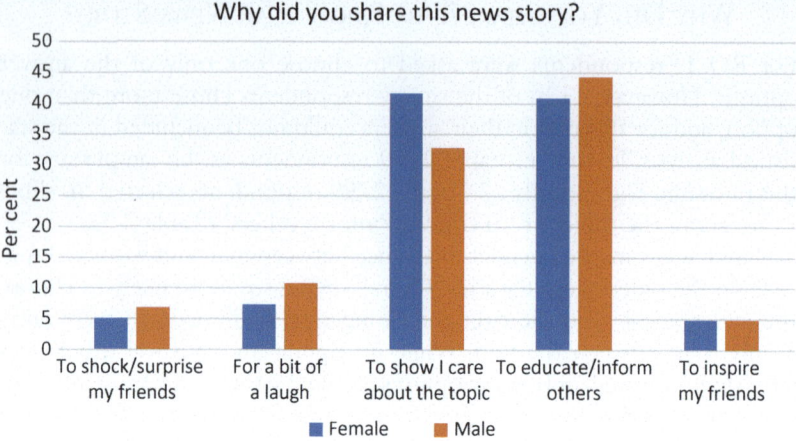

Fig. 7.1 Gender differences in motivation for sharing news from ninemsn, Sharing News Online audience survey. Image: Fiona R Martin

the experience of proximity or personal connection to the subject matter; the desire to intervene in news events and to express an opinion.

Proximity

Proximity is a key value in news production, but appears most strongly as a motivation for sharing in the survey comments for RQ1. Many of the survey respondents said they shared stories because they identified some aspect of themselves, their activities or their personal world in the subject matter, corresponding with both the on-topic and homophily models of motivation mentioned earlier. Their sense of proximity to the story ranged across personal involvement in the story (statements such as "I was there"; "I filmed it"; "I am a victim"); family interest or involvement; geographic proximity (they have lived or been near this location) and a perceived shared interest with others in animal welfare. The latter is unsurprising as domestic animals like cats and dogs figure so highly in the intimate social lives of people in the West, and also in Share Wars data about most highly shared story topics.[2]

---

[2] As our research partner Andrew Hunter argued at the start of this project, "Dogs rule. Stories about dogs are shared far more than stories about cats. Not only are dogs more share-

As is evident in the examples quoted below, the comments often provide evidence of multiple motivations for story sharing. Some refer to the existence of an 'other' for whom sharing a story about a particular topic makes sense, as evidenced in references to friends and family, and those with shared experiences. These following examples demonstrate some of the many ways respondents indicated their *personal involvement* with the story content. They have been chosen to highlight the diverse levels of involvement that prompt sharing, along with the varying emotional commitments to the story content the sharer claims, from a deeply heart-felt pleading to a light-hearted "I am a redhead".

#4597718946   19/03/2016   Male 46+   Happy; Sad
Q 1: What prompted you to share this story?
I was affected by the culprit in this story
Q 3: How did this article make you feel?
Sad that it happened and happy that the culprit has been caught.

#4663503654   17/04/2016   Female   Happy,   Sad,
Heartwarmed, Approving
Q 1: What prompted you to share this story?
I suffer from depression and it hit close to home. I felt exactly the way he described until now … I now have the courage to go speak to my friends about my struggle.

#4654900692   13/04/2016   Female 46+
Q 1: What prompted you to share this story?
I am a victim

#4664970381   18/04/2016   Female 31–35   Happy,
Heartwarmed
Q 1: What prompted you to share this story?
I'm a redhead and loved to hear of this!

able, they are more newsworthy. When we crunched the data from our first major data set in 2012, dogs featured in double the number of headlines as cats. Why dogs? They are interwoven so much tighter into the human story. In part because they are so much better at acting like humans. It turns out that animals acting like people equals sharing gold" (Walkley Foundation 2015).

#4663506748   17/04/2016   Male   46+   Happy,
Heartwarmed, Approving
Q 1: What prompted you to share this story?
I am of the same generation, I had a great friend who lost his life over there and we were able to inter him at home and very pleased to see that the same honour can be given to others.

Many stories were chosen because the sharer believed that they would prove of *interest to family or friends,* as also evident in some of the examples above. These examples show how identifying the relevance or interest for others can prompt sharing. Here the social connection is negotiated through the experience of a loved one, with whom we presume the story was shared.

#4646991777   09/04/2016   Female 46+
Q 1: What prompted you to share this story?
My husband is particularly interested in prehistoric history of the world in general and has interesting theories about Neanderthals.

#4646781909   09/04/2016   Female 31–35   Happy
Q 1: What prompted you to share this story?
My husband was one of the victims who was never paid for his 2 weeks training by 7Eleven at Toongabbie when he was a student. But he chose not to go ahead to get the claim.

The *geographic location* of the story and even the way the story exemplified some aspect of a location were sufficient to prompt its sharing. The referencing of places in the story often became a means to bridge the distance between separated families and friends. Sometimes this involved nostalgia for locations of past personal significance; at other times it became a way of demonstrating to others the natural wonders or particular characteristics of place. Once again, the importance for the sharer of identifying some aspect of themselves or their experience in the story stands out.

#4662071731   15/04/2016   Male 46+   Sad
Q 1: What prompted you to share this story?
I have a sister living in Southern Japan and posted to inform my family.

#4593113129   17/03/2016   Male   36–45   Happy,
Heartwarmed, Approving
Q 1: What prompted you to share this story?
Because I'm a proud Dane and the world needs to know how amazing
Denmark is

#4654476574   13/04/2016   Female 36–45   Sad
Q 1: What prompted you to share this story?
I was at this beach

#4654432000   13/04/2016   Female 46+   Happy
Q 1: What prompted you to share this story?
We actually stayed at here on a recent visit to Tasmania. Lovely quaint
town.

#4579386195   13/03/2016   Female 46+   Happy
Q 1: What prompted you to share this story?
I was born and raised in Melbourne. Met an American when I was 21
and have lived in the US since 1969, but "Still Call Australia Home". I
have other Australian friends that live in Canada or the US, and share
for them to see, but more important, so that my friends can see and
appreciate what "I left". Face Book has helped a lot in this regard.
Q 3: How did this article make you feel?
I like to keep up with what is happening at home.

#4654366681   13/04/2016   Female 46+   Amused
Q 1: What prompted you to share this story?
Uniquely Australian to share with o/s friends

#4608554960   24/03/2016   Male   46+   Happy,
Amused
Q 1: What prompted you to share this story?
To show my friends in USA they don't have all the stupid criminals in
their country, we have our own.
Q 3: How did this article make you feel?
RAFLMAO, what an idiot

#4576593463   12/03/2016   Female 46+   Sad
Q 1: What prompted you to share this story?
Friends, Family and I lived in this town for many years so wanted to
share the story as they may not have seen it.

Finally, references to *close feelings for animals* being the reason for sharing a story were less numerous but also more varied than expected in the survey data. They included a general commitment to animals and animal issues as much as reference to particular animal types or pets.

#4663309027   17/04/2016   Female 46+
Q 1: What prompted you to share this story?
I love dogs and a wonderful story about them is great for others to see, plus we live in an amazing and the best country in the world, and I love to show Australia to the rest of the world.
Q 3: How did this article make you feel?
Fantastic, I love dogs and we should all look after them and other animals, they have a place in this world, no harm should come to them.

#4638814711   06/04/2016   Female   46+   Happy, Heartwarmed, Amused, Approving
Q 1: What prompted you to share this story?
Especially with regard to animal issues, I feel it's important to highlight their amazing contribution to the lives of humans.

#4631184795   02/04/2016   Female   46+   Happy, Heartwarmed, Amused
Q 1: What prompted you to share this story?
My daughter loves pandas so wanted to share cute story.

#4629270041   01/04/2016   Female 46+   Disgusted
Q 1: What prompted you to share this story?
People I know who also have an extreme love of horses.

#4615153477   27/03/2016   Female   46+   Happy, Heartwarmed, Approving
Q 1: What prompted you to share this story?
Because I have held up traffic with a couple of others in Eltham, Victoria to help out an injured kangaroo, and I received abuse, also a Ute sped through the traffic and adding insult to injury, ran over its tail. Luckily a lovely girl was wrapping up the Roo's joey and saved it. Sad comment on Victorian drivers—perhaps I need to move to QLD!

#4602712695   22/03/2016   Female 46+   Happy
Q 1: What prompted you to share this story?
I sculpt goannas.

#4583936536   15/03/2016   Female   46+   Sad,
Heartwarmed
Q 1: What prompted you to share this story?
I love rabbits. I have 5 and they're out during the day and locked up
safely at night, without distress they are trained.

#4567132330   08/03/2016   Female   46+   Happy
Wanting more information
Q 1: What prompted you to share this story?
In the US we are working to restore the Monarch Butterfly population
and other pollinators.

Making an Intervention

A second factor encouraging our respondents to share the story was the
desire to *intervene in the news event*; to play a role in spreading the information gained from the news, with the associated hope of having an effect
on the outcome. It is of interest here that the set responses for this question included "to show I care" and "to educate/inform", yet many survey
respondents clearly felt that they wanted to be more specific about how
they show they care and why they were keen to amplify story information.

It is likely that a Royal Commission enquiry into institutional child
sexual abuse which reported in September 2015 had sensitised the public
to issues of child harm and sexual abuse, as many respondents express
strong views about these topics, particularly the complicity of church
workers in abusive acts. In the cases of news missing children the respondents also describe a depth of feeling about the lost child or a sense of
urgency induced by the story. More complex issues lend themselves to
respondent interventions in several ongoing issues, as, for example, with
the Sally Faulkner/60 Minutes saga (Barnard and Innis 2016; Meade
2016). This case was used by respondents to call out Channel 9 news
reporters for encouraging people to break the laws of other countries, and
to comment on issues of domestic violence and bullying.

Respondents' powerful emotional reactions to news were illustrated
where they engaged in a rant about issues that upset them. For example,
one respondent wrote a 400-word diatribe about the "type of stories
Ninemsn are running!" Another wrote 200 words, partly in capital letters,
to vent her anger about a woman who killed her child. A significant number of RQ1 comments referenced stories of political misdemeanours, with

respondents evidencing a deep mistrust of politicians, for example as "corrupt", arrogant and ripping people off.

In keeping with the preference for sharing "to show I care", news stories about missing or endangered children recurred frequently in the comments on sharing. The comments demonstrate a strong belief that the action of sharing will make a difference by enlisting the aid of others for solving the problem.

> #4647168036   09/04/2016   (age, gender not disclosed)
> *Q 1: What prompted you to share this story?*
> To get people who pray, to pray for God to help the police in all their searching, and to pray for her and her family.
> *Q 3: How did this article make you feel?*
> Very concerned for her safety, and for her family's anxiety.

> #4647693275   09/04/2016   (gender   not   disclosed)
> 36–45 Angry
> *Q 1: What prompted you to share this story?*
> To help spread the word about the missing girl in the article in the hopes that more people will know and increase the chances of someone helping police find her safe and sound.

> #4646982248   09/04/2016   Female   46+   Angry,
> Sad
> *Q 1: What prompted you to share this story?*
> So that others will know to keep a look out for the little girl, the more people know the better the chance of finding the child.

> #4664683258   18/04/2016   Female 46+   Sad
> *Q 1: What prompted you to share this story?*
> The more people who see this article may just save a life by its circulation.

Expressing an Opinion

Respondents showed a strong interest in expressing an opinion about current and ongoing news stories. Many were keen to state their views when there was uncertainty about the evolving story, or when the topic concerned systemic social or cultural problems (politicians' entitlements; domestic violence; Indigenous disadvantage; political correctness; the judicial system; the performance of the media).

#4652194964   12/04/2016   Female 46+   Sad
Q 1: What prompted you to share this story?
I shared this article because I believe that this might be a situation where post natal depression could have been a trigger. It's not an excuse by any means but maybe if mum had help with how she was feeling her baby girl might still be here. Just my opinion.
Q 3: How did this article make you feel?
Very sad because of what happened to an innocent baby. And sad because her mum might have needed help or suffered from postnatal depression. It is a very heartbreaking situation.

The comments about sharing of Sally Faulkner/Channel 9 stories show how one topic can motivate a range of affective responses through different framing of the issue. Some respondents saw the story through the prism of domestic violence. Others found the story primarily to be one about the arrogance of the Australian media. In all cases disgust was a motivating emotion, sometimes alongside anger.

#4665958363   18/04/2016   Female 46+   Disgusted
Q 1: What prompted you to share this story?
When I am too disgusted by an injustice I have to say something. In this case I find the attitude of the father of the children unacceptable, one to have failed to return the children as prescribed by an Australian Judge, then by refusing to withdraw the charges against his wife. I find him despicable and a coward.

#4664753030   18/04/2016   Male 46+   Disgusted
Q 1: What prompted you to share this story?
To show another example of the media sensationalizing another story without getting all the facts. It also shows that people don't know what the truth is anymore and are quite happy to twist the story.

#4654554022   13/04/2016   Male   36–45   Angry, Disgusted, Disapproving
Q 1: What prompted you to share this story?
To show my anger for the Australian media thinking they can go anywhere in the world and do what they want without consequence

Domestic violence issues received considerable attention during the survey period and this was reflected in the stories shared. The respondents who shared domestic violence stories were keen to not only share their personal experience but also advice on seeking help.

#4565356560   08/03/2016   Female   46+   Angry, Sad, Disgusted
Q 1: What prompted you to share this story?
I have had daughters go through abuse with their ex partners every women needs to know there is help out there

#4567880810   09/03/2016   (age, gender not dis-closed)   Angry, Sad, Disgusted
Q 1: What prompted you to share this story?
I have been in a relationship that was this bad. He tried to kill me several times and kept me and my son locked in the bedroom. He is now going to prison for aggravated assault against me. This is an inspiring story, thank you.
Q 3: How did this article make you feel?
Compassionate towards her

#4568442208   09/03/2016   Female   25–30   Sad, Disgusted, Disapproving
Q 1: What prompted you to share this story?
I have lived similar torment it takes a long time to get over and affects society and future generations in a harmful way. often these things are hard to prove later and there should be more compassion and under-standing of this sort of thing
Q 3: How did this article make you feel?
I used to live through similar. society should be less judgemental more aware and compassionate. a lot of this kind of thing is ignored and causes problems for years to come.

A strong sense of injustice and frustration about legal process permeated the comments. This was particularly the case where stories concerned the outcomes of criminal trials or prisoner releases. Respondents called for changes to law and berated police for inaction, clearly hoping that their intervention might make a difference.

The sharing of intense feelings about celebrity also motivated both respondent commendations and survey comments. Celebrity news created an opportunity for people to express this connection and in particular their relationship to musicians.

In March and April 2016 the Australian classic rock band AC/DC was forced to reschedule some of its scheduled US tour dates due vocalist Brian Johnson's hearing loss. Johnson had been advised to stop touring and performing immediately or risk total deafness. Survey comments indicated the depth of fan passions:

> #4565329958   08/03/2016   Male 46+   Sad
> *Q 1: What prompted you to share this story?*
> I have been a fan of this band since they first started, it breaks my heart to see what has happened, it broke me when Bon died, I sing there material and always will

On 10 March 2016 ninemsn announced the death of Australian entertainer Jon English and the story remained current until after his funeral on 4th April. Respondents' reactions were uniformly sad, and in comments they spoke of need to share the news to express their feeling for English as a friend, an industry colleague, a legend and an "important identity in Australia [whose death] needs to be publicised to the world!" (#4570024382).

WHAT WAS IT ABOUT THIS PARTICULAR STORY THAT PROMPTED YOU TO SHARE IT?

There were few clear differences across the sample as a whole in response to this question about content triggers. Women were, however, more likely to share a story because of the people the story was about (sig 0.027) or because the topic had interested them for a long time (sig 0.005). When analysed for age differences, the 35+ age groups were more likely to share because of the person it was about (sig 0.34), to make a stand about an issue, and to show their views. The 31–35 age group was less inclined to share a story because of the danger it warned of, and, contrary to assumptions about the power of awe-inspiring stories, all were less likely to share because the story was amazing. The 46+ age group was more likely to share because of a long-term interest in the topic, and the youngest group were less likely than others to share for this reason (see Fig. 7.2).

We decided to cross-tabulate the results for Questions 1 and 2 to ascertain the strength of the associations between the reasons for sharing and the story content that prompted sharing. Using Kendall's Tau and a 0.01 level of significance, we noted that respondents who shared their story to

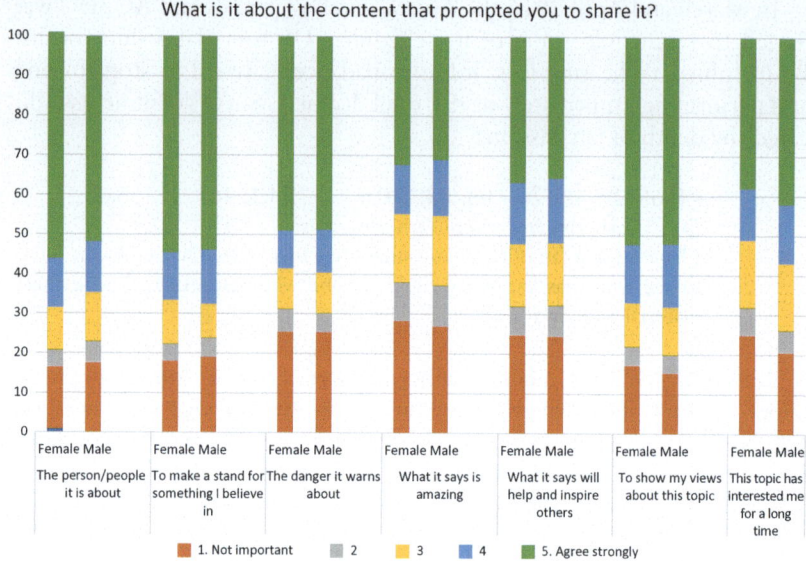

Fig. 7.2 Gender differences and degree of significance in content triggers for sharing news from ninemsn, Sharing News Online audience survey. Image: Fiona R Martin

show that they care were likely to say they did so because it showed their views about the topic (0.236), "to make a stand about something I believe in" (0.226), because of "the person/people it is about" (0.182) or because "this topic has interested me for a long time" (0.148). Those who said they shared the story to educate/inform others were likely to indicate they did so because of "the danger it warns about" (0.151).

How Did This Story Make You Feel?

When respondents were asked about the feelings they associated with stories they shared, there were again quite marked gender differences (see Fig. 7.3). Women were more likely to share stories that made them feel sad and heartwarmed, while for the men stories about which they felt angry were more likely to prompt sharing. These results were highly significant (sig. 0.01). Men were also more likely to share stories about which they felt disapproving, disgusted and amused than women.

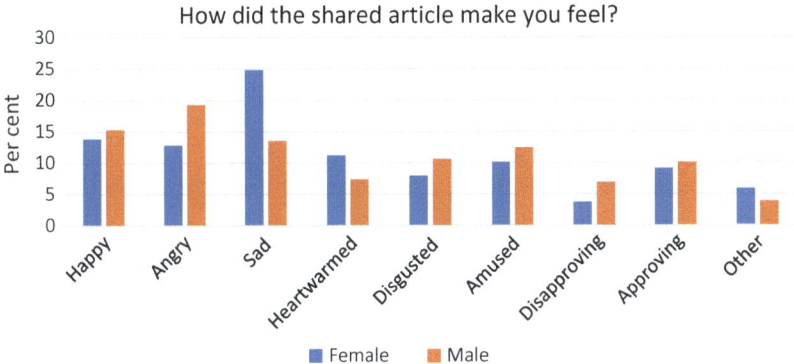

Fig. 7.3 Gender differences in affective responses for sharing news from ninemsn, Sharing News Online audience survey. Image: Fiona R Martin

Some age-related differences between the groups are worth noting. The 25- to 30-year group responses showed few differences between men and women across all the categories, except 'angry', where men were more likely to feel angry in reaction to the story they shared. The 'angry' reaction was shared with men 46+, while men 31–45 said they shared stories they found 'amusing', and men 36+ and 46+ shared stories that made them feel 'disappointed'. The oldest male group, 46+, was the only group to say they felt 'disgusted' by the story. Women in all age categories other than the 25–30 age group were significantly more likely to be sharing stories that made them feel 'sad' and women 36+ and 46+ shared stories they found 'heartwarming', and women 46+ were more likely to choose the 'other' category when answering this question.

We also looked for correlations between the reasons respondents gave for sharing a story and the feelings aroused by the story shared. Predictably our strongest correlation was between those who found the story amusing and sharing the story for a laugh (0.513). Finding the story amusing was also associated with sharing the story to shock others (0.208). Finding the story sad was significantly associated with sharing it to 'show I care' (0.270), and finding the story heartwarming was positively associated with sharing the story to inspire others (0.243). Again, using Kendall's Tau, these findings were significant at the 0.01 level.

To ascertain whether there were possible relationships between the content triggers for story sharing and the feelings our respondents claimed

Table 7.4   Correlations between content triggers and affective reactions to sharing news from ninemsn, Sharing News Online audience survey

	People	Amazing	Inspire	Interest	Views	Make a stand	Danger
Happy		0.191	0.156				
Heartwarmed		0.203	0.176				
Approving				0.137			
Amused							
Sad	0.16						
Angry					0.173	0.21	0.225
Disgusted							0.174
Disapproving							

Image: Fiona R Martin

in reaction to the story, we cross-tabulated answers to RQs 2 and 3. Again using Kendall's Tau and 0.01 significance level, our strongest results showed correlations between sharing the story to make a stand and feeling angry about the story (0.21), and sharing a story because of the danger it warned of with feeling angry (0.225) or disgusted (0.174). Sharing a story because of the views it expressed also showed a positive correlation with feeling angry about the story (0.173). People who shared because they thought a story amazing were more likely to feel happy (0.191) and heartwarmed (0.203). Sharing to inspire others was correlated with feeling happy (0.156) and heartwarmed (0.176); and sharing a story because of an ongoing interest in the topic was associated with feeling approval about the story (Table 7.4).

This table lists only our strongest positive correlations. While we recognise that correlations do not provide evidence of causation, it seems apparent that there are two emerging patterns of sharing here: feeling warm and fuzzy about stories prompts sharing of amazing and inspiring stories; and feeling angry and disgusted prompting sharing to express one's views, make a stand and warn others of danger.

As noted earlier 15% of our sample chose to answer RQ3 using the 'other' option. In doing so they appear to be seeking a more elaborated language of emotion than it was possible to offer in the survey's set answer options, and which speak to the limitations of those options. By far most of the comments were one-word affective responses, such as "horrified", "disillusioned", "heartbroken", "surprised", "shocked", "suspicious" and "sick to the stomach". Clearly the language of emotion included in the set

Table 7.5 Emotional modalities in reactions to sharing news from ninemsn, Sharing News Online audience survey

Emotional modality			%	Comment examples
Interest	Anticipation	Vigilance	17	Aware; hopeful; informed, intrigued; fascinated
Ecstasy	Joy	Serenity	5.5	Happy; relief; fantastic; awestruck
Admiration	Trust	Acceptance	10	Inspired; vindicated; relieved; admiring
Terror	Fear	Apprehension	14.5	Vulnerable; concerned; worried; scared, helpless
Amazement	Surprise	Distraction	18.5	Shocked; disbelief; alarmed; dumbfounded, confused
Grief	Sadness	Pensiveness	11	Heartbroken; nostalgic; shattered
Loathing	Disgust	Boredom	9	Sick in the guts; appalled; contemptuous; sickened
Rage	Anger	Annoyance	14	Annoyed; angry; frustrated, outraged; upset

Image: Fiona R Martin

responses was inadequate to capture the more nuanced reactions our respondents felt they experienced, and grouping this range of responses provided another set of challenges.

We decided to use Robert Plutchik's (2003) wheel of emotions as a template for organising the responses. Plutchik recognises eight emotional modalities, which we cross-referenced with the comments made in response to RQ3 (Table 7.5).

Interestingly, the modalities not represented in the survey options—those in the interest, terror and amazement spectra—were those that rated most highly, which provides something of a control for our survey options. The next most common comment response was perhaps the strongest of the surveyed emotions: rage, followed by sadness and only then admiration.

WHEN OTHERS 'LIKE' AND COMMENT POSITIVELY ON YOUR POSTS ARE YOU …?

In RQ4 and RQ5 we hoped to gauge how others responses might influence our decisions to comment on a news story. These questions referred to their general sharing responses rather than being reflections on the story they had just shared.

Table 7.6   Responses to positive commendations on news sharing from ninemsn, Sharing News Online audience survey

	Disagree (%)	Neutral (%)	Agree (%)
Pleased	32	21	47
Encouraged	35	21	44
Taken Aback	71	22	7
Honoured	58	19	23
Surprised	66	20	14
Humbled	58	21	21
Disapproving	85	11	4
Approving	43	21	36

Image: Fiona R Martin

We first asked the respondents to rate their reactions to positive comments about the stories they had shared in the past (see Table 7.6).

Overall, the majority of respondents agreed that they would feel either 'pleased' (47%) or 'encouraged' (44%) when others commend their posts. Over a third said they would approve of this response. They readily agreed that they would **not** disapprove (85%) when others react positively, or feel 'taken aback' (71%). These were the strongest reactions overall, as indicated in bold text in the above table. Most would not feel 'surprised' (66%) 'honoured' (58%), or even 'humbled' (58%) by the approving reactions of others (Table 7.6).

The only significant gender difference based on our statistical analysis was in the relative strength of agreement or disagreement with the options offered. Women more strongly disagreed that they felt taken aback, honoured, disapproving or even approving than men when others comment positively on their posts.

WHEN OTHERS COMMENT NEGATIVELY ON YOUR POSTS ARE YOU…?

We then asked respondents to indicate how they felt about negative comments occasioned by their sharing (Table 7.7).

Here there is general agreement among our respondents that negative comments have little impact on the sharing of news stories online, though there is some indication that men are less discomforted than women by negative comments. Respondents disagreed across the board that they

Table 7.7   Responses to negative commendations on news sharing from ninemsn, Sharing News Online audience survey

	Disagree (%)	Neutral (%)	Agree (%)
Annoyed	62	17	21
Hurt	71	15	14
Angry	71	16	13
Discouraged	72	15	21
Surprised	58	21	21
Reassured	74	16	10

Image: Fiona R Martin

might feel annoyed, hurt, angry or discouraged when others comment negatively on their posts. Nor was there a sense that people might be more neutrally surprised or positively reassured by disapproving reactions. There were, however, some statistically significant gender differences. Men were more likely to disagree that they felt annoyed, hurt, angry or discouraged by negative comments than the women respondents. Men were also more likely to choose the neutral option in response to 'surprised', and the women were more likely to disagree that they felt 'reassured' by negative comments on their posts.

AFFECTIVE NEWS SHARING

This study points to the shifting emotional states that we experience as we consume news, and the complexity of identifying what precisely triggers the sharing impulse. The conflict focus of news stories can provoke conflicting emotional states, as in domestic violence court cases stories that may engender fear or hate at the action, but surprise or happiness at reaching a just legal result. The major difficulty with this analysis then is the complexity of emotional responses that are triggered by reading and then deciding to share a news story. On many occasions survey respondents couldn't nominate an over-riding emotion, and talked about several competing emotions arising as they read. As on respondent noted he was: "Disgusted that they were considered for so much. Happy that they were stopped. Angry others are not aware they were caught off guard and could have been applying for similar amounts." Another was: "sentimental, empathetic, frustrated, sickened". It becomes apparent when reading the welter of affective reactions triggered by ninemsn news that the binary classification of sentiment in informatics research, characterised in Facebook's emotional contagion study, can tell us very little about what motivates people to share news or how their emotions are tied to the content they are consuming and the act of commendation.

We found that motivations, content triggers and responses to sharing are clearly influenced by gender, and sometimes by age. Some patterns follow fairly predictable gender lines. We found men to be more motivated to share news for instructional reasons, and women to demonstrate their care for others. Older men 36+ were motivated to shock, surprise and amuse those in their social media networks. Given the masculinist, heteronormative nature of newsrooms (Adams 2018) it is possible that their output reinforces these cultural differences, with issues framed in ways that encourage those affective responses and their transmission. Certainly it is possible that respondents' overall emphasis on caring and pedagogical motivations could be subject to social desirability bias, with individual respondents wanting to appear altruistic rather than provocative or entertaining. They could also be age biased, in that a younger cohort might have shown a greater tendency towards other factors.

More interesting were the qualitative responses, that suggested proximity, feeling close to a story, as well as wanting to intervene in news communication and to express an opinion were also key drivers of news sharing. While the first driver, proximity, is an 'old' news value, it appears to have renewed meaning in the unbundled world of digital information, where stories are dislocated from brands and markets. Audiences want to express their personal connection to issues, people, animals and places, the ties that bind them to the world. They also appear to want to act on news, both by mobilising and informing others and engaging in the debate.

Comment responses to RQ1 suggest ninemsn users are most motivated to share by some sense of closeness to the content they are reading: a personal identification with it, some sense of its importance to an intimate other (including friend, family members, celebrities that respondents admired and animals they valued or wanted to protect) or a geographic feeling of connectedness to place. Experiencing proximity to an issue or event then might be considered a significant precursor to wanting to share that experience of identification with others, to declare one's link to the news, and the reasons this has significance.

The desire to affect the news—that is, to make an intervention by telling others how they might take action, or to inform others with the hope that they will act on that message—was the second most important motivating factor. This speaks to users' understanding of their commendary skills and capacities, their recognition of themselves as news 'agents', who have a role in redistributing vital information to their social networks. Similarly, respondents' interest in expressing an opinion demonstrates their desire to locate themselves in the world of news, to debate political, social and cultural issues and to identify their connectedness to news actors. It is these motivations that expose online news consumers to the potential for political manipulation, via the sharing of mis- and disinformation, particularly where that content resonates with their confirmation biases.

In terms of content triggers, the story factors that motivated people to commend a news item, the results were less clear-cut. Women appear more invested than men in certain news actors and both share a strong interest in making a stand on issues they believe in as well as topicality. Men are more likely to want to entertain others and older people are more inclined to warn others of dangers. However, in correlating motive and content triggers it become apparent that these factors are intertwined, and warrant further study to understand how story consumption and selection are related to caring and pedagogical commentary intentions.

In investigating the affective responses to news sharing, our research suggests there are both obvious gender differences in the emotional states that prompt sharing behaviours, and clear emotional trajectories, with happier feelings prompting recirculation of uplifting stories, while anger and disgust prompt stories that express personal opinions, or demonstrate care for, and the desire to educate, others. That women are more likely than men to share articles that make them sad is interesting for studies of virality, which so far assume that registers of sadness are deactivating. Instead we find that this emotional state can inspire compassionate responses. A significant number of our respondents, when upset, demonstrated gestures of social concern that indicate how they feel bound to care for, or educate others. In this respect, the age bias of our sample works to highlight an under-researched aspect of online news engagement and activation, *circuits of compassion*.[3] Much attention has been paid, for example, in studies of news commenting to its incivility and aggression, and far less to the ways in which it serves to engender

---

[3] A subject of interest in television studies, particularly around audience reactions to telethons (see Tester 2001).

social solicitude or a sense of community. To the extent that news sharing is motivated by feelings of proximity and care, then, it has the potential for engendering the experience of social cohesion—or at least the sense of agency and feeling of being part of a greater networked social exchange. This sense coincides with the egalitarian potential of sharing promoted by social media platforms, which urge us to connect with others and exchange ideas as a gesture of selfless giving.

Overall, in both the survey and the comment analysis, negative emotions (sadness, anger, disgust) were stronger feelings associated with online news sharing than positive ones (heartwarmed, happy, amused). Men felt anger about the stories they shared far more than women, who were overwhelmingly more inclined to feel sadness. These findings suggest the need for more research investigating how gender, race and other forms of cultural difference are associated with affective responses on social media. This might investigate, for example, how emotional states might sponsor news sharing in different nationalities and ethnic affiliations, and affective journalism ensure broad participation in this important form of social interaction, public engagement and political activity. It would also be intriguing to explore the news sharing behaviours of different types of audiences, public service or community media users, primed in different ways to consume news to see how they respond to certain affective strategies.

More broadly we need to ask what emotions states and affective responses are central to cultivating feelings of trust in journalism in an age of disinformation. As Beckett and Deuze (2016) note, "The old idea of 'hard news' that shocks, frightens, disturbs, and alarms can leave the audience feeling alienated, disempowered, helpless and, worst of all, apathetic, insensitive, and even hostile to learning about our world." Affective reporting agendas and promotional regimes can certainly be used, as Upworthy has done to its commercial advantage, to sponsor more positive engagement with the world. Already public, civic and social journalisms are also producing news framed in more constructive, problem-solving ways than traditional news. However, the reporting agenda of traditional news, and increasingly the misleading circuits of disinformation, are the primary influences shaping our affective relationships and mediated interactions with each other. Automated news distribution technologies, for example, give the potential for weaponising "empathically optimised" misinformation and propaganda (Bakir and McStay, 2017) suggesting a grim future for the veracity of social media news. In the meantime, conflict, rather than proximity, remains the primary news value in commercial journalism, and, it appears, is the main trigger for commercial news sharing, at least in Australia among the Nine news audience. Shifting the industrial obsession with bad news will not be easy if in fact this is the form of news we are most often presented with, and value and reproduce in social exchange, even when we reject its intensity and influence.

In Search of Agency and Engagement

Together with our research into the genres, topicality and language of news sharing in the previous two chapters, this section of our news sharing study has probed the personal, social and cultural associations we have with the news we commend to others. It has enabled us to move beyond the more common uses and gratifications or social-psychological frameworks for online audience research, into the socio-cultural context of news sharing, and the ways in which subject interests, linguistic factors, gender and age, commerce and commercial editorial strategies might affect our commendary tactics. What use is it, for example, for someone to worry about a lost child in a place far from their home and how might sharing this news help them or others? What affective relations might sharing this news ever establish between users and/or news subjects? If we see the operation of commendary culture as partly rooted in our affective responses to news and information, then we can see how both news media and social media platforms benefit from the constant stoking of our concerns and anxieties. They feed our desire to have agency, as well as social and civic engagement. It is also in their interests to remove references to place in news excerpts and headlines, in order to draw us in to examining the proximity of news for our situation. By monitoring the stories we then share, and those we signal great interest in through likes, favouriting or comments, social media platforms can organise to give us more of the same, in the hope of intensifying our commendary behaviours and defining the emotional triggers to which we'll reliably respond.

This reinforcing dynamic suggests a future agenda for digital journalism research. Many audience studies of news sharing, including ours, have been conducted without reference to the significant push regimes of social media and the cultural context of media consumption. Monitoring how users' social media interactions shape their selection of shared information, and this develops over time, will be important to understanding the impact of algorithmic culture on commendary behaviour. Digging further into peoples' commendary choices, and their moments of rejecting the commendary impulse and platform use, will also help us interpret users' relationships with the affect technologies or empathic media being used to measure and marshal their input to social media systems. Only then can we decide to what extent our engagement with news sharing provides us greater agency than analogue news media, and whether it is democratic, demotic or largely algorithmically orchestrated.

Another strand of research we pursued during the Sharing News Online study was to examine the impact of social media companies on media diversity. On one hand, from the platforms, we hear the democratising rhetoric of choice: people can now find the news they want, from anywhere in the world at the time they want it, and can share that with everyone who matters, rather than just those in a geographically defined market. On the other we have the evidence from earlier chapters that news sharing is contributing to the decline of news media influence and the economic model sustaining news production, and to an increase in junk information, hate speech, misleading information and propaganda. The next chapter explores how we might think about media pluralism in light of social media oligopolies, and how we might gauge the actual impact of news sharing on the range and calibre of news sources to which we have access.

REFERENCES

Adams, Catherine. 2018. They Go for Gender First. *Journalism Practice* 12 (7): 850–869. https://doi.org/10.1080/17512786.2017.1350115.

Bakir, Vian, and Andrew McStay. 2017. Fake News and the Economy of Emotions: Problems, Causes, Solutions. *Digital Journalism* 6 (2): 154–175.

Barnard, Anne, and Michelle Innis. 2016. Australian Mother and 8 Others Face Charges in Lebanon Custody Dispute. *New York Times*, April 12. http://www.nytimes.com/2016/04/13/world/middleeast/sally-faulkner-australian-mother-child-custody.html

Beckett, Charlie, and Mark Deuze. 2016. On the Role of Emotion in the Future of Journalism. *Social Media+Society* 2 (3). https://doi.org/10.1177/2056305116662395.

Benski, Tova, and Eran Fisher. 2014. Introduction: Investigating Emotions and the Internet. In *Internet and Emotions*, ed. Tova Benski and Eran Fisher, 1–14. New York, NY: Routledge.

Berger, Jonah. 2011. Arousal Increases Social Transmission of Information. *Psychological Science* 22 (7): 891–893.

———. 2013. *Contagious: Why Things Catch On.* New York, NY: Simon & Schuster.

———. 2016. *Invisible Influence: The Hidden Forces That Shape Behavior.* New York: Simon & Schuster.

Berger, Jonah, and Katherine L. Milkman. 2012. What Makes Online Content Viral? *Journal of Marketing Research* XLIX: 192–205.

Crawford, Hal, Andrew Hunter, and Domagoj Filipovic. 2015. *All Your Friends Like This: How Social Networks Took Over News.* Sydney: HarperCollins.

Cromby, John, and Martin E.H. Lewis. 2016. Affect – Or Feeling (After Leys). *Theory & Psychology* 26 (4): 476–495. https://doi.org/10.1177/095935431 6651344.

Hansen, Lars Kai, Adam Arvidsson, Fin Årup Nielsen, Elanor Colleoni, and Michael Etter. 2011. Good Friends, Bad News-Affect and Virality in Twitter. *Future Information Technology,* pp. 34–43. *Communications in Computer and Information Science* 185. https://doi.org/10.1007/978-3-642-22309-9_5.

Hanson, Gary, and Paul Haridakis. 2008. YouTube Users Watching and Sharing the News: A Uses and Gratifications Approach. *Journal of Electronic Publishing* 11 (3). Online. https://doi.org/10.3998/3336451.0011.305.

Karppi, Tero, Lotta Kähkönen, Mona Mannevuo, Mari Pajala, and Tanja Sihvonen. 2016. Affective Capitalism: Investments and Investigations. *Ephemera: Theory and Politics in Organization* 16 (4). Online. http://www.ephemerajournal. org/contribution/affective-capitalism-investments-and-investigations.

Kramer, Adam D.I., Jamie E. Guillory, and Jeffrey T. Hancock. 2014. Experimental Evidence of Massive-Scale Emotional Contagion Through Social Networks. *Proceedings of the National Academy of Sciences USA* 111 (24): 8788–8790. https://doi.org/10.1073/pnas.1320040111.

Lee, Chei Sian, Long Ma, and Dion Hoe-Lian Goh. 2011. Why Do People Share News in Social Media? In *Active Media Technology, Proceedings of the 7th International Conference,* AMT 2011 Lanzhou, China, September 7–9, edited by N. Zhong, Vic Callaghan, Ali A. Ghorbani, Bin Hu. 129–140. Berlin/ Heidelberg: Springer-Verlag.

Leys, Ruth. 2012. The Turn to Affect: A Critique. *Critical Inquiry* 37 (3): 434–472. https://www.jstor.org/stable/10.1086/659353.

Macskassy, Sofus A., and Matthew Michelson. 2011. Why Do People Retweet? Anti-Homophily Wins the Day! Proceedings of the Fifth International AAAI Conference on Weblogs and Social Media (ICWSM). https://www.aaai.org/ ocs/index.php/ICWSM/ICWSM11/paper/viewFile/2790/3291.

Massumi, Brian, 1995. The Autonomy of Affect. *Cultural Critique,* No. 31. *The Politics of Systems and Environments, Part II* (Autumn 1995), pp. 83–109. University of Minnesota Press. http://www.jstor.org/stable/1354446.

————. 2015. *The Politics of Affect*. Cambridge, MA: Polity Press.

McStay, Andrew. 2016. Empathic Media and Advertising: Industry, Policy, Legal and Citizen Perspectives (the Case for Intimacy). *Big Data & Society* 3 (2): 1–11. https://doi.org/10.1177/2053951716666868.

Meade, Amanda. 2016. 60 Minutes Producer Sacked and Other Staff Warned over Child Abduction Story. *The Guardian*, May 27. https://www.theguardian.com/media/2016/may/27/60-minutes-producer-sacked-and-reporters-warned-over-child-abduction-story.

Morgan, Roy. 2018. Australia's Top 20 News Websites – Visitation in an Average Four Weeks over 12 Months to March 2018. http://www.roymorgan.com/findings/7595-top-20-news-websites-march-2018-201805240521.

Nielsen. 2019. Nielsen Digital Content Ratings, Monthly Tagged, January 2019, Current Events and Global News Sub-Category, Text, People2+, Census. https://www.nielsen.com/au/en/press-room/2019/nielsen-digital-content-ratings-january-2019-tagged-rankings.html.

Nikolinakou, Angeliki, and Karen Whitehill King. 2018. Viral Video Ads: Emotional Triggers and Social Media Virality. *Psychology and Marketing* 35 (10): 715–726.

Norman, Donald A. 1988. *The Psychology of Everyday Things*. New York: Basic Books.

Norman, Donald A. 2004. *Emotional Design: Why We Love (or Hate) Everyday Things*. New York: Basic Books.

Norman, Donald A., A. Ortony, and D.M. Russell. 2003. Affect and Machine Design: Lessons for the Development of Autonomous Machines. *IBM Systems Journal* 42: 38–44.

Papacharissi, Zizi. 2015. *Affective Publics: Sentiment, Technology, and Politics*. London/New York: Oxford University Press.

Peters, Chris. 2011. Emotion Aside or Emotional Side? Crafting an "Experience of Involvement" in the News. *Journalism* 12 (3): 297–316.

Plutchik, Robert. 2003. *Emotions and Life: Perspectives from Psychology, Biology, and Evolution*. Washington, DC: American Psychological Association.

Rowe, D. 2000. On Going Tabloid: A Preliminary Analysis. *Metro* 121/122: 78–85.

Serrano-Puche, Javier. 2015. Emotions and Digital Technologies: Mapping the Field of Research in Media Studies. MEDIA@LSE Working Paper #33. http://www.lse.ac.uk/media@lse/research/mediaWorkingPapers/pdf/WP33-FINAL.pdf.

Song, Sonya. 2016. *Examining Digital Consumption Trends During Breaking News Events*. A Chartbeat Study. Metrics That Matter Special Series. http://lp.chartbeat.com/rs/062-HAC-076/images/Chartbeat_Study_SONYASONG.pdf.

Steigworth, Gregory J., and Melissa Gregg. 2010. An Inventory of Shimmers. In *The Affect Theory Reader*, ed. Gregory J. Steigworth and Melissa Gregg, 1–25. Durham, NC: Duke University Press.

Tester, Keith. 2001. *Compassion, Morality and the Media*. Buckingham, Philadelphia: Open University Press.

van Ryn, Luke, and Robbie Fordyce. 2014. Facebook Emotions Can Be 'Viral' But Aren't Very Contagious. *The Conversation*, June 3. https://theconversation.com/facebook-emotions-can-be-viral-but-arent-very-contagious-27437.

Walkley Foundation. 2015, September 8. All Your Friends Like Dogs Acting Like People: Q&A with MSN's Andrew Hunter on Social Media and the News. http://www.walkleys.com/all-your-friends-like-dogs-acting-like-people-qa-with-msns-andrew-hunter-on-social-media-and-the-news/.

Wetherell, Margaret. 2012. *Affect and Emotion: A New Social Science Understanding*. London: Sage.

CHAPTER 8

Media Pluralism Policies and the Implications of Social News Sharing

Tim Dwyer

In the media pluralism policies of Western liberal nation states, access to diverse news sources is widely regarded as key to the maintenance of an informed citizenry. This assumption and its relation to the risks of concentrated private media power underpin media diversity laws across the world and is one of the central concerns of this chapter on the policymaking implications of news sharing. However, this chapter is written against the backdrop of an optimistic neoliberal proposition, frequently heard in the rhetoric of both industry professionals and politicians. That proposition is that online news sharing is somehow now capable of providing a more democratic, and therefore more relevant, form of news dissemination than the kind previously afforded by legacy media. Here, we want to consider how media researchers and policymakers might assess this claim in terms of traditional ideas of media diversity and pluralism.

In this chapter, we explore concerns about the control of social platforms over political news sharing, and new methods for measuring the social impact of sharing and attendant potential policy responses. We argue that the *Sharing News Online* research methodology (see Chap. 4) provides a useful overview of the key online *news intermediaries* reshaping the mediascape and new resources for exploring voice plurality and quality questions in digital news.

The chapter considers scholarly and regulatory policy analyses of the shift from analogue distribution to online news sharing and consumption through online intermediaries. It notes, for example, the EU's Media

© The Author(s) 2019
F. Martin, T. Dwyer, *Sharing News Online*,
https://doi.org/10.1007/978-3-030-17906-9_8

223

Pluralism Monitor study, which has introduced new ways of assessing member states' digital plurality, including broadband access, concentration of internet service and online content providers (KU Leuven (ICRI) et al. 2009; Brogi 2018). There is a high risk of broadband access being limited in some countries and of cross-ownership concentration in digital media markets, with companies like Google and Facebook dominating.

The furore arising from Facebook's alleged political bias in the US in the aftermath of the 2016 elections is a pivotal event to consider. It was claimed that Facebook's editors routinely suppressed trending conservative political news (Leonnig et al. 2017). Despite little being known about the blackbox of Facebook's algorithmic recommendation strategy, in this instance political pressure forced the company to post its internal editing guidelines for public scrutiny. The evidence that has emerged in congressional investigations regarding the purchase of US$100,000 worth of political advertising on Facebook by Russian 'Troll farms' has renewed the call for public interest interventions (Leonnig et al. 2017). These examples of regulatory impact all suggest that transnational social media companies urgently need to be regulated in the public interest.

The wider argument being made in this chapter is that caution is required in relation to simplistic claims that social media sharing is improving media diversity policies. News provision that relies on algorithms and AI more generally calls for greater scrutiny and targeted interventions in response to the conditions of an "Automated Public Sphere" (Pasquale 2015, 2017). Our suggestion is that the evolving mix of curated (human- or machine-edited) and algorithmic (computer-generated) news is stretching our understanding of media pluralism. The implications of these shifts are having a profound impact on our news diets. A combination of factors including network infrastructure, recommendation algorithms and personalisation, strong and weak ties in social networks (and related ideas of 'filter bubbles and echo chambers') all may have an impact on how people discover or access news, how deeply they engage with it and then how it shapes knowledge.

The evidence suggests that although people often have increasing access to fast internet, mobile connectivity and local and international online news, including specialist and user-generated sources, much of the high-quality news has moved behind paywalls. This, in turn, has led to the rise of freely available online sources and the concurrent risk of people consuming, at best, unreliable news or, at worst, fake news—a rapidly expanding sector designed to exploit social media users' confirmation biases with stories that are factually untrue or misleading (Turfeki 2018). Thus, the proliferation of online news does not counter an underlying tendency for consumption concentration in trusted news media markets. As Pasquale argues, "New methods of monitoring and regulation should be as technologically sophisticated and comprehensive as the automated public sphere they target" (Pasquale 2017: 1).

At the same time social media platforms are becoming more widely understood as commercial monopoly entities offering the ability to collect personal data on a massive corporate scale, and oftentimes in the service of government surveillance. There are growing calls to regulate and rein in the power of the media-tech monopolists. A series of regulatory decisions and debates (in particular in the EU, the US, Spain and Australia) have drawn attention to their power to manipulate and dominate the presentation of news media (and other) content to vast public audiences. In light of these developments in the integrity of news content, the Chairman of Ofcom, Patricia Hodgson, has publicly expressed her view that Facebook and Google are publishers, and should therefore expect greater regulation as time goes by, which apparently is at odds with the CEO Sharon White's view (Ruddick 2017; Napoli and Caplan 2017). There are even calls coming from the progressive business establishment. Liberal investor billionaire George Soros used the 2018 World Economic Forum to out Facebook as a 'menace' to society that required new forms of regulation. When Facebook Chief Operating Officer Sheryl Sandberg heard of Soros' critique, it's reported that she then ordered research be undertaken into whether Soros stood to gain financially from his comments (Confessore and Rosenberg 2018). Clearly on the defensive after the scandal of the Russian election meddling, it has also emerged that as part of its damage control and PR response the platform then "commissioned a campaign style opposition research effort by Definers Public Affairs, a Republican linked firm which gathered and circulated to reporters information about Soros' funding of advocacy groups that mobilised against Facebook" (Confessore and Rosenberg 2018).

For all these reasons we argue that it remains incumbent on democratic governments to ensure that media ownership, pluralism and diversity objectives are maintained in the instruments of media policymaking. Yet, in order for national governments to respond to way that new platform intermediaries are implicated in the distribution and consumption of online news, including through sharing news stories, they must first understand how media plurality and diversity are morphing in the new platform context (Helberger 2018). We turn now to consider the Australian context as a lens for considering these questions because of its existing high levels of ownership concentration. In our view, then, Australia has become, to invoke the popular expression, a kind of 'canary in the coalmine' of media pluralism internationally. This has recently been dramatically underscored by the findings of the main competition policy agency, the Australian Competition and Consumer Commission (ACCC), in its preliminary report of the Digital Platforms Inquiry. These have underscored the dominance of digital platforms in the Australian media landscape, and their deleterious impacts on the sustainability of a viable commercial news media sector (and in particular traditional and now online newspapers), on advertising and on consumers' personal data (ACCC 2018).

THE CONTEXT OF MEDIA PLURALISM POLICIES

The nations that have most influenced Australia's media policymaking in the past—the US and the UK—have embraced the future of media diversity far more constructively than Australia has done so. Although this can be characterised as mostly procedural in the US, and preliminary in the UK, these nations have nonetheless taken the first steps necessary to respond to transitions in the media industries accommodating media convergence in general, and more specifically changes in the news media sector.

The US has had a process of structured media ownership reviews in place since 1996, known as the quadrennial media ownership reviews (FCC 2017a). The two previous US reviews (in 2010 and 2014) concluded in 2016 (FCC 2016) and it was determined that key ownership restrictions, including on cross-media ownership, would be left in place. The cross-media rule imposes ownership restrictions based on a sliding scale that varies by the size of the market. For example, in larger markets where there are at least 20 independently owned "media voices" a media corporation can own up to two TV stations and six radio stations (or one TV station and seven radio stations) (FCC 2017a).

In its 2016 "Report and Order", the Federal Communications Commission (FCC) recognised the continuing importance of traditional media in local communities for viewpoint diversity, particularly for local news and public interest programming, and the rapidly changing ways content is accessed (FCC 2016). It argued:

We recognize that broadband Internet and other technological advances have changed the ways in which many consumers access entertainment, news, and information programming. Traditional media outlets, however, are still of vital importance to their local communities and essential to achieving the Commission's goals of competition, localism, and viewpoint diversity. This is particularly true with respect to local news and public interest programming, with traditional media outlets continuing to serve as the primary sources on which consumers rely ... the public interest is best served by retaining our existing rules, with some minor modifications. (p. 2)

The modifications referenced in the quote relate to measures to enhance innovation and viewpoint diversity, and public disclosure of agreements between media outlets about how content is shared. This has all taken place in a media landscape of far greater ownership diversity than Australia's. Although the US media rules for diversity have been to some extent mired in judicial proceedings in recent years, they nonetheless have been relatively systematic, and underpinned by generally sound public interest objectives. Yet they have continued to be attacked by the now Republican-controlled FCC, who seek to wind back the main ownership restrictions. In a new order and notice in 2017 the FCC moved to fully deregulate the existing rules for sectoral cross-ownership of newspapers and broadcast stations, local TV and radio. In her dissenting statement Commissioner Jessica Rosenworcel comments: "How do we advance journalism when algorithms are ascendant?...The solution doesn't lie in the FCC scrapping from top to bottom its policies to prevent media concentration" (FCC, 2017b: 99). The 2017 order and notice are subject to an appeal filed in 2019 by the Prometheus Radio Project petitioners in the United States Court of Appeals for the Third Circuit (Prometheus Radio v. FCC, 2019).

Meanwhile, from 2015, the main regulatory authority in the UK, Ofcom, has updated its processes for assessing media pluralism in an innovative way that sought to respond to changing media access and consumption (EPRA 2015). It undertook its own research and commissioned expert advisory reports into changing news media consumption. Ofcom has been required to review the UK's ownership rules at least every three years since 2003. The restrictions in place include:

- a rule limiting cross-media ownership of newspapers and TV at a national level to 20% (the 20/20 rule),

- requirements for the appointment of a regional TV news (Channel 3) provider and
- a rule for administering a media public interest test in relation to mergers.

The last point refers to a media-specific pluralism test overseen by the Secretary of State, who was given powers under the 2003 Communications Act to intervene in the cases of media mergers found to be against the public interest. Ofcom and the Competition and Markets Authority (CMA) both have a role in advising the Secretary in relation to the question of whether or not "there is a sufficient plurality of persons with control of media outlets" (Humphreys 2009: 207).

Recognising that ongoing deregulation may have adverse impacts on media pluralism, and therefore media concentration, Ofcom is required to undertake a review of ownership patterns every three years. In its most recent statutory review, Ofcom concluded the rules needed to be retained to protect pluralism. Yet the regulator also foresaw that this would require ongoing reassessment if the importance of TV news and newspapers continues to decline (Ofcom 2015).

In this new framework developed for assessing plurality in news and current affairs content, Ofcom has in place a range of quantitative and qualitative indicators. These are designed to assess the availability of news sources, their consumption and their impact on users. It includes metrics for assessing the number of providers, their internal plurality their reach, share of consumption, news habits and sources, and the personal importance of a source using a bespoke 'share of references' metric.

The UK government, through Ofcom, has recognised that online news access is increasingly important as a news source, and that plurality concerns continue in the online world. There is an active ongoing debate in relation into how the current rules can be further extended to online media, including the administration of the mergers' public interest test and the national cross-media ownership rule. Similarly, the debate in the UK (as it is at the EU level) concerns extending regulation to online providers around questions of 'online harm', conceived broadly as forms of disinformation.

A large proportion of people now access news only via Facebook (Gottfried and Shearer 2016; Reuters 2017). In the US, estimates suggest around 43% of the population use this source for news, and it is far more popular than either Twitter or Reddit, the other networks where users

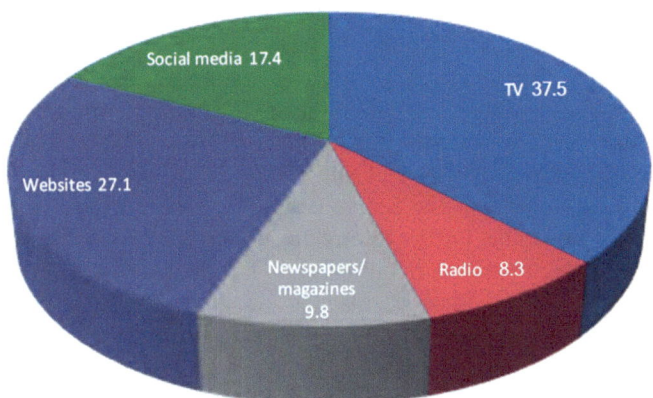

Fig. 8.1 News Brands used via Online Platforms in the week before the survey (%). Survey response to question, "Which, if any, of the following have you used to access news in the last week? Please select all that apply." Image: Reuters 2017/ News and Media Research Centre, Uni of Canberra Fig. 3.2 (Watkins et al. 2017: 30). Courtesy of Sora Park

report high exposure to news (Matsa and Shearer 2018). This pattern of social media dominance can be seen around the world, including in the UK and Australia. Not surprisingly, the results of the research on access to online and social media news sources depend on the specific questions being asked of survey and poll participants. For example, in research conducted for the Australian component of the 2017 Reuters News Study, 27% of respondents, when asked to name their 'main source of news', nominated 'online media' while 17% nominated 'social media'. Around 37% nominated 'TV', and approximately 10% 'newspapers and magazines' (Reuters 2017: 30). This indicates that TV, radio and newspapers remain in a dominant position in Australia (see Fig. 8.1). Conversely, the Pew Research Center in the US notes in a recent study that "the percentage of people who get their news from TV is falling across all categories, as online news consumption increases … but the gap between online and TV news consumption was narrowing" (Pew 2017). Fifty-seven per cent of Americans were 'often' getting news on TV, while "38 percent were often getting news online—a 19 point gap". By mid-2017 "50% of Americans were often getting news from TV, and 43% were often getting it online" (Pew Research 2017).

The key point made by the authors of the Australian 'Digital News Report' was that it is no longer appropriate to assume a relationship between the number and diversity of news sources and the health of liberal democratic society in an era of networked news distribution and a "scarcity of news consumer attention for—rather than a scarcity of access to—this content" (News and Media Research Centre 2017). In these circumstances, the authors recommended to the Senate Committee on the Future of Public Interest Journalism that further research be undertaken to establish the relationship between the number and diversity of news sources in the contemporary public sphere and how that affects civic engagement.

While that kind of research is, of course, very important, their diagnosis of the so-called 'filter bubble' effect in the report is open to critical interpretation. They noted that, on the basis of the survey of Facebook users that they had undertaken, more than half (52%) agreed or strongly agreed that "they often see news stories that they are not interested in" (News and Media Research Centre 2017). Yet, this is problematic because it relies on the survey participants' self-assessment that the news they are exposed to in their news feeds is news they would 'not normally use'. Our research in the Sharing News Online project indicates that overwhelmingly people share news that they personally find 'shareworthy', and that they care about what certain news stories mean within their social networks (see Chap. 6). In other words, their socio-cultural context of news sharing *is* the filter bubble, in Pariser's original sense of the term (Pariser 2011).

Questions about consumer's specific news diets are usually an important preliminary step for understanding the relative values we might ascribe to different sources. Ofcom's News Consumption 2018 Report indicates that at a platform level 64% of UK adults say they use the internet for news. Social media is now the most popular type of online news, used by 44% of UK adults, followed by 37% for other online internet sources. Interestingly while 76% of respondents said they used Facebook for news 43% of that group "said they only knew the original source of news stories posted by other people they follow on Facebook some of the time" (Ofcom 2018a). In releasing two qualitative studies into news consumption in 2018, as part of the Share of References metric survey, CEO of Ofcom, Sharon White, noted that 24/7 news availability has changed "former consumption patterns based around habit and routine". Furthermore, the online landscape shaping that consumption, including sharing on social media platforms using mobile devices, is presenting challenges for news audiences and regulators (Ofcom 2018b).

This means that regulators such as Ofcom need to find new ways of monitoring these changing practices, and new rules will need to be developed to respond to them depending on market conditions, and concentration of voices needs to be factored into maintaining pluralism. She noted,

> The fluid environment of social media certainly brings benefits to news, offering more choice, real-time updates, and a platform for different voices and perspectives. But it also presents new challenges for readers and regulators alike—something that we, as a regulator of editorial standards in TV and radio, are now giving thought for the online world. (Ofcom 2018b)

News consumption in now a process of reading news in social media feeds scrolling and swiping through various sources. News consumers are reading 'breaking news' and notifications, shared news and stories with various types of content. White noted that the commissioned research "shows only 39% consider social media to be a trustworthy news source, compared to 63% for newspapers, and 70% for TV" (Ofcom 2018b).

Taking this changing consumption into account in policy is even more important when we know these platforms are not neutral: their algorithms manipulate what news content people see (see Fig. 8.2). Although ulti-

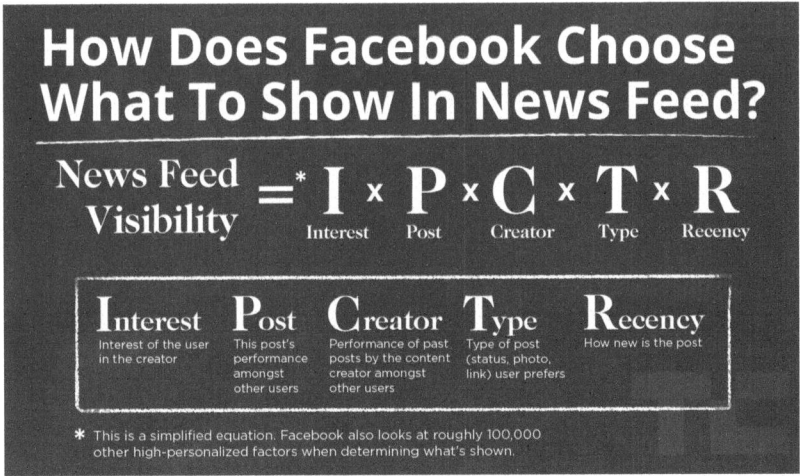

Fig. 8.2   A rough equation of how Facebook calculates what to show in the news feed. Image: Techcrunch/'Facebook puts friends above publishers in "News Feed Values" and ranking change', Josh Constine (2016)

mately shrouded in commercial confidentiality, there are a number of analysts and firms that closely monitor the Facebook newsfeed for the way in which it evolves. This has consequences for audiences, whether that's in terms of knowing that Facebook's algorithm is making judgements about accounts that overshare clickbait/fake news stories, or when the algorithm on Facebook demotes 'lower-quality' news sites, or that it prioritises news stories depending on how people 'react' to stories. Facebook itself disclosed in 2016 that posts from friends and family will get a higher priority on users' News Feeds followed by posts that 'inform' and posts that 'entertain'. This is tacit acknowledgement by Facebook that the satisfaction of audiences is prioritised ahead of news publishers, app developers, advertisers and 'even its own monetization'. Other ranking factors include posts that represent all ideas and posts with "authentic communication" (basically less 'spammy' content) as preferenced by users by the data it feeds back to the constantly evolving algorithm (Constine 2016). The qualitative news consumption research commissioned by Ofcom indicates that algorithm-led preferences and social media friends "shaped the content that individuals consumed as opposed to more transparent differences driven by conventional newspaper loyalty" (Revealing Reality 2018). The idea that news (and other content) is "different for different people" underscores that online news consumption is increasingly incidental and indeed serendipitous (Fletcher and Nielsen 2018). The research also found that for many users content was blurred when accessed via social media networks and that "many were unable to distinguish between advertising, social content, entertainment and news" (Revealing Reality 2018).

Ofcom has introduced assessment mechanisms to take into account qualitative contextual factors. The proxies they use for impact include impartiality, trust, reliability and the ability of news sources to sway an opinion. Ofcom's innovative 'share of references' is used to compare consumption of news across different platforms with different consumption measures (Barnett 2013). It is, in effect, a cross-media metric that looks at consumption in terms of who owns the news source. Ofcom asks, "Which news sources are you using nowadays?" Frequency of use is also important, but the metric is silent in relation to the duration of news consumption. In the 2018 survey the share of references metric indicates that at a platform level, internet sources have a 41% share, followed by TV at 34%, radio at 16% and offline newspapers at 9%. In terms of the share of reference of specific sources of news, use of the BBC is over three times more than the next traditional news provider at the wholesale (ITV) and retail (ITN) levels or the main intermediary, Facebook (Ofcom 2018a).

Under this approach, online intermediaries such as search engines or social networks are considered a separate category of growing importance when looking at media consumption metrics, where they may not necessarily be a producer of a news title or a separate brand. These kinds of aggregated metrics are necessary to allow regulatory agencies working in the public interest to track changes in patterns of news consumption and the diversity of available news sources. It is not without its critics. Steven Barnett's assessment of the Ofcom 'share of references' framework is that it is hopelessly biased towards television news, arguing that the measure "takes no account of the power to persuade, or the opinion-forming impact of print and online media". He also noted that the metric "takes no account of the power to set news agendas' and 'it takes no account of the power to influence policy makers—parliamentarians, think tankers, civil servants, regulators" (Barnett 2013). In other words, although it was an important first step in the right direction to track the morphing consumption of news sources across platforms, Ofcom's metric is incapable of assessing the operation of 'real world' power and influence. As we will argue later in this chapter, what is required to address this deficit is a metric that is capable of tracking recurring, influential and interlinked news sources across platforms and news sites. Only in this way is the diffusion of news voices, and the relative power of particular corporations, and therefore media plurality, able to be empirically accounted for across brands and outlets.

Responsible public policymaking obliges governments and their agencies to monitor these developments, gathering the information needed to evaluate whether or not the current policy intent remains. If so, governments must figure out how to develop regulatory tools (including web traffic analysis software and news data analytics) to secure that intent. As Moore argues in relation to the impact of platform power on news media consumption, it is not "until we better understand and communicate the dilemmas they raise" that effective policy responses will be able to be found (Moore in Helberger 2018).

Moving Beyond Short-Term Political Motivation

Let's fast forward to the deregulatory context of Australian 'media reform' in mid-2017, when media policies were in the spotlight once again. Alternative modes of achieving diversity objectives became prominent as key bargaining chips in those debates. It was evident that the making of media policies is always, inevitably, going to be politicised; this is referencing the idea that media systems will always be shaped by competing political interests, "to inscribe their own values and objectives on the possibilities facilitated by a complex combination of technological, economic and social factors" (Freedman 2008: 1).

Australian media policies display some clear similarities and differences from other Western 'North Atlantic' frameworks. The similarities are that from the mid-twentieth century, there has been substantial international support for plurality of media ownership. Policies designed to limit the number of media outlets owned or controlled by one proprietor have been seen as a precondition for achieving a diverse range of viewpoints. The assumption has been that concentrated ownership confers undemocratic power on 'influential' owners to sway governments and advance their own private interests. But while the power of major media groups has long been recognised—particularly during elections—ruling political parties increasingly make significant policy changes only with an eye to the impacts on their media allies. Consistent with other Western nations, Australia's media ownership rules have become incrementally deregulated since the 1980s. This has seen media ownership in Australia become steadily further concentrated alongside the rise of neoliberal ideologies. In a sense, they represent a worst-case scenario of media concentration.

The Australian media policy omelette cannot simply be unscrambled, but forward-thinking diversity rules could help prevent further concentration of ownership. The Turnbull government and its Communications Minister, Mitch Fifield, were very vocal in their desire to see ongoing deregulation. Yet their proposed changes were neither future looking nor future proofing. Serious attempts at systemic reform to tackle a changing media landscape were last seen in the Convergence Review in 2012. Its proposed changes, including the idea of a Content Service Enterprise (where regulation of content was to be applied equally regardless of the platform it was delivered on), were too threatening to the interests of incumbent players and the review was binned.

Prior to the cross-media laws being introduced in 1987, limits had applied to the numbers of media-specific outlets within a single sector. This meant media groups such as John Fairfax Holdings and the Herald and Weekly Times had previously been able to accumulate media outlets across platforms like newspapers, TV and radio. But it was considered not to be in the public interest to allow this kind of concentration of influence. Later, in the deregulatory spirit of the times, successive Australian Coalition governments from 1996 attempted to repeal laws aimed at tackling media concentration. Yet it took until 2006 for this goal to be achieved when the conservative Howard government removed the main cross-media ownership restrictions. This allowed TV/newspaper/radio mergers with a 'two-out-of-three' media sector limit, and introduced metropolitan and rural/regional voice limits under the so-called '5/4 voices' test. The latter refers to the minimum number of media groups (or 'voices') allowed in metropolitan and regional markets respectively.

In spite of ongoing attempts, and largely due to a lack of industry consensus, conservative governments have been unable to remove the final ownership restrictions. Finally, in 2017, the Turnbull government announced that a consensus had been reached. The proposed changes to media ownership—axing the 'two-out-of-three' rule and the 75% 'reach' rule—were strategically buried under more headline-grabbing measures. These include the removal of licence fees for commercial TV networks, the introduction of gambling ad restrictions on free-to-air licencees and granting pay TV expanded access to sporting events previously on the anti-siphoning list. Restricting gambling ads during daytime viewing has a clear community benefit, but the wider voice benefits of diversity that flow from retaining restrictions on the further concentration of ownership are far more consequential for all Australians.

MEDIA CONCENTRATION

Media concentration has been a steady feature accompanying the rise of capitalist media markets throughout the nineteenth and twentieth centuries (Baker 2007; Dwyer 2010). Digital media convergence has only accelerated that pattern of consolidation, and this industrial trend is not going away in the foreseeable future. The argument that needs to be made is that the measures and mechanisms that governments put in place should be directed towards future proofing for media diversity and pluralism. The Australian news media industries are among the most concentrated in the world, with the two largest 'newspaper' companies owning over 90% of the market (Dwyer 2017). Consequently, this recognition should be the foundational knowledge upon which future policy interventions are constructed. Neoliberal politicians and financial media commentators wishing to feather their own nests tend to hyperbolically paint the current period as one of media corporations being allowed to either 'merge or fail', but this is a false dichotomy. The question is not whether or not media laws and policy are further deregulated to allow mergers, and thus allow incumbent players to scale up. Rather, the point is that transitional and new mechanisms (or new to some markets) are required to ensure future diversity and to prevent untrammelled media concentration. One of the first steps for governments responsible for media diversity is to have a closer understanding of the forces of change in the media industries, based on the best available understanding of these industries and their audiences.

There are precedents to be found in other media systems around the world. Recognising that these forces in commercial media systems influenced external pluralism, the German Constitutional Court from the 1980s sought to control private media monopoly markets. It established the KEK, or Kommission zur Ermittlung der Konzentration im Medienbereich (Commission for the Investigation of Concentration in the Media), in order to maintain plurality of voices (Czepek et al. 2009: 235).

Australia's media landscape is an outlier as one of the most highly concentrated in the world—behind Egypt and China, according to one international assessment (Molineaux et al. 2016). While there are still some ownership controls and local content requirements that remain in place, these will not stop further media concentration. The rules that a single person cannot control more than two radio stations or more than one television station in a single market will not stop cross-media mergers In regional markets there is still a requirement of 21 minutes of local content a day—a fairly low bar, most agree. However, with the removal of the 'two-out-of-three' rule, News Corporation Australia, for example, which already owns more than two-thirds of the print media sector, is now potentially allowed to buy up all the traditional categories of media (TV, radio and print) in any single market. In cities such as Brisbane, Adelaide and Hobart, where there is already only one daily newspaper, the consequences of further concentration are stark. With the removal of the 'two-out-of-three' rule, Australia has already seen the beginning of further mergers: one of the largest free-to-air commercial television networks, Nine Entertainment, has now taken over the largest independent print media group, Fairfax Media. Commentators note the potential loss of quality journalism and mourned the passing of a leading brand and mastheads (Muller 2018). It capped off a decade of major job loss in the news media, during which more than 3000 journalists were let go or made redundant across Australia (Zion et al. 2018).

In addition to industry strategies, Australia needs to have a comprehensive review of how news is now consumed across online and traditional media. This would serve as a precursor to media diversity policies that tackle the changing news environment. The UK's Ofcom and the European Commission have made significant inroads into monitoring, researching and updating voice pluralism policies (EUI/CFMP 2018). Australia needs to take similar decisive action. This is even more urgent for Australia given the parlous state of its media pluralism and diversity.

Ofcom, at the request of Culture Secretary Karen Bradley, decided that a full takeover of BSkyB by 21st Century Fox was not in the public interest. However with the Fox bid being supplanted by US giant Comcast, her decision no longer applied. It remains valid to note that if media pluralism and the dominant influence of Rupert Murdoch's companies on the news is a big concern in the UK, then the same issue is front and centre in Australia's highly concentrated news sector. The removal of the 'two-out-of-three' rule can only make Australia's media more concentrated in Murdoch's hands—for example, when News Corporation came perilously close to buying the ailing Ten Network in 2017. Fortunately they were gazumped by the giant US network TV corporation CBS. Commentators speculate that the next potential takeover target could be commercial free-to-air Seven West Network, which would remove a significant voice in the Australian media.

Radical changes in the news media sector urgently demand new policy responses to accommodate an industry in transition. Simply removing the last major remaining bulwark against the concentration of media voices was not the solution. It will not lessen the impact of internet hegemons Facebook and Google on news business models—they control around 90% of the growth in the online advertising market (ACCC 2018). That horse has long since bolted, even though the rule continued to prevent further media concentration. The 2017 'media reform package' outed the government doing deals with the incumbent commercial TV networks and News Corp's Foxtel. It was widely seen as a short-sighted political play, and not a serious attempt to tackle structural change in the media industries by looking at ways to maximise diversity for audiences.

'Media Reform' or Doing More Political Deals?

The breakthrough in negotiations with the Senate crossbenchers that the conservative government had been chipping away at over media reform finally arrived in 2017. The deregulatory legislation, the Broadcasting Legislation Amendment (Broadcasting Reform) Bill 2017, required 38 votes to pass the Senate, where the Coalition controlled only 29 votes. It had already secured the support of three crossbenchers and four One Nation senators, but was waiting for just two votes to get it over the line—until Nick Xenophon struck a deal.

After protracted negotiations with Xenophon and his NXT party, the Coalition arrived at a quid pro quo deal that saw the repeal of the remaining cross-media diversity rules, after the government agreed to NXT's proposal to introduce funding grants for small and regional publishers. Clearly, though, they were not the 'substantial quid pro quo' for public interest journalism that Xenophon has trumpeted, which had previously included tax breaks. The main features of the bill were:

- repeal of the 'two-out-of-three' rule and the 75% reach rule;
- the creation of a one-off A$50 million innovation fund for smaller and regional publishers, whose turnover is between A$300,000 and A$30 million. This is capped at $1 million per publisher and available from mid-2018; and
- the creation of 200 cadetships and 60 scholarships.

Another sop that the government announced was that it would direct the ACCC to conduct an enquiry into the advertising practices of Google and Facebook and their impact on journalism. Funding for these publishers would require them to meet specific eligibility criteria, including membership of the Australian Press Council and having ethical guidelines in place. It would need to be for the purposes of news production, and civic and public interest journalism from a local perspective, and the Australian Communications and Media Authority would oversee the distribution of the funds.

Recipient entities of the grants must be majority Australian-owned, pass an independence test and not be affiliated with a political party, union, super fund or lobby group. These eligibility criteria mean some publishers will not have access to these meagre funds. For example, offshore-controlled or -owned online publications such as *The Guardian* and BuzzFeed, or a publisher like The New Daily, which is closely affiliated with super funds, would most likely not be eligible.

Other horse-trading led to amendments that assist community television, a welcome rescue measure for the sector. It included a controversial measure—a A$30 million gift to Fox Sports for women's and niche sports—a commercial broadcaster that can be accessed by less than 30%

of the Australian population. A major A$90 million gift to commercial free-to-air broadcasters in the form of licence fee removals raises the question of whether something was given in return. The obvious quid pro quo was the agreement secured to remove gambling advertising in prime time.

In the wider frame of high industry concentration and the dominance of US-based hegemons, Xenophon's measures were a minimalistic band-aid response, and which will do nothing to prevent further concentration of Australia's media landscape.

Proposed tax breaks for genuine public interest journalism reporting the news and informing the public had the potential to help keep some small players afloat, but these were jettisoned in the negotiations to gain support for the amendments. Similar ideas resurfaced in the ACCC's preliminary report in late 2018. The more innovative, globally leading recommendation in that report was for the creation of a regulator with powers to oversee the impact of algorithms (ACCC 2018).

On the face of it since the main beneficiaries of the innovation fund and training funds would be News Corporation and Fairfax Media competitors, this seemed like a positive measure in the dire state of the newspaper industry. Yet most commentators saw it as drop in the ocean compared with the resources of the dominant two companies. The major problem of longer-term concentration remained, and only a complete redesign of the regulatory framework would render it fit for the twenty-first century. The opportunity for a root-and-branch analysis of media consumption by Australian audiences, an agency tasked to effectively do that and tracking the transitioning news industries, with commensurate resources and diversity mechanisms has, once again, been sidestepped.

These deals with key stakeholders followed a decade of attempts by conservative governments to dismantle media ownership restrictions. They were minor funding measures that did virtually nothing to address the underlying problem of an increasingly concentrated media landscape (where the vast bulk of the eyeballs are anyway). The more serious mechanisms that had been ventilated in the Senate Select Committee Inquiry into the Future of Public Interest Journalism—such as direct financial subsidies—have not got a look in.

A 2014 study prepared for the London School of Economics (LSE) looked at countries with direct financial support for their news industries (the Nordic countries, the Netherlands, Austria, France). The support was for up to 50 years, no matter the party in power. The report concluded that:

> Policymakers can support private media organisations with mechanisms such as tax relief or even direct subsidies to specific media companies. Such support need not compromise media independence if safeguards such as statutory eligibility criteria are in place. (Schweizer et al. 2014)

The authors' view was that the reality of convergence meant support of private media should be extended to online media. Public funding of private media has occurred for decades in Europe and the US, and as the authors of the LSE report note, "media policy has several options at hand to financially support news organizations and help them in tackling the media crisis" (Schweizer et al. 2014). Serious diversity mechanisms such as indirect tax measures and direct measures like subsidies did not pass muster in the historically cosy relations between politicians and media proprietors in Australia. Real alternatives with impact are possible. In the Swedish subsidy scheme, for example, eligible print or digital newspapers need to have less than 30% market share. While subsidies contribute only 2–3% of total industry revenue, they amount to 15–20% of revenue for weaker titles that are their main beneficiaries. For a handful, the subsidy represents up to 33% of total earnings.

Of greater importance to the survival of smaller publishers, these minor funding measures do very little to address the concern that 90% of new online advertising spending is controlled by Google and Facebook. So why doesn't the government introduce a levy on these two players to fund public interest journalism as suggested by the Senate Select Committee on the Future of Public Interest Journalism?

The main journalist's union, the Media Entertainment and Arts Alliance (MEAA), made this suggestion, and many others in a comprehensive and holistic submission to the Senate Select Committee Inquiry. They made recommendations for sustaining public interest journalism and, as a by-product, media voice pluralism:

1. Restore and increase funding to public broadcasting.
2. Tax incentives and other forms of support for rural and regional news outlets.
3. More rigorous taxation of news aggregators.
4. Consideration of a levy to raise funds for "digital disruptors" to be invested into public interest journalism.
5. Consideration of direct and indirect government subsidies to media, with safeguards to protect editorial integrity from being compromised.

6. Creation of a media diversity fund.
7. Tax deductibility for news subscriptions.
8. Industry assistances to retrain and re-educate journalists, along with innovation grants and other forms of assistance to maintain editorial staffing levels.
9. Funding for counselling and assistance to media workers as they transition out of secure work.
10. Extension of charitable or tax-exempt status to public interest journalism.
11. Encourage the establishment of foundations or not-for-profit media outlets.
12. Further investigation about how to extend workplace protections and collective bargaining to freelance journalists who work as independent contractors with poorer pay and less job security than permanent staff journalists.
13. Defamation law reform. (Submission, p. 3)

Another influential report that was cited by the MEAA and other submitters was the Canadian parliament's Standing Committee on Canadian Heritage which has similarly recommended a range of support measures for sustainable public interest journalism, including:

1. Tax deductibility for digital advertising in Canadian-owned media platforms.
2. Five-year tax credits for print media companies to compensate for investing in capital and labour in digital media.
3. Ensuring foreign news aggregators are subject to the same tax obligations as Canadian media.
4. Through expansion and increased budget for the Canadian periodical fund (which provides assistance and rewards innovation and industry initiatives to Canadian publishers, magazines and non-daily newspapers to ensure the public has access to a range of Canadian publications) make daily and free newspapers eligible to participate in the fund, offer support for online distribution of magazines and newspapers including greater support for ethnic and indigenous media.
5. Apply a 'diversity of voices' test to ensure there is no dominance in any media market.
6. Change the definition of a registered charity to include not-for-profit media and/or foundations.

It can be seen that there are many measures and instruments that can be put in place to support media industries at a time of rapid change and financial uncertainty. As I suggested at the outset of the chapter, the first step is to fully understand the new online media distribution context, and what it means for media pluralism. Accompanying the rise of online news outlets, the commodification of news information—or news metadata—is now a basic determinant of the shape and characteristics of news provision. In our view it is critical for policymakers to study the ways in which social media companies and their satellite social metadata intermediaries are transforming news commodification, production and distribution though their use of algorithmic/AI information processing (Dwyer and Martin 2017).

A New Register of News Commodification

In our previous research we have documented a new register of news commodity, social media sharing metadata and its integration into earlier articulations of news as information and audience commodities (Dwyer and Martin 2017). We have also mapped the diversity of actors that comprise the social media news sharing ecology, an interdependent system of industrial players, practices, processes and technologies that together reinforce the power of news sharing analytics to shape the future of journalism in subtle and not always visible ways. In this way, we have shown that it is not only Facebook swallowing the news media, but Facebook, its friends and associates. We note that while journalists' attention is rightfully on the dubious uses of news analytics to value them and their work, it may be less alert to the consequences of social media sharing gradually reshaping newsroom practices and resource allocation across the globe.

Much of this algorithmic, platform-centred re-ordering of news distribution has arguably been to the detriment of earlier forms of independent, citizen-focused news provision (Van Dijck et al. 2018). Yet news sharing developments are often hyped as the saviour of journalism, and shrouded in the constitutive free market ideologies of Silicon Valley. In this sense, understanding the operation, possibilities and limits of social media sharing analytics for journalism, and for media research, is a priority for those who would hope to use these tools in more innovative ways, as we have sought to do; to understand changes to news consumption, audience participation and information re-use.

Our investigation of what these tools might otherwise be useful for, apart from telling us what is trending somewhere and whom we should read about it, has fruitfully shown us the possibilities of a new empirics of media diversity and voice pluralism. It's for this reason that we advocate the use of computational techniques, metrics and tools for enhancing public policy interventions, to replace some of the ageing twentieth-century media pluralism and diversity toolkit. This is not to argue that older mechanisms designed for diversity and policy outcomes, such as limits on the number and kinds of outlets, should be entirely jettisoned.

Using News Analytics for Pluralism Assessment Research

Given that current media policy is based more closely on traditional political economic measures of media pluralism such as ownership and control, or of market share and reach in geographical markets, we argue that news analytics must be a factor in future policymaking to acknowledge the primary role of global platforms in news distribution, consumption, evaluation and redistribution.

At the beginning of the chapter, we noted that the history of media pluralism policymaking has been premised on a positive correlation between the number and diversity of news media outlets, and the quality of any given democracy. The dominance of legacy print and broadcast news media throughout the twentieth century justified that interpretation, and the equation of ownership and control measures to the overall state of media diversity and pluralism. However, as the authors of a submission to Senate Inquiry into the Future of Public Interest Journalism state:

> In an era now characterized by the networked distribution of news-based media content, and a scarcity of news consumer attention for—rather than a scarcity of access to—this content, it is no longer appropriate to assume a relationship between number and diversity of news sources and the health of liberal democratic society. (Watkins et al. 2017)

In a sense this is an extension of the long-running access and exposure debates in the research of media audiences (Napoli 2011). Certainly audience consumption metrics will only ever provide part of the picture of digital media influence, with monitoring of independent news sources, cross-ownership and media concentration still essential. The Reuters researchers, in their submission to the Senate Inquiry, recommend further research "to establish a relationship between the number and diversity of news sources in the contemporary public sphere and how this shapes civic engagement" (Watkins et al. 2017).

Analytics could help in developing a more effective media policy framework for monitoring digital media pluralism. Related to the uncoupling of link between the number of media outlets and the overall level of voice diversity arising from new modes of network distributed news, that have occurred with the rise of the network, this realignment calls for new policy mechanisms to respond to these changed industrial circumstances. This includes the financial circumstances and the ability of both old and new media companies to survive. Obviously the larger the media company the better placed it will be to cross-subsidise their own various operations. We will explore these alternative mechanisms shortly, but first there's a need for more detailed discussion of the way people are accessing news on social networks and how journalism practice has responded.

As many scholars have previously noted, the more people access and share news on social media, and the more journalists take their cues on what to publish from social media analytics, the greater the shift we will see in media power relations with implications for political process. This makes the increasing market dominance of the GAFAM, their subsidiaries, partners and allied services an important narrative in the reconfiguration of the news media industries (see Boczkowski 2013) and the shaping of media influence into the future. While there are clear media diversity benefits from people publishing to, and commenting on, social media, there are major risks in having more of the public inform themselves through those platforms—particularly with the rise of fake news and concerns about its effect on political bias in the US and French national elections.

In these respects, there are serious media diversity questions associated with the rise of social media platforms as news providers, not in the least who controls the future of traditional news players, who will fund news production, and with what political and social outcomes in mind. Social media companies do not have the historic association with democratic process and media accountability of traditional news media, as was evidenced during the recent debate about Facebook's allegedly biased coverage of US elections (Manjoo 2016). Academic studies suggest that people exposed to limited public affairs information as news may be disadvantaged as citizens (Pariser 2011; Tewksbury and Rittenberg 2012). Recent Australian research (Thomas et al. 2016) also suggests inequalities in access to online news as well as digital literacy and ability may spark new manifestations of a digital divide.

Normative policy frameworks for sustaining pluralism have a long history in national media policy (Dwyer and Martin 2010; Dwyer et al. 2011), but this form of policy has so far had only minor effect on the operation of these new media gatekeepers. So while question of what is 'sufficient pluralism' in the digital age remains unresolved among media scholars (Gibbons 2015) we argue it could be addressed by further empirical study, using, for example, social news sharing data.

Different historic conceptions of media pluralism might shape that study in different ways. For example Denis McQuail, in his book *Media Performance: Mass Communication and the Public Interest*, provided a broad normative anchor for understanding the various dimensions of a pluralistic media system. McQuail summarises these 'dimensions of difference' as political, geographical, social and cultural. He argues, "The degree of correspondence between the diversity of society and the diversity of media content is the key to assessing performance" (McQuail 2010: 162). This statement triggers many questions about how we might then analyse the diversity of any one media system, about measuring for example, representation, access, available content choices and impact for audiences. In contrast investigating more recent conceptions of voice pluralism, including Couldry's (2010) idea of voice as 'process and value' and Crawford's (2016) algorithmic agonism, suggests we examine how the significance of any one voice is recognised by social sharing analytics, or how the design and automation of digital media platforms operate to promote certain voices above others. Intrinsic to a critical media studies perspective is the need to examine how ideas of marketisation, quantification and choice remain central to ideas of voice pluralism in media regulation and policy (Karppinen 2013).

In light of our earlier Likeable Engine study, we argue the computational analysis of big news content datasets promises to revitalise the study of media pluralism. The first steps in researching the diversity of multi-platform news content provision and identifying the challenges for regulation have already been undertaken (Doyle 2015; Van Hoboken 2015; Ohlsson et al. 2016). Sjøvaag has mapped levels of media diversity in the changing digital infrastructure of distribution, production and reception, and the impact of 'global superplayers' as the ground for future policy interventions (Sjøvaag 2016). Other market-oriented researchers have begun to use news analytics to ask more nuanced questions such as, 'how diverse is the news that people are consuming around the time of major breaking news events?' like the Paris attacks, the San Bernardino shootings or the presidential debates (Song 2016). The intention there is to drill down into the data, to explore the relations between social and search traffic 'referrers' (e.g. Google, Facebook and Twitter) and to better understand the 'traffic' patterns of news stories being consumed.

Social media analytics methods could supplement interesting new approaches to measuring media pluralism emerging in Europe from dialogue between scholars and regulators. The European Commission's Media Pluralism Monitor (MPM) (KU Leuven [ICRI] et al. 2009) has been developed through scholarly work (Valcke et al. 2015).

In the UK, after an enquiry by the House of Lords (2014), the regulator launched its Measurement Framework for Media Plurality (Ofcom 2015), which has also been critiqued by media and regulatory scholars (Barnett and Townend 2015). These new approaches to assessing news media pluralism take into account industry, technology and audience consumption trends. The normative drive in European media pluralism—promoting a heterogeneity of media outlets, owners, and content—has arguably been much broader than the more practical notion of 'media diversity' seen in a country like Australia (Hitchens 2016), where law and policy are based on structural measures of ownership and control, and neglect online news, the public service broadcasters, pay TV and community media. Yet regardless of their ambit none of these pluralism-measuring mechanisms takes account of the ways in which news is now accessed and shared via social media.

As Gibbons (2015) notes there is a need for more sophisticated monitoring and assessments of plurality risks, and social media news sharing should be a part of that process, given it is now a mainstream aspect of news culture. We agree with Karppinen that the EU's Media Pluralism Monitor (MPM), unlike existing empirical metrics for assessing media pluralism and diversity, offers a "more comprehensive and holistic approach' to examine pluralism 'in all its complexity" (2015).

Our research suggests news analytics work could be usefully paired with the European MPM approach (which investigates cultural, political, geographic and ownership factors, as well content types and genres) and/or the Ofcom measurement framework (which examines media availability, consumption, impact and contextual factors). For example, providing governments were willing to shoulder the cost of licensing and analysing 'raw' social media sharing data, they could calculate risks to pluralism in terms of:

1. Availability (or in MPM terms 'supply' or 'distribution'), based on which news providers are most or least shared;
2. Consumption (or in MPM terms 'use'), based on where audiences are accessing news stories, including the reach of different platforms' offerings; their relative share of consumption, and the extent of user multi-sourcing across platforms; and
3. Impact or influence—based on its level of recirculation or sharing, social velocity, geographic spread, presence of commendations and comments.

A major caveat to the application of social media analytics-based study is gaining access to data that can present a comprehensive picture of the social and cultural diversity of pluralistic societies. In the West, with its dependence on US-owned and -controlled platforms and services, our view of social media diversity is somewhat culturally reductive. As we noted in Chap. 2, the analytics tools discussed so far under represent, for example, the cultural dispersal of news across non-Western platforms (in north Asia, for example, via Chinese Weibo and WeChat services, South Korea's Naver and Kakao, or Japan's Line, which is also used in Taiwan and Indonesia).

Another issue is establishing measures of 'sufficient pluralism' to assess. Here the definition put forward by Ofcom (2015) and subsequently endorsed by the House of Lords in the UK has practical merit. They suggest that future policy assessments for digital media pluralism need to be equipped to identify:

- The range of independent media voices
- The reach and share of those voices across demographics
- The absence of voices in key markets
- Consumers' active use from a range of independent news providers
- Any one news source having too high a share of consumption
- Conditions of relatively free entry into media markets

In terms of using analytics to assess ideas of 'sufficiency' or 'media performance', we make two key observations. First, media performance assessment of online news stories needs to correlate the kinds of most shared stories against our received assumptions about quality, voice and public interest or public affairs news. That is, any genre and topic assessment of most shared news stories should continue to have a relation to previous value assessments of news content. News stories that deal with politics, civics, economics and business, or that have significant social and material consequences for audiences, should be assumed to play an important part of such assessments.

Second, we consider that there is value in considering the diversity of online news sharing in terms of socio-demographic indicators of high-profile social media accounts, or digital influencers, as these can assist us in investigating the relative representation of various ethnicities, the presence of minority, community and public service media, local and regional media in the sharing media system, and public participation in via comments. Alternatively, analytics could be used to examine the presence of diverse social media participation around an event of national significance, as MIT Lab is doing in its Electome analysis of Twitter participation during the 2016 US presidential elections.

Valcke et al. (2015: 132) suggest socio-demographic indicators of media pluralism "concern social approaches to the range of media available to citizens" (including active media use by citizens and social composition of the media workforce), and that risks can be identified not only in the diversity of media types and genres, but in political, cultural and geographic media pluralism. They further note that socio-demographic indicators in the "basic domain" of policy, that of ownership and control, are typically "less often conceptualized and implemented in the literature on media pluralism" (p. 132). Certainly, analysing participation in social news sharing is fraught with ethical and practical difficulties, not in the least in trying to associate individual accounts with defined political preferences, and real world identities, locations, age, gender or ethnicity factors. However simply isolating the social and cultural groups that do speak openly, and those that choose not to, gives us a deeper understanding of how participatory voice diversity might be theorised in the social media era, beyond the algorithmic reasoning of the social metadata services that are increasingly shaping our news flows.

INTERVENTIONS IN THE PUBLIC INTEREST

So while many, and we would count ourselves in this group, argue that cross-media ownership restrictions founded on clear numerical voice limits in black letter law are the 'gold standard' version of genuine laws and policies for diversity, there are various ways of achieving diversity. In the past rules regulating the ownership and control of media outlets have, of course, been the principal levers. Yet diversity in the number of media voices in a market or geographical area can be achieved in other ways, as we have discussed in this chapter.

Recognising alternative policy levers is arguably a far more visible part of the regulatory tool kit in neoliberal times. This chapter has provided an account of how news data analytics provide twenty-first-century ways and means of accurately tracking media pluralism and news diversity. The diversity mechanisms discussed in this chapter have become prominent alternatives at a juncture in the history of the internet (Abbate 2017), when diversity is "vaguely cited as both...the cause of media difficulties and the excuse to do nothing about the core issue of media diversity" (Ludlam 2017).

Former Australian Greens Senator Scott Ludlam, in his parliamentary Second Reading speech rejecting the repeal of cross-media amendments, noted that the proposed changes in the conservative ruling party's policies did not "address the issue of increasing digital media consumption and the difficulties that traditional media platforms are having in bringing in ad or subscription revenue to actually keep the doors open. Nor do they equip the sector with a framework to embrace the further changes to come" (Ludlam 2017).

Given the rise of algorithms and AI in online intermediaries and social media newsfeeds, and the consequences of this for news pluralism, there is a clear need for more active assessments and monitoring by governments and their agencies. Social media are using algorithms and profile data to tailor audiences' news feeds. As Pasquale argues, our usage of the internet is actively personalised by the Silicon Valley platforms, and this means that our exposure to content is shaped by our own usage (Pasquale 2015: 79). The dynamics between traditional media publishers and platform intermediaries need to be more fully understood for new media policy responses (Helberger 2018). Advertisers can therefore target individuals directly, and this, of course, has become a powerful electioneering tool, including allowing the supply of fake news or disinformation. Transitional arrangements will therefore require laws that deal with the specific changes in news distribution and consumption via platform intermediaries. As argued in this chapter, new modes of network distributed news call out for new policy and regulatory mechanisms to respond to these changed industrial circumstances.

The provision of news based on algorithms and artificial intelligence means that feedback loops from this computational mode of distribution are now embedded in these systems. Layered onto this new way of discovering our news and combined with "split-second posting/sharing culture" (Gilmour 2017) are fundamental restructurings in news and information industry ecosystems. These developments are challenging news as a public good, as behemoth private interests in platform capitalism recast the news and information industries (Srnicek 2017).

Perhaps we need to take a lead from the laws before the US Congress that require disclosure of political advertisements or so-called 'dark advertising' on social media platforms. It's proposed that digital platforms with more than one million users would be required to create a public database of all 'electioneering communications' by persons or groups that spend more than $US10,000 on online political ads (Shaban and Gold 2017). The proposed law (which is an online version of existing offline media laws) would require particulars regarding the target audience, ad view counts, date and time of the ads, and, importantly, the purchaser. But these proposed regulations can be seen as just one small component, albeit a very important part, of the re-regulation of big media, discussed at the beginning of this chapter. Given the political will governments and regulatory authorities can require accountability and enforce existing and new laws in the long-term public interest.

The Cambridge Analytica scandal that broke in early 2018 was arguably one of the loudest alarm bells for accountability and transparency in an automated public sphere.[1] Law makers in Washington suddenly realised that the unauthorised use of an estimated 87 million Facebook users' personal data had far-reaching consequences for democratic processes. Facebook CEO Mark Zuckerberg's subsequent congressional testimony

---

[1] As noted in Chap. 4 the Cambridge Analytica/Facebook scandal was breaking news in April 2018, even though the activities themselves took place pre-2015, and the data breach had been consciously withheld by Facebook management from public view for two years. This story was of Snowden-esque proportions and led to widespread coverage of the scale of the breaches and their implications (see, for example, Meyer 2018).

was generally perceived as a calculated PR exercise shaped by spin doctors. The question that many are now asking, though, is what kinds of regulation will this lead to, if any.

In the following chapter we will consider how algorithmic virality, as one of the defining features of online news sharing distribution in the attention economy, acts to deprioritise and displace media plurality in commercial media platform ecosystems.

REFERENCES

Abbate, Janet. 2017. What and Where Is the Internet? (Re)Defining Internet Histories. *Journal of Internet Histories: Digital Technology, Culture, and Society* 1 (1–2): 8–14.

Australian Competition and Consumer Commission. 2018, December. *Digital Platforms Inquiry. Preliminary Report.* https://www.accc.gov.au/focus-areas/inquiries/digital-platforms-inquiry/preliminary-report.

Baker, C. Edwin. 2007. *Media Concentration and Democracy: Why Ownership Matters (Communication, Society and Politics).* New York: Cambridge University Press.

Barnett, Steven. 2013. Media Plurality Series: Is Ofcom's Share of References Scheme Fit for Measuring Media Power? LSE, *Media Policy Project Blog,* December 4. http://blogs.lse.ac.uk/mediapolicyproject/2013/12/04/media-plurality-series-is-ofcoms-share-of-references-scheme-fit-for-measuring-media-power/.

Barnett, Steven, and Judith Townend, eds. 2015. *Media Power and Pluralism: From Hyperlocal to High-Level Policy.* Basingstoke, Hampshire, UK: Palgrave Macmillan.

Boczkowski, Pablo. 2013. The Continual Transformation of Online News in the Digital Age. *Communication & Society* 25: 1–26.

Brogi, Elda. 2018, November. Personal Interview, Centre for Media Pluralism and Freedom. EUI, Florence.

Confessore, Nicholas, and Matthew Rosenberg. 2018. Sheryl Sandberg Asked for Soros Research, Facebook Acknowledges. *The New York Times,* November 29. https://www.nytimes.com/2018/11/29/technology/george-soros-facebook-sheryl-sandberg.html.

Constine, Josh. 2016. Facebook Puts Friends Above Publishers in "News Feed Values" and Ranking Change. *Techcrunch,* June 29. https://techcrunch.com/2016/06/29/facebook-news-feed-change/.

Couldry, Nick. 2010. *Why Voice Matters: Culture and Politics After Neoliberalism.* London and New York: Sage.

Crawford, Kate. 2016. "Can an Algorithm Be Agonistic"? Ten Scenes from Life in Calculated Publics. *Science, Technology and Human Values* 41 (1): 77–92.

Czepek, Andrea, Mellanie Hellwig, and Eva Nowak. 2009. Pre-Conditions for Press Freedom in Germany. In *Press Freedom and Pluralism in Europe: Concepts and Conditions*, ed. Andrea Czepek, Melanie Hellwig, and Eva Nowak. Bristol, UK and Chicago, USA: Intellect Books.

Doyle, Gillian. 2015. Why Ownership Pluralism Still Matters in a Multi-Platform World. In *Media Pluralism and Diversity: Concepts, Risks and Global Trends*, ed. Peggy Valcke, Miklos Sukosd, and Robert Picard, 297–309. Basingstoke, Hampshire, UK: Palgrave Macmillan.

Dwyer, Tim. 2010. *Media Convergence*. Maidenhead: Open University Press.

———. 2017. Why Media Reform in Australia Has Been So Hard to Achieve. *The Conversation*, May 12. https://theconversation.com/why-media-reform-in-australia-has-been-so-hard-to-achieve-77392.

Dwyer, Tim, and Fiona Martin. 2010. News Diversity in Online Media Systems: A Preliminary Report on the Concept of "Voice". In *Content, Channels and Audiences in the New Millennium: Interaction and Interrelations*, ed. Elena Vartanova, 116–142. Moscow: Faculty of Journalism, Lomonosov MSU – MediaMir.

———. 2017. Sharing News Online: Social Media News Analytics and their Implications for Media Pluralism Policies. *Digital Journalism* 5 (8): 1080–1100.

Dwyer, Tim, Fiona Martin, and Gerard Goggin. 2011. News Diversity and Broadband Applications: Challenges for Content and Distribution. *Telecommunications Journal of Australia* 61 (4): 65.1–65.11.

EPRA. 2015, December 2. Ofcom Concludes Its Work on the Measurement Plurality Framework. European Platform of Regulatory Agencies. Strasbourg, France. https://www.epra.org/news_items/ofcom-concludes-its-work-on-the-measurement-framework-for-media-plurality.

EUI/CMPF, Elda Brogi, Iva Nenadic, and Mario Viola De Azevedo Cunha. 2018. *Monitoring Media Pluralism in Europe: Application of the Media Pluralism Monitor 2017 in the European Union, FYROM, Serbia & Turkey*. Florence: European University Institute.

FCC. 2017a. *FCC's Review of Media Ownership Rules*. Washington, DC https://www.fcc.gov/consumers/guides/fccs-review-broadcast-ownership-rules.

———. 2017b. *Order on Reconsideration and Notice of Proposed Rulemaking*. 17–156. Released 16 November. pp. 1–100. Washington, DC.

Federal Communications Commission (FCC). 2016. Second Report and Order, 16-107. Released 25 August. Washington, DC.

Fletcher, Richard, and Rasmus Kleis Nielsen. 2018. Automated Serendipity. *Digital Journalism* 6 (8): 976–989. https://doi.org/10.1080/21670811.2018.1502045.

Freedman, Des. 2008. *The Politics of Media Policy*. London: Polity.

Gibbons, Thomas. 2015. What Is 'Sufficient' Plurality? In *Media Power and Pluralism: From Hyperlocal to High-Level Policy*, ed. Steven Barnett and Judith Townend, 15–30. Basingstoke, Hampshire, UK: Palgrave Macmillan.

Gilmour, Dan. 2017. A New Chapter: News Co/Lab, Medium. October 4, 2017. https://medium.com/@dangillmor/a-new-chapter-news-co-lab-a95e0af0a27f.

Gottfried, Jeffrey, and Elisa Shearer. 2016. News Use Across Social Media Platforms, 2016. Pew Research Center. May 26, 2016. http://www.journalism.org/2016/05/26/news-use-across-social-media-platforms-2016/.

Helberger, Natali. 2018. Challenging Diversity: Social Media Platforms and a New Conception of Media Diversity. In *Digital Dominance: The Power of Google, Amazon, Facebook, and Apple*, ed. Martin Moore and Damian Tambini, 153–175. New York: Oxford University Press.

Hitchens, Lesley. 2016. Reviewing Media Pluralism in Australia. In *Media Pluralism and Diversity: Concepts, Risks and Global Trends*, ed. Peggy Valcke, Miklos Sukosd, and Robert Picard, 252–266. Basingstoke, Hampshire, UK: Palgrave Macmillan.

House of Lords. 2014. *Select Committee on Communications (Media Plurality Report)*. London: House of Lords/Stationary Office.

Humphreys, Peter. 2009. Media Freedom and Pluralism in the United Kingdom (UK). In *Press Freedom and Pluralism in Europe: Concepts and Conditions*, ed. Andrea Czepek, Melanie Hellwig, and Eva Nowak. Bristol, UK and Chicago, USA: Intellect Books.

Karppinen, Kari. 2013. *Rethinking Media Pluralism*. New York: Fordham University Press.

———. 2015. The Limits of Empirical Indicators: Media Pluralism as an Essentially Contested Concept. In *Media Pluralism and Diversity: Concepts, Risks and Global Trends*, ed. Peggy Valcke, Miklos Sukosd, and Robert Picard, 287–296. Basingstoke, Hampshire, UK: Palgrave Macmillan.

KU Leuven (ICRI) et al. 2009. *Independent Study on Indicators for Media Pluralism in the Member States – Towards a Risk-Based Approach*. Brussels: European Commission. http://ec.europa.eu/information_society/media_taskforce/doc/pluralism/pfr_report.pdf.

Leonnig, Carole, Tom Hamburger and Rosalind Helderman. 2017. Russian Firm Tied to Pro-Kremlin Propaganda Advertised on Facebook During Election. *The Washington Post*, September 6. https://www.washingtonpost.com/politics/facebook-says-it-sold-political-ads-to-russian-company-during-2016-election/2017/09/06/32f01fd2-931e-11e7-89fa-bb822a46da5b_story.html.

Ludlam, Scott. 2017. Second Reading Speech. Broadcasting Legislation Amendment (Broadcasting Reform Bill) 2017. Commonwealth of Australia. Parliamentary Debates. Senate Official Hansard. No. 7. 22 June, pp. 4854–4860.

Manjoo, Farhad. 2016. Facebook's Bias Is Built-In, and Bears Watching. *Technology*. *The New York Times*, May 11. https://www.nytimes.com/2016/05/12/technology/facebooks-bias-is-built-in-and-bears-watching.html.

Matsa, Katerina Eva, and Elisa Shearer. 2018, September 10. *News Use Across Social Media Platforms 2018*. Pew Research Center. https://www.journalism. org/2018/09/10/news-use-across-social-media-platforms-2018/.

McQuail, Denis. 2010. *McQuail's Mass Communication Theory*. 6th ed. Los Angeles: Sage.

Meyer, Robinson. 2018. My Facebook Was Breached by Cambridge Analytica. Was Yours? *The Atlantic*, April 10. https://www.theatlantic.com/technology/archive/2018/04/facebook-cambridge-analytica-victims/557648/.

Molineaux, Julienne, Donald Matheson, Merja Myllylahti, Sean Phelan, Peter Thompson, and Geoff Lealand. 2016. *Submission to the NZ Commerce Commission Inquiry into the Merger Between NZME Ltd and Fairfax Media Ltd.* https://www.comcom.govt.nz/dmsdocument/14481.

Muller, Denis. 2018. A Modern Tragedy: Nine-Fairfax Merger a Disaster for Quality Media. *The Conversation*, July 26. https://theconversation.com/a-modern-tragedy-nine-fairfax-merger-a-disaster-for-quality-media-100584.

Napoli, Phillip. 2011. *Audience Evolution: New Technologies and the Transformation of Media Audiences.* New York: Columbia University Press.

Napoli, Phillip, and Robyn Caplan. 2017, May. Why Media Companies Insist They're Not Media Companies, and Why They're Wrong. *First Monday* 22 (5).

News and Media Research Centre. 2017. Submission to the Select Committee on the Future of Public Interest Journalism. (No. 50), 22 June. University of Canberra.

Ofcom. 2015, November. *Measurement Framework for Media Plurality.* London: Ofcom.

———. 2018a. *News Consumption in the UK, 2018.* Jigsaw Research. London: Ofcom.

———. 2018b. Read All About It...Without Even Realising. Ofcom.org.uk. *News and Updates*, July 13. https://www.ofcom.org.uk/about-ofcom/latest/features-and-news/news-research.

Ohlsson, Jonas, Johan Lindell, and Sofia Arkhede. 2016. A Matter of Cultural Distinction: News Consumption in the Online Media Landscape. *European Journal of Communication* 32 (2): 116–130.

Pariser, Eli. 2011. *The Filter Bubble: What the Internet Is Hiding From You.* New York: Penguin.

Pasquale, Frank. 2015. *The Black Box Society: The Secret Algorithms that Control Money and Information.* London: Harvard University Press.

———. 2017. The Automated Public Sphere. Legal Studies Research Paper, Number 2017-31. University of Maryland, Francis King Carey School of Law. http://ssrn.com/abstract=3067552.

Pew Research Center. 2017, September 8. People Are Watching a Lot Less TV News (Especially Local TV) as They Get More News Online. http://www.

pewresearch.org/fact-tank/2017/09/07/americansonline-news-use-vs-tv-news-use/.

Reuters. 2017. *Digital News Report*. Oxford: Reuters News Institute. https://reutersinstitute.politics.ox.ac.uk/sites/default/files/Digital%20News%20Report%202017%20web_0.pdf.

Revealing Reality. 2018. *Scrolling News: The Changing Face of Online News Consumption*. A Report for Ofcom. London. https://www.ofcom.org.uk/__data/assets/pdf_file/0022/115915/Scrolling-News.pdf.

Ruddick, Graham. 2017. Ofcom Chair Raises Prospect of Regulation for Google and Facebook. *The Guardian*, October 11. https://www.theguardian.com/media/2017/oct/10/ofcom-patricia-hodgson-google-facebook-fake-news.

Schweizer, Corrine. et al. 2014, March. *Public Funding of Private Media*. LSE Media Policy Brief, No. 11. London, UK: London School of Economics and Political Science.

Shaban, Hamza, and Matea Gold. 2017. Facebook, Google and Twitter Face Proposed Bill Targeting Shadowy Political Ads. *The Washington Post*, September, 22. https://www.washingtonpost.com/news/the-switch/wp/2017/09/22/facebook-google-and-twitter-could-face-a-new-law-targeting-shadowy-political-ads/.

Sjøvaag, Helle. 2016. Media Diversity and the Global Superplayers: Operationalising Pluralism for a Digital Media Market. *Journal of Media Business Studies* 13 (3): 170–186. https://doi.org/10.1080/165522354.2016.1210435.

Song, Sonya. 2016. Examining Digital Consumption Trends During Breaking News Events. A Chartbeat Study. *Metrics That Matter Special Series*. http://lp.chartbeat.com/rs/062-HAC-076/images/Chartbeat_Study_SONYASONG.pdf.

Srnicek, Nick. 2017. *Platform Capitalism*. Cambridge, UK and Malden, MA: Polity Press.

Tewksbury, David, and Jason Rittenberg. 2012. *News on the Internet: Information and Citizenship in the 21st Century*. New York: Oxford University Press.

Thomas, Julian, Jo Barraket, Scott Ewing, Chris Wilson, Ellie Rennie, and Julie Tucker. 2016. *Measuring Australia's Digital Divide. The Australian Digital Inclusion Index*. Melbourne: Swinburne University of Technology/Telstra. https://digitalinclusionindex.org.au/wp-content/uploads/2016/08/Australian-Digital-Inclusion-Index-2017.pdf.

Turfeki, Zeynep. 2018. It's the (Democracy-Poisoning) Golden Age of Free Speech. *Wired.com*, January 16. https://www.wired.com/story/free-speech-issue-tech-turmoil-new-censorship/.

United States Court of Appeal. 2019. Prometheus Radio v. FCC. Third Circuit. On Petition for Review of an Order of the FCC. Reply Brief. Filed 12 April.

Valcke, Peggy, Miklos Sukosd, and Robert Picard. 2015. Indicators for Media Pluralism. In *Media Pluralism and Diversity: Concepts, Risks and Global Trends*, ed. Peggy Valcke, Miklos Sukosd, and Robert Picard, 121–138. Basingstoke, Hampshire, UK: Palgrave Macmillan.

Van Dijck, Jose, Thomas Poell, and Martijn De Waal. 2018. *The Platform Society: Public Values in a Connective World*. New York: Oxford University Press.

Van Hoboken, Joris. 2015. Search Engines, Pluralism and Diversity: What Is at Stake and How to Move Policy Forward. In *Media Pluralism and Diversity: Concepts, Risks and Global Trends*, ed. Peggy Valcke, Miklos Sukosd, and Robert Picard, 341–357. Basingstoke, Hampshire, UK: Palgrave Macmillan.

Watkins, Jerry, Sora Park, Caroline Fisher, R. Warwick Blood, Glen Fuller, Virginia Haussegger, Michael Jensen, Jee Young Lee, and Franco Papandrea. 2017. *Digital News Report: Australia, 2017*. Bruce: News and Media Research Centre, University of Canberra.

Zion, Laurie, Merrilyn Sherwood, Penny O'Donnell, Tim Marjoribanks, Matthew Ricketson, Andrew Dodd, and Monika Winarnita. 2018. New Beats Report: Mass Redundancies and Career Change in *Australian Journalism*. Melbourne. La Trobe University. http://www.newbeatsblog.com/wp-content/uploads/2016/12/New_Beats_Report.pdf.

CHAPTER 9

Understanding Viral News Sharing

Tim Dwyer and Fiona Martin

The idea of 'virality', the rapid, epidemiological spread of socially engaging information, has been central to debates about the value of shareworthy news, and how we measure social sharing's impacts on societies. In our research to evaluate the impact of news sharing we have considered several interrelated dimensions of news virality: social velocity (speed of sharing over time); the number and/or types of people reached; the geographic distance a shared story covers; the emotional factors that stimulate rapid commendation and the wider political, social or cultural impacts of that diffusion. We have also charted how editorial interest in more systematic identification and coverage of potentially 'viral' news stories underpinned the embrace of data analytics services in newsrooms.

As Berger and Milkman (2012) have noted viral content most commonly is unusual and/or arouses our emotions. However, beyond that examples of viral content or 'contagious' media events are as diverse as the users of the internet. Instances of viral social media have been observable long enough now for particular age and social groups to recall their own iconic examples. Viral videos range from Susan Boyle's unexpected breakthrough on *Britain's Got Talent*, Dave Caroll's consumer fight-back success, *United Breaks Guitars (1 & 2)*, and the mega-hit music videos such as Luis Fonsi's *Despacito* (6.2 billion views) or Psy's *Gangnam Style* (3.3 billion views) to the millennial poseur drone skiing stunts of YouTube 'digital influencer' Casey Neistat, or the curious culinary habits of 'mukbang' celebrities (TV eaters) in South Korea. Other examples that we could more confidently describe as news, such as Donald Trump's tweets,

© The Author(s) 2019
F. Martin, T. Dwyer, *Sharing News Online*,
https://doi.org/10.1007/978-3-030-17906-9_9

ISIS beheadings or the death of Osama Bin Laden implicate geo-political relations and have instantaneous global impacts. Social media platforms provide a lingua franca for news sharing, and the relative 'hardness' or 'softness' of the story or event is a sliding scale. The term 'virality' has had currency in marketing contexts for decades, and has applied to the spread of mobile phone apps, including hugely popular games like *Angry Birds* (Kirby and Marsden 2007; Keogh 2016).

In this chapter, we use the term 'viral' in relation to the rate, reach and wider significance of news media events on the internet and social media networks or platforms. We consider the implications of viral news for the formation of public opinion in different political, social and cultural contexts: China, the US and Australia. By presenting several viral event case studies, this chapter seeks to diagnose the significance of this mode of news distribution for generating public understanding of the event's meaning and political responses to its impacts. We also argue that while viral news events might have commonalities, they also demonstrate their own unique characteristics and patterns of sharing based on national political and cultural characteristics, together with the specifics of the events themselves, which generate diverse repercussions. For example, the catastrophic explosions in the Chinese city of Tianjin in August 2015, which killed well over a hundred people and cost in excess of $6 billion in damages, clean-up and market disruption, became a global news event partly due to the graphic eyewitness video footage distributed online. This disaster was the most viewed news event on a social media platform at that time (Dwyer and Xu 2015). However the wealth of citizen discussion and debate about what caused the blasts and what effects they had triggered a rapid 'anti-rumour' campaign by Chinese authorities seeking to quell criticism of the official response and to suppress inaccurate claims about the accident (Zeng et al. 2017).

In China, viral media news events symbolise ongoing transformations in the country's news media industries, as social media use rewrites the controlled patterns of communication that have been in existence for hundreds of years, and accelerates the extraordinary pace of economic and social change in that country. In early 2019 as this chapter was being finalised, the country had 772 million internet users, constituting just over half of its total population and a burgeoning social media landscape. Mobile connectivity has reached 753 million Chinese smartphone users and news sharing is inevitably a key activity via mobile apps (CNNIC 2018). It is difficult to disagree with Wang Huning, political theorist and member of the Politburo Standing Committee of the Communist Party of China, when he noted in his first public speech that China's digital economy was on a "fast train" to online development and innovation (Needham 2017). It is reportedly the largest e-commerce market internationally and home to one in three of the world's start-ups valued at over $US1 billion (Woetzel et al. 2017). From 2017, Chinese leader Xi Jinping publicly spoke of his goal of developing China as a "cyber superpower" (Freedom House 2018).

Yet China's tight control of political talk online, its detention of online dissidents, constraints on citizen journalism, real name registration cyber-security law and suppression of virtual private networks (used to avoid censorship) led to Freedom House labelling the country the world's worst abuser of internet freedoms for the third year in a row (Freedom House 2017).

The crackdown by the Chinese government on the news sharing after the Tianjin disaster contrasts with the aftermath of the Boston Marathon bombing, which saw a quarter of adult Americans, and over half of all 18- to 29-year-olds, say they followed the news about the explosions and the hunt for the bombers on social media platforms including Facebook and Twitter (Pew 2013). Here the local police and FBI used social media to call out to the public for information, to send out updates and to correct rumours. Thousands of spectators were asked to comb their mobile phone photos for possible images of the suspects. Boston became a textbook case of how to use social media sharing for community policing. It also became a case study in the pros and cons of crowd-sourcing investigations.

This chapter argues for ongoing comparative assessment of viral news events that takes account of platform affordances, distribution infrastructures and platform adoption, as well as nuanced modes of cultural intermediation and politico-regulatory contexts. The intention is not to simply apply information science analysis or theories of network and diffusion to our examples of viral news media events, although we will use graphs where they help to clarify some aspect of virality and social media. Rather we want to explore different political and cultural components of these events, and in so doing help us better understand mass-scale news sharing over social media as cultural and political economic phenomena.

VIRAL NEWS MEDIA EVENTS

As we noted earlier, the launch of Facebook's 'Like' button a decade ago heralded a new era of accelerated social media news sharing. Social media platforms need content to go viral—it's an important element of their business models to encourage people to boost content, and especially content which might signal widespread, commonly held tastes and interests. From a marketing perspective, corporates are particularly keen for brand-related content to be virally shared to increase the likelihood of product evaluation and purchase (Apkinar and Berger 2017).

Viral news is the result of the circular, popularity reinforcing dynamics of sharing technologies, and news media's subsequent promotion of highly shared stories. Internationally social networking platforms like Weibo, WeChat, QQ, Cyworld, Mixi, VKontakte, LinkedIn, SnapChat and Instagram have all in their own ways allowed audiences to decide which stories will be selected for mega-amplification, and then their algorithmic systems of content valuation then make more visible stories that are already being highly shared. Of course, news industry use of data analytics, as we've seen already, introduces a further feedback loop where news editors will see high social sharing as a signal that they should feed these stories back into the news mix, in response to their evident newsworthiness. News media visibility then accelerates and extends a story's spread, and gives it further legitimacy, ensuring further circulation beyond the original social networks. A loop like this ensures that there is a steady stream of viral news media events making its way into the news feeds of any platform that uses algorithmic curation. So our choice of which events to share becomes a kind of 'best of' selection, influencing the velocity at which stories diffuse, and the overall reach into the myriad of internet-worked distribution platforms.

We can draw some conceptual sense of how virality operates from studies of media consumption and the genealogy of the term 'media event': the vent staged as spectacle. In the mid-1990s McKenzie Wark (1995) explored the dynamics of 'weird global media events', the mediatised circulation of political spectacles via satellite television, that connected audiences worldwide in interpreting these events through shared (or oppositional) histories, ideologies, metaphors and affective responses. He notes, for example, how the news footage of Wang Weilin, the worker who confronted a line of Chinese army tanks alone in Tiananmen Square in 1989, risking being crushed in the process, came to stand in for the greater unrecorded chaos and complexity of the protests. As Wark argues this footage became a metonym for dissent that quickly fed back via television broadcast into the Communist Party's response to the protests and its censorship protocols, into the mythology of the struggle and eventually into the constraints on Baidu's search-engine results, which erase this incident from popular discovery. Virality then has universal symbolic meaning at its base, and the possibility of transcending immediacy and particularity. It operates as witness, interpretation and reframing of media events, and can be cultivated, in order to mobilise audience action or spread propaganda.

Using an audience studies perspective to understand the way we focus on and share information about certain media events, Karen Ross and Virginia Nightingale (2003) found that traditionally, media sharing involved people being audiences in different types of communicative environments:

> Contemporary urban life depends on the media for the fast and efficient sharing of information. The media enable people who may otherwise have no direct contact to share access to the knowledge base on which their everyday lives are grounded ... The changing media landscape has, therefore, enabled a dramatic expansion in the range and nature of the media spaces where communicative engagement is practised. (2003: 5)

Ross and Nightingale were interested in how media events sutured audiences in the act of consumption, for example in subcultures and fandom, and argued there were five aspects of audience engagement in media events that had attracted research attention:

- the audience participants as individuals,
- participants' audience activities as part of the media event,
- the media time/space of the event,
- the media power relations that structure the event and
- the mediatised information with which people engage. (2003: 7)

While all these aspects are pertinent to our consideration of how and why viral news circulates on social media platforms, some will have different emphases in online contexts. The notion of audience agency and activism that might be read into points 1, 2, 4 and 5 needs to be differently inflected in social media research than it previously has been in analogue media studies. As Ross and Nightingale themselves argued, " 'Net-work' is more obviously purposive than much television viewing" (2003: 161). Citizenship research indicates that new media contexts for distribution have altered traditional audience formations, and political agency now operates in different ways for digital citizens (Isin and Ruppert 2015). New internetworked perspectives on media events can be found in a special section of the journal *Media Culture and Society*, where Frosh and Pinchevski, for example, revisit the seminal text by Dayan and Katz *Media Events: The Live Broadcasting of History* (1992). They argue that while there has been much debate about the spatial effects of broadcast events, including how they act as "privileged site[s] of shared symbols and values" little attention has been given to their temporality, their 'liveness' and the way this is reconfigured by mobile technologies of witnessing like smartphone posting to social media. As Frosh and Pinchevski note the domestic uptake of "mobile digital technologies gives rise to multiple temporalities and trajectories of events through the media" (2017: 135) endowing all recorded moments with potential 'eventfulness', an immanence of importance just waiting for its viral media context to be declared. Unlike broadcast events, mobile witnessed events are distributed and decentred:

> The multiplication of media devices capable of transmitting to others through networks means that there is no stable single perspective associated with the orchestration of the event. The 'center' of the event is highly dynamic, fluctuating with the spreading and dissemination of feeds, streams, posts, tweets, images, and so on, which as such constitute the event both as a duration and as an aggregation. It is a bottom-up making of the event rather than the top-down orchestration of broadcasting. (2017: 137)

Social media–mediated viral events also have a different 'eventness' than the focused, discrete narrative structures of broadcast events, emerging from networks of mediating agents, whose actions go on to shape the multiplicity of subsequent televisual renderings. From this perspective it is harder, though not impossible, for professional news media to dominate the historical narrative of an event.

Nahon and Hemsley (2013) also mask the distinction between bottom-up or top-down events, the first being triggered organically, perhaps by the work of a citizen journalist or the everyday documentation of local happenings, and the latter having a more professional curatorial or staged promotional dimension. Their approach to analysing internetworked virality provides us with a framework for analysing media events via two often competing perspectives:

> ... first, a technical, quantitative perspective that helps us explain network structures and gives us ways to identify, describe, and visualise viral events;

and second, a more qualitative social perspective, wherein we examine the qualities of specific viral events and draw on well-known existing social theories to describe virality as a social process and outline its effects in our current and future societies. (2013: 13)

In our analysis we also want to foreground the distinction between 'entertainment' virality, epitomised in Kim Kardashian's publicity strategies (Hershkovits 2016), and 'news and information' virality. This distinction is in some ways artificial (and dare we say, 'fake', to factor in producer intentionality), but nonetheless requires we investigate the different editorial motivations for recirculating viral content (boosting website traffic or informing a public sphere). Of course sometimes there is no easy alignment towards a bottom-up or top-down trigger, let alone a clear distinction to be made about whether the event can be characterised as 'entertainment' or 'news'. Viral content may begin as popular within a bounded network, and only escape to the epidemiological when it achieves broader newsworthiness, perhaps by being presented in a different context. So while this analysis will foreground the bottom-up making of the events by multitudes, we recognise that there are hierarchies of production at work, and that professional media organisations will often be in positions of power in the final constitution of events for public consumption.

Nahon and Hemsley's (2013) definition of 'virality' remains useful because it focuses our attention on the story that works qua a viral news media event:

Virality is a social information flow process where many people simultaneously forward a specific information item, over a short period of time, within their social networks to different, often distant networks, resulting in a sharp acceleration in the number of people who are exposed to the message. (2013: 16)

Following this they provide a process for identifying and tracking 'virality' by analysing:

1. the human and social aspects of information sharing from one to another,
2. the speed of spread,
3. the reach in terms of the number of people exposed to the content and
4. the reach in terms of the distance the information travels by bridging multiple networks.

Without slavishly applying this formula to our analysis of news virality, we recognise it is useful to examine the role each factor plays in shaping the dimensions of different events, together with the intersection of human commendary and information network effects that contribute to their amplification. The following case studies highlight these constituent factors which vary along their 'axes of influence' of event witnesses and other digital stakeholders.

THE TIANJIN DISASTER

The devastating explosions in the Tanggu area of Tianjin in August 2015, which claimed the lives of over 100 people including 19 firefighters, and injured many hundreds of civilians and displaced thousands living nearby, triggered a nationwide online conversation in China. The disaster became the most viewed news event on a social media platform to that time, with the hashtag #Tianjin Tanggu massive explosion attracting 3.32 billion views on Sina Weibo (weibo.com), China's primary microblogging platform, along with 3.62 million comments and 420,000 followers in the month of the event (Dwyer and Xu 2015). However, the widespread social sharing of video and general public chatter online, including rumours about the effects of the blasts, triggered a government crackdown on posts about the accident, with removal of posts, and closure of accounts. '#Tianjin Tanggu massive explosion' became a banned search term on Sina Weibo. The official response to citizens' news sharing was a clear example of how the Communist Party of China (CPC) both attempts to, and is *able to*, control the flow of information on commercial socially networked platforms.

In the West, one of the most shared accounts of the event was a mobile video shot from a nearby apartment video, which captured three successive explosions and which spectacle, along with the witnesses amazed responses, led it to be broadcast by television networks worldwide (BBC News 2015a). The most highly shared material in China included more affective responses to the accident. For example, in the immediate aftermath of the explosions, one of the most shared posts was a screenshot of a heartbreaking conversation between two firefighters on WeChat, the country's most popular instant messaging tool (see Fig. 9.1) (Chiu 2015).

The screenshot shows brief, almost staccato, messages, as each tries urgently to respond to the other. The man closest to the blaze asks his friend to look after his father, and to visit his mother's grave in case he

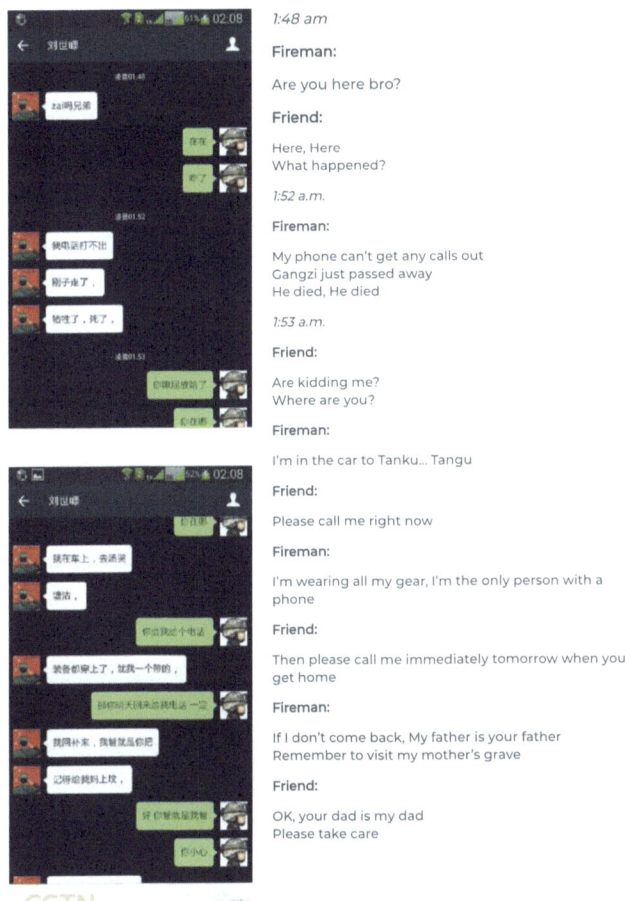

1:48 am

Fireman:

Are you here bro?

Friend:

Here, Here
What happened?

1:52 a.m.

Fireman:

My phone can't get any calls out
Gangzi just passed away
He died, He died

1:53 a.m.

Friend:

Are kidding me?
Where are you?

Fireman:

I'm in the car to Tanku... Tangu

Friend:

Please call me right now

Fireman:

I'm wearing all my gear, I'm the only person with a
phone

Friend:

Then please call me immediately tomorrow when you
get home

Fireman:

If I don't come back, My father is your father
Remember to visit my mother's grave

Friend:

OK, your dad is my dad
Please take care

Fig. 9.1 WeChat conversation between two firefighters during 2015 explosions in Tianjin. (Chiu 2015). Source: CTGN America

doesn't make it back alive, expressions of filial piety that would resonate in the collective consciousness. Even their avatars signal national and workplace pride, one showing a salute to the Chinese flag, the other an icon of a helmeted rescue worker. The recirculation of this WeChat conversation mobilised the compassionate response we discussed in Chap. 6, showing how sadness may not act as a de-motivating factor in triggering news sharing, but rather a suturing one.

WeChat, owned by the Shenzhen-based Tencent Holdings, is marketed as Weixin on the mainland and is China's largest social network, with close to one billion active monthly users (Tao 2017). It offers users arguably the world's most comprehensive social networking platform ecology, with transactions ranging from content sharing, to shopping and mobile payments, as well as what is emerging as the country's default, officially sanctioned personal ID system. According to the China Media Project, Tencent was the first news portal to provide a news brief of the event, even ahead of the Weibo account of the *People's Daily*, historically the main official CPC news publisher (Xiao 2015).

Another highly shared item—this time on Sina Weibo—was a popular cartoon named the "world's coolest retrograding", a possible reference to the vectorisation and re-colouring of an image taken near the scene, of a fireman walking towards the blast as others leave the area. It was retweeted more than 700,000 times, attracting more than 57,000 comments and 300,000 likes within hours of the event (see Fig. 9.2) (Demon 2015). The image, which highlights the fireman in red and orange while fleeing civilians are rendered in black and white, clearly struck a chord with the public in the way it represented the risk taken by emergency

Fig. 9.2 The fireman cartoon that went viral on Weibo. Source: *The Conversation*, 'Tianjin disaster takes social news sharing to new levels in China' (Dwyer and Xu 2015)

services people, and their particular sacrifice in dealing with the after-math of the explosions.

Sina Weibo, the Chinese social media service closest in form to Twitter, is a critical infrastructure for public comment in China. Owned by tech-nology giant SINA and Alibaba, the e-commerce corporation, Sina Weibo is the oldest and most popular microblogging network in China, with over 90% of its users accessing by mobile phone. An early 2010 survey of users found that the majority of people used the service to see what others were saying about news and public affairs and to talk about it (Zhang and Negro 2013). By 2015, as China Watcher and foreign policy scholar David Wertime tweeted the morning after the Tianjin blast, "[With] breaking news or a crisis—facts scarce, stakes high, time tight—Weibo is still default digital public square in China" (Wertime 2015).

Shortly after the disaster rumours about death count, and the cause and effects of the blasts, emerged in posts referring to "terrorist attacks", "shops looted", "no survivor within 1 kilometre of the site" and "sodium cyanide leaking into city's sewage", which were widely dispersed. A day after the disaster, the top-trending hashtag on Sina Weibo was "#塘沽爆炸真相#"—"Tanggu explosion truth" (Tiezzi 2015). With the surge in news sharing, China's internet regulators busied themselves monitoring, removing and rebutting what they called "unhealthy" posts on social media platforms including Weibo and WeChat.

Rumours, not surprisingly, were the main source of unease for the reg-ulators. However, they also censored citizen complaints about the failure of the local, government-controlled station Tianjin TV to cover the acci-dent (BBC News 2015b). In this regard, we can understand the term 'rumours' not as inaccurate information, but rather as "unofficial informa-tion that results from collective uncertainty in society when reliable infor-mation is not available" (Zeng et al. 2017). According to China's internet watchdog, the Cyberspace Administration of China, Chinese officials dis-played "zero tolerance" towards online rumours during and after the Tianjin events (CAC 2015). More than 360 social media accounts on Weibo and WeChat were investigated, resulting in 160 being permanently shut down and 200 more suspended. Fifty 'rumour-mongering' sites were investigated in further detail, leading to 18 of these accounts being revoked.

But this action by the CAC was not limited to bottom-up rumour-mongering or even varieties of citizen journalism. The WeChat account of the *Zhengzhou Evening News*, a municipal-level local newspaper, was forced to close for a week after the account circulated information that there would be a reshuffle in the Tianjin government leadership, a controversial news item to publish in a country where so much of the information flow is centrally controlled.

The open access of social media platforms has rendered the production and dissemination of 'speculative' content both free and instantaneous; while the exponential growth in access to social media is the actual mechanism that allows content to go viral. There were legitimate reasons for the actions taken by the CPC to control the flow of information arising from these events. Some of the messaging created panic and fear among online users affected by the disaster and the Government in Beijing was acting responsibly to control the crowds. Yet the problematic proliferation of rumours led to a push for more transparency and timely release of information from the government and state-run media. Chinese Premier Li Keqiang said: "Rumours will fly if authorities do not release enough up-to-date information" (Gov.cn 2015). He requested that the rumours stop, and that government agencies not fail to disclose sufficient relevant information.

China's news industry, like many others, is experiencing rapid change as social media rewrites the patterns of communication that have been in existence for hundreds of years. The China Internet Network Information Center (CNNIC) predicts that increasingly online news will be algorithmically recommended to users in a more individualistic way, exploiting data collection and mining techniques to push popular news to a user via a model that combines social network links, and digital browsing traces (CNNIC 2017).

China has the world's largest internet community and the most mobile users. The widespread use of mobile phones and web use has developed with the expansion of the middle class in China, which includes the new, old, marginal and "entrepreneurial" middle classes (Goodman 2015). While traditional media is simultaneously under attack and reinventing itself, new media enterprises are often the most nimble, strategic and innovative in this space.

By late 2017 the country's online population had reached over 700 million, around half of its total population (CAC 2015). Expanding 4G mobile network use has further facilitated the use of social media networks and growth in social media platforms and markets is central to this change; these powerful intermediaries are reconfiguring how news is produced and distributed. The eventual roll-out of 5G networks will continue to reshape these powerful intermediaries in China and elsewhere. More than 90.8%

of China's internet users have taken up instant messaging services including WeChat. More than 200 million people—almost ten times the population of Australia—are registered on microblogging services including Sina Weibo. The tension between innovative social media distribution businesses and a government with no intention of giving up control is forging the new mass-scale connective news sharing culture in China.

QLDFLOODS

One of the best examples internationally of social news sharing research has been undertaken by researchers at Australia's Queensland University of Technology (QUT) who, under the aegis of their 'media ecologies project', tracked the unfolding of significant media events on social media in order to better understand the political dynamics of changing digital media landscapes. One of the key events they analysed was major floods in South East Queensland during January 2011, which took 35 lives and destroyed natural and built environments over 78% of the state, and the capital Brisbane. An area the size of Germany and France combined was estimated to have been covered by flood waters (Bruns et al. 2012: 11). Over 2.5 million people were affected and the damages bill was estimated at over $AU5 billion (Queensland Floods Commission of Inquiry 2012). Australian and international media covered the crisis, with sensational images of cars and houses being carried away by the raging torrents.

Social media, and most prominently Facebook and Twitter, played a central role in the crisis communications management used to mitigate the devastating impact of the disaster. Information about the floods spread very rapidly on social media, indeed virally over a few days, and was frequently the *principal* source of information for mainstream media to then report for the 24-hour news cycle. Some of this material was generated by official sources. As Flew et al. note, the Queensland Police Service Media Unit (QPS Media):

> … reported a tenfold increase in the number of followers on its Facebook page (from 17,000 to 165,000) over the 24 hours following the 10 January 2011 Toowoomba flash floods. (Flew et al. 2013: 5–6)

Much of the messaging circulated on Facebook and Twitter was generated by citizen eyewitnesses or people retweeting official information. The phenomenon Bruns calls "gatewatching" (2005, 2018), the personal monitoring and selection of information to feed to one's own networks of interest, was an important aspect of that citizen reporting and news valorising, even if people were simply retweeting a news update from the media or emergency services (Bruns 2005). News sharing was a critical activity of these social media users; they may have shared a link to a story, and image or video, to a Facebook post or some other official (government) or unofficial source (e.g. for fundraising), but they were essentially amplifying and shaping the public sphere reaction to that event.

The Twitter hashtag #qldfloods became a central coordinating mechanism used by authorities and citizens. As a well-understood coordinating feature of the Twitter platform, hashtags provide a relatively open mechanism for "conversation and update threads between users even if these users are not already 'following' one another in the social network" (Bruns et al. 2012: 13) and "a rallying point for ad hoc publics" (Bruns 2018: 115). Between the critical disaster dates of 10th and 16th January, more than 35,000 tweets using the #qldfloods hashtag were sent to disseminate or locate information to help save lives (see Fig. 9.3). There were spikes

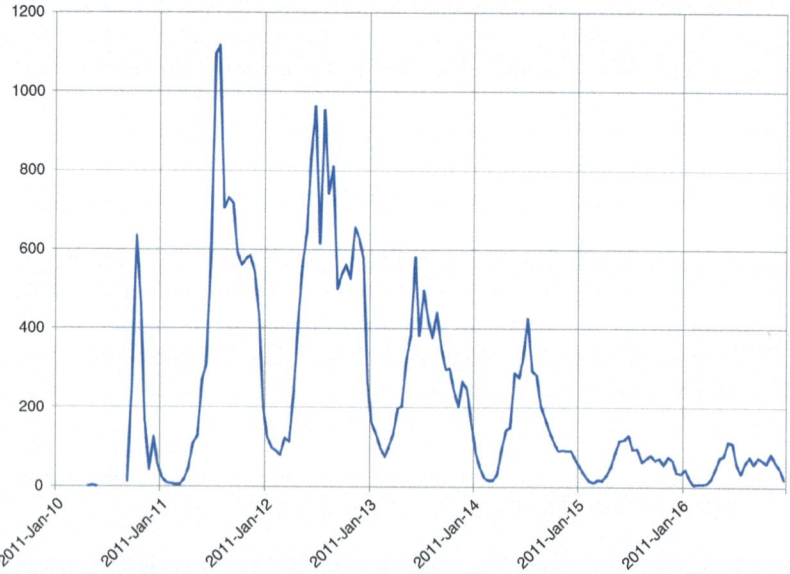

Fig. 9.3   #qldfloods tweets per hour, 10–16 January 2011 (Bruns et al. 2012). Courtesy of Axel Bruns

and troughs in these posts, with the highest number of tweets/retweets occurring on 11 January 2011 (and specifically between 12 pm and 2 pm with 1100 tweets per hour), when the Brisbane River burst its banks (Bruns et al. 2012: 23). The research team observed in their report of the crisis that "50–60% of #qldfloods messages were retweets (passing along existing messages, and thereby making them more visible); 30–40% of messages contained links to further information elsewhere on the Web" (Bruns et al. 2012: 7).

The authors note that a maximum number of users (almost 7000) tweeted on 12 January, explaining the peak in terms of maximum international and national media attention for the crisis (Bruns et al. 2012: 24), which highlights the amplifying dynamic that occurs between "mass" and distributed media platforms, and the operation of "shared awareness" (Bruns 2018: 118) that occurs when citizens, journalists and other communications professionals work to make visible each other's messages.

The QUT team's analysis contributed several important dimensions to the study of viral news media events. First, the research indicates that a number of key Twitter users dedicated their accounts to disseminating #qldfloods tagged messages. In so doing they amplified the emergency messages, taking them to much wider audiences than would otherwise have been the case. The main 'amplifiers' were two media organisations: @abcnews, the Australian Broadcasting Corporation's public service media news account; and @couriermail, the account of News Corporation's major Brisbane-based daily newspaper, the *Courier-Mail*. These and other media organisations used their Twitter accounts to disseminate news stories and information resource links, including eyewitness photos and videos, boosting the social velocity of citizen and emergency services posts. The main emergency service coordinating agency on Twitter was the Queensland Police Service Media Unit @QPSMedia. The Police Service Media unit played the key role in providing detailed situational information and advice to assist those in harm's way from the flood waters. @QPSMedia was also engaged in countering misinformation and rumour-mongering using a series of #Mythbusters tweets. As Bruns et al. observed @QPSMedia "played a crucial role in enabling affected locals and more distant onlookers to begin the difficult process of making sense and coming to terms with these events, even while they were still unfolding" (2012: 8).

Second, the research found that a coordinating agency can effectively direct the flows of information online by prioritising certain official and citizen information sources and that there is scope for official agencies to play an even greater role in crisis communication and emergency management, by using social media platforms. The Queensland Police, in its own analysis of the disaster, also noted the dissemination capacity of platforms: "social media sites are free and robust which can handle volumes of traffic much larger than agency websites" (Queensland Police Service 2012: vii) and the importance of using them to receive feedback and engage its online community. However, the need for emergency services to understand the dynamics and usefulness of hashtagging, and the development of follower networks are important take-away messages from this crisis.

Third, the QUT researchers in their analysis of the #qldfloods message distribution and the variety of media formats shared, from links to resources, images and videos, suggest Twitter is a critical platform "for disseminating information and furthering the flow of news and other material across multiple media platforms" (2012: 7). Figure 9.4 shows the different types of tweets which correspond to the unfolding crisis, from the original tweets to subsequent retweets and URL dissemination, with

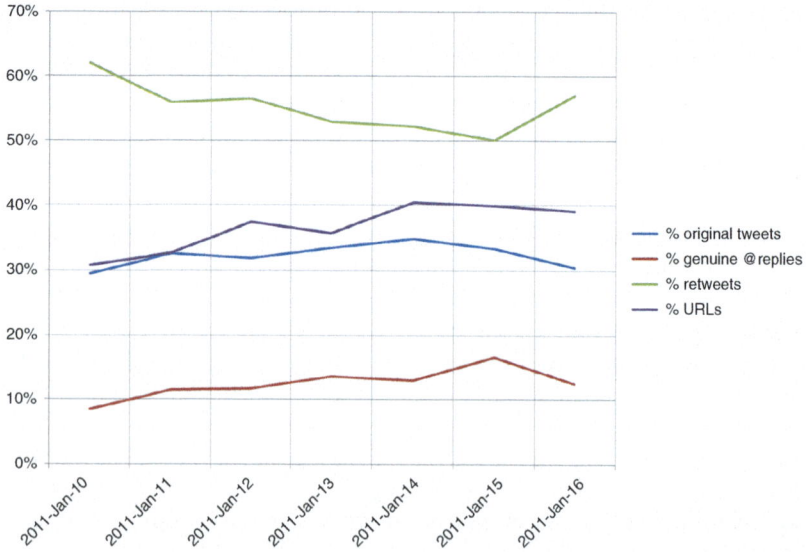

Fig. 9.4 #qldfloods tweet types, 10–16 January 2011 (Bruns et al. 2012). Courtesy of Axel Bruns

the level of retweets suggesting the ongoing importance of the hashtag to amplifying messages.

The researchers found that Twitter networks both used and became a source for the mainstream media, with their engagement depending on their proximity to the disaster. They noted: "Social media users around the world shared a wide range of flood-related media resources via *Twitter*… users closer to the site of the disaster shared their own experiences and observations, often by including photographs and videos in their tweets" (Bruns et al. 2012: 7). This crowd-sourcing of information to assist others, and to contribute to the management of the crisis by emergency service organisations, is an important insight into the way social media can used to convey information in times of a disaster. However as Flew et al. point out the use of such participatory networks in crisis communication also raises issues of *coordination* for agencies managing flows of information across a distributed media ecology, and the need for them to maintain *authority* and *trust* in their messaging, especially in terms of any citizen sources they might choose to recirculate (2013: 6).

As the QUT team was able to observe from their extracted Twitter corpus, there was a gradual increase in messaging as the crisis unfolded over the week, followed by a decline as the crisis subsided, leaving only the affected flood victims with "a relatively direct relation to the floods events and most involved in sharing further information about the floods and their aftermath" (Bruns et al. 2012: 26). During this period, the amplification and spread of messaging performed key social functions for those affected, aside from enabling their news acquisition. It assisted with communal sense making around the event and the negotiation of participant roles during the emergency, for example in providing ways for people to understand aspects of the emergency response and to express their gratitude to emergency services (Shaw et al. 2013). This case study of the #qldfloods viral media news event indicates that social media played a critically important role in assisting the responses of emergency services organisations. It also demonstrated how citizens could work with government authorities and their agencies to assist others in the face of a natural disaster.

THE BOSTON MARATHON BOMBINGS

On one level the Boston Marathon bombing on 15 April 2013, which killed three people and injured more than 260, was one of several terrorist attacks in recent years where authorities have been able draw on crowd-sourced information to the benefit their investigation and the information of wider publics. Yet, on another, it has been recognised as a defining moment in the short history of social media's contribution to the transformation of news gathering and distribution.

On that day, two pressure-cooker-styled bombs had been detonated near the finish line of the world-renowned marathon event, which had attracted approximately 23,000 entrants. The detonation was timed to coincide with the completion of the race, and the placement to create chaos where hundreds of assembled spectators had gathered to celebrate the arrival of those finishing the event.

The speed of the spread of this breaking news event, its social velocity, was a clear measure of its virality. According to Topsy, a Twitter analytics company, at around 4 pm on the day of the bombing there were approximately 300,000 mentions on Twitter of 'Boston explosion'. By 4.30 pm 'Boston Marathon' mentions had spiked to 700,000 (Stern 2013). #BostonMarathon became the main trending hashtag on the Twitter platform. As with disastrous news media events in general, the public were quick to share images and videos of what they were witnessing on social media—especially on Reddit, Facebook and Twitter, but also other image- and video-sharing outlets such as 4Chan, Instagram, Flickr, YouTube and Vine. Quickly people began to crowdsource their investigation of the perpetrators and victims of the bombing. By the end of the night on the day of the bombing, the event had around three million followers on Reddit/r/findbostonbombers trying to sleuth out who was behind the bombing and to develop explanations for their motives.

A documentary account of the bombing called *The Thread* describes how the most hare-brained 'wild west' theories emerged on social media—including one that had Beyonce and rapper Jay Z as the culprits (Kew Media 2015). The usual suspects named the usual suspects: dark-skinned black males, Middle Eastern people and Muslims. The Murdoch-controlled *New York Post* ran with a conspiracy theory sourced from Reddit. Author Jonathan Fitzgerald, writing an account of the attack for *Time* magazine, noted:

> The false identification of the perpetrators first on Reddit and then on the front page of *The New York Post*, the hasty and lazy reporting by cable news networks, the threats against Muslims here in Boston, serve as a perfect example of how instant news culture can do very real harm. (Fitzgerald 2014)

The Boston Police Department (BPD) quickly called for people to come forward with any information or media content they may have to assist its investigation. It also tweeted out from the official account @ Boston_Police updates based on a press conference and other developments. The tweet below (see Fig. 9.5) from the BPD bureau chief of public information, Cheryl Fiandaca, shows how the account was used to inform the public of events from the moment of the explosions.

As if to quickly refute Surowiecki's wisdom of crowds thesis, however, a university student, Sunil Tripathi, was wrongly identified on Reddit as one of two suspects in a surveillance image released by the FBI (Surowiecki 2005). Tripathi had been missing for about a month, and his families' social media posts attempting to locate him quickly attracted an outpouring of race hate. One account noted how "the family of the missing 22 year old saw the false accusations spiral out of control and received a barrage of phone calls in what some people described as 'vigilante justice' perpetuated by social media" (Ziv 2015). Boston police eventually released the names of the actual suspects, brothers Dzhokhar and Tamerlan Tsarnaev. The Reddit user who created the subreddit r/findbostonbombers posted

Fig. 9.5 Screenshot of Boston Police Department's Twitter reporting of Boston Marathon explosion

a mea culpa over his role in the incorrect identification of Sunil Tripathi (Abad-Santos 2013).

So social media attention turned to the brothers and the manhunt that was fully underway, and soon their full backstory was emerging with little regard for principles of natural justice. The extreme haste and vigilantism of the social media discovery process pointed to the ethical problem of how platforms should manage content regulation. The frequently heard defence of 'we're just a platform' yet again rang hollow as the media-like role of the platforms came to the fore, with journalism and (in)justice taking centre stage. The volume of material about the bombings solicited from the public, and the sheer velocity at which social media debates unfolded, rendered this event as a kind of watershed for the public dissemination of news and information in a terrorist attack.

The Tsarnaev brothers were finally identified, tracked and captured "through the grand scale dissemination and collection of information, photos and videos through social media" (Haddow and Haddow 2015). After a police shoot-out, Tamerlan Tsarnaev was dead, his brother Dzhokhar was injured, but on the run. A manhunt ensued and thousands of police officers zoomed in on and searched Watertown Massachusetts. Both the FBI and the Boston Police Department posted several images of Dzhokhar on social media, including this tweet (see Fig. 9.6) which generated about 11,500 retweets, and mobilised citizens in the search for the fugitive.

As with the Queensland floods, authorities in Boston realised that social media platforms were important tools for crowd-controlled crisis management. Haddow and Haddow note that:

> the FBI and Boston PD used Twitter to reach out to the public to inform them of what was going and what to do. The public found out in real time what was going on as soon as law enforcement did. They were given updates throughout the event. News conferences were tweeted out and shared on Facebook as they occurred. (2015)

Another similarity with the Queensland floods case was that the authorities in Boston used social media to issue instructions and correct misinformation that was circulating. The BPD's Cheryl Fiandaca, a former TV news journalist, is reported to have used the Department's Twitter handle ten times during about 90 minutes, to tweet posts including: "Boston Police confirming explosion at marathon finish line with injuries" and

Boston Police Dept. ✓
Follow ⌄
@bostonpolice

#WANTED: Updated photo of 19 year-old Dzhokhar Tsarnaev released. Suspect considered armed & dangerous.

6:32 AM - 19 Apr 2013

12,472 Retweets **746** Likes   😊🐣🦋⚓️🌀🐵👤👢🍑

💬 209   🔁 12K   ♡ 746

Fig. 9.6 Screenshot of Boston Police Department tweet about the Boston Marathon bombing suspect. Courtesy of Boston Police Department

"BPD asking people not to congregate in large crowds". Accounts of the social media usage during the event have noted that when several news sources, including Associated Press and CNN, incorrectly reported that a suspect was in custody, the BPD tweeted to correct the information. When Dzhokhar Tsarnaev was finally apprehended, the BPD tweeted, "CAPTURED!!! The hunt is over. The search is done. The terror is over. And justice has won. Suspect is in custody." Twitter users retweeted this approximately 144,000 times. The BPD also tweeted triumphantly:

> The Boston Police Appreciates the love and support of the USA GOD BLESS AMERICA. BOSTON STRONG! (Swann 2013)

According to this public relations expert the Boston PD Twitter account had 54,000 followers before the Marathon, and then subsequently acquired over 330,000 during the crisis; finally reaching 49 million people within five days (Swann 2013). Other researchers using big data and qualitative methods noted that nearly eight million relevant tweets were sent by 3.7 million people from the start to the finish of what has become known as 'the Boston Marathon bombings'.

Yet these authors warned of some Twitter users that "Malicious entities exploit the vulnerable emotions of people during crisis to make their rumours viral" (Gupta et al. 2013). The same study found that of the millions of tweets sent during this period, 29% were rumours and fake content, around half were people's opinions and only 20% conveyed factual information (Schultz 2013).

In this respect, the Boston Marathon is not dissimilar to most socially mediated viral events, which now are likely to spawn all manner of inaccurate claims, rumours, disinformation and digital tampering with original content. To this end international agencies have been working on a range of information verification projects, from an automated media verification assistant app (Cameron 2018) to training for journalists to recognise fraudulent information (Ireton and Posetti 2018). Each seeks to allow journalists to control, if not the spread of information online, then at least that which they will share and give legitimacy to in the process.

RETHINKING VIRAL SOCIAL MEDIA NEWS EVENTS

The viral events discussed here indicate that with the rise of social media networks, news and information is no longer centrally controlled in, or by, traditional news media cultures. Yet neither is it dominated by bottom-up DIY news work, organically generated by concerned citizens. On the contrary, social media users can be motivated to spread information for their entertainment, or by narrow self-interest, and even malice. In every case of virality, news sharing is now a dynamic process involving bottom-up audience participation and sharing, and top-down, professionally constructed interventions across media platforms, each intersecting in negotiations about veracity, authority and trust.

While social media platforms are often a sword hanging over the future of news media relevance and legitimacy, are we still able to categorically claim that "eye-witness citizen reportage" brings unalloyed public benefit? (Allan 2014). As Stuart Allan, a scholar of citizen-led reporting, notes, other available terminology to describe the activities of smartphone-armed people in crisis or disaster situations includes "amateur photo sleuths", "online vigilantes", "digital witch hunts" and "conspiracy nuts" (Allan

2014: 136). So, the answer to our rhetorical question needs to be a resounding 'no'. However, assessing the citizen reporting components of these viral news media events does serve to focus our thinking about the role and purposes of social media. The ethics of chasing a 'scoop', of who legitimises decision making and process judgements, and the possibility of betraying victims in the name of breaking news must all be weighed in that assessment. Appraising the relative contributions of crowd-sourced rumours and revelations is now always part of the mix.

Analysing the stakeholders of viral media news events, and their motivations for engaging in online news sharing, engenders an important set of questions for media research. By analysing social media participation over a series of crisis events, we may get a sense of the patterns of engagement, the discursive tendencies and genres, and the points at which official intervention could usefully assist emergency management. As the QUT floods study noted, "If current crisis events can be reliably identified from trends in Twitter data, for example, this would constitute a valuable new information input for emergency services, adding to their existing range of sources" (Bruns et al. 2012: 10). Studies in social media listening by government authorities, emergency services and media organisations might illuminate how best to work with communities to elicit critical information and mobilise crisis responses. Another area of research might examine how the traditional media, especially local publications, best act as disseminators and investigate their capacity to manage crisis communications across multiple platforms.

A common theme to emerge in these examples of viral news media events is the impact of social network structures themselves on how news sharing is amplified. The hashtag convention adopted by several major platforms, for example, allows audience participatory practices to inevitably shape and pattern the way that news and information becomes accessible, and interpreted (Nahon and Hemsley 2013: 83). From this perspective the power of individuals to identify and categorise viral news media events to capture our attention and to inspire social flows of information becomes central to how people then share information, and the consequences of their sharing practices. The so-called power-law of distributed attention dictates that a few messages will get the majority of attention faster than all others, be they videos, posts or tweets. So *who* you are in a network and *what* control you have over the distributive tendencies in that network have real consequences for *how* content will spread.

Viral news media events, as we have seen, are mostly a narrative about lack of control. However, one new controlling network distribution mechanism that needs to be recognised as determinative is the gatekeeping role of news feed algorithms in the public sphere; serving us news based on the kind of news that we have all tended to personally prefer.

REFERENCES

Abad-Santos, Alexander. 2013. Reddit's 'Find Boston Bombers' Founder Says 'It Was a Disaster' But 'Incredible'. *The Atlantic*, April 22. https://www.theatlantic.com/national/archive/2013/04/reddit-find-boston-bombers-founder-interview/315987/.

Apkinar, Ezqi, and Jonah Berger. 2017. Valuable Virality. *Journal of Marketing Research* 54 (2): 318–330.

Allan, Stuart. 2014. Witnessing in Crisis: Photo-Reportage of Terror Attacks in Boston and London. *Media, War & Conflict* 7 (2): 133–151. https://doi.org/10.1177/1750635214531110 London: Sage.

BBC News. 2015a. Tianjin Explosion Video Captures Fear of Eyewitnesses. Courtesy Dan van Duren. August 14. https://www.youtube.com/watch?v=993wlZ6XFSs.

———. 2015b. China Silences Netizens Critical of "Disgraceful" Blast Coverage. August 13. https://www.bbc.com/news/world-asia-china-33908168.

Berger, Jonah, and Katherine L. Milkman. 2012, April. *What Makes Online Content Viral?* 192–205. XLIX: Journal of Marketing Research.

Bruns, Axel. 2005. *Gatewatching: Collaborative Online News Production*. New York: Peter Lang.

———. 2018. *Gatewatching and News Curation: Journalism, Social Media, and the Public Sphere*. New York: Peter Lang.

Bruns, Axel, Jean E. Burgess, Kate Crawford, and Frances Shaw. 2012. *#qldfloods and @QPSMedia: Crisis Communication on Twitter in the 2011 South East Queensland Floods*. Brisbane: QUT, ARC Centre of Excellence for Creative Industries & Innovation (CCI).

Cameron, Lori M. 2018. Digital Forensics Meets Social Media: When Breaking News Hits Your Feed, A "Media Verification Assistant" Can Help Separate Fact From Fiction. *IEEE Computer Society*, May 22. https://publications.computer.org/internet-computing/2018/05/22/social-media-verification-assistant/.

China Internet Network Information Center (CNNIC). 2017, July. *The 39th China Statistical Report on Internet Development*. http://cnnic.com.cn/IDR/ReportDownloads/201706/P020170608523740585924.pdf.

———. 2018, August. *The 42nd China Statistical Report on Internet Development*. China Internet Network Information Center. http://www.cnnic.cn/hlwfzyj/hlwxzbg/hlwtjbg/201808/P020180820630889299840.pdf.

Chiu, Lisa. 2015. This Text Exchange from a Fireman at Tianjin Explosion Will Bring You to Tears. *CGTN America*, August 13. https://america.cgtn. com/2015/08/13/this-text-exchange-from-a-fireman-at-tianjin-explosion-will-bring-you-to-tears.

Cyberspace Administration of China (CAC). 2015. The State Administration of the Internet Has Investigated and Prosecuted 50 Websites for Spreading Fire and Explosion Accidents Involving Tianjin Port. August 15. http://www.cac.gov. cn/2015-08/15/c_1116265229.htm.

Demon [妖妖小精]. 2015. The World's Coolest Retrograde. *Sina Weibo*, August 13. https://www.weibo.com/2185608961/CvB9xbq0O?type=comment#_rnd1532767356270.

Dwyer, Tim, and Weiwei Xu. 2015. Tianjin Disaster Takes Social News Sharing to New Levels in China. *The Conversation*, August 24.

Fitzgerald, Jonathon D. 2014. Boston Marathon Bombings: Making Sense of the Social Media Blitz. Time.com, April 21. http://time.com/69726/social-media-boston-marathon-bombings/.

Flew, Terry, Axel Bruns, Jean E. Burgess, Kate Crawford, and Frances Shaw. 2013. Social Media and Its Impact on Crisis Communication: Case Studies of Twitter Use in Emergency Management in Australia and New Zealand. Paper Presented to the ICA Regional Conference: Communication and Social Transformation, 8–10 November 2013, Shanghai, China.

Freedom House. 2017. China Report. In *Freedom on the Net 2017*. https://freedomhouse.org/report/freedom-net/2017/china.

———. 2018. China's Cyber Superpower Strategy: Implementation, Internet Freedom Implications, and U.S. Responses. September 28. https://freedom-house.org/article/china-s-cyber-superpower-strategy-implementation-inter-net-freedom-implications-and-us.

Frosh, Paul, and Amit Pinchevski. 1992. *Media Witnessing: Testimony in the Age of Mass Communication*. London: Palgrave Macmillan.

———. 2017. Media and Events After *Media Events*. *Media Culture & Society* 40 (1): 135–138. https://doi.org/10.1177/1063443717726007.

Goodman, David S.G. 2015. Locating China's Middle Classes: Social Intermediaries and the Party-State. *Journal of Contemporary China* 25 (97): 1–13.

Gov.cn. 2015. Li Keqiang: Rumours Will Fly If Authorities Do Not Release Enough Up-to-Date Information (in Mandarin). August 16. http://www.gov. cn/guowuyuan/2015-08/16/content_2913800.html.

Gupta, Aditi, Hemank Lamba, and Ponnurangam Kumaraguru. 2013. $1.00 Per RT #BostonMarathon #PrayforBoston: Analysing Fake Content on Twitter. In Proceedings of eCrime Researchers Summit (eCRS), 17–18 September, San Francisco CA. USA. https://doi.org/10.1109/eCRS.2013.6805772.

Haddow, George, and Kim Haddow. 2015. Social Media and the Boston Marathon Bombings: A Case Study. *Physical Security & Emergency Management*, June 4. http://scitechconnect.elsevier.com/social-marathon/.

Hershkovits, David. 2016. How Kim Kardashian Broke the Internet with Her Butt. *The Guardian*, December 18. https://www.theguardian.com/lifeand-style/2014/dec/17/kim-kardashian-butt-break-the-internet-paper-magazine.

Ireton, Cherilyn, and Julie Posetti, eds. 2018. *Journalism, 'Fake News' & Disinformation. Handbook for Journalism Education and Training.* Paris: United Nations Educational, Scientific and Cultural Organization.

Isin, Engin, and Evelyn Ruppert. 2015. *Being Digital Citizens*. London/New York: Rowman and Littlefield.

Keogh, Brendan. 2016. Paying Attention to Angry Birds: Rearticulating Hybrid Worlds and Embodied Play through casual iPhone Games. In *The Routledge Companion to Mobile Media*, ed. Gerard Goggin and Larissa Hjorth, 267–275. London: Routledge.

Kew Media. 2015. Trailer for The Thread. Documentary, Director Greg Barker. https://www.youtube.com/watch?time_continue=123&v=s4cd_thaLcA.

Kirby, Justin, and Paul Marsden, eds. 2007. *Connected Marketing*. London: Routledge.

Nahon, Karine, and Jeff Hemsley. 2013. *Going Viral*. Cambridge, UK: Polity Press.

Needham, Kirsty. 2017. The Next Frontier for Internet Giants. *The Sun-Herald*, December 10. Sydney: Fairfax Media.

Pew Research Center for the People and the Press. 2013. Most Expect 'Occasional Acts of Terrorism' in the Future. April 23. http://www.people-press.org/2013/04/23/most-expect-occasional-acts-of-terrorism-in-the-future/.

Queensland Floods Commission of Inquiry. 2012, March. Queensland Floods Commission of Inquiry Final Report. http://www.floodcommission.qld.gov.au/__data/assets/pdf_file/0007/11698/QFCI-Final-Report-March-2012.pdf.

Queensland Police Service. 2012. Disaster Management and Social Media – A Case Study. Media and Public Affairs Branch. https://www.police.qld.gov.au/corporat-edocs/reportsPublications/other/Documents/QPSSocialMediaCaseStudy.pdf.

Ross, Karen, and Virginia Nightingale. 2003. *Media Audiences: New Perspectives.* Maidenhead, UK: Open University Press.

Schultz, Colin. 2013. In the Wake of the Boston Marathon Bombing Twitter Was Full of Lies. *Smithsonian.com*, October 24. https://www.smithsonianmag.com/smart-news/in-the-wake-of-the-boston-marathon-bombing-twitter-was-full-of-lies-5294419/.

Shaw, Jean Burgess, Kate Crawford, and Axel Bruns. 2013. Sharing News, Making Sense, Saying Thanks: Patterns of Talk on Twitter During the Queensland Floods. *Australian Journal of Communication* 40 (1): 23–40.

Stern, Johanna. 2013. Boston Marathon Bombing: The Waves of Social Media Reaction. *ABC News Technology Review*, April 16. http://abcnews.go.com/

blogs/technology/2013/04/boston-marathon-bombing-the-waves-of-social-media-reaction/.

Surowiecki, James. 2005. *The Wisdom of Crowds*. New York: Random House.

Swann, Patricia. 2013. How the Boston Police Used Twitter During a Time of Terror. *Public Relations Tactics*, May 24. http://apps.prsa.org/Intelligence/Tactics/Articles/view/10197/1078/How_the_Boston_Police_Used_Twitter_During_a_Time_o#.Wk6dplJL0yk.

Tao, Li 2017. WeChat Poised to Become China's Official Electronic ID System. *South China Morning Post*, December 26. http://www.scmp.com/tech/social-gadgets/article/2125736/wechat-poised-become-chinas-official-electronic-id-system.

Tiezzi, Sharon. 2015. The Tianjin Explosion, As Chronicled on Chinese Social Media. How Sina Weibo Brought the News Story to Millions. *The Diplomat*. https://thediplomat.com/2015/08/the-tianjin-explosion-as-chronicled-on-chinese-social-media/.

Wark, McKenzie. 1995. *Virtual Geography: Living with Global Media Events*. Bloomington: Indiana University Press.

Wertime, David. 2015. [With] Breaking News or a Crisis... Twitter, August 12, 11.20 am. https://twitter.com/dwertime/status/631530756259606533.

Woetzel, Jonathan, Jeongmin Seong, Kevin Wei Wang, James Manyika, Michael Chui, and Wendy Wong. 2017. China's Digital Economy: A Leading Global Force. McKinsey & Company. August 2017. https://www.mckinsey.com/featured-insights/china/chinas-digital-economy-a-leading-global-force.

Xiao, Han. 2015. The Chinese Media and the Tianjin Disaster. Media Beat. *China Media Project*, August 20. http://chinamediaproject.org/2015/08/20/chinese-media-and-the-tianjin-disaster/.

Zeng, Jing, Chung-hong Chan, and Fu King-wa. 2017. How Social Media Construct "Truth" Around Crisis Events: Weibo's Rumor Management Strategies After the 2015 Tianjin Blasts. *Policy and Internet* 9 (3): 297–320. https://doi.org/10.1002/poi3.155.

Zhang, Zhan, and Gianluigi Negro. 2013. Weibo in China: Understanding Its Development Through Communication Analysis and Cultural Studies. *Communication, Politics and Culture* 46 (2): 199–216.

Ziv, Stav. 2015 How Social Media Changed News Coverage After the Boston Marathon Attack. *Newsweek*, April 15. http://www.newsweek.com/how-social-media-changed-reporting-wake-boston-marathon-attack-322416.

CHAPTER 10

The Future of Journalism in a Sharing Ecology

Tim Dwyer and Fiona Martin

The contours of news media ecologies are changing before our eyes, as social media platforms grow in influence. Inevitably the platformization of media and communications is transforming the material conditions under which consumers and citizens will be able to access news and information. Where news is found, how it is discovered, liked and shared on social media, platforms' different commendary cultures and commodification strategies are all factors central to these changes. News sharing transforms not only the way news is distributed, but where it is seen, who is likely to access it, how it is valued, what our reactions are to it and how these reactions are exploited for commercial gain.

In Logan Paul, for example, we see the perfect storm trooper for socially networked, affective capitalism and lifestyle influencer news making. With annual earnings of $US14.5 million, and nearly 19 million followers, Paul is one of the top ten YouTube earners according to *Forbes*, alongside alt-right provocateur PewDiePie, the *Dude Perfect* sports channel and Paul's younger brother Jake, a blogger and rapper who sat at number two on the list of highest-paid stars, with $US21.5 million. Only a year after Logan's Aokigahara suicide forest stunt, he was again in the news for joking that he and his YouTuber mates would "go gay" for the month of March, as one of their New Year resolutions (Barr 2019). Predictably his comments were shared exponentially, sparking anger across the globe from individuals and

© The Author(s) 2019
F. Martin, T. Dwyer, *Sharing News Online*,
https://doi.org/10.1007/978-3-030-17906-9_10

groups who called out their inaccuracy and insensitivity. Paul generated other lesser sensations during 2018 when he ate Tide Pods, a detergent capsule, as another stunt and claimed to support the flat earth movement. He then arranged a streamed, pay-per-view boxing match between himself and KSI, another popular YouTuber. The latter was a demonstrably lucrative spectacle which brought in around $US8 million, including merchandise sales (Webb 2018). In his endless quest for attention, Paul cares little about the veracity of his reporting or the type of commendary reaction he attracts, only that he attracts it. Opprobrium and outrage are as valuable as admiration, as long as they generate views, share counts and comments.

The real power of social sharing platforms, as we've revealed in this book, is not simply in their acquisition of, and control over, our personal data, but in their capacity to lock users into a creative contract, an evaluative quid pro quo and cultural politics of sharing news and information. In providing ordinary citizens the means to network, share and publish news, immediately and globally with little cost, social media companies have given the world access to more voices, and more opinions than ever before. On their platforms, ordinary people enjoy the benefits of networking, self-promotion, news discovery and community building, along with other socio-technological affordances of international connectivity. They can shape news agendas as never before, as long as they can mobilise enough of a public groundswell to make their interests algorithmically visible and measurable. Online news sharing has been critical in the mobilisation of political movements, like Hong Kong's Umbrella Revolution and the global #MeToo declarations, which exposed systematic sexual assault and harassment in the workplace (Lee et al. 2015; Manikonda et al. 2018).

At the same time, though, individuals are being enlisted as reviewers, mediators and redistributors of news, giving platforms access to analyse and monetise their most intimate and personally inflected communications. The social cost of these activities in personal data capture, targeted advertising and organised manipulation is yet to be calculated. At the same time they are being given the tools to flag harmful content, so invited to regulate the sharing of news and information, but without any assurance of transparency about what will happen as a result of their efforts. Users' relative agency to shape news production and circulation obscures a clear imbalance in the economic value of commendary exchanges, and the probability that this dynamic is also undermining and exploiting the professional news media, destabilising its revenue base and undermining the already tenuous trust relationship between citizens and journalists.

THE CHALLENGES TO PUBLIC INTEREST JOURNALISM

As we have discussed throughout this book, the news media industries are now in a state of unremitting contestation for markets, revenues, visibility and authority, a struggle involving the social sharing platforms and their interlinked industry actors, competitor publishers, active audiences and governments.

The first issue for publishers is that news has been 'atomised', as more people turn away from traditional bundled journalism forms, such as newspapers, and towards online discovery via search, aggregators and social media, and arriving at stories via recommended links instead of browsing news homepages or apps. The 2018 Reuters Digital News report found 65% of respondents "prefer to get news through a side door, rather than going directly to a news website or app" (Newman et al. 2018: 14). Meanwhile, even though the proportion of people using social media as a source of news has fallen in many countries recently, 23% of respondents to the Reuters international Digital News survey said that they used social media as their main news gateway (p. 7).

The drift to digital discovery has been accompanied by people's relative unwillingness to pay for online news and disruption of media business models. While there is evidence of an upswing in paying audiences as more publications introduce paywalls, the figures in many countries are discouraging. In the UK only 7% of adults on average have paid for online news, in Germany 8% and in France 11% compared to 16% in the US, 20% in Australia and 30% in the Nordic countries (Newman et al. 2018: 22–23). As a result, news paywalls of various types (freemium, metered and hard) are becoming more popular, with 66% of European publications overall operating some model, including 71% of newspapers and news magazines—although most digital-born publications still offer free access to their product (Cornia et al. 2017). Paywalls are part of a trend towards more diversified revenue models, with a clear shift away from advertising as a central revenue pillar, and towards subscriptions or membership (Deloitte 2018). Yet as the UK's Cairncross Review notes, many publications are finding it hard to switch from relying on advertising to subscription, with some finding it difficult to capitalise on audience data to build these new relationships (2019: 39–55). The report argues the decline in news revenues has seen significant cuts in coverage, particularly to regional and local news.

The loss of advertising to Google and Facebook has caused major disruption to the news media. In the US platforms have captured the majority of growth in digital advertising, and 57.7% of online advertising spend (Silber 2018), a pattern replicated across the globe. In response to the loss of ad revenue, news companies, particularly newspapers, have shed jobs and closed operations. In the last decade, US newsroom employment has declined by 23% (Grieco 2018). In Canada 30% of all journalism jobs have been lost since 2010 and 27 daily papers have ceased publication (Public Policy Forum 2017). In the UK over a quarter of frontline journalism jobs have disappeared (Cairncross 2019: 15) while in Australia newspaper jobs had fallen 37% during the 2011–2017 financial years (MEAA 2018).

As platforms have taken more of a role in digital news distribution, the legacy news media has tried to adapt to their ascendancy, taking part in platform publishing initiatives and integrating social media routines and design standards into their production regimes. For Jose Van Dijck et al. (2018: 56–63) many of the economic changes underway in the news media landscape can be explained in terms of two factors. One is the 'datafication' or analytics dependence of online news production and distribution, which is driving new editorial and audience development approaches. This is the dynamic associated with the rise of the metadata commodity. The other is a contest between 'networked' and 'native' publishing strategies. The former involves new media hosting their own content, and encouraging audiences to visit it, while the native strategy is more like BuzzFeed's approach, which is to publish more content on multiple third-party platforms. A major Tow Center study of over a thousand US and Canadian newsrooms found that 83% had made major or minor changes to adjust to socially mediated news environments (Rashidian et al. 2018). Yet it also found that social media companies' "mercurial behavior, and rapid changes to their own businesses, make formulating long-term strategy for publishers nearly impossible" (par. 7).

The development of news business models and more varied dependence on diverse revenue streams, including subscription, paywalls, events and even shopping, are the critical factors that will determine publishers' longer-term survival. Even now, a decade into social media disruption, these are works in progress. Neil Thurman and colleagues found that after two decades of investment and experimentation in digital distribution, many newspapers may have a larger number of readers for their print products than they do for desktop accesses to their online edition, although the balance tips well to digital figures when you count mobile visitors

(Thurman et al. 2018). In light of that reach, they ask why the revenue generated by digital is significantly lower than print: "the relative contribution made by digital output to the total revenues of the publishers in our sample that are reliant mainly on news businesses, averages out at little more than a fifth: 21 percent at Fairfax, 28 percent at the New York Times Co., 26 percent at Gannett and 13 percent at Postmedia"? (p. 5). The answer comes in the greater slice of digital revenues going to advertising intermediaries, the lower cost of digital advertising inventory, the difficulty of placing ads in mobile real estate and consumers' reluctance to pay for online news. But they locate the main problem as the low audience engagement with online news. Time spent on reading news is 80 times higher with UK print editions than their digital counterparts.

The transition to mobile could provide new ways of relating to audiences and new revenue models, as it involves new means of capturing and patterning user data (Dwyer 2018b) and metadata. Smartphones are now the most common way to consume news online, whether that involves addictively checking your Instagram feed, being pushed daily news email updates, discovering, sharing or discussing news on messaging apps (WhatsApp, Facebook Messenger, WeChat, Line, Kakao, Viber, etc.), or via your preferred news app (Newman et al. 2017). However, the market is still evolving with an early push towards multi-platform app-delivered news having fallen off. In 2018 only 31% of digital-born publications offered apps on both Android and iOS, down from 42% in 2017 (Pew Research Center 2018). Certainly, the need to constrain the cost of app development and maintenance, and to place bets on where the audience actually is, rather than trying to reach them on every platform, is starting to impinge on news companies convergent publishing strategies.

With most research showing that platforms provide little in the way of shared revenue in return for content hosting (Myllylahti 2018), there is no doubt that the future of news journalism cannot be dependent on social media exposure. And yet other strong revenue streams that might cover digital publishing costs have not emerged from industry transformation. Subscriptions, product sales and events are providing some income to offset the transition to online publishing, but they are rarely sufficient to fill the gap left by lost advertising. For years, the news media have tried to absorb the cost of digitalisation—of hosting and streaming content, software infrastructure and development, newsroom metrics services and community management—on gradually depleting resources. In the process newsrooms' initial enthusiasm for social media publishing has been somewhat muted. In some senses news sharing, which initially seems like a demonstration of renewed interest in journalism, a means of knowing what the audience like and wanted, now represents a reminder of where the editorial and economic power has shifted, and another cudgel in the armament of increased productivity, where journalists must do more with less.

It is true that the transnational hosts of our news sharing activities have launched various projects to improve journalism's precarious prospects. However, there is some scepticism about the significance of these rescue efforts given their modest scope and platform revenue focus. As media researcher Victor Picard notes:

> Google has pledged $300 million over three years (per yearly average, less than 1 percent of its 2017 profits) for its recently launched News Initiative to combat misinformation and help media outlets monetize news content. Facebook has launched a $3 million journalism "accelerator" (about .007 percent of 2017 revenues) to help 10 to 15 news organizations build their digital subscriptions using Facebook's platform. (Picard 2018)

Arguably these companies are primarily driven by the cost-efficient dynamic of audience publication, data capture and targeted advertising rather than, in the first instance, the creation of more expensive general news products. Despite publisher complaints, they have not moved to increase the revenue share that news companies receive from co-publishing arrangements like Instant Articles or AMP. They have also resisted attempts in countries like Germany and Spain to make them pay for the news they host, with Google News threatening to shut down in Europe in response to the EU's plan to introduce a 'link tax', Article 11, to help fund public interest journalism (Waterson 2018). So, there is no strong sense in which platforms appear genuinely invested in the maintenance of a diverse news media sector, beyond its entanglement in their own news services.

Further the effect of the fake news scandals which the platforms have hosted has certainly not helped public confidence in journalism. Eighty-six per cent of those journalists interviewed by the Tow Center felt that social media misinformation had "contributed to a decline in trust in journalism" (Rashidian et al. 2018, par 14). Interestingly while Reuters researchers find trust in news overall has remained relatively stable year to year at 44%, trust in social media news sits at only 23%, with respondents in Europe and Asia relatively keen (60% and 63%) to see governments intervening to address misinformation.

Nation states are now making clear statements about their desire to regulate platform power in the public (and also political) interest. The UK's Cairncross review (2019: 10–11) has recommended a code of conduct to govern the commercial relationships between publishers and platforms, state funding and tax relief for local journalism, and regulation of platforms efforts to control misinformation. Meanwhile a House of Commons enquiry (2019) into disinformation has also argued that social media companies should be regulated as a new category of media entity, to ensure they are held responsible for the content and advertising they host, while the media regulator Ofcom has drawn up options for regulating content (Ofcom 2018). In the US, there have been calls to break up the tech companies, and debates about possible regulatory measures playing out during both the congressional enquiry into Russian interference in the 2016 elections, and the subsequent probe into data privacy. In Australia, the competition regulator, the Competition and Consumer Commission (ACCC), has filed an interim report recommending more regulatory controls over, and greater monitoring of, how Google and Facebook are operating in digital news and advertising markets, and how they are collecting and using personal data (ACCC 2018).

At the heart of the Cairncross and ACCC enquiries is the fate of public interest journalism, and the negative impact of platforms on the supply of original, professional news and information production. The precarious state of the new media that we describe above is an unexpected consequence of our enthusiasm for social media news sharing, but the impacts will play out differently in each country according to the history and functions of its media system. In Australia, where we are based, the fate of digital media diversity hangs in the balance as the news media sector shrinks in response to Facebook and Google's stranglehold on advertising revenue, and increased digital competition. The 2018 merger between two of the country's major news companies, Nine Entertainment and Fairfax Media, was widely anticipated when the federal government repealed its main anti-concentration laws (Dwyer 2018a). When the merger was finally approved by the ACCC, it created Australia's largest media company—and presumably the loudest private media voice with the most political clout. Yet this convergence does not guarantee the long-term viability of Nine Entertainment's constituent publications in the face of collapsing profits and the continued market disruption of the Silicon Valley juggernauts.

The Nine deal will allow its new media entity to pool assets and cut back office duplication and other more expensive aspects of its news operations, such as public interest investigative reporting. It is selling off Fairfax's regional network of news publications, putting the future of local news in doubt. Nine also plans to streamline the management of its assets and to adapt its national advertising to address its main commercial competitor, Rupert Murdoch's News Corporation, and a rapidly evolving digital news market in which *The Guardian*, the *New York Times*, the BBC and other international brands are jostling for attention. News Corporation is itself transitioning to a future where it will be controlled by Disney, as part of its own survival strategy in the face of the FAANG (Facebook, Amazon, Apple, Netflix and Google) onslaught. From this perspective, Australia's Nine-Fairfax merger is a cautionary tale of media concentration and the reduction of voice diversity, given the emerging contexts of digital news production and distribution, and the everyday practices of online news sharing.

THE QUESTION OF ONLINE NEWS DIVERSITY

A key question we raised in Chaps. 1, 4 and 8 is whether social media sharing has heralded a new era of diversity in news consumption. Despite the obvious loss of news outlets and journalists, signalling a loss of professional content and source diversity, the answer is complex, with social and cultural factors adding nuance to the economic picture.[1]

Social media news sharing does expose news consumers to greater diversity of news brands than they would normally use. Reuters Institute researchers found "more people agree that they often see news from sources they wouldn't normally use (...35%) than disagree (27%)" with 36% of respondents non-committal (Fletcher 2017). They found social media users accessed more news brands than non-users, and were more incidentally exposed to different news brands than non-users. They also noted the agency of users in curating news feeds: a quarter have blocked or actively added sources to manage what news they receive.

Social sharing can also incidentally expose users to new voices and ideas. More than two-thirds of US teenagers, for example, say social media "help people their age interact with individuals from diverse backgrounds, find different points of view or show their support for causes or issues" (Anderson and Jiang 2018). Social media companies have also undoubtedly provided platforms for local and marginalised voices that the legacy media have failed to represent. Twitter has been home to extraor-

---

[1] See Philip Napoli (2011) on the definition of diversity measures.

dinary forms of networked advocacy journalism, from the Black Lives Matter movement in the US to the Indigenous X collective in Australia. Twitter's capacity to help users marshal special interest publics, and to connect with journalists, one of the largest user groups (Jan Kamps 2015), makes it an excellent tool for political news sharing and campaigning. Similarly, as Cairncross notes, "Facebook offers a hub for local groups, with more speed, versatility and local involvement than local publishers offer" (2019: 80). The affordances of social media for local reporting and discussion underscore the imperative for small news publishers to reinvent their civic role and connect more deeply with their communities. It also points to central challenge for the news media in learning to listen to and engage with these groups, with the aim of sharing their news with wider audiences.

However, in at least one respect the diversity of what ordinary users can see and can share online is very much in the hands of social media companies and their content regulation and ranking algorithms. Automated filters act to examine all online content, in the first instance to check that posts meet content standards, and to flag them for a human moderator where that issue is in doubt. However, inconsistencies in the application of those systems has seen Facebook move to censor the posts of Rohingya activists witnessing the genocide in Myanmar, and to suspend the accounts of feminist activists sharing examples of the abuse they have received online (Leetaru 2017). In Germany, under the Network Enforcement Act, Facebook and Instagram have censored the work of artists and culture jammer Barbara, and Twitter has blocked the account of a satirical magazine which parodied the words of a far right, anti-immigration political group (DW 2018). These anomalies have led civil society to question how filters and editorial policies operate to gatekeep what we are allowed to see online, and to marginalise the sharing of information about the forms of violence perpetrated on the vulnerable.

There is also strong public concern about news feed algorithms acting to reinforce users tastes and commendary interactions, evidenced in debates about the existence of filter bubbles and echo chambers. Facebook's Adam Mosseri argues that the company promotes sites that are trusted by a wide variety of different types of readers (Montti 2018). However, it also ranks by relevance to user preferences, predictions based on past interactions, and a range of other factors that tailor content to an individual's interests. This means unless users deliberately widen their social network, or occasionally favour content that is not to their taste, a recommendation formula based on user feedback will gradually narrow the topic diversity of what content is served up. In contrast, researchers studying the operation of news recommendation systems argue "a truly diversity preserving recommendation engine will rather over-represent the 'minorities' and under-represent the 'majorities' to counter this narrowing effect of the distribution over time" (Möller et al. 2018: 971).

The larger problem of Facebook's historic dominance of news sharing and referrals is that it has a significant isomorphic structuring impact on news value and how it is produced. From Caplan and boyd's perspective "Facebook increasingly writes the rules, or code, that defines which content succeeds or fails in no small part because Facebook is now playing an outsized role in how people access news content" (2018: 5)—as well as how news publishers respond to that dynamic, and how they then develop strategies to use social media to attract attention. This power to set the terms of news visibility and value further legitimises its metrics and approach to measuring journalistic worth.

Danish researchers from the Center for Journalism at the University of Southern Denmark (Van Dalen 2018) have conducted useful news diversity research into sharing practices on social media, with a view to investigating the influence of Facebook news feed algorithm changes on the sharing of a newspaper's Facebook posts and the diversity of those posts. Their conceptualisation of sharing practices includes the familiar dimensions: 'diversity of content as sent' and 'diversity of content as received'. More innovatively, however, they add a third intermediary factor for online news—'diversity of content as shared'.

Their research began with the 'news gap' assumption that we challenged in Chap. 4: that political stories were less likely to be shared than 'non-political' (or, as we categorised it more broadly, 'non-public affairs'). They were expecting that 'diversity as shared' would less closely reflect political diversity (based on content analysis of the mentions of specific political parties) than 'diversity as sent'; that is, when Facebook changed its algorithm to prioritise information from friends, they expected that political information would be shared less, and that 'diversity as shared' would decrease.

Their dataset comprised two Danish national broadsheet newspapers and two Danish regional newspapers. They collected around 20,000 posts and just under three million interactions (shares, likes and comments). The data was collected in the wake of two major changes to the news feed algorithm. We've already mentioned the best known one, in January 2018 which prioritised friend and family posts over public content. The second is less well known: in March 2018, the algorithm was tweaked to prioritise local news, first in the US, so that readers could now see topics that had a more direct impact on them or their community (Berger 2018).

Just as with our genre and topicality study, the Danes found that there were more interactions with newspapers' political content than with its non-political content on Facebook. However they also found that Facebook's prioritising of friend posts led to a decrease in shared political information (especially after the March 2018 changes). Third, diversity as shared less closely reflects political diversity than diversity as sent. Fourth, prioritising information from friends seemed to lead to a decreased 'diversity as shared' (Van Dalen 2018).

This research is a recent example of the structuring power of algorithmic curation for social news sharing. In fact Helberger (2018) rightly argues that this is social media platforms' chief source of communicative power, and the main problem with solving the issue of diminishing structural diversity in our media landscape. Social media, as she argues, are not concerned with the supply of diverse media but with controlling our exposure to available information. Platforms "stage encounters with media content, affect the 'findability' of content, order and prioritise existing content, manage and direct user attention as a scarce resource, and influence the choices consumers make" (162). In this respect, social media are not seeking to promote media diversity but user agency—leaving us to make our own choices about the news we choose to read and share, choices they then seek to monetise.

THE MYTH OF USER AGENCY

Facebook has argued that we determine the news we're exposed to by the people we choose to network with, and the sources we choose to follow. Facebook Australia's News Partnerships Lead executive, Andrew Hunter, and our industry partner in the *Sharing News Online* ARC research project, has argued that "People define their networks" and thus what appears in their news feed through their consumption choices (Hunter 2018). He conveniently leaves out the significant work the platform does to alert people to certain relationship and source opportunities, and to structure news feeds according to its own aggregated signals and rankings data. As Elvestad and Phillips argue: "the key issue in a news feed is placement. People are more likely, by a very high margin, to click on stories at the top of their news feed and that is dictated by the algorithm, which in turn is guided by your past behaviour and the behaviour of those you link to…it is Facebook that decides which of the stories in your feed you are most likely to click on" (Elvestad and Phillips 2018: 24). Hunter also fails to account for the reasons we might hesitate to share certain news, for example because of the context collapse that occurs when work, social and cultural relations overlap. In such a space, it may not be appropriate to share some ideas or to comment frankly on others news because of the negative connotations for one or other group of contacts—the spiral of silence theory (Hampton et al. 2014). Others may prefer a bundled approach to news consumption and so not subscribe to their preferred publication/s on social media—leaving their feeds lacking key communicative signals about their regular information tastes. So, Facebook's corporate perspective on news feed diversity tends to rely on an optimistic sense of news user agency that downplays the realities of algorithmic nudging, social group structures and cultural conventions.

This choice paradigm also draws on another myth embedded in the expression 'social networks', which is ascribing everyone an interest in news sharing. Hunter writes, "One of the ways people connect is by sharing news. Observing, comprehending and discussing a common set of stories each day helps us understand the world" (Hunter 2018). In reality people vary greatly in their news consumption habits, with some being junkies and others increasingly news avoiders, including younger people, people who find the news depresses them or makes them angry or those who do not trust the media (Elvestad and Phillips 2018). In exploring the claim that that news personalisation might "improve plurality, diversity and ultimately democracy" Elvestad and Phillips also question the extent to which news sharing might promote political polarisation (2018: 16–22). They cite for example the capacity of populist movements and analytics-based campaign companies like Cambridge Analytica to use social media for propaganda purposes, promoting certain types of highly affective and manipulative news sharing.

Van Dijck et al. roundly critique Facebook's tendency to assert users are primarily responsible for accessing a diversity of news sources and assessing their veracity, as this is work which used to be the province of professional editors and public debate. They argue "platformization tends to transform the accuracy and comprehensiveness of news from a *public value* to a *personal value*" (2018) minimising the role that, say, institutions might play in ensuring the quality and veracity of news media. Indeed the myth of user agency imagines users have significant time and resources for news evaluation, when the reality may be that people chance on snippets in their news feed and quickly browse the story, without exploring further how it relates to other news.

We would question the practical liberty of all people to freely build their own 'Daily Me' news diet on social media. A better term to describe the systems they are working with might be "user-customised recommender systems" (Elvestad and Phillips 2018). In one respect, as in social domains more generally, people create their social and cultural arrangements, and their taste preferences, within the limits of available resources (see Bourdieu 1984). So their arrangements are fundamentally tempered by their platform literacies or 'technacy', the broader sense of having the capacity to critically evaluate technological affordances and risks. Beyond that they are very much part of a digital media system that operates to service the economic needs of the keystone ecosystem species, Facebook, YouTube, Instagram and Twitter. A more accurate take on user agency might be to acknowledge that media diversity and pluralism is defined by the economics, politics and culture of your chosen social platform/s.

A critical media ecology analysis allows us to better assess the interlinked impacts of atomised, personalised social news on the composition and diversity of our news diet. By analysing the interplay of structuring actions taken by all the relevant stakeholders in the social media sharing ecosystem—platforms, content placement services, analytics companies, regulators, news providers and users—we can build a more detailed picture of how journalism is being reshaped by the collection, and trade in metadata about news sharing, and what this means for the future of public interest reporting.

More deeply theorised sociological reflections on the meaning of new media infrastructures and the roles of news sharing practices in society will eventually bring us closer to a longue durée understanding of networked media transformations. Couldry and Hepp's notions of "deep mediatization and the media manifold" (2017: 53–56) is one such meditation on both the choices and complexity of digital media communications. The changing significance of social media news sharing is intimately connected with the ways we negotiate our ever-changing, technologically dependent lives, cultures and societies. In Couldry and Hepp's work, news sharing is part of the wave of digitalisation that followed after electrification and mechanisation and has emerged as central to the institutionalisation and materialisation of our mediatised lives, in that all aspects of sociality are now pre-mediated. From that perspective, there is no way to completely opt out of social media sharing, or the datafication of our contemporary existence, as these processes are inescapably embedded in the communications routines and the social, political and economic lives of millions. We have little choice other than to try and resist the colonial aspects of connectivity and to reshape the limited ways in which we work with, and through these technologies.

RETHINKING SHARING: COMMENDARY CULTURE AND GLOBAL NEWS CONVERSATIONS

To re-think our relationships with the Silicon Valley giants, and their many digital collaborators, it is crucial—as we have done here—to unpick the masking rhetoric of sharing that allows platforms to harvest and exploit our communicative exchanges, while simultaneously enlisting and undermining the old systems of media that have some pretence to democratic and civic purpose. Public debates about how to manage platform power would benefit from a critical, socio-culturally nuanced use of the term, and the assertion of news sharing as something more than personal expression. Sharing news online is something we do for the benefit of our networks and our societies, as a way of contributing to our mutual interpretations of reality, ethics and political process. In generating this social data, it is increasingly clear that we need control over its uses, for example, via the development of so-called personal or national "data markets" (Srnicek 2018). Such markets could include blockchain-based technologies for individuals to grant permission to access personal data, and some incentives to recognise unpaid social media labour.

For journalism, the meaning of news sharing also needs re-appraisal, to re-locate it as one element of a broader digital news production strategy and a central pillar in a new relationship with audience. Social sharing is no longer a proxy for consumption, but rather part of a broader shift in the interaction between journalists, editors and news consumers; a shift which favours editorial moves to better understand how social connectedness, engagement and participation can be cultivated to improve citizen trust in the news. Rather than counting shares and likes as a measure of their worth, journalists now need a deep awareness of commendary behaviour, culture and politics, one that may guide them in the restructuring of industry and profession that lie only just ahead. As a preliminary step down that path, we can re-imagine the role of information sharing in news media, and study its broader meanings for sociology, cultural studies and political communication.

Back in 2004, American technology writer Dan Gillmor famously suggested in his book *We the Media* that legacy media companies would not survive the transition to digital unless they started a conversation with users. Gilmour's high-publicised claim focused researchers on the growth of citizen journalism, and those 'amateurs' who wanted to make media as well as the participatory turn more broadly, particularly the media's development of so-called comments sections. However social media news sharing is also a form of conversation between citizens about the news that they value. It has arguably had a far broader impact on the way we now consume news than either citizen reporting or commenting, given that sharing also amplifies the spread of journalism, gives it personal legitimacy and evaluation, and may also include discussion or critique of the item being shared. As news sharing seeks to capture others' attention, it also commands their response. This reciprocal dynamic positions commendary cultures, from Facebook and Instagram to Reddit and WeChat, as dialogic and generative, rich in possibility for communication across geographic, political and cultural barriers.

News sharing presents fertile territory for future research on the ways we communicate globally about the wicked problems that we face as a species: climate change, immigration, human rights and even how to communicate civilly online. It is, as we've demonstrated, a highly political activity and so offers clues about what motivates us to act on problems and what we find proximate enough to care about. The news we share also contains indicators of the conflicts we face in values, ideologies, aspirations, hopes and fears and how we might negotiate these better. However, we must have cooperation from Facebook and other platforms for this research, and permission to use analytics tools to capture and explore public discussion in ways that are ethically rigorous, open and agreed. We need to *share* these aims and responsibilities, not have private companies as the only arbiters of how our everyday communicative data will be studied.

There are some issues that platforms, governments, journalists and civil society need to work together on, in order to ensure safe and trusted environments for news sharing. It is vital for citizens and journalists to have free, encrypted means to share news without surveillance, as a means to communicate safely about contentious issues. For dissidents and activists, mainstream social media sharing is now a dangerous landscape, from which speaking out can signal their location and prompt organised harassment or detention. It is also important that social media platforms act to reduce the spread of hate and misinformation, in cooperation with information professionals. Following the 2019 New Zealand mosque shooting where one of the attackers livestreamed his video on Facebook, which was then recirculated in edited form by political extremists and news organisations worldwide (Bogle 2019), it is clear that we not only need better reporting and moderation procedures for harmful content, but also clear editorial guidelines for those who would seek to represent it. Finally, if platforms truly care about free speech principles from a human rights perspective, they will spend more time on the problems of effective, well-valued human content moderation and community management, and ways to make their environments more safe and secure platforms for the type of discussions we need to share, rather than the misinformation we need to control.

At the heart of the news sharing business is a struggle for control over the distribution of everyday meaning and a global debate about to what extent nations can sustain diverse, pluralistic, information agendas. Journalists have an important role in these contests, as originators and professional intermediaries of the news we share. In a time of proliferating deep fakes, propaganda and hate speech they need a critical attitude to using social media metrics as a measure of public worth, a strong grip on verification procedures and a clear understanding of the ethical issues involved in recirculating risky content. Given that what we share online is only a fragment of the ideas, opinions and subject matter that we value, the future of journalism is still in exploring the whole of that terrain, looking past its metrified traces, into the rich social and cultural connections beyond.

References

ACCC. 2018, December. *Digital Platforms Inquiry: Preliminary Report.* Australian Competition and Consumer Commission. https://www.accc.gov.au/system/files/ACCC%20Digital%20Platforms%20Inquiry%20-%20Preliminary%20Report.pdf.

Anderson, Monica, and Jingjing Jiang. 2018. Teens' Social Media Habits and Experiences. Pew Research Center, November 28. https://www.pewinternet.org/2018/11/28/teens-social-media-habits-and-experiences/.

Barr, Sabrina. 2019. YouTuber Logan Paul Criticised for Saying He's 'Going Gay' For One Month. *Independent,* January 12. https://www.independent.co.uk/life-style/logan-paul-criticism-backlash-gay-podcast-impaulsive-youtube-apology-a8724296.html.

Berger, Jessica. 2018. Facebook Changes News Feed (Again), Offers Suggestions to Publishers. International News Media Association, March 12. https://www.inma.org/blogs/social-media/post.cfm/facebook-changes-news-feed-again-offers-suggestions-to-publishers.

Bogle, Ariel. 2019. Social Media Deserves Blame for Spreading the Christchurch Video, But So Do We. *ABC News*, March 19. https://www.abc.net.au/news/science/2019-03-19/facebook-to-blame-for-christchurch-live-video-but-so-are-we/10911238.

Bourdieu, Pierre. 1984. *Distinction. A Social Critique of the Judgement of Taste*. Cambridge, MA: Harvard University Press.

Cairncross, Frances. 2019, February 12. The Cairncross Review: A Sustainable Future for Journalism. Department for Digital, Culture, Media & Sport, UK Government. https://www.gov.uk/government/publications/the-cairncross-review-a-sustainable-future-for-journalism.

Caplan, Robin, and danah boyd. 2018, January–June. Isomorphism Through Algorithms: Institutional Dependencies in the Case of Facebook. *Big Data & Society*: 1–12. https://doi.org/10.1177/2053951718757253.

Cornia, Alessio, Annika Sehl, Felix Simon, and Rasmus Kleis Nielsen. 2017. Pay Models in European News. Factsheet May 2017. Reuters Institute for the Study of Journalism.

Couldry, Nick, and Andreas Hepp. 2017. *The Mediated Construction of Reality*. Cambridge, UK: Polity.

Deloitte. 2018. TMT Predictions 2018: What's Ahead for Technology, Media and Telecommunications? https://www2.deloitte.com/cy/en/pages/technology-media-and-telecommunications/articles/tmt-predictions.html.

DW. 2018. *Facebook Slammed for Censoring German Street Artist*. DW Akademie. https://www.dw.com/en/facebook-slammed-for-censoring-german-street-artist/a-42155218.

Dwyer, Tim. 2018a. Starter's Gun Goes Off on a New Phase of Concentration as Nine-Fairfax Lead the Way. *The Conversation*, July 30. https://theconversation.com/starters-gun-goes-off-on-new-phase-of-media-concentration-as-nine-fairfax-lead-the-way-100592.

———. 2018b. Privacy from Your Mobile Devices? Algorithmic Accountability, Surveillance Capitalism and the Accumulation of Personal Data. In *Handbook of Mobile Communication, Culture and Information*, ed. Rich Ling, Gerard Goggin, Leopoldina Fortunati, Sun Sun Lim, and Li Yulin. London: Oxford University Press.

Elvestad, Eiri, and Angela Phillips. 2018. *Misunderstanding News Audiences: Seven Myths of the Social Media Era*. London/New York: Routledge.

Fletcher, Richard. 2017. Social Media and Incidental Exposure. Reuters Institute for the Study of Journalism. http://www.digitalnewsreport.org/survey/2017/social-media-incidental-exposure-2017/.

Gillmor, Dan. 2004. *We the Media: Grassroots Journalism by the People, for the People*. Sebastopol, CA: O'Reilly Media.

Grieco, Elizabeth. 2018. Newsroom Employment Dropped Nearly a Quarter in Less Than 10 Years, with Greatest Decline at Newspapers. Pew Research

Centre, July 30. https://www.pewresearch.org/fact-tank/2018/07/30/ newsroom-employment-dropped-nearly-a-quarter-in-less-than-10-years-with-greatest-decline-at-newspapers/.

Hampton, Keith, Rainie Lee, Weixu Lu, Maria Dwyer, Inyoung Shin, and Kristen Purcell. 2014. Social Media and the 'Spiral of Silence'. Pew Research Center, August 26. https://www.pewinternet.org/2014/08/26/social-media-and-the-spiral-of-silence/.

Helberger, Natali. 2018. Challenging Media Diversity – Social Media Platforms and a New Conception of Media Diversity. In *Digital Dominance: The Power of Google, Amazon, Facebook and Apple*, ed. Martin Moore and Damian Tambini, 153–175. New York: Oxford University Press.

House of Commons. 2019. Disinformation and 'Fake News': Final Report. Eighth Report of Session 2017–19. Digital, Culture, Media and Sport Committee. February 14, 2019.

Hunter, Andrew. 2018. Facebook Australia's Andrew Hunter 'People Define Their Networks'. *Mediaweek*, August 9. https://mediaweek.com.au/facebook-andrew-hunter-people-define-networks/.

Jan Kamps, Haje. 2015. Who Are Twitter's Verified Users? *Medium*, May 25. https://medium.com/@Haje/who-are-twitter-s-verified-users-af976fc1b032.

Lee, Paul S.N., Clement Y.K. So, and Louis Leung. 2015. Social Media and Umbrella Movement: Insurgent Public Sphere in Formation. *Chinese Journal of Communications* 8 (4): 356–375. https://doi.org/10.1080/17544750.2 015.1088874.

Leetaru, Kalev. 2017. How Social Media Can Silence Instead of Empower. *Forbes*, October 14. https://www.forbes.com/sites/kalevleetaru/2017/10/14/how-social-media-can-silence-instead-of-empower/#48d103e7ba18.

Manikonda, Lydia, Ghazaleh Beigi, Huan Liu, and Subbarao Kambhampati. 2018. Twitter for Sparking a Movement, Reddit for Sharing the Moment: #metoo Through the Lens of Social Media. ArXiv.org. Cornell University.

MEAA. 2018. Media, Entertainment and Arts Alliance Submission to the Australian Competition and Consumer Commission's Digital Platforms Inquiry. April 2018. Australia Competition and Consumer Commission.

Möller, Judith, Damian Trilling, Natali Helberger, and Bram van Es. 2018. Do Not Blame It on the Algorithm: An Empirical Assessment of Multiple Recommender Systems and Their Impact on Content Diversity. *Information, Communication & Society* 21 (7): 959–977. https://doi.org/10.1080/13691 18X.2018.1444076.

Montti, Roger. 2018. Facebook Discusses 4 Parts of Their News Feed Algorithm. *Search Engine Journal*, February 14. https://www.searchenginejournal.com/ facebook-news-feed/237593/.

Myllylahti, Merja. 2018. An Attention Economy Trap? An Empirical Investigation into Four News Companies' Facebook Traffic and Social Media Revenue.

Journal of Media Business Studies 15 (4): 237–253. https://doi.org/10.1080 /16522354.2018.1527521.

Napoli, Philip M. 2011. Exposure Diversity Reconsidered. *Journal of Information Policy* 1: 246–259.

Newman, Nic, Richard Fletcher, Antonis Kalogeropoulos, David A. Levy, and Rasmus Kleis Nielsen. 2017. *Digital News Report 2017*. Oxford: Reuters Institute.

———. 2018. *Digital News Report 2018*. Oxford: Reuters Institute.

Ofcom. 2018. Addressing Harmful Online Content: A Perspective from Broadcasting and On-demand Standards Regulation. UK Office of Communications, September 18. https://www.ofcom.org.uk/__data/assets/ pdf_file/0022/120991/Addressing-harmful-online-content.pdf.

Pew Research Center. 2018, June 6. Digital News Fact Sheet. https://www.journalism.org/fact-sheet/digital-news/.

Picard, Victor. 2018. Break Facebook's Power and Renew Journalism. *The Nation*, April 18. https://www.thenation.com/article/break-facebooks-power-and-renew-journalism/

Public Policy Forum. 2017, January 2017. The Shattered Mirror: News, Democracy and Trust in the Digital Age. Ottawa, Canada. https://shattered-mirror.ca/wp-content/uploads/theShatteredMirror.pdf.

Rashidian, Nushin, Pete Brown, and Elizabeth Hansen with Emily Bell, Jonathan Albright, and Abigail Hartstone. 2018. Friend and Foe: The Platform Press at the Heart of Journalism. Tow Centre for Digital Journalism, June 14. https:// www.cjr.org/tow_center_reports/the-platform-press-at-the-heart-of-journalism.php.

Silber, Tony. 2018, December 31. Facebook Ad-Spend Growth from National Marketers Is Slowing, Intelligence Firm's Data Shows. https://www.forbes. com/sites/tonysilber/2018/12/31/facebook-ad-spend-from-national-marketers-is-slowing-intelligence-firms-data-shows/#558585a31591.

Srnicek, Nick. 2018, May/June. The Social Wealth of Data. In Duncan McCann et al., eds. Social Wealth Funds in the UK. *Autonomy* (3): 68–71. http:// autonomy.work/wp-content/uploads/2018/10/SOCIALWEALTHFUND_ AUTONOMY.pdf.

Thurman, Neil, Robert Picard, Merja Myllylahti, and Arne Krumsvik. 2018. On Digital Distribution's Failure to Solve Newspapers' Existential Crisis: Symptoms, Causes, Consequences and Remedies. In *Routledge Handbook of Developments in Digital Journalism Studies*, ed. Scott A. Eldridge and Bob Franklin. London: Routledge.

Van Dalen, Arjen. 2018, October 31. Diversity as Shared: Changes in Facebook's News Feed Algorithm and the Diversity of Shared News Stories. Paper Presented to ECREA Pre-conference, Information Diversity and Media Pluralism in the Age of Algorithms. Università della Svizzera Italiana, Lugano, Switzerland.

Van Dijck, Jose, Thomas Poell, and Martijn De Waal. 2018. *The Platform Society: Public Values in a Connective World*. New York: Oxford University Press.

Waterson, Jim. 2018. Google News May Shut Over EU Plans to Charge Tax for Links. *The Guardian*, November 19. https://www.theguardian.com/technology/2018/nov/18/google-news-may-shut-over-eu-plans-to-charge-tax-for-links.

Webb, Kevin. 2018. The 10 Highest-Paid YouTubers of 2018 Include the Paul Brothers and a 7-Year-Old Toy Reviewer – Here's the Full List. *Business Insider*, December 5. https://www.businessinsider.com.au/highest-paid-youtube-stars-2018-12.

SHARING NEWS ONLINE SURVEY

Sharing News Online Survey

ninemsn and the University of Sydney are studying why people share news on social networks and we'd really like your help. This short survey will take 5 minutes. If you're willing and interested, please read the detailshere, and tick the box to show you consent to be part of the study

☐ I agree

1. Why did you share this news story? Please tick the most relevant answer.

☐   To shock/surprise my friends/family
☐   For a bit of a laugh
☐   To show I care about this topic
☐   To educate/inform people
☐   To inspire people
☐   Other

2. What aspect of the story content made it worth sharing?
Circle the score that shows whether you strongly disagree, disagree, are neutral, agree or strongly agree with each of these statements.

	strongly disagree	disagree	neutral	agree	strongly agree
The person/people it is about	1	2	3	4	5
This is an issue I want to make a stand about	1	2	3	4	5
The danger it warns about	1	2	3	4	5
What it says is amazing	1	2	3	4	5
What it says will help and inspire others	1	2	3	4	5
To show my views about this topic	1	2	3	4	5
This topic has interested me for a long time	1	2	3	4	5

3. How did this article make you feel? Please tick the most relevant answer.
☐   Happy
☐   Angry
☐   Sad
☐   Heartwarmed
☐   Disgusted
☐   Amused
☐   Disapproving
☐   Approving
☐   Other

4. When others 'like' and comment positively on your posts, how do you feel?
Circle the score that shows whether you strongly disagree, disagree, are neutral, agree or strongly agree with each of these responses.

	strongly disagree	disagree	neutral	agree	strongly agree
I feel pleased	1	2	3	4	5
I feel encouraged	1	2	3	4	5
I feel taken aback	1	2	3	4	5
I feel honoured	1	2	3	4	5
I feel surprised	1	2	3	4	5
I feel humbled	1	2	3	4	5

5. When others make negative comments about your posts, how do you feel ?
Circle the score that shows whether you strongly disagree, disagree, are neutral, agree or strongly agree with each of these statements.

	strongly disagree	disagree	neutral	agree	strongly agree
I feel annoyed	1	2	3	4	5
I feel hurt	1	2	3	4	5
I feel angry	1	2	3	4	5
I feel discouraged	1	2	3	4	5
I feel surprised	1	2	3	4	5
I feel reassured	1	2	3	4	5

6. Thinking generally about the news you share on social media, are you more likely to share a story because it...

Circle the score that shows whether you strongly disagree, disagree, are neutral, agree or strongly agree with each of these statements.

	strongly disagree	disagree	neutral	agree	strongly agree
Echoes my own experience	1	2	3	4	5
Affirms my opinions and beliefs	1	2	3	4	5
Makes me laugh	1	2	3	4	5
Is relevant for a problem I face	1	2	3	4	5
Expresses my political views	1	2	3	4	5
Has shock value	1	2	3	4	5

7. Overall, what part does sharing stories play in your life?

Circle the score that shows whether you strongly disagree, disagree, are neutral, agree or strongly agree with each of these statements.

	strongly disagree	disagree	neutral	agree	strongly agree
It's a way of making friends	1	2	3	4	5
It's a way of exploring ideas	1	2	3	4	5
It helps me improve my profile	1	2	3	4	5
It helps me keep in touch	1	2	3	4	5
It shows others I care	1	2	3	4	5
It expresses how I feel	1	2	3	4	5
It's about being a good citizen	1	2	3	4	5
It's for my own amusement	1	2	3	4	5

8. About you…

8.1 Age
> 30
31-45
46-65
66<

8.2 Gender
M
F

8.3 Postcode
Overseas
Australia

8.4 Country
Overseas
Drop down list of countries
Australia
NSW
Vic
SA
Qld
WA
Tas
ACT
NT

Index[1]

[1] Note: Page numbers followed by 'n' refer to notes.

The manufacturer's authorised representative in the EU is Springer
Nature Customer Service Centre GmbH, Europaplatz 3, 69115 Heidelberg,
Germany. If you have any concerns regarding our products, please
contact ProductSafety@springernature.com

Printed and bound by CPI Group (UK) Ltd, Croydon, CR0 4YY
29/04/2026
02099471-0012